WHITE RECONSTRUCTION

White
Reconstruction

DOMESTIC WARFARE AND THE LOGICS OF GENOCIDE

Dylan Rodríguez

FORDHAM UNIVERSITY PRESS   NEW YORK   2021

Library of Congress Control Number: 2020915796

Printed in the United States of America

23 22   5 4 3 2

First edition

Contents

Preface and Acknowledgments

Coming up in Alexandria, Virginia (a nearby suburb of Washington, DC), during the Reagan-Bush years, i was shaped by the expressive racism and anti-Blackness of Northern Virginia white liberals as well as the organic white supremacist politicization of emergent Young Republican assholes. Yet what may have been most personally (and thus politically-intellectually) formative about this period was the degree to which i experienced the subtleties and ideological seductions of multiculturalist white supremacy (as defined in Chapter 1).

This book is significantly shaped by a long-cultivated disgust with the cultural-political regimes of multiculturalism, compulsory diversity, and inclusivist American optimism, as well as their many derivative overtures. Yet throughout this same period, i have been privileged with teachers, mentors, classmates, friends, and co-conspirators who obliterate the political and cultural frameworks of multiculturalism/diversity/inclusivity through their caring, deep, collective commitments to other forms of creativity, movement, scholarship, and praxis: Black radicalism, Third-World liberation and anti-colonialism, radical feminism, carceral abolitionism, Indigenous decolonization and self-determination, critical trans radicalism, and queer radicalism, to name a few. At the risk of overreliance on a profane political dichotomy, i can profess to the reader that this upbringing and collective education has convinced me that i can (usually) tell who is full of shit and who is ready to fight.

Bluster aside, i cannot claim to have ever been fully *outside of* the regimes of multiculturalist white supremacy, which hail so many who fall within certain gendered racial class profiles. To the contrary, i live and work in the toxicities of these regimes even as i oppose and despise them. As a result, i write, think, talk, move, and teach for the sake of joining many of you in the service of an unending charge: Our critical, radical gestures must somehow participate in creating possibilities for collective exercises of radical, creative, political-cultural genius that demystify White Being and incite (or even productively weaponize) other insurgent practices and methodologies of human life. This is difficult, scary, and beautiful work. And if more people do not attempt to engage in it, many more will disappear.

I have come to realize that anyone who generously reads my writing and patiently considers my words is a partner in the historical present. This is not a benign partnership, nor is it one to which i can simply affix or deduce static, prescriptive responsibilities. At best, we will have reason to talk, argue, create, and consider our positioning and movement within and beyond these different places. Perhaps we can find ourselves together in dangerous times, finding beauty and creating joy in the process of surviving another fight. I thank you in advance and offer the following pages as the first of a two-book series addressing what i have chosen to call, with the encouragement of my late colleague and friend Clyde Woods, White Reconstruction. Around 2009, Clyde—sitting next to soon-to-be Fordham University Press editor Richard Morrison—cajoled me into writing this book after i casually used the phrase in response to one of his typically challenging questions. *White Reconstruction* is the first of a two-book sequence, to be followed by *White Reconstruction II*, a shorter narrative text that is multivocal and speculative, mixing polemic, fantasy, theory, and fictions of the now, the future, and the recent past. We miss you, Clyde.

Maraming salamat to current and former students—graduate and undergraduate—who have (or will soon) become my colleagues, teachers, and co-conspirators. They have profoundly influenced how i think, what i do, and how i do it: Martha Escobar, Ren-Yo Hwang, J. Sebastian, Angelica (Pickels) Camacho, Loubna Qutami, Luis Trujillo, Arifa Raza, Casey Goonan, Lucha Arévalo, Aaron Alvarado, Orisanmi Burton, Cinthya Martinez, Lawrence Lan, Alejandro Villalpando, Justin Phan, Jolie Chea, M. T. Vallarta, Jalondra Davis, David Chavez, Cameron Granadino, Aundrey Jones, Jules Smith, David Chavez, Tania Hammidi, Juli Grigsby, John Maldonado, Kenneth LeBleu, Jocelyn Romero, Damon Cagnolatti, Lorena Macias, Kaelyn Rodriguez, Roberto Labrada, Gaby Ocon, Brittnay Proctor, Joana Chavez, Azadeh Zohrabi, Kevin Cosney, Joshua Mitchell, Kehaulani Vaughn, and Sormeh Hameed.

A community of people continually embraces me with their love and labor. Their radical creativity and political courage push me to think, speak, and fight beyond what i would otherwise dare. I thank Critical Resistance (http://criticalresistance.org/), Scholars for Social Justice (http://scholarsforsocialjustice

.com/), the Abolition Collective (http://abolitionjournal.org), and Southern California Library (http://www.socallib.org/) for including me in their extended, increasingly global collectives of organizers, teachers, activists, artists, researchers, and makers. Yusef Omowale and Michele Welsing from Southern California Library are stalwart custodians and defenders of community-accountable knowledges and archives, and they have enabled the work of many people mentioned in this preface and cited throughout these pages. The formation of the Blackness Unbound core working group at the University of California, Riverside in 2018 germinated a critical energy that pushed me through the final stages of writing this book.

I am privileged to be supported by people who possess the magical ability to apprehend the best possibilities of anything i say, write, or think, reflect it back to me with generosity and critical insight, and dare me to do better.

The people who have worked, fought, suffered, and grown with and alongside me at the University of California, Riverside have nourished a sense of defiant political-intellectual autonomy that encourages and periodically challenges me to thrive and create to the best of my capacity. It is impossible to thank them enough for their collective camaraderie. Everywhere i have turned, there has been someone with whom i can laugh, think, rage, conspire, and reflect: João Costa Vargas, Sarita See, Jodi Kim, Erica Edwards, David Lloyd, Mariam Lam, Amalia Cabezas, Tamara Ho, Michelle Raheja, Vorris Nunley, Crystal Baik, Jeff Sacks, Jayna Brown, Traise Yamamoto, Keith Harris, Freya Schiwy, Alessandro Fornazzari, Donatella Galella, Stephen Cullenberg, the late Emory Elliott, Eddie Comeaux, Allison Hedge Coke, Cherysa Cortez, Devra Weber, Pat Morton, Judith Rodenbeck, Ricky Rodriguez, Cathy Gudis, Emma Stapely, and Jonathan Walton, among others. There are some who came through UCR for too short a time, but whose contributions to the community of critical and radical practitioners were indispensable. They remind me that to be in these institutions is not necessarily to be of them. Thank you to Nick Mitchell, Ashon Crawley, Eric Stanley, Fred Moten, Maile Arvin, Deb Vargas, Laura Harris, and the late Lindon Barrett.

Being part of The Anti-Colonial Machine has afforded me the privilege of vital, intensive critical conversation over a few focused days on an almost annual basis since 2011. Key parts of this book are informed by the meals, seminars, workshops, and panels we convened in different places. I am grateful to Atef Said, David Lloyd, Fred Moten, Stefano Harney, Denise Ferreira da Silva, Colin Dayan, J. Kameron Carter, Mark Harris, Sora Han, and the late Nasser Hussain, whose wicked sense of humor we miss dearly.

I often refer to the teachers, mentors, and (young) elders who have exemplified principled, courageous, and consistent support for those of us attempting to engage in radical interdisciplinary and counter-disciplinary scholarship. These are just some of the people who have firmly guided, subtly informed, or otherwise enabled and deeply encouraged my thinking and praxis: Robert Allen, Rick Bonus, Oscar (Oca) Campomanes, Angela Y. Davis, Ruthie Gilmore, Avery Gordon, Ted Gordon, Joy James, Robin DG Kelley, Lisa Lowe, Martin Manalansan, Chris Newfield, Margo Okazawa-Rey, Gary Okihiro, Laura Pulido, H. L. T. Quan, Barbara Ransby, Beth Richie, David Roediger, Neferti Tadiar, James Turner (whose measured words on the science and art of intellectual guerilla warfare echo every day), Robert Warrior, and Sunn Shelley Wong.

Friends, colleagues, (extended) family, and loved ones have cultivated, challenged, demanded, or otherwise influenced the work that shaped this book. *Malaki and utang na loob ko sayo*: João Costa Vargas, Viet Mike Ngo, Connie Wun, Damien Sojoyner, Shana Redmond, Sarah Haley, Tashiri Askari (Harrison), and Raman Prasad. I am enriched and emboldened by my connections to Patrick Alexander, Patrick Anderson, Juliann Anesi, Hannah Appel, Nerissa Balce, Jared Ball, Alisa Bierria, Melissa Burch, Keith Camacho, Sylvia Chan-Malik, Dennis Childs, Charmaine Chua, George (Gio) Ciccariello-Maher, Cathy Cohen, Marshall Eddie Conway, Glen Coulthard, Ofelia Cuevas, Iyko Day, Andrew Dilts, Nada Elia, Keith Feldman, Rod Ferguson, Nicole Fleetwood, Mishuana Goeman, Sandy Grande, Susila Gurusami, Zoë Hammer, Davíd Hernández, Rachel Herzing, Marc Lamont Hill, Daniel Hosang, Ashley Hunt, Adrienne Hurley, Anthony Jerry, Imani Kai Johnson, Ronak Kapadia, Kehaulani Kauanui, Tiffany Lethabo King, Scott Kurashige, Laura Liu, Brian Lovato, Jenna Loyd, Toussaint Losier, Sharon Luk, Curtis Marez, John Marquez, Natasha McPherson, Erica Meiners, Eli Meyerhoff, Anoop Mirpuri, Scott Morgensen, Nadine Naber, Jecca Namakkal, Tamara K. Nopper, Ben Olguín, Isaac Ontiveros, taisha paggett, Naomi Paik, Jason Magabo Perez, Cornel Pewewardy, Josh Price, Junaid Rana, Khalil Saucier, Stuart Schrader, Micol Seigel, Orlando Serrano, Rashad Shabazz, Mario Sifuentez, Nat Smith, Sandra Soto, Dean Spade, David Stein, Dominque Stevenson, Eric Tang, Lee Ann Wang, Alex Weheliye, Ni'Ja Whitson, Randall Williams, Tiffany Willoughby-Herard, Craig Willse, Stephen Wu, and K. Wayne Yang. A shout out to these good people for inviting me to publish early versions of the ideas developed in this book: Paisley Currah, Monica Casper, Andrew Dilts, Perry Zurn, Moon-Kie Jung, João Costa Vargas, Eduardo Bonilla-Silva, Tavia Nyong'o, and John S. W. Park.

Apologies to anyone i failed to mention!

I have followed Richard Morrison from press to press. He is the baddest editor around. David Martinez is not only the smartest copy editor and indexer on the planet, but also has close reading skills that equate to superpowers.

Love and gratitude to the close branches of the family tree: Anthony Bayani Rodríguez, Yumi Belanga, (Ate) Chari Arespacochaga, Realista Rodríguez, Edgardo Rodríguez, Antonio (Kuya Ton) Tiongson, Jr., Alessia Belanga, and Emilia Rodríguez.

Most of all, giant kisses to the most important people in my life: Setsu Shigematsu, Taer Rodríguez Shigematsu, and Saya Rodríguez Shigematsu, who deal with my shit and humble me with theirs every day.

Dylan Rodríguez
June 2020

Introduction

"The Cause Is Effect": Inhabiting White Reconstruction

Before/Beyond November 2016

We are in the fray of yet another moment in the long history of the United States as a project of anti-Blackness and racial-colonial violence. The ascendance of white nationalism, white supremacist terrorism, and white fascist statecraft prior to, during, and beyond the election of Donald Trump has authorized a proliferation of racist, misogynist, and transphobic state and extra-state terror. When i began working on this book in the late-2000s, few imagined and far fewer anticipated the intense aggregation of reaction against the (neo) liberal post-racial "hope" of post–civil rights, post–racial humanism crystallized in the symbolic and institutional matter of the Obama presidency. As i write this introduction a decade later, a complex totality of cultural-institutional movements actively imagine, publicly advocate, and *openly plan* the neutralization and extermination of Black people; invasive and degrading enforcement of gender and sexual normativity; cultural and ecological genocide of Indigenous peoples; focused militarization against border crossers from Central America, Mexico, the Caribbean, and the Middle East; and other forms of tactical and strategic infrastructure-building that extend the epochal delusions shaping what Sylvia Wynter references as "techno-industrial Progress and national-racial Manifest Destiny" (a.k.a. Civilization, a term i will capitalize throughout this book when referencing the ongoing half-millennium of hemispheric conquest).[1]

It should be clear by now that whatever stubborn social-historical antagonisms the alleged post-racial society was projected to displace or eliminate may have been inadequately conceptualized or improperly defined. *White*

1

Reconstruction is a response to some of these urgent critical failures. This book is animated by an archive of radical thinkers whose work facilitates a critical re-engagement with a number of concepts and keywords—"racism," "white supremacy," "multiculturalism," "mass incarceration," "genocide," and so on—while also nourishing the development of some alternative terms (re) introduced and used throughout this book, including White Being, multiculturalist white supremacy, genocide poetics, and domestic war. I rely on a combination of analytical, archival, and theoretical methods that are expressed in different traditions of creative and radical praxis, from twentieth-century anti-colonialism and Black (feminist) radicalism to twenty-first-century abolitionism and Indigenous anti-colonialism and decolonization.

White Reconstruction focuses on the conditions of possibility for the most recent and current revivals and rearticulations of White Being's ascendancy, and offers a frame through which to understand how these mobilizations shape, strengthen, and sustain the foundational regimes of anti-Blackness and racial-colonial violence that constitute the contemporary United States and its globality from the scales of the systemic to the intimately interpersonal. Throughout this study, i posit anti-Blackness and racial-colonial power as distinct, though significantly coterminous (and often symbiotic) formations of dominance that constitute the conditions of sociality, state formation, epistemic and ontological coherence, and economic and ecological sustainability within the long hemispheric projects of Civilization, conquest, settlement, and modernity. I follow João Costa Vargas and Moon-Kie Jung's definition of anti-Blackness as

> structured, ubiquitous, and perduring disadvantages for Black people and structured advantages for nonblacks . . . in the realms of ontology (how individuals constitute and define themselves as such), sociability (lived social experience), and access to resources. . . . The likelihood of social and physical death is a direct function of antiblackness.[2]

Anti-Blackness, in this conceptualization, is the epistemic, aesthetic, ontological, and political condition of colonial, chattel, and modern socialities and not merely a secondary expression or consequence of otherwise non-anti-Black social formations. To the extent that anti-Blackness constitutes sociality as such, it also tends to serve as the assumptive, undertheorized premise for counter-hegemonic, reformist, radical, and even revolutionary struggles against the oppressive, exploitive, and fatal power/institutionalities of Civilization. That is, anti-Blackness may be fortified and reproduced by such struggles even as they aspire toward new forms of freedom and being.

The notion of racial-colonial power/violence draws from the thought of Haunani-Kay Trask (Kanaka Maoli) and Frantz Fanon, among others:

In our subjugation to American control, we have suffered what other displaced, dislocated people, such as the Palestinians and the Irish of Northern Ireland, have suffered: We have been occupied by a colonial power whose very law, policy, cultural institution, and collective behavior entrench foreign ways of life in our land and on our people. From the banning of our language and the theft of our sovereignty to forcible territorial incorporation in 1959 . . . we have lived as a subordinated Native people in our ancestral home.[3]

The singularity of the colonial context lies in the fact that economic reality, inequality, and enormous disparities in lifestyles never manage to mask the human reality. Looking at the immediacies of the colonial context it is clear that what divides this world is first and foremost what species, what race one belongs to.[4]

This book rests on the premise that racial-colonial power and anti-Blackness— in their state-organized and extra-state forms—are aggressive, long-historical violations of intimacy across forms of kinship, spirituality, community, and collective bodily integrity. The fray at hand reflects an extended, asymmetrical hemispheric conflict that has been historically cultivated by the colonial and carceral practices of Civilizational dominance that continuously fabricate new modalities of white self-vindication. This cultivation of declared, undeclared, and culturally normalized asymmetrical warfare generally posits all other forms of being—human and otherwise—as actual or potential targets of domestication, expropriation, liquidation, occupation, (coerced) assimilation, and generalized subjection to White Being's symbolic, economic, biological, epistemic, scientific, and cultural ascendancy.[5]

Thus, the notion of "White Reconstruction" does not attempt to give title to a compartmentalized, exceptional moment of white supremacist rejuvenations. Rather, it references a historically persistent, continuous, and periodically acute *logic* of reform, rearticulation, adaptation, and revitalization that shapes white social and ontological self-and-world-making within the aspirational, present-tense and violently future-oriented humanist projects of Civilization/Manifest Destiny/Progress, and so on. White Reconstruction crystallizes and mobilizes this logic through an ensemble of cultural and political projects, narrative structures, ideological tendencies, and state formations that rely on, while actively reproducing, the distinct and dense national, hemispheric, and global violences of anti-Blackness and racial-colonial power.

While White Reconstruction neither began nor culminated in the electoral events of November 2016, and although its logics of (anti-)social formation are inseparable from the long emergence of a hemispheric and global white supremacist modernity, it is nonetheless possible to identify its period-specific intensities. In this sense, the term "White Reconstruction" also provides an alternative conceptualization and naming of the long half-century that is commonly referenced as the "post–civil rights" period.[6] In fact, it was precisely such a renaming and rethinking that the late Black radical scholar Clyde Woods had in mind when he encouraged the development of this project.

Robert Allen's "Post–Civil Rights" Re-Narrative

As longtime *Black Scholar* editor Robert Allen recounts in his classic study *Black Awakening in Capitalist America*, the decade following the official abolition of U.S. apartheid (landmarked by the Civil Rights Act of 1964 and Voting Rights Act of 1965) was characterized by a comprehensive institutional struggle to reconfigure and sustain white supremacy in the context of an anti-Black, colonial social formation in crisis. For Allen, the struggle for white supremacist reconfiguration and sustainability was galvanized by a coalescence between state and extra-state (philanthropic, corporate, and other private) actors: the mandate to refurbish, reinvent, and strategically amplify the political and social repression of Black radicalism and other forms of insurgent Black life.

Throughout this period (and of course, well prior to it) Black people, within and beyond their various and complex forms of liberation struggle, exemplified multiple models of self-determination and human being that potentially abolished the ascendancy of *white* human being, while also resonating with (and often emboldening) other oppressed peoples' revolutionary and anti-colonial/decolonial imaginaries. Allen's book documents and rigorously analyzes how a confluence of institutional mobilizations, led by an ensemble of "America's corporate elite"—including the Ford Foundation, Urban Coalition, National Alliance of Businessmen, Carnegie Foundation, and Rockefeller Foundation—responded to the U.S. and diasporic Black-led revolt that flourished in the 1960s and early 1970s. Writing with a sense of alarmed urgency, Allen says,

> In the United States today a program of *domestic neo-colonialism* is rapidly advancing. . . . This program was formulated by America's corporate elite . . . because they believe that the urban revolts pose a serious threat to economic and social stability.[7]

Black Awakening provides a durable, indispensable examination of a militarized and counterinsurgent racist state busily reforming its criminalization, policing, and carceral infrastructures in order to broaden its cultural and juridical capacities to wage domestic war. The brilliance of Allen's insight is his focus on the somewhat less conspicuous, though equally calculated, strategies of domestic white humanitarianism and philanthropy that were simultaneously producing the ideological and institutional blueprint for an embryonic U.S. nonprofit industrial complex.[8] This generally coordinated confluence of strategic planning across corporate, state, and civil society institutions was not only "designed to counter the potentially revolutionary thrust of the recent [B]lack rebellions in major cities across the country,"[9] but was also a defense of the integrity of White Being in-and-of-itself at a historical conjuncture in which its hemispheric ascendancy was destabilized by the successful overthrow of the Jim Crow apartheid social form.

To the extent that the ascendancy of White Being composes the foundational grammars for white modernity's symbolic, cultural, economic, and epistemic coherence under the teleologies of Civilization and progress, Allen's text clarifies the scale, intensity, and ambition of reconstructive labor that emerges among an ensemble of groups and organizations when White Being is pushed into momentary retreat. Thus, alongside the socially transformative possibilities of creative Black political and cultural productions that composed what Nikki Giovanni and Manning Marable reference as the United States' "Second Reconstruction" (1945–2006), there has been an equally protracted, overlapping series of struggles to counteract, neutralize, and/or liquidate liberation-oriented feminist, queer, anti-colonial/decolonial, Black radical, and antiracist mobilizations of thought, organization, creative community, and collective (self-defensive) rebellion throughout the still ongoing "post–civil rights" moment.[10]

Black Awakening lucidly narrates how the organic intellectuals and professional planners of white civil society and the U.S. racist state scrambled through the 1970s to convene their collective political and economic capital, shared interests, and infrastructural capacities to countervail and coopt the revolutionary social trajectories incited by the dense liberationist movements that posed imminent and direct threats to the dominance of global U.S. modernity and its foundational ordering in the ascendancy of White Being. Put another way, Allen illustrates how the struggle to remake White Being in the throes of the post-apartheid socio-juridical crisis (including its iterations through institutional mandates of multiculturalism, diversity, and inclusivity) affirm rather than undermine the totality of anti-Blackness.

A crucial "soft" directive became central to the institutional and political methods of White Reconstruction during this period: Liberal and progressive blocs within the racist state and white civil society had to clearly delineate the horizons of post-apartheid political reforms in a manner that reproduced White Being's ascendancy while *desegregating* its institutional, phenotypic, and ideological expressions. The liberal-progressive tendencies of the racist state and white civil society were tasked with cultivating a desegregated American Dream that was ideologically inclusive of the Black and nonwhite masses while simultaneously rearticulating, diversifying, and strengthening the logics of anti-Blackness and racial-colonial dominance on which that dream was/is based.

Principal to this directive was the reproduction of racial capitalism and its constitutive violence, an agenda significantly accomplished through programs of class and cultural assimilation that have since taken the form of diversity and affirmative action programs, foundation and nonprofit funded campaigns for piecemeal policy reform and delimited versions of social change, and various privately and publicly funded academic research grants, scholarships, and high-profile fellowships.[11] By way of prominent example, the Ford Foundation played a central role in shaping the development of college- and university-based African American Studies and Ethnic Studies programs, departments, and initiatives such that these institutionalizations helped neutralize Black and "Third World" student protest while containing the epistemological and pedagogical implications of Black radicalism's epistemological and scholarly interventions.[12] Similarly, liberal shifts in K–12 and college curricula, periodic piecemeal reforms of racist state policing/criminological/carceral practices, and hundreds of successful local, statewide, and national electoral campaigns for public office contributed to a disciplining of political imaginaries that established the framework for White Reconstruction as an emergent political, cultural, and racial capitalist project.

I offer this short meditation on the durable insights of *Black Awakening in Capitalist America* to signify how a body of (Black) radical scholarship and activist study has enabled the construction of this book's primary thesis: that the ascendancy of White Being toxifies the emergence, reproduction, *and formal disassembly* of American apartheid, that this ascendancy permeates the cultural politics and (carceral) statecraft of white liberalism and reaction alike, and that anti-Blackness, racial-colonial violence, and domestic war not only survive periods of reform, but are the relations of dominance on which such reforms rely, and through which they often articulate.[13]

Dreadful Dream: White Being, White Supremacy, and the (Non-)Hegemonic

Over the course of the current half-century of White Reconstruction, the global U.S. racist state metastasizes with dooming brilliance as it invents, dismantles, and reproduces its changing protocols of immiseration and terror.

Never quite reducible to institutionalizations of white racial monopoly and American apartheid, the historical systems and infrastructures of gendered anti-Blackness and racial-colonial violence flex and "reform" at variable paces, from the incremental to the maddening. Mounting anecdotal and empirical evidence accrues: believable (non)fictions of racist conspiracy buzzing beneath the coldly official accounts of Black, Brown, Indigenous, and queer casualties, all of which indicate how desegregation, equal opportunity, diversity, tolerance, multiculturalism, colorblindness, and *inclusion* in the Civilization experiment are the Master's experiments, engineered to reproduce the society structured in anti-Black sociogeny and racial-colonial dominance.[14]

There is a dream of reconstruction that recurs in the white social imaginary: This dream shapes and sharpens white nation-building while displaced and targeted peoples surge into labors of lifesaving creativity. The insurgent peoples—whose collective personhood may itself be a primary method of rebellion—generally realize their liberation is an act of war, or at least a collective threat against the rising tide of white invitation into the experiment, as they simultaneously recognize that there may be no "outside" to the promiscuous institutional reaches of a resurgent White Reconstruction.

Contrary to reductive academic, journalistic, popular cultural, and liberal-progressive common sense formulations of white supremacy as an exceptional, irrational (hateful), and/or reactionary/extremist political subjectivity, a rigorous definition of the term encompasses the deeply historical, normalized relations of gendered anti-Blackness and racial-colonial violence, evisceration, and denigration that have characterized the emergence of Civilization and its coercive iterations of global modernity in the long post-conquest epoch. White supremacy is conceptualized in this book as a *violence of aspiration* and *logic of social organization* that invents, reproduces, revises, and transforms changing modalities of social domination and systemic, targeted physiological and ecological violence.[15] This domination and violence occurs through the planning, imagination, (re-)planning, and institutionalization of group-based human and cultural hierarchies, spanning the environmental and economic to the epistemic and aesthetic. I distinguish the conceptualization of white supremacy from both anti-Blackness and racial-colonial power in the sense that the latter forms of dominance are not fundamentally aspirational, but are the long existing, *pre-aspirational* conditions through which white supremacy is made fathomable and coherent.

White supremacy, as posited here, is animated by the dynamic narrations, global aspirations, and militarized mobilizations of White Being. Guided by Sylvia Wynter's radical critique of European and Euroamerican humanism, White Being is the militarized, normative paradigm of human being that inhabitants of the ongoing half-millennial civilizational project have involuntarily inherited as a violent universal. Wynter's framework rethinks the Marxist formulation of class struggle "in the terms of a 'politics of being': that is, one waged over what is to be the descriptive statement of the human, about whose master code of symbolic life and death each human order organizes itself."[16] White Being—as a narrative, ceremonial practice of human being that pivots on relations of dominance with other beings (human and otherwise) and aspirational mastery over the wildness and unknowabilities of nature and the physical universe—should not be conflated wholesale with "white people." Rather, it must be apprehended through its mobilizations of legitimated violence and colonial-chattel entitlement that, in turn, build the historical apparatuses of white embodiment as active practices and institutionalizations of sociality.

Fanon's surgically incisive meditation remains ever-relevant: The epidermalized, physiologically activated structure of power that inheres in white bodies (however white bodies are socio-politically formed and institutionalized in a given moment) is simultaneously the amplification and rewriting of politics, economy, and Eurocentric Marxist notions of "substructure" and mode of production. In continuity with the previously cited passage from *The Wretched of the Earth*, Fanon writes,

> This compartmentalized world, this world divided in two, *is inhabited by different species*. . . . In the colonies the economic infrastructure is also a superstructure. The cause is effect: you are rich because you are white, you are white because you are rich. This is why a Marxist analysis should always be slightly stretched when it comes to addressing the colonial issue.[17]

Fanon's language of "species" difference is generally compatible with Wynter's conception of the divergent "genres" of human being that antagonize White Being's marshaling of a universalized, violently monopolistic, "genre-specific" humanity: following Wynter's feminist and diasporic Black radical critique while also echoing Jasbir Puar's and Rey Chow's (queer) materialist explications of the "ascendancy of whiteness," i am interested in tracing how White Being's operationalized ascendancy is articulated across the grammars and vernaculars of race, civilization, nation, culture, religion, rationality, evolution, genetics, aesthetics, and economic development as foundational violence in the service of Civilization's racial order (a.k.a. humanism).[18]

Wynter's autobiographical account of confrontation with this order provides a useful point of departure for the critical analytical labor i am attempting to undertake in this book:

It's not a matter of someone getting up and suddenly being racist. It is that given the conception of what it is to be human, to be an imperial English man or women, you had to be seen by them as the negation of what they were. So *you*, too, had to *circumcise* yourself of yourself, in order to be fully human.[19]

The condition of such intensive, intimate racial violence is white supremacy's mobilization as a social logic that assembles while coordinating an ensemble of juridical, cultural, economic, political, and militarized regimes. Here, white supremacy is conceptualized as a productive, creative historical totality that exceeds its common political categorization as a far-right wing ideology—in fact, white supremacy coheres the fields of politics and culture in-and-of-themselves.[20]

In such a conceptual and analytical context, White Reconstruction cannot be defined as a form of social equilibrium or "hegemony." Rather, it is best analyzed as a historically specific, relatively coherent coalescence of efforts to *achieve* a condition of hegemony. The most recent and current expression of White Reconstruction entails the internally contested rearticulations and co-ordinations of juridical, cultural, economic, political, and policing/domestic warfare apparatuses that attempt to address the potentially explosive contradictions between the official dismantling of apartheid segregation and its *de facto* persistence as a logic of carceral social ordering, while sustaining the national and global logics of the U.S. social-political form as a racial chattel, settler colonial order.[21]

At stake in this historically specific struggle for hegemony is the production, refurbishing, and/or reorganization of political alliances, gendered racial statecraft, cultural common sense, and social identities (convened as "historical blocs," in the language of Antonio Gramsci) for the sake of defending and sustaining White Being's ascendancy in the face of the unsustainability and structural obsolescence of classical, rigidly exclusionary, apartheid-based white supremacy.[22] Stuart Hall crystallizes the classical conception of hegemony in his 1986 essay "Gramsci's Relevance for the Study of Race and Ethnicity":

"[H]egemony" is a very particular, historically specific, and temporary "moment" in the life of a society. It is rare for this degree of unity to be achieved, enabling a society to set itself a quite new historical agenda, under the leadership of a specific formation or constellation of social forces. . . . There is nothing automatic about them. They have to be actively constructed and positively maintained. Crises mark the beginning of their disintegration. . . . [W]e must take note of the multi-dimensional, multi-arena character of hegemony. It cannot be constructed or sustained on one front of struggle alone (e.g., the economic). It represents a degree of mastery over a whole series of different "positions" at once.[23]

On the one hand, the juridical dismantling of American apartheid prefaces a sustained, even epochal "crisis" in the gendered racial ordering of the United States. Echoing Hall's definition, the disestablishment of formalized white institutional monopoly in various social, political, and economic fields disrupts the terms of a historical white supremacist "unity" that has been convened around and through apartheid racial power, including state-sanctioned civil violence, militarized and legally enforced white geographic, economic, and social entitlements, and a formally segregated racist state. On the other hand, this momentous shift is not best characterized as a crisis of *disintegrating* hegemony, if hegemony is defined as "the winning of consent, [and] the taking into account of subordinate interests" within a broader attempt by the aspiring hegemonic bloc "to make itself popular."[24]

Hall reads Gramsci's conception of hegemony as a form of social power and civil order in which "there is no pure case of coercion/consent—only different combinations of the two dimensions," in which the formation of effective consensual rule "encompasses the critical domains of cultural, moral, ethical and intellectual leadership."[25] Complicating and confounding any such conception of hegemony, however, are the historical continuities of different peoples' *asymmetrical* subjection to the anti-Black, racial-colonial violences of a political and national-cultural modernity that consistently relies on imminent, threatened, and normalized exercises of coercive (state) power as the primary methods for establishing the *pre-conditions* for economic development as well as an aspirational social and political order. Within these temporally and geographically overlapping genealogies of asymmetrical violence, the notion of "consensus" is a fundamental fraud: Domestic and hemispheric war—as an expression of anti-Blackness and racial-colonial power—is the overwhelming (if not exclusive) modality of rule over people whose access to the entitlements of citizenship, property, recognized political subjectivity, and even humanity itself is variously marginal, obstructed, disrupted, or simply nonexistent.

By way of paradigmatic example, the construction of Jim Crow apartheid in the emergence of U.S. modernity can only be apprehended as the establishment of a non-hegemonic social order due to its reliance on a totality of legally legitimated and culturally sanctioned gendered anti-Black violence/disfranchisement/carceral displacement/state terror as its primary method of order and sociality. Such a form of rule did not consider African-descended people to be proper subjects of "consent" and contingently categorized other racially marked and colonially displaced/occupied peoples—Indigenous and Aboriginal peoples, Mexicans, Filipinos, Chinese, Puerto Ricans, and so on—as variably marginal to or fundamentally alienated from white (American) modernity's fabricated "domains" of culture, morality, ethics, and intellectuality. As such, the presumed constituencies of white "leadership" were structured in complex relations of cultural and juridical racial-colonial subjection and ontological anti-Blackness.[26] Under the modern U.S. apartheid order, Black people were the subjects of non-hegemonic "coercion" via an ensemble of protocols and institutionalized practices of direct physiological, spiritual, and discursive evisceration that extinguished any context or possibility for hegemonic "consent." Juridical/religious/scientific degradations and nullifications of being, state-condoned sexual assault, mob violence, lynching, and other forms of systemic state and civil violence constituted the ruling apparatus of post-emancipation, anti-Black segregation and, alongside other historically overlapping regimes of dominance, sustained the dynamic historical conditions of anti-Black, racial-colonial domestic war.[27]

Given the various genealogies and long historical continuities of coercive power that persistently puncture and disrupt the possibilities for constructing consensual relations of state authority and popular consent to a modern social order—including but not limited to land displacement and conquest, settler colonial occupation, ecological and cultural genocide, chattel enslavement, legal non-personhood, and violently enforced gender normativity—the consensual basis of "hegemony" has *always* been overwhelmingly reserved for the geographies, publics, and privileged collective subjectivities of White Being, including non-citizen, immigrant, and even "undocumented" white Europeans.[28]

As a modern liberal iteration of a settler colonial society that reproduces foundational relations of genocidal land, cultural, and ecological conquest, White Reconstruction presumes the militarized occupation of Indigenous geographies and consistent political compartmentalization and/or disavowal of a distended colonial sociality.[29] Trask's enduring diagnosis of the "New World Order" remains as incisive as it is succinct:

> Unremittingly, the history of the modern period is the history of increasing conformity, paid for in genocide and ecocide. The more we are made to be the same, the more the environment we inhabit becomes the same: "backward" people forced into a "modern" (read "industrial") context can no longer care for their environment. As the people are transformed, or more likely, exterminated, their environment is progressively degraded, parts of it destroyed forever. Physical

despoliation is reflected in cultural degradation. A dead land is preceded by a dying people. . . .

The secrets of the land die with the people of the land. This is the bitter lesson of the modern age. Forcing human groups to be alike results in the destruction of languages, of environments, of nations.[30]

Trask, Wynter, and Fanon enmesh, enrich, and radically recontextualize Hall's critical interpretation of hegemony by focusing on the irruptions and interruptions of (white) Western modernity's alleged transition to non-coercive rule. These thinkers demand an ongoing confrontation with the modern (New World) order as a condition of perpetual, dynamic anti-Black and racial-colonial violence. Among others cited throughout this book, Trask, Wynter, and Fanon collectively demonstrate how any working conception of U.S. hegemony tacitly presumes the fundamentally *non-consensual* power of conquest, chattel, anti-Blackness, and racial-colonial war as the conditions of possibility for modern power, sociality, and politicality. Analyzed alongside the ongoing formation of the United States within the resilient global Manifest Destiny mandates of white settler–conquest, there is little conceptual room to consider the apartheid, racial-colonial U.S. social order as a "hegemonic" order at all—that is, unless the notion of hegemony is explicitly defined as a *racially provincialized* relation of consent that has generally been reserved for social-political intercourse among non-enslaved, non-segregated, non-colonized, "free" (non-incarcerated) white social subjects and their (nonwhite/colonized) correlates, surrogates, and designees.[31]

Multiculturalist White Supremacy

Jodi Melamed's *Represent and Destroy* plumbs the tensions within critical conceptualizations of U.S. racial-colonial power, tracing the serial racial formations of a "formally antiracist, liberal-capitalist modernity" that emerged "as white supremacy gradually became residual after World War II."[32] Following the movements of racial hegemony from "racial liberalism (1940s to 1960s)" and "liberal multiculturalism (1980s to 1990s)" to "neoliberal multiculturalism (2000s)," Melamed argues that these serial cultural-political institutionalizations have cohered U.S. sociality since the mid-twentieth century as "unifying discourses for U.S. state, society, and global ascendancy and as material forces for postwar global capitalist expansion."[33] Her discursive-historical framework offers a helpful corrective to the subtly misleading periodizations of racial formation presented by Michael Omi and Howard Winant in their classic text *Racial Formation in the United States* (1986),[34] as well as in Winant's subsequent work, including *The World Is a Ghetto* (2001) and *The New Politics of Race* (2004).[35] Melamed explicitly parts ways with Winant when she contends that the "racial break" of the post–World War II years marked the onset of an authentically new relation of global racial power:

> Although I agree with Winant that the racial projects of white suprem-
> acist modernity have continued after the racial break, I argue that the
> break itself instantiated a new worldwide racial project that complexly
> supplemented and displaced its predecessor: a formally antiracist,
> liberal-capitalist modernity articulated under conditions of U.S. global
> ascendancy.
>   . . . I theorize the racial break as complete in the sense that its
> contradictions and tensions have given rise to [this] new worldwide
> racial project . . . that revises, partners with, and exceeds the capacities
> of white supremacy without replacing or ending it.[36]

Under the conditions of this global rupture in racial power formations, "for-mal" or "official" antiracism leaps into prominence as a "nonredistributive" discourse that is continuously, dynamically absorbed into the differential, in-tertwined, and generally symbiotic institutional structures and sociopolitical relations produced and otherwise impacted by the U.S. state and the appara-tuses of global capitalism.

Resonating with the work of Dean Spade, Nicholas Mitchell, Roderick Fer-guson, and other critical theorists of gendered, sexual, and racial normativities within academic, juridical, and other contemporary institutional formations, Melamed proposes that[37]

> [O]fficial antiracisms—the freedoms they have guaranteed, the state
> capacities they have invented, the subjects they have recognized, and
> even the rights they have secured—have enabled the normalizing
> violences of political and economic modernity to advance and
> expand.[38]

By conceptualizing racial liberalism "as a mode of normative power" that "de-cisively sutured an official antiracism to U.S. governmentality," Melamed constructs a dynamic framework through which to analyze shifts in the tex-ture of hegemonic racial power via the post–Jim Crow racial state and emer-gent neoliberal capitalism.[39] In this context, she argues that the shift from racial liberalism to liberal multiculturalism in the 1980s was catalyzed by a central ideological-political contradiction shaping the late–Cold War globality of the United States and adjoined regimes of transnational capitalism: "official anti-racist discourse had to take US ascendancy for granted and remained blind to the inequalities of global capitalism despite its racial organization." Melamed illustrates how, by subsuming the (already structurally and conceptually delimited) egalitarian aspirations of racial liberalism to the commodifying tenets of liberal multiculturalism, the U.S. racial order was defined in the last two decades of the twentieth century by a "pluralist framework [that] took for granted the primacy of individual and property rights at the cost of collective and substantive social rights."[40] Jodi Kim further extends this genealogy by conceptualizing the Cold War as "not only a historical period, but also an epistemology and production of knowledge," clarifying how the particular version of racial pluralism that emerged in the 1980s produced discursive and material militarizations against perceived and fabricated threats to "individual and property rights"—these, in turn, further activated the policing, carceral, and punitive juridical apparatuses of the gendered racist state in ways that indelibly marked the field of racial power.[41]

The most recent and concurrent racial formation, Melamed goes on to argue, is that of neoliberal multiculturalism, which deforms prior liberal notions of normative (and therefore commodified and constricted) "antiracist equality" by averting reference "to concrete human groups" and instead coding "multicultural formalism" as "an economic order of things."[42] Crucially, she suggests that these sequential racial formations have "signaled white supremacy's partial deactivation" as liberal-to-neoliberal racial power has generally displaced direct relations of white racial domination in the mutually reinforcing domains of statecraft, jurisprudence, and civil society.[43] Her study provides an extended cultural materialist analysis of the institutional transformations and discursive rearticulations of racist state and state sanctioned violence under the aegis of official antiracism (emblematized in the rise of the post-apartheid U.S. racial state). In so doing, Melamed's work provides a sound theoretical basis for critical examination of gendered racial-colonial power in its complex historical continuities—that is, as a form of rule, militarization, jurisprudence, cultural production, institutionality, and modern liberal statecraft that exceed historically compartmentalized conceptions of racial and racial-colonial domination.

The latter tendency is exemplified in Omi and Winant's now-canonical periodization of the post–World War II era as a "transition from racial despotism to *racial democracy* . . . from domination to hegemony. In this transition, hegemonic forms of racial rule—those based on consent—eventually came to supplant those based on coercion."[44] While the authors qualify their periodization by conceding that "[b]y no means has the United States established racial democracy in the 21st century, and by no means is coercion a thing of the past," they nonetheless insist that "hegemony is a useful and appropriate term with which to characterize contemporary racial rule."[45] While the preceding section of this introduction questions the adequacy of the hegemony concept to addressing the continuous, durable violences of anti-Blackness and racial-colonial power in the modern period, i will elaborate this schematic critique by way of collegial departure from Melamed's (as well as Omi and Winant's) book here.

In my view, Melamed's analytical and narrative reframing of the post–World War II racial break invites a closer reading of white supremacy's dynamic presence—that is, its continuities—as a logic of power and violence that is shaped by racial-colonial power and anti-Blackness generally, including and especially in white supremacy's liberal and officially antiracist forms. While my approach in this book subtly differs from Melamed's in its conceptualization of white supremacy as a logic of dominance that constitutively *exceeds* particular state, economic, and/or social forms animated by a "hollow ideology of force used to dominate nonwhites and appropriate global resources," i am in agreement with her contention that serial racial formations have (perhaps temporarily) decentered *official* white supremacy as the primary discursive expression of post–World War II global racial modernity.[46] The question i raise here is whether and how white supremacy's continuities—and continuous violences—*define* rather than recede from the socialities, institutions, cultural logics, and statecraft of what Melamed names as the periods of liberal and neoliberal multiculturalism (1980s-2000s).

Manning Marable's *Race, Reform and Rebellion* creates productive conceptual and theoretical friction with Melamed's historicization of hegemonic racial liberalisms. Examining the complex legacies and internal contradictions of U.S.-based Black freedom struggle in the post–World War II period (the Second Reconstruction), Marable develops the study through a historical critique of twentieth-century Black liberationist, anti-apartheid, and antiracist political movement, suggesting that

> A Third Reconstruction at some future point is historically probable, given the gross structural failures of the Second Reconstruction to abolish permanently high rates of unemployment for [B]lacks, Latinos, and low-income whites, or to resolve the dire conditions of poor health care, inferior public schools, and urban decay which plague all national minorities and millions of white Americans.[47]

Moving from a critical analysis of how "[t]he prime beneficiary of the gains from the Second Reconstruction was the [B]lack elite," Marable devotes much of the book's penultimate chapter to a detailed account of the layered forces of reaction, repression, and resurgent conservatism that assembled in response to the limited political, legislative, electoral, and cultural victories of the movement that overthrew US apartheid.[48] Marable's text demonstrates that while white supremacy's primary institutional expressions may have substantially *shifted* during this period, it did not significantly *recede* from U.S. social life during the post–World War II (or post-1960s) era.

In fact, Marable's study reveals the creep and spread of anti-Black reactionary elements across the institutions, cultural structures, and political discourses of state and civil society, illustrating how they both cultivated and infiltrated an ensemble of forces that attacked the legacies of the Second Reconstruction. For Marable, the Carter and Reagan presidential administrations were conjoined in their rollback of the economic, educational, and legislative gains secured by the Black freedom struggle. He further documents the expansion of white supremacist organizations and organized anti-Black violence across the United States throughout the 1970s, evidencing how such violence included, but was not limited to, militia-type warfare against progressive Black organizations, assassinations of Black political leaders, mass white supremacist rallies, periodically successful (and always politically impactful) electoral campaigns by self-identified white supremacist candidates, white supremacist infiltrations of local police forces, and widespread legally sanctioned police torture and killing of Black civilians. The book further outlines how "COINTELPRO-type repression of [B]lack radicals, revolutionary nationalists and Marxists also resurfaced during these years," while paying special attention to increased occurrences of the "most prevalent form of American racist violence . . . lynching: hangings, castrations, shootings, and other acts of racially motivated random violence."[49]

White Reconstruction lingers in the narrative-theoretical tension between Melamed's genealogy of racial liberalism/liberal multiculturalism/neoliberal multiculturalism and Marable's tracing of the Second Reconstruction and its aftermath. Following Marable, the Second Reconstruction, when apprehended alongside the global surge of (Black) liberationist, (Indigenous and Third World/Global South) anti-colonial, self-determination, anti-capitalist, feminist, and radical democratic movements throughout the middle decades of the twentieth century, forms the extended cultural-political context for a resurgent white supremacist reaction that has generally articulated with while periodically differentiating itself from the ensembles of post–World War II liberal racial modernity. This book frames the overlapping, intertwined resurgences, rearticulations, and "reforms" of gendered white supremacy, anti-Blackness, and racial-colonial power within a particular period of White Reconstruction that continues to unfold in critical tension with the ensembles of liberal multiculturalism and neoliberal multiculturalism alike.

Here and in Chapter 1, i introduce and elaborate *multiculturalist white supremacy* as a distinguishing technology of White Reconstruction that emerges through the discursive regimes and institutional rearticulations of liberal and neoliberal multiculturalism. The notion of multiculturalist white supremacy indexes how the logics, protocols, compulsory normativities, and gendered racial violence of hegemonic institutions—and of the anti-Black, racial-colonial social formation generally—become increasingly capacious, flexible, and promiscuously inclusive as monopoly-based systems of racial dominance (for example, apartheid Jim Crow and other versions of "classical" white supremacy) are abolished and displaced in the name of (liberal, teleological, national-to-global) racial progress. Within the mobilizations and institutional technologies of multicultural white supremacy, the "diverse" social subjects (who are also the commodified demographic objects) of these conditions of capaciousness, flexibility, and promiscuous inclusivity are solicited as living evidence of a liberal modern racial telos. They, in turn, inhabit the paradigms, methods, and relations of power that constitute the foundational violence of White Being, including but not limited to its conquest, colonial, racial chattel, and neoliberal imperial distensions.

Critical Methods for "the Millennium of Man"

Thus far, i have attempted to build a conceptualization of White Reconstruction as a historically pervasive logic of reform/rearticulation/adaption/revitalization that periodically surges into the aspirational hemispheric-to-global projects of White Being (Civilization, Manifest Destiny, civil rights progress/desegregation, and so on). Considered in the context of the recent and ongoing half-century, White Reconstruction references a specific mobilization of institutional rhetorics, cultural and discursive regimes, political-juridical strategies, and (militarized) racial statecraft that 1) sustain anti-Black and racial-colonial (domestic) war as the condition of racial capitalism and the U.S. social formation, and 2) constitute a political and cultural field of distinctly *post-apartheid* struggles for hegemony that are strategically, unevenly, and inconsistently inclusionist, diversity directed, and/or multiculturalist in form. These post-apartheid struggles for hegemony are significant in their newness, largely because they are waged on or in proximity to the normative

racial statecraft of liberal/desegregated racial-colonial "recognition," in which
people historically targeted by formalized protocols of categorical alienation
and exclusion from the racial chattel settler state are non-consensually subjected to the novel and constantly changing mandates, processes, and compulsory rituals of pluralist inclusion and accommodation into proper national
personhood (citizenship).

Glen Coulthard (Yellowknives Dene) crystallizes the centrality of liberal
recognition to Indigenous peoples' exposure to the post-1980s iterations of the
Canadian nation-state:

> [I]nstead of ushering in an era of peaceful coexistence grounded on
> the ideal of *reciprocity* or *mutual* recognition, the politics of recogni-
> tion in its contemporary liberal form promises to reproduce the very
> configurations of colonialist, racist, patriarchal state power that
> Indigenous peoples' demands for recognition have historically sought
> to transcend.[50]

For Coulthard, the pageantry and public exercises of liberal recognition (for
example, voting rights, formal equality under the law, citizenship status, compulsory multiculturalism and "diversity" mandates, state apologies, and/or
piecemeal financial redress for past atrocities) extend rather than replace, repair, or even mitigate the ensemble of state and cultural practices that sustain
colonial occupation and war as Canada's condition of national coherence and
sovereignty. The implications of this critique are vast: The invasive premises
of the liberal extension of politicality (and full sociality) permanently delineate, disrupt, and redefine the structures and discursive regimes of citizenship,
freedom, bodily integrity, and personhood as they are contingently accessed
by the non-normative (non-)subjects and targets of the anti-Black, racial-
colonial settler state. In this context, criminal law, policing, electoral politics,
border militarization, corporate media, carceral schools, foundation and think-
tank funded academic research agendas, prisons, jails, reservations, detention
centers, and other such institutions signify the relations of *coercive power* that
overdetermine White Reconstruction's struggles over hegemony (as the mediated, *non*-coercive power of consent).

Put differently, the cultural-political terrain of White Reconstruction's particular form of hegemonic struggle is distinctive because the conditions of
anti-Blackness, racial-coloniality, and domestic war are the precedents and
foundations on which a logic of *white/multiculturalist solicitation* anticipates
the bodily presence and delimited inclusion of human groups previously mar-
ginalized or excluded from the domain of political coalitions, historical blocs,

and social subjectivities within the modern (post-conquest, post-emancipation) U.S. nation-building project.[51]

The following chapters examine White Reconstruction's ensemble of war, insurgency, consent, and solicitation through a combination of three analytical and methodological approaches. One approach entails symptomatic readings of specific historical moments, archival texts, and political-cultural geographies within the contemporaneous, ongoing half century of White Reconstruction's most recent (and current) re-emergence. This symptomatic method encompasses discursive analysis as well as informed, creative, and periodically speculative explication of the events, cultural productions, political formations, and inhabited places that contextualize the logics of White Reconstruction in its moments and sites of enactment. How do the power formations of White Reconstruction look/feel/read in their instances of articulation? How can intensive analytical readings and re-narrations of such instances provide political-intellectual tools for understanding the forms of anti-Black and racial-colonial power/dominance that constitute (rather than contradict or displace) the institutionalized narratives of the liberal, multiculturalist racist state at the same time that they galvanize (multiculturalist) white supremacist statecraft and populist white nationalist political cultures?

A second methodological strategy involves a re-periodization of the projected white/multiculturalist subject(s) of White Reconstruction: Most acutely, i am interested in cultivating a deeper understanding of how the ascendancy of White Being is conceived, operationalized, periodically institutionalized, and (violently) defended amidst the formal desegregation of apartheid white institutionalities *across multiple historical contexts.* This form of engagement addresses the conceptual, ontological, and historical premises of White Reconstruction through theorized re-narrations of prior (pre-1960s) archival moments in the entwined historical lives of anti-Blackness, racial-colonial violence, and ascendant White Being. I argue that the core value of protecting and sustaining White Being's ascendancy not only defines the post-U.S. apartheid social formation, but also permeates the historical totality of white nation-building and white supremacist globality. The interwoven regimes of liberal racial statecraft, white racial subject formation and ontological (re) assembly, and systemic state and extra-state violence are some of the technologies of reconstruction that empower White Being as an invasive aspiration to global universality (Civilization).

The third analytical and methodological approach of this book is generally aligned with Michel Foucault's notion of "genealogy" as a theorized historical tracing that "[dispenses] with the constituent subject . . . to arrive at an analysis which can account for the constitution of the subject within a historical framework." Foucault describes this method as

> [A] form of history which can account for the constitution of knowledges, discourses, domains of objects etc., without having to make reference to a subject which is either transcendental in relation to the field of events or runs in its empty sameness throughout the course of history.[52]

In critical dialog with Foucault's framing, i conceptualize White Reconstruction less as a discrete historical periodization than as a *mobilized and militarized narrative structure* that attempts to rearticulate, police, and pacify the violences, crises, and irreconcilable antagonisms of a post-apartheid, post-conquest "society structured in dominance."[53] The genealogical approach allows for rigorous analytical, narrative, and archival practices that are not restricted to traditional disciplinary knowledge forms and methodologies (for example, scientific empiricism, archival and archaeological object study, strict differentiation between "primary" and "secondary" texts, and so on). Further, a critical and capacious approach to genealogy allows for the creative and attentive consideration of every imaginable cultural-political text, including those that might otherwise be deemed too mundane, ordinary, unrefined, or uninteresting to serve as focal points of scholarly analysis and/or critical knowledge making. Foucault argues for a counter-/anti-disciplinary disposition in the production of an insurgent historical episteme (that is, a form of historical knowledge that displaces and demystifies official, hegemonic histories):

> [W]e can give the name "genealogy" to [the] coupling together of scholarly erudition and local memories, which allows us to constitute a historical knowledge of struggles and to make use of that knowledge in contemporary tactics. . . .
>
> Genealogies are . . . not positivistic returns to a form of science that is more attentive or more accurate. Genealogies are, quite specifically, antisciences. . . . Genealogy has to fight the power-effects characteristic of any discourse that is regarded as scientific.
>
> Compared to the attempt to inscribe knowledges in the power-hierarchy typical of science, genealogy is, then, a sort of attempt to desubjugate historical knowledges, to set them free, or in other words to enable them to oppose and struggle against the coercion of a unitary, formal, and scientific theoretical discourse.[54]

While i embrace Foucault's approach to genealogy, i qualify my appropriation of his method with a critical rejoinder. In this book, the work of archival explication is simultaneously engaged in a demystification and disruption of the presumed epistemological agent and subject (that is, the active knowledge producer) of Foucaultian genealogy—what i have elsewhere referenced as the subject position of *white academic raciality*.[55]

As conceptualized here, white raciality is simultaneously an epochal, disciplining knowledge-project and a laboriously constructed epistemic subject position (fabricated as the essential bearer of and respondent to epistemology as such). As both epistemological project and collective subjectivity, white raciality inhabits a position structured in global histories of systemic power and dominance, articulated through post-conquest and modern discourses of white (European and euroamerican) racial "transparency." For Denise Ferreira da Silva, the "transparency thesis" is a narrative of ontology and epistemological agency that yields white raciality as the "transparent 'I,'" a transcendent subject of history that is crystallized through the violently universalized notions of Man, mankind, humanity, Civilization, and human nature (et al.). Silva describes the "transparent 'I'" as "the representation of the subject historicity presupposes and (re)produces," which in its constitutive—that is, *inhabited*— white raciality "emerges always already in a contention with [racial] others that both institute and threaten its ontological prerogative."[56] In transparency, the white racial being constantly produces (fabricates) their own mastery over both the external forces of the material-natural world and the ontological/ physiological differences signified by racial others.[57]

The narrower problem of white *academic* raciality surfaces in Foucault's genealogical method. As the unspoken, assumptive agential and mediating epistemic position that is prepared to engage (and perhaps rescue, translate, or otherwise recuperate) "desubjugated" and "insurgent" knowledges, white academic raciality assumes a posture of generally unquestioned authority both *within* the archival methodologies of the modern academic disciplines, and *against* that regime of disciplinary hegemony in the production of "critical" interdisciplinary, trans-disciplinary, and counter-/anti-disciplinary knowledges—for example, Foucault's (and Nietzsche's, etc.) "genealogy."[58] White academic raciality occupies the nexus of disciplinarity, counter- disciplinarity, and racial transparency as the veritable monopoly position for the making of proper knowledges as such.

The genealogical method of this book reads white raciality against its self- enunciations in White Reconstruction, with special attention to its vindicating articulations of post-apartheid white collective subjectivity and multicultur- alist institutionality. This approach attempts to demystify the stranglehold of white academic raciality on the recognition and critical reproduction of archives and counter-archives alike. What if white raciality—including its academic variations—was subjected to *others'* intrusive, disruptive, and epistemically destructive genealogical narratives? Of course, it is possible to trace how people on the alienated margins of the Civilization-academic coalescence have *always* engaged in some version of this critical-creative practice as a matter of cultural survival and interdisciplinary liberation praxis—the point is to breathe freely and think openly while performing that work, which by necessity must be experimentally rigorous and rigorously experimental.

While white academic raciality occupies a virtual monopoly position in the institutionalization of official knowledge, it is both possible and necessary to form a genealogical method that actively displaces this long-standing, white supremacist knowledge position. Ashon Crawley reminds us that the university, as a primary site of epistemic and institutional "struggle and contestation," accretes "settler-colonial logics and logistics and antiblack racism." Thus the university, "in its normative function and form, is against the flourishing of abundance."[59] As i have tried to clarify elsewhere, white raciality is not reducible to "white people," as it encompasses piecemeal inclusions of non-white racial others and is also appropriated as a paradigm for power, rule, and knowledge-making within the parameters of modern nation-building, identity formation, and cultural production.[60] White raciality is adapted, appropriated, and—oft-tacitly—naturalized by other beings as the template for proper/respectable *human* being.

In the following chapters, i attempt to model a critical tracing of the long archival knowledge regime of white raciality that embraces a methodological commitment to the obsolescence of white academic raciality as such. Such an approach, i contend, can illuminate and facilitate the "flourishing abundance" of thought, praxis, and being that Crawley invokes as an antithesis to the university's normative institutionality. This labor invites a wondrous possibility that Foucault obliquely invokes but cannot consummate in his vast body of work: White academic raciality gravitating (or pushed) toward irrelevance, as its claims to transparency and epistemic essentiality are expunged by the unavoidably physiological, inherited modalities of knowing that are constituted across layered, overlapping epochs of gendered, racial-colonial and anti-Black violence.

Dian Million (Tanana Athabascan) gestures to an Indigenous feminist episteme formed in—and critically, rigorously informed by—gendered colonial violence, radically departing from rituals of knowledge production that replicate the assumptive authorship/authority of white academic raciality:

Indigenous women [participate] in creating new language for communities to address the real multilayered facets of their histories and concerns by insisting on the inclusion of our lived experience, rich with emotional knowledges, of what pain and grief and hope meant or mean now in our pasts and futures. [This] is also to underline again the importance of felt experiences as community knowledges that interactively inform our positions as Native scholars, particularly as Native women scholars.[61]

Million's thesis on knowledge formation is both anti-colonial (contributing to a displacement and destruction of white epistemic transparency) and decolonial (forming a premise for liberated, self-determining Indigenous life and knowledge). I privilege her account on its own terms while also recognizing its resonances with other political-intellectual traditions that situate the conditions and substance of epistemology within accumulated/collective experiences of flesh, body, spirit, ecology, and revolt against systemic, oppressive violence.[62]

This book's conceptualizations, theoretical arguments, and methods are shaped by such radical traditions, including the anti-colonial and decolonizing (feminist) praxis exemplified by Million's work, the creative labors of Black (diasporic, feminist, and queer) radicalism, contemporary (late-1990s to present) carceral and policing abolitionist praxis, antiracist and radical liberationist movements/insurgencies/rebellions, and other forms of interdisciplinary/counter-disciplinary knowledge that annihilate the assumptive epistemic ascendancy of white raciality. Traversing the Pelican Bay (CA) Prison Hunger Strike and Chicago's We Charge Genocide (see Chapters 4–5) to Idle No More, The Movement for Black Lives/Black Lives Matter, and the Standing Rock Water Protectors (#NoDAPL), as well as grass roots rebellions against anti-Black police violence during and prior to Summer 2020, there is no shortage of collective knowledges and cultural productions that repudiate the coercive globality of white raciality. This collective genius enunciates the transformative possibilities already present in insurgent peoples' memories, art, extra-academic scholarship, and un/decolonized archives. Following Million, such creative scholarly activist labors thrive in intimacy with rage, disgust, principled hatred, love of collective peoplehood, urgent desire for escape/freedom, systemic racialized premature death, and other affective and physiological modalities of knowing that are utterly common to people working within various traditions of radical, liberationist, and revolutionary praxis.[63]

David Lloyd argues that "since its inception in the late eighteenth century, aesthetic philosophy has functioned as a regulative discourse of the human on which the modern conception of the political and racial order of modernity rests."[64] If the condition of the aesthetic (and thinking about aesthetics) coheres in the disciplinary and violent (that is, robustly "regulative") relations of power, dominance, authorship, and authority that define the ascendancy of White Being, then it is incumbent on other beings to identify, creatively theorize, and re-narrate its textual body. Following Nicole Fleetwood's framing of Black aesthetic praxis as "a performative field where seeing race is not a transparent act; it is itself a 'doing,'" it becomes possible to both trace and radically confront the violence of ascendancy through insurgent re-inhabitations of the (collective) act of textual/visual/cultural production.[65] Here, i am guided by Fleetwood's nuanced explication of Blackness, the Black body, and Black life as "always already troubling to the dominant [white, Western] visual field," a critical methodological and theoretical approach that places a vital emphasis on "the productive possibilities of this figuration through specific cultural works and practices."[66] One productive possibility of such an aesthetic, epistemic, and analytical centering of insurgent Black being is the invigoration of an archival *reading and narrative practice* that demystifies and potentially obliterates White Being as such.

The archive of white raciality is peculiarly accessible and multi-disciplinary, surfacing in U.S. Congressional records (Chapter 2), human rights jurisprudence (Chapter 4), body art (Chapter 3), and state counterinsurgency strategies (Chapters 1 and 5). As this archive surrounds and permeates the cultural structures of white Western modernity and the ongoing Civilization project, i contend that the texts of white raciality can and must be subjected to purposeful, intellectually principled and rigorous methods of disarticulation. Such a critically aggressive posture is both justified and necessary because the worldly, aesthetic, and discursive coherence of white raciality is mutually dependent on the long historical production of multiple, violently oppressive and dehumanizing totalities—exploration, colonial national sovereignties, racial chattel property relations, patriarchal racial capitalism, racial-colonial sexual violence, cultural and ecological expropriation, epistemological conquest, and so on. Here, i am committed to a project that subjects white raciality to a *leveling*, that is, a critical re-narration against its own generalized terms of (liberal, rational, teleological) self-valorization, progress, and global humanitarian/humanist subjectivity. In this context, the contemporary moment of White Reconstruction indexes a longer archive of white raciality that must be critically—relentlessly—theorized and traced.

Katherine McKittrick's archival dance with demons is instructive here, as it moves on the (other-)worldly surfaces of Black women's collective historical encounter with an unfathomable—though persistently narrated—white racist, anti-Black misogyny. Read alongside Million, her critical theory of methodology expands and multiplies the temporalities and locations of epistemology as such:

> [T]he demonic invites a slightly different conceptual pathway—while retaining its supernatural etymology—and acts to identify a system (social, geographic, technological) that can only unfold and produce an outcome if uncertainty, or (dis)organization, or something supernaturally demonic, is integral to the methodology.[67]

McKittrick's radical Black feminist "demonic grounds" form an altogether different conception of spatiality and geography, centering a genealogy of "the historical spatial unrepresentability of [B]lack femininity" in order to rethink human geography against the ways it has been conceived, inhabited, and reproduced through the regimes of white academic raciality.[68] Spurred by Wynter's unparalleled critique of Western humanism, McKittrick's methodology reveals as it rejects the racial-colonial power of white raciality ("Man") as both an epistemological *position* and actively inhabited epistemic *project*.[69]

> [Wynter's] demonic model serves to locate what [she] calls cognition *outside* "the always non-arbitrary pre-prescribed," which underscores the ways in which subaltern lives are not marginal/other to regulatory classificatory systems, but instead integral to them. This cognition, or demonic model, if we return to the nondeterministic schema described above, makes possible a different unfolding, one that does not *replace* or override or remain subordinate to the vantage point of "Man" but instead parallels his constitution and his master narratives of humanness.[70]

On the other side of the demonic is the archival mundaneness of evil, that is, Man's evil. This archivally mundane evil conditions and is actively produced in the ascendancy of White Being and the oppressive convenings of white academic raciality. A critical archival labor can and must be undertaken on this other side, informed by the demonic as it tells stories of evil's origins, speculates about terror's genesis, and excavates the sinister thoughts lurking behind the smiling/smirking faces that rearticulate master narratives, old and new.

These archival engagements are guided by a counter-disciplinary insurgency against the coercive universality of Wynter's European "Man," the genre of human being that is forcibly imposed on the rest of humanity as the universalized template for the species. Following Wynter, the primary terms of any genealogy of White Being's ascendancy must encompass the racial geography and paradigmatic power relation of the New World slave plantation as well as the West's peculiar genre of human being, "Man." She writes,

> [The New World slave plantation is] a dominant *logic*, and it's a specific *cultural* logic, but it is also an ethical logic, a paradoxical realpolitik and a secular one that is in the process of emerging. It is this reasons-of-state ethic/logic that is going to bring in the modern world, what I call the millennium of Man. *We have lived the millennium of Man in the last five hundred years* [emphasis added]; and as the West is inventing Man, the slave-plantation is a central part of the entire mechanism by means of which that logic is working its way out. But that logic is total now, because to be not-Man is to be not-quite-human. Yet that plot, that slave plot on which the slave grew food for his/her subsistence, carried over a millennially *other* conception of the human to that of Man's.[71]

In the raging internal antagonism of Civilization—Wynter's ongoing "millennium of Man"—there is an insurgent, proto-revolutionary "conception of the human" that is inhabited, nourished, and collectively sustained by the enslaved. For Wynter, the enslaved (that is, incarcerated, deracinated, denigrated captive Africans in the New World) produce modalities of communion, kinship, and physiological-cultural reproduction (via creative genius) that permanently disrupt Man's colonial anti-Black universalization.

White Reconstruction apprehends white academic raciality as a fiction that is simultaneously produced by and constitutive of the epochal project of Civilization, within which U.S. nation-building is arguably the paradigmatic modern expression. In this sense, the most recent iteration of White Reconstruction is "new" only in the sense that it marshals the post-apartheid technologies of racial liberalism—specifically, the piecemeal, compulsory, and/or disciplinary inclusion of non-normative bodies into normatively white supremacist, heteronormative institutional spaces—in the service of sustaining the ascendancy of White Being well into the twenty-first century.

Irruption

The dreadful genius of White Reconstruction lurks in the creative, selective (temporary?) disruption of white bodily monopoly in the administration of the United States nation-building project, structured in the manifest dreams of global Civilization. Changing institutional ensembles selectively reconstitute personnel and protocols under the ideological umbrellas of "diversity," "inclusion," "equity," "tolerance," and "mutual respect."[72] In so doing, there is a reassembly of long-familiar relations of dominance, legitimated state terror, and misery-making, guided by the nation-building imperatives of gendered racial criminalization, colonial occupation and displacement, and normalized (domestic-to-global) carceral war.[73] Within this extended moment, the long relations of chattel, frontier, patriarchal, and heteronormative violence thrive within a vexed racial common sense. *White Reconstruction* attempts to cultivate a counter-disciplinary intimacy with the historical violence of gendered anti-Blackness and racial-coloniality for the sake of contributing to dynamic and growing irruptions of critical, radical, and abolitionist praxis.

The notion of *irruption* is multifaceted: In ecological terms, it references a sudden increase in an animal population within a specific geography as a result of migration or displacement; somewhat more commonly, irruption suggests a forcible or violent intrusion.[74] The following pages are a study of and tribute to the spectrum of irruptions that define the long half-century of White Reconstruction. Irruptive surges of human movement/immobilization/dispersal, collective radical creation and critique, and various formations of community within movements of insurgency and revolt are the constant rebuttals to the lasting cultural-economic consequences of what Lewis Gordon names "institutionalized dehumanization" and what Saidiya Hartman, Zakiyyah Iman Jackson, and others apprehend as the perpetual subjection of Black (human) being to the criminalizing violence, abjection, and ontological vulnerabilities of the epochal chattel institution.[75] Many of these irruptions seek the abolition and/or revolutionary transformation of systemic immobilization and misery, prisons, defunded and policed schools, militarized borders, and state occupied streets and skies. Focused, densely strategized and theorized praxis radically inhabits, invades, and infiltrates the carceral sites of White Reconstruction, drawing from multiple wellsprings of decolonial sovereignty, Black radical creativity, feminist organizing methods, and transformative queer rearticulations of place/body/subjectivity, among other living traditions. Such are the primary indications of systemic and collectively experienced distress, that is, of White Reconstruction as an ensemble of projects that attempt to normalize the (anti-)sociality of gendered, racialized, targeted peoples' differentiated "state-sanctioned or extralegal . . . vulnerability to premature death."[76] Each of this book's chapters attempts to address different, related inhabitations of this historical present tense.

The aftermath of U.S. apartheid's formal abolition has been overwhelmed by a juridical and narrative national-cultural vindication of "Civil Rights" as the vessel of fully actualized gendered-racial citizenship. This fraud has facilitated rather than interrupted the expansion and proliferation of a domestic war-waging regime. For the sake of momentary simplicity, consider the prevailing national narrative: The half-century legacy of Civil Rights victory rests on an always fragile but persistent common sense notion that national political culture ("America") and reformist law and statecraft (let us call this "The Dream") have definitively, irreversibly endorsed official racial equality. Bound by this narrative-political arc, the racist state's mechanics shift and multiply to rearticulate a condition of normalized anti-Black, racial-colonial violence that is condoned or even applauded by the institutionalized regimes of Civil Rights. Under the terms of this political-cultural regime, the early twenty-first-century crises of racist state violence—from homicidal anti-Black policing to the ecological toxification of indigenous and Black ecologies—are not best understood as tragic deviations from an otherwise rights-respecting liberal sociality. Rather, such crises index how the post-1960s Civil Rights regime is entirely compatible with—if not directly complicit in—a still-emerging culture and statecraft of criminalization and proto-genocidal violence that *affirms* the nationalist dream of post–Civil Rights "citizenship." The racial/racist state is constantly called upon to legislate, protect, and serve the Civil Rights Citizen even as it is the subject of militant demands for reform that will align it with the Civil Rights versions of America and The Dream. (This contradiction yields ever increasing layers of gendered racist statecraft in the post-optimist's Age of Obama-Trump.)

A growing archive of critical scholarship and journalism, as well as a diversity of civil society–based activisms continually navigate the fallout of White Reconstruction as if it is akin to an accumulating set of legal and civil violations, ideological betrayals of the Civil Rights dream, or mean-spirited institutionalizations of suffering for otherwise innocent (queer/dark-skinned/poor) people. Critical scholars and teachers, nonprofit and nongovernmental advocacy organizations, legal campaigns, and mass protest mobilizations energetically spread progressive discourses of social and economic justice, antiracism, accountability for sexual violence, civil/human rights protection, and redemptive citizen-personhood against the ugliness, abuse, and sickness that seem to perforate and puncture The Dream. Yet there remains an overwhelming cultural and political insistence that the last half-century is a time of generalized racial progress, even as proliferating spectacles of atrocity betray the omnipresence of unspectacular racial-colonial, anti-Black violence across the American totality. In the pages that follow, i will attempt to contribute a theorized counter-narrative of the historical present tense that departs from such liberal-progressive narratives and their various derivations.

White Reconstruction fixates on the structural and symbolic rearrangements of gendered anti-Blackness and racial-colonial violence that have seemingly replaced prior "classical" models of institutionalized and state-formed racial dominance. Each chapter focuses on specific moments and texts in the long archives of anti-Blackness, racial-colonial dominance, and ascendant White Being in order to analyze and explicate the largely under-theorized conditions of the contemporary iteration of the white reconstructionist dream. I intend for this critical scholarly labor to contribute to a deeper appreciation of the origins, methods, and radical creativity of the different forms of insurgent collective genius that galvanize within and against the deadly Civilization experiment.

Chapter 1, "'I Used Her Ashes': Multiculturalist White Supremacy/Counterinsurgency/Domestic War," frames the critical study of White Reconstruction in continuity with this Introduction. Departing from a reflection on how critical scholarly work on "the body" and "embodiment" is redirected by Hortense Spillers' indispensable explication of Blackness, gendered chattel captivity, and "flesh," the chapter considers the disrupted sociality of the body under conditions of anti-Blackness and racial-colonial power. Close attention to the nuances of Cedric Robinson's formulation of "racial capitalism" provides a vital elaboration and extension of this critical framing and further contextualizes the analytical and theoretical method of this book. The chapter attempts to illustrate the implications of these critical theoretical structures by closely reading and counter-narrating the Los Angeles Police Department's "Join LAPD" diversity recruitment initiative. Departing from a moment of Black revolt against the normalized, juridically sanctioned violence of the LAPD, the chapter concludes with a preliminary conceptualization of abolitionist praxis that considers its anchoring in the Black radical tradition while gesturing to its capacity to inform and influence other liberationist visions.

A dense history of gendered racial atrocity and unrecoverable loss is woven into the fabric of Civilization and its ascendant modern national signifier, the United States of America. Generations, family trees, cultural communities, and ways of life are permanently altered and periodically liquidated through the mandated racial violence of American progress and hegemony. Yet, many of the most intensified and spectacular forms of U.S. racist state and state-sanctioned violence are narratively compartmentalized into bygone periods of land conquest, racial colonization, chattel slavery, and apartheid segregation. This discursive and historiographic (in fact, epistemic) compartmentalization constitutes another layer of Man's violence and signifies the endurance of white (academic) raciality as a transparent origin point of hegemonic knowledge structures that persist well beyond their moments of inception. A radical reconsideration of the cultural and epistemological productions of anti-Blackness and racial-colonial dominance as the providence of a tragic "past" is indispensable for the larger labor of addressing these genealogies of terror as part of a historical present tense.

Chapter 2, "'Let the Past be Forgotten . . .': Remaking White Being, from Reconstruction to Pacification," attempts to build a critical genealogy that addresses white supremacy as a primary logic of racial power in its "liberal," philanthropic, and reformist iterations. The chapter focuses on two geographically distended (but fundamentally related) moments in global white supremacy's living archive, spanning the late nineteenth to early twentieth centuries: The late nineteenth-century testimonials culled by the Freedmen's Bureau in the aftermath of the reunited white nation's repression of Black Reconstruction, and the early twentieth-century chronicling of U.S. colonialist "pacification" and neocolonial nation-building in the Philippines. This meditation on turn-of-the-twentieth century white reconstructionist statecraft opens into a conception of white supremacy as a formation of power that traverses global circuits of trauma, fatality, and social disruption, each of which is central to—in fact, historically determinant of—the present-tense of Civilization. I argue that the logics of anti-Blackness and racial-colonial violence form the conditions of white supremacist sociality, and thus comprise the ascendancy of White Being within projects of racial reform as well as in liberal racial modernity more generally.

At the time of this writing, national and global conversations about white nationalism and white supremacist populism/fascism are anxious and widespread. The reactionary social dreams affirmed and institutionally empowered by the 2016 election of Donald Trump have provoked a spectrum of responses that demand a course-correction of the racist state and a revivified commitment to the ideological premises and promises of both America and The Dream. Often ignored in the outraged din of responses to this nightmare of governance, however, is the extensive evidence that such political-ideological positions have historically functioned as the generalized framework through which *respectable* national-political forms unfold. While Trumpism catalyzes and legitimates reactionary white (overwhelmingly male and masculinist) violence through various symbolic, state, and extra-state (as well as extra-legal) methods, this moment of aggressive white nationalism overlaps with prior periods of multiculturalist white supremacy that anticipate the emergence of contemporary post-racialism.

Chapter 3, "Goldwater's Tribal Tattoo: On Origins and Deletions of Post-Raciality," makes use of Silva's conception of "raciality" to define "post-raciality" as both an enabling condition of White Reconstruction and the necessary pre-condition for the articulation of early twenty-first-century "post-racial" dis-course. Here, post-raciality is the historical and discursive precedent for twenty-first-century post-racial political rubrics and social rhetorics; that is, post-raciality establishes the framework through which disavowals of racial dominance come to facilitate rather than forestall, repair, or prevent racist state and state-condoned violence. I argue for a critical genealogy of post-raciality that relies on forms of creative, critical, speculative archival and narrative en-gagement that trace the intimate and public texts and markings of white racial state figures—here, exemplified by 1964 Republican Presidential candidate and multiple-term U.S. Senator Barry Goldwater. This tracing—presented as a counter-narration of White Being's disturbing, grating, morbidly (and unin-tentionally) comedic, and sometimes bizarre archival body—demystifies post-racial discourse while situating it within the longer continuities of racial dehumanization, anti-Blackness, and logics of racial-colonial genocide.

To consider anti-Black and racial-colonial genocide as structuring logics of the post-1970s social order is to ignite collective debate, reconsideration, and potentially substantial refiguring of "left" political commitments and agendas that understand themselves to be progressive, radical, transformative, revolu-tionary, or liberationist. *White Reconstruction* embraces counter-Civilization readings of insurgent human (as well as extra- and non-human) archives as a way of honoring the creativity endemic to endangered practices of human be-ing against the fatal ascendancy of White Being.

An analytical centering of anti-Black and racial-colonial *genocide* in the contemporary moment incites a critique of political vernaculars, activist para-digms, academic research agendas that may generate incisive rejoinders to the reformist logics of the White Reconstruction period. From the National Ur-ban League and the Civil Rights Congress to incarcerated Georgia and Peli-can Bay prison strikers, there is a far-reaching body of scholarly writing, policy reports, documentary film, grassroots publications, art, investigative journal-ism, editorials, organized protest, and other forms of knowledge production that address the institutional practices and normalized cultural structures of anti-Black and racial-colonial genocide. This living archive refutes the liberal American common sense that compartmentalizes the "time" of genocide to the (distant) past. To the contrary, the archive illuminates the multiple, complex forms that racial violence, social liquidation, and life-curtailment have assumed in the distended aftermath of chattel slavery, land conquest, and classical white supremacist nation-building.

Chapter 4, "'Civilization in Its Reddened Waters': Anti-Black, Racial-Colonial Genocide and the Logic of Evisceration," reconsiders how the modern concept of genocide provides an incomplete rubric for apprehending the historicity of gendered anti-Blackness and racial-colonial violence. "Genocide," as a modern conceptual and jurisprudential formulation, is the impasse of the racial: To invoke its terms already suggests exceptionality and absolute abnormality, yet the formations of anti-Blackness and racial-colonial power, in all their iterations, rest on logics of the genocidal that collapse into regimes of normalcy/normativity, universality/humanism, and sociality/civil society. In this sense, "genocide" is a discursive regime that invokes, but cannot fully engage, the layered, historical violence of Civilization as a global order.

Critically departing from the hegemonic legal (United Nations) and academic discourses on genocide, the chapter moves to consider several examples of radical praxis that appropriate and rearticulate genocide discourse in confrontation with the fundamental, fatal violences of anti-Blackness and racial-colonial power. I argue that these *genocide poetics* not only reflect the insufficiency of liberal-progressive activist and juridical/rights-based vernaculars for communicating the everyday violence of anti-Blackness and racial-colonial dominance, but also inaugurate a critique of hegemonic human rights rhetoric. Genocide poetics can and must be rigorously engaged and critically appreciated as moments of artistry and creativity, where "genocide" is repurposed as a weaponized poetry of freedom-seeking insurrection and radical self-determination, mobilized in an irruptive announcement of emergency against a state of normalcy.

To think radically while thinking long-historically requires constant recognition of how seemingly bygone, past-tense violences continually shape the present and often (re)appear in the world as if they never left at all. Consider how those who have differently inherited and/or survived the anti-Black, racial-colonial past cannot escape its practices of power, including its languages, images, institutional legacies, and intertwining pathways of ecological, psycho-social, physiological, and communal damage. Such coerced heritages impose a political-intellectual and ethical burden on scholarly activists, academics, artists and creative cultural workers, journalists, independent scholars, legal professionals, teachers, students, and everyday critical thinkers of all kinds: The existing and/prevailing terms of critical political and cultural discourse must be analyzed, debated, and dynamically challenged in order to avert the pitfalls of (white/multiculturalist) liberal appropriation.

Chapter 5, "'Mass Incarceration' as Misnomer: Domestic War and the Narratives of Carceral Reform," closely examines how "mass incarceration" has become an early twenty-first-century keyword of shared grievance, national moral outrage, and liberal humanist alarm that simultaneously disavows and re-narrates (anti-Black) carceral warfare. This chapter argues that such keywords distort and misapprehend the systemic violences cultivated in the gendered chattel-colonial statecraft of the United States while effectively displacing other scholarly, theoretical, and insurgent activist languages of revolt.

As a phrase that invokes a sense of historical crisis, "mass incarceration" induces a multiculturalist liberal-progressive coalescence that reifies reformist notions of unfairness, systemic bias, racial disparity, and institutional dysfunction. Under the fraudulent terms of an emergent national narrative, the fallout, misery, and asymmetrical casualties of domestic war can be resolved and repaired through vigorous internal auditing, aggressive legal and policy shifts, and rearrangements of carceral, juridical, and policing infrastructure. The chapter contends that such reformist measures reproduce—and ultimately enhance—the tactics and technologies of gendered racist criminalization, police occupation, and human capture that constitute the militarized cultural, juridical, and institutional infrastructures of domestic warfare. Thus, the contemporary narrative of mass incarceration endorses an intensification of policing as both a premise and method of carceral reform.

Finally, the Epilogue, "Abolitionist Imperatives," departs from a historical mandate that conceptualizes abolition as a creative, imaginative, speculative collective labor grounded in Black radicalism and its speculative praxis. As it builds, solicits, and urges collective labors toward a radical departure from the delimited political horizons imposed by White Reconstruction, abolitionist praxis is invigorated by creativities of struggle, revolt, and community that seek the end of White Being's ascendancy and the liberation and revitalization of incarcerated, displaced, occupied, criminalized, and oppressed peoples' existence as such and beyond.

While the first five chapters explicate White Reconstruction as an ensemble of cultural and political projects, narrative structures, ideological tendencies, and state formations that attempt to sustain the globality of White Being in response to late twentieth- and early twenty-first-century liberationist insurgencies, the epilogue moves from the understanding that such insurgencies do not *merely* seek to exterminate and/or transform particular institutionalizations of gendered anti-Blackness and racial-colonial violence. Rather, these creative movements anticipate and enact the abolition of White Being in its globality, that is, an obliteration of White Being's ascendancy as the normative paradigm of human being within a global racial modernity that has been formed through the foundational power relations of transatlantic racial chattel, land

and ecological conquest, and (proto-)genocidal warfare. The epilogue situates abolitionist praxis as an expression of the creative genius of those who have insurgently thrived as the descendants and inheritors of particular, differentiated conditions of historical vulnerability to Civilization and its dehumanizing violence. Given the periodic gestures to such collective, critical, creative genius in the prior chapters, the epilogue reflects on the conditions for and implications of this archive of insurgent insight/knowledge as an incitement toward radical, abolitionist futurity.

1

"I Used Her Ashes"

*Multiculturalist White Supremacy/Counterinsurgency/
Domestic War*

Introduction: Body, Flesh, and the Problem of (Racial) Determination

This chapter invokes the racial body as a discursive site, material mobilization, and biopolitical production of white supremacy's aspirational technologies, constantly shaping as it is altered by infrastructures and institutionalizations of domination and violence.[1] The body is the historical and physiological material on and through which "race" works as a production of power in its most intimate and broadly systemic forms. Focusing on the body as a geography of gendered violence thus requires an analytic departure from the privileging of subjectivity/identity (or notions of the racialized "self") in the historical theorization of anti-Blackness and racial-colonial power.[2]

Karen Barad's conceptual and theoretical work girds this framing, enabling a critical method that apprehends the violences of gendered anti-Blackness and racial-colonial dominance as simultaneous productions and performative mediations of bodies in their complex "material-discursive" presence. Stipulating that "any robust theory of the materialization of bodies would necessarily take account of *how the body's materiality*—for example, its anatomy and physiology—*and other material forces actively matter to the processes of materialization*" (emphasis in the original), Barad's approach shifts the terms and methods through which power (and the subjectivities presumed to inhabit its various frictions and movements) is analyzed within particular human—and extra-human—ecologies and socialities.[3] Barad continues,

What is needed is a robust account of the materialization of *all*
bodies—"human" and "nonhuman"—and the material-discursive
practices by which their differential constitutions are marked. This
will require an understanding of the nature of the relationship
between discursive practices and material phenomena, an accounting of "nonhuman" as well as "human" forms of agency, and an
understanding of the precise causal nature of productive practices
that takes account of the fullness of matter's implication in its
ongoing historicity.[4]

Barad's insistence on an engagement with both nonhuman and human bodies illuminates the contestation and policing of racialized biological, symbolic, and cultural differentiations of the human while also disrupting the
categorical, abstracted treatment of the whole, healthy, coherent body as a
universally inhabited (white, colonial) entitlement. Monica J. Casper and
Paisley Currah help clarify the analytic and theoretical impetus for a historicized centering of geographies of the racial body when they argue that "the
edifice of any particular knowledge project is built around the specter of the
body it calls forth (or erases); that vision in turn sets its ontological, epistemological, and methodological limits."[5] Elaborating a critique of interdisciplinary traditions that "center the phenomenological concept of embodiment,"
they write,

> [T]he body may be interpellated by various schemes and arrangements
> that can circumvent the self entirely. Disentangling the study of the
> body from that of the self reveals new biopolitical (and what Achille
> Mbembe calls necropolitical) processes that produce commodities,
> track inventories, collect and collate data, and distribute reproduction,
> life, trauma, and death among collectivities, social networks, and
> populations. . . . Placing bodies at the center of stories of knowledge
> formation thus reveals how the notion of bodies as whole organisms—
> and indeed, their very integrity—is destabilized.[6]

The logics of gendered anti-Blackness and racial-colonial power surface in
changing regimes of systemic, institutionalized, and culturally normative
(state) violence that expose profiled, targeted, criminalized, and otherwise vulnerable bodies to specific forms of "destabilization," that is, exposure to ensembles of dominance that disrupt the capacity to presume bodily integrity as
a social or existential entitlement.

The selective, socially reproduced *non-presumption* of the body's physiological coherence calls forth Hortense Spillers's indispensable conceptualization

of the captive African's inhabitation of "flesh" as the nadir of sociality, constantly haunting Civilization's modern edifices:

> I would make a distinction in this case between "body" and "flesh" and impose that distinction as the central one between captive and liberated subject-positions. In that sense, before the "body" there is the "flesh," that zero degree of social conceptualization that does not escape concealment under the brush of discourse, or the reflexes of iconography. Even though the European hegemonies stole bodies—some of them female—out of West African communities in concert with the African "middleman," we regard this human and social irreparability as high crimes against the *flesh*, as the person of African females and African males registered the wounding. If we think of the "flesh" as a primary narrative, then we mean its seared, divided, ripped-apartness, riveted to the ship's hole, fallen, or "escaped" overboard.[7]

Spillers affixes critical attention on the captive chattel African "body's" perpetual contingency as such: Humanism's access to the body as a symbol, historical geography, physiological entity, and site of study is preempted by the long relations of captivity and chattel; Civilization is the violation of Black flesh, the pre-emptive, ontological disruption of the body's universality as a signifier of realized human being. This critical rejoinder undermines any presumption of the (Black, African) body's coherence as a historical discursive artifact, and further complicates the assumptive quality of the "social" that frames critical discussions of social determination. The latter part of this chapter will revisit the present tense of Spillers's "flesh" in the context of fatal policing and the responses of surviving kin to the systemic, juridically valorized "seared, divided, ripped-apartness" of Black fatality. For now, i ask the reader to apprehend flesh in its (Afro-descended, racialized Black) present tense continuities, that is, as the long historical condition of possibility for sociality as well as the physiological material through which White Reconstruction renders its logics of violence legible, accessible, and potentially (though not universally) consensual.

To paraphrase Stuart Hall, race is not reducible to class relations, nor is it an epiphenomenal reflection of a social formation's economic substructure or mode of production. At the very least, race is the embodied social experience "through which class is lived," and "the medium in which class relations are experienced."[8] Extrapolating Hall's formulation, race not only signifies the material historicity of the body—its contested physiology, social agency, historicity, and nonuniformity—within particular socialities and economic orders, it also *determines* the geographies and systemic logics of social formations in ways that are generally (though not always) symbiotic with logics of economic determination.[9]

In what follows, i examine the problems of determination, sociality, and (dis) embodiment in relation to three central technologies of contemporary White Reconstruction: (anti-Black) policing, domestic war (counterinsurgency), and multiculturalist white supremacy. Guided by Cedric Robinson's historical conceptualization of racial capitalism, the chapter considers the context and implications of the Los Angeles Police Department's "Join LAPD" diversity campaign alongside the racist state's ongoing militarization against and criminalization of Black life. I contend that the discursive contours and institutional strategies of White Reconstruction betray the fragility of White Being's ascendancy even as they sustain and reproduce the carceral violence of the U.S. social form.

Substructure of Skin: Robinson's Racial Capitalism and Disruptions of "The Body"

Robinson's classic study of the "social and ideological consequences" of the "emergence of racial order in feudal Europe" illuminates how racism (as a relation of power) and racialism (as an epistemic structure of human differentiation) constitute the militarized discursive foundations of the Civilization project. Part I of *Black Marxism* exhaustively details the permeating prevalence of racial violence *qua* proto-racial differentiation within intra-European modalities of conflict and emergent social organization prior to the genesis of transcontinental colonial and chattel conquest. Crucially, this historicization of European development demonstrates how the violence, ritualized animus, and systemic subjection that have come to be attributed to the "irrationality" of racism were not a corollary, epiphenomenal, or thinly ideological expressions of this aspiring global civilizational order, but were fundamental to it. Robinson succinctly posits that,

> The tendency of European civilization through capitalism was . . . not to homogenize but to differentiate—to exaggerate regional, subcultural, and dialectical differences into "racial" ones. As the Slavs became the natural slaves, the racially inferior stock for domination and exploitation during the early Middle Ages, as the Tartars came to occupy a similar position in the Italian cities of the late Middle Ages, so at the systemic interlocking of capitalism in the sixteenth century, the peoples of the Third World began to fill this expanding category of a civilization reproduced by capitalism.[10]

Robinson lays bare how the preconceptual elements of global anti-Blackness and racial-coloniality—and by careful extrapolation, the contingent aspirational expressions of white supremacist globality—were formed in and through Europe's internal tribal and proto-racial antagonisms in the transition from feudal provincialism to proto-capitalist Civilization and ultimately, capitalist modernity.[11] The endemically racialist structuring of the European civilizational project precipitated the white supremacist telos of Civilization as the worldly manifestation of the white body's militarized, disease-enabled accession to earthly dominance as well as its self-narrated mastery of nature and savagery.[12]

Following Robinson, the invasive-expansive imagination of white globality (Wynter's millennium of Man) was overdetermined at its origins by a logic of proto-racial differentiation and the naturalization of oppressive relations among European ethnic, tribal, and national groupings. White supremacy, in this historical genealogy, is an aspirational expression of the developmentalist narratives and coercively enforced global protocols of European capitalist modernity and the larger historical geographies of its peculiar notions of civilizational progress. In this sense, white supremacy is both a sophistication of the endemic European racialism of which Robinson writes, as well as a marshaling of global communion on which the (internally contested) emergence of a colonialist, conquest-driven European/white global dominance was and is based.

To the extent that projections of Civilization require an imagination of the civilized and civilizing body—a working conception of its capacities, potentials, fashioning, and phenotype—it is vital to distinguish the singularity of white supremacy as something more than a benign or "inevitable" self-differentiation of white Europeans from their nonwhite others. As a uniquely oppressive and generally genocidal imagination of the transcendence and unique sanctity of the white body situated at the explosive historical convergence of emergent capitalism, the Enlightenment, and chattel colonial conquest, white supremacy is the articulation of a Civilizational condition as much as a racial destiny. (This is also its logic of social organization expressed at an epochal and global scale.) Thus, if we conceptualize racial power as a socially determining force—productive of bodies, geographies, economic relations, and socialities—then white supremacy is an epochal articulation of this historical racial determination that fortifies the collectively experienced—that is, collectively inhabited and experienced—ascendancy of white life and bodily integrity.[13]

Tiffany Lethabo King helpfully centers the figure of the *conquistador* in a crystallization of ascendancy's violent production of the human within the Civilization project:

To become or "ascend" to Whiteness is to enact a self—or self-actualize—in a way that requires the death of others. The position of the conquistador is tethered to the process of "ascending to whiteness," or becoming human under the terms required by multiple versions of the human that keeps the category an exclusive and privileged site of unfettered self-actualization.[14]

The white body's projected biological and psychic gratification—formed through the discursive construction of its needs and desires in the extended moment of conquering, mastering, or otherwise waging war on all other beings—fulfills the fundamental requirements of Civilization's protocols: This gratification (and the dynamic, persistent need to satisfy it) animates enunciations of the white body's historical telos, including and beyond its paradigmatic narrations/militarizations in hemispheric chattel slavery and Manifest Destiny. Further, the historical ensemble of Civilization's protocols produces the white body's peculiar historicity as the module of a massive global fatality: The racial body of white supremacy is at once the signification, valorization, and material introduction of Other bodies' structured susceptibility to disarticulation, dispersal, and extinction. In this framing, white supremacy is fundamentally more than an ideological consequence of the racialist European Civilizational project: Rather, it is its organic elaboration. In this elaboration, it forms the ideational matrix through which (white) Civilization and the millennium of Man are rendered conceptually coherent and politically compelling. Robinson clarifies,

> What concerns us is that we understand that racialism and its permutations persisted, *rooted not in a particular era but in the civilization itself*. And though our era might seem a particularly fitting one for depositing the origins of racism, that judgment merely reflects how resistant the idea is to examination and how powerful and natural its specifications have become. . . . As an enduring principle of European social order, the effects of racialism were bound to appear in the social expression of every strata of every European society no matter the structures upon which they were formed. *None was immune.*[15]

As a civilizational animus that emerges from Europe's endemic primordial racialism, white supremacy constitutes the historical telos of the white body's destiny and fulfillment.

In sum, notions of "internal" racial difference both predated and actively formed the conceptual premises, human geographies, and material social relations through which the (white) Western Civilizational order cohered itself as an aspirational global project: ". . . from its very beginnings, this European civilization, containing racial, tribal, linguistic, and regional particularities, was constructed on antagonistic differences."[16] As a historical schema, Robinson's genealogy of European racialism shows how the apparent irrationality of racial violence is actually the *perpetual condition of historical possibility* for the (allegedly) rationalist logics of economic, national, and Civilizational development into and beyond the modern period. Thus, "European civilization is not the product of capitalism. To the contrary, the character of capitalism can only be understood in the social and historical context of its appearance."[17]

Robinson's racial capitalism calls to mind a persistent "racial project" within the long historical logics of White Reconstruction that traverses various historical geographies: the racial differentiation of populations, subjects, and bodies that ostensibly belong to the same economic "class," such that a unified class identity cannot be posited as a self-standing, or even temporarily stable, historical actor.[18] Hall's re-reading of Antonio Gramsci's work provides a helpful analytical lens through which to apprehend Robinson's genealogy:

> [T]here is the question of the non-homogeneous character of the "class subject." Approaches which privilege the class, as opposed to the racial, structuring of working classes or peasantries are often predicated on the assumption that, because the mode of exploitation vis-a-vis capital is the same, the "class subject" of any such exploitative mode must be not only economically but politically and ideologically unified. . . . Gramsci's approach, which differentiates the conditional process, the different "moments," and the contingent character of the passage from "class in itself" to "class for itself," or from the "economic-corporate" to the "hegemonic" moments of social development, does radically and decisively problematize such simple notions of unity. Even the "hegemonic" moment is no longer conceptualized as a moment of *simple* unity, but as a process of unification (never totally achieved), founded on strategic alliances between different sectors, not on their pre-given identity. . . . This begins to explain how ethnic and racial difference can be constructed as a set of economic, political or ideological antagonisms, within a class which is subject to roughly similar forms of exploitation with respect to ownership of and expropriation from the "means of production."[19]

Read through Hall's framework, Robinson's concept of racial capitalism helps clarify another significant historical and theoretical formation: Racial power/difference is a *determinant* rather than a derivative or outcome of economic modes of production, and therefore generates primary rather than secondary antagonisms within particular social formations. In this paradigmatic shift, racial capitalism provides a historical analytic through which to comprehend how discursive technologies of the body are implicated in the generative processes of sociality, economy, statecraft, and ecology across different racial geographies.[20] Robinson's study anticipates the possibility, if not the likelihood, of variations of racial warfare as the coterminous modalities (alongside colonial/capitalist formations) through which the Wynterian millennium of Man reproduces its worldly dominance as a *white* globality—the ascendancy of White Being—in excess of the parameters, protocols, and logics of capitalist globality. Racial capitalism, as it is constituted in violence, war, and human bodily differentiation, equips a conceptual elaboration of white supremacy that situates its continuities in the recent, still-unfolding unfolding half-century of White Reconstruction.

Many noteworthy and significant contemporary scholars of race replicate archetypal renditions of white supremacy that conflate its power with past-tense social formations of "racial dictatorship" and literal white power monopolies.[21] In opposition to this stubborn tendency toward theoretical and political compartmentalization, i conceptualize white supremacy here as an aspirational logic of ongoing, present-tense social formations, including and especially those that appear to have transcended the cultural and political delimitations of classically recognized racist social arrangements like franchise and settler colonialisms, racial apartheid, and *de jure* segregation. White supremacy, apprehended in its present tense, shapes the socially determining powers that condense at the material surface of the white body and crystallize through the historical imaginary of the white social-historical subject.[22]

The intersecting political genealogies of white supremacy (traced across the knowledge productions of religious and theological discourse, political philosophy, canonical Western literatures, hegemonic racial modes of economic organization, and so on) convene in multiple, apparently contradictory, or politically inverted social forms, from racial chattel slavery and settler colonialism to "post–civil rights" neoconservatism, multiculturalist liberalism, and post-racial Obamaism.[23] The complexity of white supremacy, in this sense, induces a critical method that does not reduce race to an outcome of economic determinations, and differentiates the aspirational logic of white supremacy from the processes of "racialization" and "racial formation."[24]

Conceptualizing white supremacy as a productive logic of social organization brings attention to its *compulsory narrative structure*. As sociality's story of normativity, white supremacy shapes the discursive and political (i.e., "material") parameters of historicity in-and-of-itself, animating the visions and aspirations of an anti-Black, racial-colonial Civilization project from the Treaty of Tordesillas (1494) to the War on Terror. To address white supremacy as a social-historical and narrative logic is to highlight the tensions and contradictions—as well as the congruencies and symbioses—between its sociopolitical, economic, and discursive productions (including constructions of "the body" across scales of institutionality, physiology, and phenotype).

The critical labors of Wynter, Robinson, Hall, Spillers, and others yield at least six implications for this book's explication and critical theorization of White Reconstruction:

The white body's emergence as the disciplinary prototype of the "human" (a.k.a. the abstracted and racially idealized model against which other people's humanity is to be measured, ranked, and/or disputed) is not merely the imprint of the Enlightenment era's racial and proto-racial articulations of rationality, civil subjectivity, and self-possession, but is the cumulative consequence of Europe's own internal racial violences and social transformations since at least the eleventh century; these violences and transformations are no less responsible for forging the disciplinary power of the "white human" than are the traumas of racial conquest, colonialism, and slavery.

The production of the disciplinary white human is inseparable from the *a priori* sanctity (hence *singular* "humanness") of the white body: The global institutionality and systemic enforcement of white existential entitlement to health, bodily integrity, and freedom of movement—as well as the white social body's relative alienation from and exceptionalist narrations of group-based premature death—is inseparable from this singular humanness. (That is, even the actuality of premature death among the white poor and socially dislocated is culturally and/or empirically incongruous with the systemic death of their Black, Brown, and Indigenous "class" analogues.)

The social determinations of race have, across different historical periods and social formations, worked *on* and *through* the body as both its primary social-discursive "raw material"; in this sense, the body is the physiological, inhabited mediation of anti-Blackness, racial-coloniality, and derivative forms of racial power more generally—in this sense, the body is both a site of signification for racial meaning and an active agent in the production of (and insurgency against) relations of violence, carceral/colonial war, and systemic dominance.

In tension with some reductive interpretations of Marxist dialectical historical materialism, the social determinations of race are not subsumable to the economic logics of accumulation, surplus value, and labor exploitation, but are constitutive of Civilization as a long half-millennial (capitalist) project, and produce (and are not merely produced by) Civilization's genocidal, imperial, colonial, chattel, and carceral regimes.

Robinson's and Wynter's historical genealogies of Civilization/the millennium of Man facilitate a theorization of the ascendancy of White Being as the durable, generally unspoken foundation of civil society as such, including its post-apartheid expression through narratives of liberal racial transformation.[25]

Contemporary institutional (racial/racist state) articulations of multi-culturalism, diversity, and inclusivity (per multiculturalist white supremacy) do not reflect the obsolescence of white supremacy, race, and/or racism. Rather, they indicate the historical continuities and discursive-political complexities (including the internal ideological contradictions) of white supremacist social formations. These institutional rearticulations are formed in the foundational relations of anti-Blackness and racial-colonial power, and generally normalize those relations while narratively disavowing them.

Departing from these six implications, the following sections of this chapter offer an initial archiving and critical genealogy of White Reconstruction. While my chosen examples focus on the contemporary policing regimes of the anti-Black and racial-colonial state, this privileging of domestic militarism invites other analytical foci and is not necessarily intended as an assertion of theoretical or political primacy.

"Join LAPD": Multiculturalist Policing as Remarshaled Domestic War

The anti-Black, racial-colonial logics of militarization, criminalization, and patrolling are central to the construction, reproduction, and institutional co-herence of modern social formations. Domestic war emerges as a general de-scriptor of the conditions through which the U.S. nation-state establishes sovereignty and sustains its apparatuses of political rule and (aspirational) cul-tural hegemony within these durable conditions of sociality. The production of normalized conditions of direct state violence against targeted people, com-

munities, and geographies—from surveillance and police terror to criminalization, displacement, incarceration, and legally/culturally sanctioned state
torture, homicide, and (proto-)genocide—is fundamental to the national project, and is the tacit premise of legibility for generic American notions of freedom, democracy, safety, (civil) rights, and civil society.

For the purposes of this discussion, i situate a contemporary notion of
domestic war in conceptual and ideological affinity with the latter twentieth-
century paradigm of warfare canonized by the U.S. Army in its *Counterinsurgency* field manual. The most recent (2006) edition of the manual juxtaposes
"insurgency" and "counterinsurgency" in a manner that provides a useful definitional context for my purposes. Crucially, as a state-formed conceptual
framework, *Counterinsurgency* can be read against its own grain: Consider
the field manual as a present-tense archive that indexes (and in fact operation-
alizes) non-traditional, politically directed warfare as a modality of racial
statecraft that is versatile, durable, and transnational (inclusive of the domestic
realm):

> 1–2. Insurgency and its tactics are as old as warfare itself. Joint doctrine
> defines an *insurgency* as an organized movement aimed at the over-
> throw of a constituted government through the use of subversion and
> armed conflict. Stated another way, an insurgency is an organized,
> protracted politico-military struggle designed to weaken the control
> and legitimacy of an established government, occupying power, or
> other political authority while increasing insurgent control. *Counterin-
> surgency* is military, paramilitary, political, economic, psychological,
> and civic actions taken by a government to defeat insurgency. . . . [A]
> key paradox: though insurgency and [counterinsurgency] are two sides
> of a phenomenon that has been called revolutionary war or internal
> war, they are distinctly different types of operations. In addition,
> insurgency and [counterinsurgency] are included within a broad
> category of conflict known as irregular warfare.
>
> 1–3. Political power is the central issue in insurgencies and counterin-
> surgencies; each side aims to get the people to accept its governance
> or authority as legitimate. Insurgents use all available tools political
> (including diplomatic), informational (including appeals to religious,
> ethnic, or ideological beliefs), military, and economic—to overthrow
> the existing authority. . . . Counterinsurgents, in turn, use all instru-
> ments of national power to sustain the established or emerging
> government and reduce the likelihood of another crisis emerging.[26]

The U.S. Army's inventory of counterinsurgency operations anticipates how the martial institutionalization of relations of dominance—via military, policing, carceral, governmental, and other formalized modern regimes—does *not* always rely on white bodily monopoly (or even majority) within apparatuses of soldiering, administrative leadership, and bureaucratic management.

A critical genealogy of White Reconstruction requires close examination of the *non-normative*—nonwhite, queer, non-Christian, and so on—iterations of white supremacy within contemporary institutionalizations of diversity, inclusion, and multiculturalism. Such non-normativities are constitutive of (rather than incidental or exceptional to) the protocols, planning, and statecraft of contemporary counterinsurgency/domestic war, extending and complicating rather than disrupting or abolishing the historical ensembles of anti-Black and racial-colonial state violence.

Consider the Los Angeles Police Department's conspicuous efforts to augment and publicly signify the demographic diversity of its officers in the immediate aftermath of the late-1990s Rampart Division scandal, a massive police corruption case that implicated over 70 officers, led to the reversal of more than 100 false criminal convictions, and resulted in close to 150 civil lawsuits against the city.[27] Addressing the Rampart debacle, a June 2001 federal consent decree mandated that the City of Los Angeles and the LAPD remediate what U.S. Attorney General Janet Reno and the Civil Rights Division of the Department of Justice called a "a pattern or practice of unconstitutional or otherwise unlawful conduct that has been made possible by the failure of the City defendants [City of Los Angeles, Board of Police Commissioners of the City of Los Angeles, and the LAPD] to adopt and implement proper management practices and procedures."[28] Notably, the terms of the decree—which was lifted in 2013—allowed the city, the Board, and the LAPD to admit no culpability.[29]

Under the leadership of Chief William Bratton, the LAPD engaged in a series of piecemeal internal reforms and public relations campaigns that included sponsorship of the 2006 Gay Games Sports and Cultural Festival (a national initiative to increase the numbers of out gay cadets), co-sponsorship of the Tenth Annual International Criminal Justice Diversity Symposium (2006), and the ongoing "Join LAPD" recruitment initiative.[30] It is difficult to overstate the extent to which Bratton, the former New York Police Department commissioner who intensified the police harassment of Black and Latinx residents under the rubrics of "broken windows" and "zero tolerance" policing, is reviled by criminalized people in the cities in which he has reigned as the head police administrator. Abolitionist organizer and scholar Rachel Herzing succinctly details the broad implications of Bratton's policing paradigm:

Under zero tolerance, also sometimes called suppression policing, use of police sweeps has become commonplace as police forces remove entire elements of communities from the streets—the homeless, queer and gender non-conforming people, sex workers, day laborers, youth— explaining that their very presence causes disorder. Stop-and-search tactics have deeply engrained the logic of racial profiling in the practice of policing, as individual cops are given discretion to assess who is suspicious and worthy of stopping.

The rise in the use of zero tolerance policing has coincided with the increased militarization of law enforcement, creation of special- ized policing units, longer sentences, a tripling of the U.S. prison population, and the increased use of solitary confinement within prisons.[31]

While Bratton exerted enormous influence on the infrastructure and street- level martial protocols of the early twenty-first-century LAPD, the department's public-facing mission of domestic militarist inclusivity was also shaped by a 2009 RAND Center on Quality Policing study that instructed it to "identify ways to streamline and prioritize applicants in the recruiting process that can meet both recruiting and diversity goals" while encouraging it to "tailor media . . . to attract diversity target groups."[32]

As of this writing, the pedantic visual solicitation of a diversified (cisgender women, Latinx, Black, LGBTQ, and so on) cadet profile pervades the adver- tising and social media platforms of the Join LAPD campaign: In addition to sponsoring highway billboards across Southern California, the recruitment ini- tiative encompasses a widely visited Facebook page, "@joinlapd" Twitter and Instagram accounts, a devoted YouTube channel, and a self-standing "joinlapd .com" website (see Figures 1 and 2) that is distinct in substance and design from the LAPD's official site. Between the subtle photographic display of the rain- bow gay pride flag on the windshield of an LAPD squad car and an Instagram commemoration of 2019 International Women's Day, Join LAPD provides a living archival index of racial state multiculturalism as a logic of martial reart- iculation that expands as it reforms the logics and protocols of domestic (car- ceral) war and what Stuart Schrader identifies as the localized distensions of U.S. counterinsurgency.[33] Here, the imperatives of militarized, gendered ra- cial policing are compounded through rhetorical and ideological turns toward demographic, identity-based inclusivity in the hiring and mobilization of do- mestic militarism's on-the-ground personnel.

By 2015, Join LAPD's operationalization of the reformist diversity mandate helped to double and triple the ratios of "Latino" and "Asian" officers relative

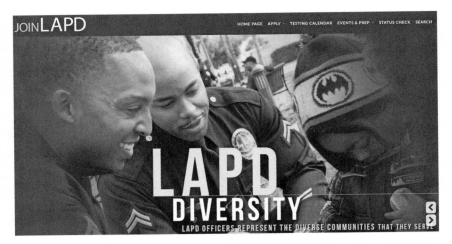

Figure 1. Recruitment image featured on "LAPD: Diversity" website (https://www.joinlapd
.com/diversity-our-city-and-department)

Figure 2. "LAPD Hiring Seminar" (www.joinlapd.com)

to the department's early 1990s demographics, while simultaneously yielding a *decrease* in the representation of Black LAPD personnel. While rigorous explanations for the latter trend exceed our purposes here, it is worth questioning whether domestic war's multiculturalist, diversity-and-inclusion–directed rearticulations serve to empower rather than disrupt the logical and historical continuities of anti-Black police violence, sustaining a culture of alienation between police forces and their projected constituencies of potential Black cadets. At a minimum, the visual apparatus of police multiculturalism projects a statecraft of domestic warfare/counterinsurgency that is enriched and legitimated by the seemingly instantaneous *availability and eagerness* of non-normative police bodies and visages.

Join LAPD's discursive artifacts affirm and amplify Mark Neocleous's contention that "bodily tropes surround the ideology of state power, serving to legitimize the state and the exercise of the most extreme forms of violence."[34] Read within the logics of White Reconstruction, Join LAPD signifies the formation of a visual curriculum that attempts to decontextualize, deflect, and disavow the racist state's dense ensembles of anti-Black and racial-colonial power. Max Felker-Kantor's historical analysis of the LAPD in the intervening years between the 1965 Watts rebellion and 1992 Los Angeles uprising contextualizes the lurking absurdity of this diversity-oriented rearticulation:

> Racial targeting was central to the LAPD's expansion of police power and efforts to control the streets at all costs. Residents of color, because the police viewed them as disorderly and lawless, had long been the subjects of the LAPD's police power. As African American and Mexican migrants reshaped Los Angeles's racial geography during the postwar era, they confronted a police force intent on maintaining Los Angeles's reputation as the nation's "white spot." As part of a system of racialized punishment that was rooted in Los Angeles's history of settler colonialism and racism, the growth of police power in the decades after the 1960s was organized around the aim of controlling the city's black and brown populations. Intensified police power and racially targeted policing were not incidental but mutually constitutive.[35]

Analyzed in the context of the 2001 federal consent decree and the post–World War II history of its foundational role in the establishment and enforcement of Los Angeles's geographies of criminalization and racial dominance, the LAPD's twenty-first-century diversity recruitment efforts can and should be decoupled from two of its implied promises: 1) a substantive or fundamental alteration of the LAPD's policing/counterinsurgency methods (for example, gang task forces and databases, SWAT, gendered racial profiling, and juridically condoned killing of civilians), and 2) a decisive withdrawal of police mobilizations against (queer and transgender) sex workers, unhoused people, undocumented communities, and criminalized Black and Brown youth.[36]

The Join LAPD initiative reflects the racist state's concession that white supremacist policing must undergo substantive reform to remain politically and institutionally viable. This discursive and curricular process, rendered compulsory by federal state intervention as well as ongoing grass roots resistance, rebellion, and periodic retaliation from people and communities most acutely vulnerable to police violence, entails a reform and/or dismantling of the white supremacist policing regime's classical elements—including (but not limited to) the optics and nationalist theater of white (male) police officers patrolling, detaining, humiliating, intimidating, harassing, abusing, torturing, and assassinating LA residents targeted by racialized, sexualized, and gendered criminal/suspect/gang profiles. Yet, the piecemeal phenotypic and demographic diversification of the policing body may intensify rather than dissipate white reactionary attachments to domestic war and the militarized institutionality of the racist state: In September 2019, a Join LAPD advertisement appeared on *Breitbart*, the self-described Alt-Right website brought to international prominence by former executive chairman Steve Bannon, featuring (since disgraced) professional troll Yiannopoulos among its cast of writers. (LAPD administrators and spokespeople apologized in the face of wide criticism, suggesting that a marketing algorithm was to blame for the ad's placement.)[37]

Journalist Tim Arango casually affirms that the LAPD's multiculturalist refurbishing sustains rather than interrupts the force of racist state violence in the opening lines of a 2018 article bearing the subtitle "'This Is Not Your Grandfather's LAPD'":

> It's been a long time since Los Angeles was ruled by its Police Department, when its chief was more powerful than the mayor, when its officers were mostly white men who patrolled poor, minority neighborhoods in the style of an occupying military.
>
> *Even as police shootings in the city remain stubbornly high, and many poor black and Latino residents, especially young men, still complain about heavy-handed tactics,* the force has become gentler in recent times, and its demographics more reflective of the city.[38]

The ACLU's 2008 study of the LAPD (*A Study of Racially Disparate Outcomes in the Los Angeles Police Department*) offers vast evidence that diversity-and-inclusion oriented recruitment and hiring practices do not significantly alter the gendered racist protocols, methods, and outcomes of everyday policing, nor do they induce a shift in the actions and decision making practices of police actors, regardless of their individualized social identities. While there is a longer history of Black, Latinx, and other nonwhite officers dissenting and periodically defecting from the police departments by which they are employed, the ACLU report suggests that increased demographic diversity among police officers is entirely compatible with the protocols of racial criminalization:[39]

> The results of this study raise grave concerns that African Americans and Hispanics are over-stopped, over-frisked, over-searched, and

over-arrested. After controlling for the violent and property crime rates in the specific reporting district and a host of other variables, we find that:

> Per 10,000 residents, the black stop rate is 3,400 stops higher than the white stop rate and the Hispanic stop rate is almost 360 stops higher.
>
> Relative to stopped whites, stopped blacks are 127% more likely to be frisked and stopped Hispanics are 43% more likely to be frisked.
>
> Relative to stopped whites, stopped blacks are 76% more likely to be searched and stopped Hispanics are 16% more likely to be searched.
>
> Relative to stopped whites, stopped blacks are 29% more likely to be arrested and stopped Hispanics are 32% more likely to be arrested.

All of these disparities are statistically significant ($p. < .01$).[40]

A body of qualitative, anecdotal, and statistical evidence indicates that initiatives such as Join LAPD are modest revisions of a white supremacist institutional phenotype, modeling a method of racial reform that has gained traction since the successful mid-1990s neoconservative attacks on affirmative action.[41] The LAPD has, in this way, become a state platform for a public theater of bodily spectacle that performs the obsolescence of old-school white supremacist policing while retaining a paradigmatic commitment to juridically sanctioned, culturally legitimated anti-Black, racial-colonial domestic warfare.

As the multiculturalist approach to police recruitment accumulates discursive and bureaucratic momentum, the anti-Blackness and racial-colonial logic of law-and-order remains a primary determination of the LAPD's on-the-ground operations. Damien Sojoyner's study of the symbiotic interactions between policing, criminal justice, and public schools in Los Angeles County suggests that the widely shared liberal-progressive activist and academic conceptualization of the "school-to-prison pipeline" is not only an analytically fraudulent metaphor, but also misapprehends how under-resourced, Black, and Latinx schools are *already* criminalized, actively policed carceral sites ("enclosures"). Sojoyner frames the ramping of the LAPD's militarized repressive capacities in the latter decades of the twentieth century as a precursor for the symbolic, ideological, and political maneuvers of Join LAPD and other such publicity/recruitment campaigns:

> Although the presence of police and representatives of the criminal justice system have had a sordid past in the lives of Black people, the

type of repression that was ushered in during the late 1960s and early 1970s and enhanced during the 1980s and 1990s was formerly relegated only for moments deemed "states of emergency" (that is, riots, massive political demonstrations). Yet, in this new epoch, the extreme and excess became normalized as a continual presence within Black communities.[42]

The formation of Los Angeles–based organizations such as Coalition to End Sheriff Violence in LA Jails, Dignity and Power Now, Critical Resistance Los Angeles, and Black Lives Matter Los Angeles critically accompanied the aspirational post-2001 diversification of the LAPD's policing phenotype. The emergence of this counter-police, abolitionist and proto-abolitionist work during the 2000s enacts various forms of grassroots response to what Sojoyner describes as the cultural normalization of the LAPD's racialized militarization and occupation, that is, the "intentional attack upon those ordinary and everyday spaces that had proven to be fertile in the development of Black culture, resistance, and organized dissension: schools."[43]

Los Angeles has long boasted the largest jail system in the United States (and, according to the ACLU, the world), a carceral toll overwhelmingly borne by Black and Latinx people (including youth, undocumented migrants, and those jailed while awaiting trial).[44] Prior to and since the issuance of the 2001 federal consent decree, the fact of the LAPD's implication in multiple high-profile scandals and incidents has not only rendered the notions of both "scandal" and "incident" inadequate, but has also rendered obsolete conventional narratives of the gendered racist state's official embodiment. By way of example, the investigation and criminal proceedings that exposed the depth and scope of the Rampart scandal implicated a prevalence of Black and Latinx officers as its central planners and co-conspirators.[45] Almost a decade later, LAPD crowd control officers—many of them Mexican-descended and Latino—physically brutalized and chemically attacked immigrant rights activists and other civilians during a peaceful 2007 May Day gathering at MacArthur Park.[46] Such widely publicized and visually circulated police violence, considered alongside the mundane and unremarkable tactics of the LAPD's everyday patrolling and occupation of the city's Black and Brown geographies, compels a re-reading of Join LAPD's soliciting displays of uniformed queer, Black, Brown, Asian, and cisgender women's bodies. As the multiculturalist future-vision of urban counterinsurgency and law-and-order, the campaign exemplifies how the institutional logics and inhabitations of anti-Black, racial-colonial state violence are not reducible to the uniformed, reactionary white cop.

Political scientist and Black Lives Matter Los Angeles (BLMLA) chapter co-founder Melina Abdullah (former Chair of Pan-African Studies at California State University-Los Angeles) concisely illustrates the diversified LAPD's continued post-consent decree implication in racist state terror in a September 2017 radio interview with KPFK (90.7 FM, Los Angeles):

> There is no shortage of police killings here. LAPD leads the nation in killing its residents. Out of the last five years, it's led the nation in killings every single year except for when Los Angeles County Sheriff's Department surpasses it. So when we talk about LA County, it's the most deadly place, in terms of police killings, in the entire nation.[47]

BLMLA's public discourse further dismantles the ideological pretensions of Join LAPD in a widely circulated 2017 petition addressed to LA County District Attorney Jackie Lacey, who in 2012 became the first African American elected to the office. Titled "Prosecute Police Who Kill Our People," the missive explicates as it radically reframes Lacey's role in normalizing the fatal consequences of racist police impunity:

> During her terms in office, nearly 300 Los Angeles County residents have been killed by police, including #EzellFord, #KendrecMcDade, #JohnHorton, #NephiArreguin, #MichelleShirley, #RedelJones, #WakieshaWilson, #JRThomas, #KeithBursey, #JesseRomero, #EdwinRodriguez, #KennyWatkins, #BrendonGlenn, #BrotherAfrica, #ZelalemEwnetu, #CarnellSnell and literally hundreds of others. In the case of Brendon Glenn, the officer was actually recommended for charges by the Los Angeles Police Department. NO OFFICER HAS EVER BEEN CHARGED FOR THE KILLING OF A RESIDENT BY LACEY.
>
> Los Angeles Police Department, Los Angeles County Sheriffs, and the policing units throughout the County lead the nation in the killing of community residents. For at least the last five years, LAPD and LA County Sheriff have led the nation in police killings. Yet, the District Attorney has not charged a single officer in any of these killings. The message sent to Los Angeles County law enforcement units is that they can kill residents and get away with it. Police cannot be relied on to hold themselves accountable, this is the work of the District Attorney.[48]

As it continues to kill Black and Brown civilians with effective juridical sanction, the LAPD's assimilation into a statecraft of diversity reflects a pair of mutually reinforcing institutional logics. On the one hand, Join LAPD represents an externally (federal consent decree) coerced departure from a densely white

male heteronormative officer profile that became a political and tactical lia-
bility in the aftermath of the 1992 LA rebellion: The policing phenotype—the
signifying body of law enforcement—became increasingly incompatible with
the changing form of the racial state in its various scales of iteration (local,
state, regional, and national). On the other hand, the LAPD's contingent institutionalization of personnel diversity articulates with the historical cultural
and juridical mandate to facilitate, sustain, and enhance gendered racist counterinsurgency, criminalization and domestic war as a primary condition of
urban social (dis)order.

"That's Wakiesha! She's going to stay with you!"

Analyzed as a period-specific racial state strategy, Join LAPD re-embodies as it
proliferates a climate of fatal hostility. Here, i am concerned with how a moment of Black insurgency punctures the normalization of domestic war through
shared distress, a collective grieving that refuses death's closure by enacting
abnormality in a loving weaponization of cremated Black flesh against the ascendancy of the badge. In such moments of rebellion, the violent mystery of
police valor collapses into the densities of gendered anti-Blackness, awakening
radical defiance of the normalized abnormal that tortures the survivors.

Sheila Hines-Brim, aunt of Wakiesha Wilson, did not accept the LAPD's
explanation that there was "no evidence any force was used" when her 36-year
old niece died in police custody on Easter Sunday 2016. As BLMLA members
mobilized around Wilson's case in support of Hines-Brim and Wilson's mother
Lisa Hines, the LA City Council voted unanimously in December 2017 to
settle their case against the city for $298,000. As part of this financial settle-
ment, the Los Angeles Police Commission denied any LAPD culpability in
Wilson's death and, as noted above, LA County District Attorney Jackie Lacey
refused to file criminal charges against the killers.[49]

Hines-Brim, whose unrelenting demand for accountability remained un-
quenched by the settlement and undeterred by the LAPD's denials, radically
altered the normalized/abnormal relations of gendered racial bodily integrity,
anti-Black state induced death, and white supremacist governance at the Police Commission's May 8, 2018 meeting. Disrupting the racist state's procedural
ceremony of engagement with the (Black) community and Wakiesha Wilson's
surviving kin, Hines-Brim cast her niece's remains as a perpetual curse on
LAPD Chief Charlie Beck:

> [Wakiesha] Wilson's aunt, Sheila Hines-Brim attended the meeting
> with Wilson's mother, Lisa Hines. Throughout the meeting, some

attendees were directed to leave due to multiple interruptions. Hines-Brim proceeded towards Los Angeles Police Chief Charlie Beck and threw a white, powder-like substance at him.

"That's Wakiesha," Hines-Brim exclaimed as she walked away, "That's Wakiesha! She's going to stay with you!"

The meeting quickly ended. Police officers proceeded to arrest Hines-Brim. Fire crews were urgently called to identify the substance and whether it was dangerous. Joshua Rubenstein, the police department's spokesman, shared that although it doesn't seem hazardous, the department has not confirmed what it was.

Hines-Brim was arrested on charges of suspicion of battery on an officer. She shared after her release, "I used her ashes so they can be with him, so he can feel her, because he murdered her. They covered it up."[50]

Hines-Brim memorializes Spillers's account of captive African flesh in the act of scattering her niece's ashes into Charlie Beck's deadpan visage. As Beck feels, smells, and breathes Wakiesha Wilson's burned, mourned, assassinated flesh, the body of the police is reduced to something beneath despicability, as that which must be radically decentered, cursed, and disrupted—perhaps also toxified, infected, and haunted—in the presence of flesh's survivors and inheritors. This revolt against the mystified white police body signifies a rejection of multiculturalist white supremacy's solicitations—rather, it dwells on the unforgivable matter of Black casualty as a fabricated, ritualized fundament of sociality, security, and jurisprudence.

White Reconstruction institutionalizes the partial, piecemeal, contingent incorporation of nonwhite and non-normative subjects and bodies into the millennial ascendancy of White Being; these processes attempt to discipline, selectively assimilate, and otherwise dissipate insurgent modalities of human being that persist within and against the violent and violating supremacy of Man. The operational tendencies of White Reconstruction—exemplified by Join LAPD—involve interplay between 1) the actuarial (predictive and anticipatory) routines of institutional protocol, discursive rationalization (of reform, repression, contradiction, and so on), and disciplinary-to-punitive statecraft (jurisprudence, policing, criminalization, and so on), and 2) the aspirational and experimental (hence speculative) dimensions of a period-specific statecraft, which orchestrates domestic warfare and gendered racial reform as a complex and simultaneous totality (counterinsurgency as diversity, and vice versa).

The tension between these operational modalities—the actuarial, the aspirational, and the experimental—indicates the presence of a *speculative cultural algorithm* within White Reconstruction's ensemble of labors and institutional-izations. This algorithm—speculative in its experimental, aspirational relation to both hegemonic and martial/coercive power—attempts to coordinate the shifting, reforming terms of White Being's ascendancy (a notion fully examined in Chapter 2) with the foundational conditions of sociality and institutionality, that is, Civilizational anti-Blackness and the racial-coloniality of the modern order.

The implementation of diversity mandates, compulsory tolerance and sensitivity protocols, and other "post–civil rights" multiculturalisms signifies the (possibly momentary) obsolescence of classical white supremacy as an order of violence that is based primarily or even predominantly on monopolistic and exclusionary institutionalizations of the white social body. Post-racial, multiculturalist, diversity-valorizing Americanism remains central to the racial narrative telos of the twenty-first century, even and especially amidst white supremacist and "white nationalist" reaction. As the planners, administrators, and armed officers of the racist state continually test the cultural algorithms of White Reconstruction, there is neither respite nor security from the recalibrations of domestic, hemispheric, and global anti-Blackness and racial-colonial warfare.

The flexible genius of multiculturalist white supremacy is its capacity to sustain, transform, and elaborate the aspirations of ascendancy while claiming the moral-political high ground of diversity, inclusion, and equity—this virulent suppleness indicates white supremacy's sustainability across institutional mandates while exhibiting the strength of its resistance to cultural and political obsolescence. In this iteration, white supremacy breaks the conventions of its classical apartheid logic and re-operationalizes within the normative political and cultural structures of (post-segregation, post-apartheid, "post-racial") democracy, liberal humanism, and (national) progressivism.

Conclusion: Obsolescence, Abolition

White Being, as an ontological, epistemic, and political-cultural formation, constitutes a historically durable and dynamic narrative of global dominance that is capable of hailing other racial beings. How does White Being *work* when peoples long targeted by its discursive, aesthetic, political, religious, and military regimes for denigration, expulsion, exploitation, elimination, and subjection are suddenly afforded opportunities to be enfolded into its ensembles of empowerment and affirmation, whether by virtue of rights, citizenship, marriage, or some other form of Civilizational sovereignty? How does White Being offer these political affinities and reformed institutionalizations of power through notions of good life—including promises of access to the privileges and entitlements of the modern liberal political order and its trappings of pleasure, physiological health, and recognized social-historical subjectivity?

The contemporary period of White Reconstruction is characterized by the extrapolation of white supremacy's contours: The sociality of racist subjection transcends and survives—and in moments of political crisis, conjures—the intentional obsolescence of classical white supremacist social forms. Modalities of social determination are never absolute or closed, and the multiple, overlapping circuits of institutionalized fatality and bodily subjection generated by white supremacist social logics are vulnerable to disruption, implosion, and explosion. Abolitionist praxis attempts to inhabit this vulnerability through sustained acts of insurgent, collective creativity. Here, "abolition" is a narrative and practical-theoretical rubric in the Black radical genealogy that capaciously resonates with multiple, interrelated liberationist political desires—slavery abolition, anti-colonialism, Black liberation, radical feminist anti-violence, queer and trans challenges to violent normativities, and so on.

Abolitionist praxis instigates principled and irreconcilable antagonisms toward the systems of dominance inaugurated by conquest, colonialism, and transatlantic chattel slavery, stressing the radical possibilities of community, revolt, sociality, kinship, and self-making in the experimentation, vision, and planning of Civilization's undoing. If, as Black radical thinkers such as David Walker, Ida B. Wells, Angela Y. Davis, George Jackson, Assata Shakur, and many others have articulated repeatedly over the last two centuries, the praxis of abolition embraces an overarching, internally complex struggle for modalities of human existence that are unapologetically *free* from the systems, epistemologies, and institutionalities of gendered anti-Black and racial-colonial dehumanization, then how might abolition cultivate the growth of vital and versatile analytical and organizing tools in the contemporary period of White Reconstruction? How can abolitionist praxis foster radical confrontation with multiculturalist white supremacy in a manner that does not replicate the institutional and interpersonal logics of white supremacist dominance, including systems of gendered racial bodily and sexual violence, valorizations of heteronormative family and sexuality, and proto-patriotic normalizations of colonial, neo-colonial, and racist settler states?

I conclude this chapter by gesturing to a historically grounded conceptualization of critical, collective praxis that significantly relies on the generous critical instruction of the Black radical tradition. Robinson writes,

> The resoluteness of the Black radical tradition advances as each generation assembles the data of its experience to an ideology of

liberation. The experimentation with Western political inventories of change, specifically nationalism and class struggle, is coming to a close. Black radicalism is transcending those traditions in order to adhere to its own authority. It will arrive as points of resistance here, rebellion there, and mass revolutionary movements still elsewhere. But each instance will be formed by the Black radical tradition in an awareness of the others and the consciousness that there remains nothing to which it may return. Molded by a long and brutal experience and rooted in a specifically African development, the tradition will provide for no compromise between liberation and annihilation.[51]

Abolition emerges through the long, complex genealogies of Black radicalism, including and especially its feminist, self-determining, queer, guerilla, anticarceral, diasporic, and counter-/anti-Civilization mobilizations of being and community. If abolition is understood as a form of praxis that is simultaneously instructed by and ethically and politically accountable to the practical, theoretical, and pedagogical labors of the Black radical genealogy, then its collective labors may be inhabited as perpetual incitement to rebellion and militantly collective insurgency against the dominance of White Being as the often unspoken framework through which humanity is itself averred. In this sense, abolition via Black radicalism is both a creative praxis of reimagined, speculative futurity and an exemplification of the "praxis of human being."[52]

Chapters 2 and 3 re-read the overlapping archives of the anti-Black and racial-colonial geographies of White Reconstruction to consider how White Being struggles to self-narrate its acute confrontations with abolitionist possibility. The ongoing, contemporary half-century of White Reconstruction encompasses a sustained scramble to postpone the end of the millennium of Man, steeped in a culture of political immediacy that obscures this period's continuities with other historical and archival moments. The next chapter initiates a symptomatic study of two such continuities in order to demonstrate how the logics of White Reconstruction can be traced across geographies, texts, and temporalities.

2

"Let the Past Be Forgotten . . ."

Remaking White Being, from Reconstruction to Pacification

White Supremacy as Social-Historical Form

The ascendancy of White Being is a perpetual state of global emergency of vacil-lating intensity for those who encounter white European modernity and eu-roamerican Civilization as inherently hostile projects. W. E. B. Du Bois, in the devastating contemplation that opens his essay "The Souls of White Folk," writes,

> High in the tower, where I sit above the loud complaining of the human sea, I know many souls that toss and whirl and pass, but none there are that intrigue me more than the Souls of White Folk.
>
> Of them I am singularly clairvoyant. I see in and through them. I view them from unusual points of vantage. . . . I see these souls undressed and from the back and side. I see the working of their entrails. I know their thoughts and they know that I know. This knowledge makes them now embarrassed, now furious! . . . My word is to them mere bitterness and my soul, pessimism. And yet as they preach and strut and shout and threaten, crouching as they clutch at rags of facts and fancies to hide their nakedness, they go twisting, flying by my tired eyes and I see them ever stripped,—ugly, human.[1]

This chapter attempts to honor while enacting Du Bois's situated declaration of clairvoyance through a tracing and re-narration of the stories told in the ar-chives of White Being's reconstructionist moments.

The complex totalities of anti-Blackness and racial-colonial power are the perpetual historical conditions through which the aspirational global projects of white supremacy are rendered feasible, legitimate, and normative.

59

As a historical technology of dominance, system of social ordering, and dense discursive site of worldly imagination and subject/identity formation, white supremacy is a contingent aspiration to mastery—of spirit, nature, and land as well as of self, savage, and slave. Of San Domingo's colonial formation by way of chattel slavery, C. L. R. James writes,

> From the underworld of two continents they came, Frenchmen and Spaniards, Maltese, Italians, Portuguese and Americans. For whatever a man's [sic] origin, record or character, here his white skin made him a person of quality and rejected or failures in their own country flocked to San Domingo, where consideration was achieved at so cheap a price, money flowed and opportunities of debauchery abounded.
>
> No small white was a servant, no white man did any work that he could get a Negro to do for him.[2]

James traces the sociality of the New World's global coloniality in the transatlantic conquest, incarceration, trafficking, and enslavement of Africans and Afro-descended people. In this sense, he offers an origin story of white supremacy, told through a lexicon and narrative structure that coheres in the subjection of Black people (and of Black personhood) to the anti-sociality of chattel fungibility. Following James, the ontological, discursive, and material formation of white supremacy is formed in the *a priori* of what Vargas and Jung conceptualize as the "structured, ubiquitous, and perduring" violence of anti-Blackness, which permeates "the realms of ontology (how individuals constitute and define themselves as such), sociability (lived social experience), and access to resources" while generating persistent differentiation between Black and "nonblack" social positions (see Introduction).[3]

This chapter proposes a critical genealogy of White Reconstruction that bridges archives, geographies, and temporalities while sustaining a conceptualization of white supremacy as an aspirational, contingent power that shapes global projects of violence and dominance: Civilization and savagery; modern white nation-building and land displacement, empire (cultural, physiological), genocide, and ecocide; humanist transcendence and anti-human depersonalization; white civil personhood and social/civil death.[4] Roy Harvey Pearce's classic study of the U.S. imagination of the "Indian" considers the centrality of the Civilization-savagery circuit in the sustenance of the white national *telos*:

> American pity and censure, American progressivist certainty of manifest destiny, American agrarian idealism and quasi-metaphysical faith in private property—each was authenticated by that understanding [of "savagism"], as each contributed to its authentication. . . . This,

at least, is the way it was with Americans at the beginning of their national history. They could fully and honestly comprehend the Indian only in terms of that theoretical understanding of savagism which was possible to them in their time.[5]

Stephanie E. Smallwood's history of transatlantic trafficking in enslaved Africans, on the other hand, illuminates the circuitry of property relations and racial chattel, establishing an analytic baseline for the conditions of white civil society's (and capitalist political economy's) emergence:

> On the ship at sea the logic of commodification reached its nadir. It was here, on the ocean crossing, that the practices of commodification most effectively muted the agency of the African subject and thereby produced their desired object: an African body fully alienated and available for exploitation in the American marketplace.[6]

Working within the historical tension created by a simultaneous reading of Pearce's and Smallwood's exemplary studies, it becomes possible to fathom how white supremacy's overlapping circuits of opposition are *epochal* outcomes of cultural, institutional, and militarized labors that have, in turn, been integral to the formation of socialities, state systems, and political economies (from slave and settler societies to apartheid "democracies") since the dawn of the New World.[7]

White supremacy, in this historicized and narrativized context, is a historically dynamic, aspirational logic of social organization that exceeds its more common conceptualization as a narrowly reactionary ideological or political tendency. Following the lead of Tiffany Willoughby-Herard, i am interested in how specific archival and geographic sites of white supremacy indicate a globality of power/dominance/imagination:

> [G]lobal whiteness . . . denaturalize[s] the existence, spatiality, and temporality of the white settler colonial nation, and to insist, as [B]lack radical movements do, that addressing racial politics as if it can be confined to national borders is a point of departure at best. . . . [R]acial politics and its border-crossing features help create and sustain mythic national borders. Thus global whiteness . . . can be better understood as the geographic contiguity that results from shared and enduring commitments to white nationalism as well as attempts to deny those commitments.[8]

In continuity with Chapter 1, the following sections work from the premise that white supremacy is not reducible to a past tense political artifact, extremist ideological articulation, irrational enunciation of "hate," or essentialist or chauvinistic discourse of white raciality. By engaging in a form of critical genealogy that demystifies and epistemically decenters white (academic) raciality, this archival re-narration attempts to explicate white supremacy as a primary expression of racial power as such.[9] To address white supremacy as an aspirational social-historical form is to simultaneously narrate and analyze the tensions and contradictions—as well as the congruencies and symbioses—between its durable *animus* (which seems to persist across historical periods) and its dynamic (and often internally contradictory) *mobilizations* across scales of institutionality, physiology, and phenotype. This is to argue, in part, for a counter-disciplinary (and periodically anti-disciplinary) methodology, analytical premise, and theoretical approach to apprehending and tracing white supremacy in its global complexity.

This chapter works across temporally overlapping though geographically disparate archives of White Being's reconstructive tendency: the late nineteenth-century Reconstruction-era testimonials of the Freedmen's Bureau and the early twentieth-century U.S. racial-colonial state's account of militarized "pacification" and U.S. proctored nation-building in the Philippines. This critical reading and meditation does not rely on traditional historical or historiographic methodologies. Rather, my approach attempts to re-read white supremacy's mundane self-chronicling, and hence its official and quotidian self-narrations, against a critical analytic that defines white supremacy as a constitutive aspirational logic of social formation, statecraft, and nation-building. What productive theoretical and political work might be enabled by re-reading these archives as chapters in the constantly unfolding memoir of White Being? If the white supremacist animus is not merely provincial, regional, or even national in its self-conceptions and political aspirations, but is in fact a Civilizational ambition that seeks the re-making and re-mapping of the world, how can we make sense of its internal continuities across different historical moments?

"A Power and Glory Dazzling to the Imagination": White Being and Speculative Historicity

White supremacy's modern post-conquest and post-emancipation form is anchored in the archive of the white racial subject's self-definition as a liberated social entity, entitled to the presumption of bodily integrity over and against the subjection of racial others to immediate danger, terror, and fatal disarticulation.[10] It is the perpetual violence of (white) freedom, and *not* the grueling matter-of-factness or "bare life" of nonwhite others' unfreedom, that reproduces white supremacy as a compulsory and indelible logic of the national form.[11] The Thirteenth Amendment to the U.S. Constitution, commonly valorized as the decree that emancipated enslaved Africans, serves as a central point of historical departure in this context:

> Neither slavery nor involuntary servitude, *except as a punishment for crime whereof the party shall have been duly convicted*, shall exist within the United States, or any place subject to their jurisdiction.[12]

Reading the Thirteenth Amendment as the decisive recodification of state-sanctioned, juridically endorsed slavery exposes the matrix of modern white nation-building. In addition to naturalizing the discursive, institutionalized, systemic affinities between anti-Blackness, criminal jurisprudence, carceral punishment, and racist state sovereignty, the Thirteenth Amendment rests on a legal redefinition of the (implicitly Black) "convict" as a civil non-being available for enslavement. Yet, this juridical availability is culturally codified as a *progressive* leap in the liberal racial *bildungsroman* of U.S. nationhood.

As a punitive ritual of justice, the amendment pivots on the systemic logic of a racial chattel state, wherein the governance of enslaved Africans defines the singularity of white civil subjectivity's broader racial-colonial political monopoly. That is, citizenship and national-historical subjectivity are not simply designated as the exclusive entitlement of whites, but must be materially secured, socially practiced, and legally defined over and against the bodily proximity of captive Africans. Put another way, the Thirteenth Amendment inaugurates a state of permanent carceral war against Black people (profiles, bodies, and geographies) that unfolds in a generalized symbiosis with protracted conditions of racial-colonial conquest. Anti-Blackness as protracted carceral warfare, in the modern period, is the (conceptual and material) condition of violence on which other forms of racial-colonial state power (against non-Black people and places) rely as a persistent, foundational template of subjection. The land and ecological displacement of Native peoples and political economic subordination of other racially marked and pathologized populations can and must be analyzed in relation to the amendment's formalization of an anti-Black power relation that shapes and unevenly proliferates the infrastructure of anti-Black (state) violence across differentiated (Black and non-Black) racial positions, subjects, and geographies.[13]

At the cusp of U.S. Reconstruction, the Thirteenth Amendment accomplished two interrelated shifts in the institutional and cultural formation of racial chattel violence: First, it nominally transferred the legally sanctioned entitlement to construct and mobilize a regime of carceral chattel punishment from the generalized domain of white plantation society to the formal domain

of the racist state; by reforming (that is, *not abolishing*) slavery as such, the Thirteenth Amendment permanently inscribed the relation of racial chattel slavery on "post-emancipation" U.S. statecraft. Second, the amendment definitively
assigned the incarcerated captive to the state as its material (chattel) property
and bodily possession; in this sense, the (Black, emancipated) convict/slave
was/is more than an *object* of formalized carceral state violence or *subject* of
resistance and revolt against racial criminalization-as-slavery, but is also the
physiological conduit for White Being's historicity in its fullest sensorial capacities. Saidiya Hartman's now-canonical explication of the enslaved African's
subjection to relation of fungibility is deeply instructive:

> The relation between [white] pleasure and the possession of slave
> property, in both the figurative and literal senses, can be explained in
> part by the fungibility of the slave—that is, the joy made possible by
> virtue of the replaceability and interchangeability endemic to the
> commodity—and by the extensive capacities of property—that is, the
> augmentation of the master subject through his embodiment in
> external objects and persons. Put differently, the fungibility of the
> commodity makes the captive body an abstract and empty vessel
> vulnerable to the projection of others' feelings, ideas, desires, and
> values; and, as property, the dispossessed body of the enslaved is the
> surrogate for the master's body since it guarantees his disembodied
> universality and acts as the sign of his power and dominion.[14]

Following Hartman's framing, the emancipated Black convict/slave, along with
their fungible "freedom," calibrate the white supremacist state's nation-building
capacities in the aftermath of emblematic white national trauma—intra-racial
civil war—and thus stages white civil society's exercises of social entitlement
and flexible access to state-condoned racial violence/terror.

This complex production of U.S. nationhood and citizenship near the turn
of the twentieth century was integral to the emergence of a social form that
was already intensely global in its aspirations. The white supremacist conquest
fantasy of Manifest Destiny, by way of paradigmatic example, exceeded the
parochial geographic and political boundaries of the national project and emblematized a delusion of divinely ordained white globality. U.S. Representative J. H. Harmanson (Louisiana), speaking in 1847 at the height of Manifest
Destiny's ideological renaissance, punctuates his Congressional speech on the
Mexican War as such:

> The political philosophers and philanthropists of the old world have
> looked on us with wonder, and with the liveliest hopes for humanity,

as they see the influence of our new civilization gradually winning its way into the hearts and minds of men the world over. . . . This is what our Union, our Constitution with its compromises, is doing for ourselves and the human race. . . .

Who is there not proud of being called a citizen of this mighty republic, reared, as if by magic, to a power and glory dazzling to the imagination? Already has its policy elevated the African from a state of barbarism to one of intelligence, happiness, and comfort before unknown to the race. Yes, I may safely add, unknown to the laboring white race of Europe. . . .

Yes, sir; I believe that African slavery in the South, instead of being a political evil, *is* a great political advantage, not only to us but to the world. I believe it has been, and will be, *one of the principal instruments in emancipating the white race. . . .*

Let our Union progress in its mission. Let it stretch its arms to the Pacific, and control the commerce of that ocean. . . . Let our agricultural States, both slaveholding and non-slaveholding, wheel into our great national army, on its march to a more perfect civilization, and break down all obstacles to our intercourse with the world . . . May God, in his infinite wisdom, direct that power, when lodged with us, to the security of virtue, happiness, and freedom to man.[15]

Slavery, in this rendition of Manifest Destiny's telos, enacts a productive and ethical national violence: It forcibly "civilizes" the African to a status of unfree "happiness," while potentially fulfilling the potentials of a global white (American) freedom. Thus, when the Thirteenth Amendment first designated the "duly convicted" as a category of (non)human available for formal subjection to the bodily punishment of slavery, it was revising and elaborating—again, not abolishing—the essential violence that constituted racial chattel: fungibility, disposability, exchangeability, and categorical exposure to white (state) violence for the sake of a national-racial destiny. In fact, this essential violence elaborates Vargas and Jung's crystallized definition of anti-Blackness, to the extent that it constitutes a material and historical touchstone for the ontological, physiological, and juridical evisceration of Black positioned people/bodies in the hemispheric production of modernity.

I am privileging this transitional moment in the statecraft and cultural structuring of racial chattel slavery—the movement and vacillation between Manifest Destiny's rationalization and emancipation's recodification—in order to scrape the surfaces of the white supremacist Civilization project and induce an archival encounter with the terror of white historicity in-and-of-itself.

A genealogy of white supremacist animus is necessarily different from an outline of white supremacy's institutionalizations of oppressive dominance. While its accumulated labors and technologies certainly require the constant work of historical inventory, white supremacy is not reducible to its institutional or ad hoc expressions.

This is where the endemic methodological and theoretical slipperiness of tracing the trajectory of white supremacy *as an aspirational social logic* can find some creative traction in speculative re-narrations of its archive—that is, a subjection of its discursive materials (texts, orations, records, maps, poems, paintings, and so on) to disintegrating counter-readings of White Being, including demystifying interpretations of the various iterations of the white human being as the assumptive subject of knowledge, politicality, sociality, and modernity, et al.

To engage white supremacy's archive is to confront a speculative historicity: The past constantly infiltrates and shapes the present, twisting the presumed linearity of time into knots and tangles through technologies of violence, ceremonies of White Being (for example, national anthems, federal holidays, monuments to white national ascendancy, and so on), and narratives of world-making that eradicate any feasible distinction between fiction and historical truth.[16] Of this confrontation, Paula Gunn Allen writes, "Like our sisters who resist in other ways, we Indian women who write have articulated and rendered the experience of being in a state of war *for five hundred years.*"[17] While Sarah Haley's speculative Black feminist historiographic/narrative praxis unfolds somewhere on the obverse of this chapter's confrontation with White Being, her active inhabitation of archival violence exemplifies the risks and possibilities of a counter- and anti-disciplinary method:

> A speculative accounting of the lives of Nancy Morris and Adeline Henderson grounded in and elaborated from a range of archival documents is not an attempt to romanticize women's lives or relationships and does not remedy archival gaps or offer a redemptive reading, but instead *enables a historical musing upon the emotions, ambivalences, and intimacies that might have marked their experiences in the context of overwhelming violence.*[18]

What might it mean to follow Haley by similarly "musing" on the archive of the anti-Black, racial-colonial state as a global memoir of White Being and its reconstruction? Guided by the work of Allen, Haley, and others, this chapter considers how white supremacy's most excessive and extensive violences never quite displace or truly separate from the massive historical aspirations to which they are attached, whether Manifest Destiny, "democracy," or the infrastructures and epistemological labors of (white) modernity. Rather, these violences are tethered to a durable sociality, characterized in part by relations of fatal and immanently fatal dominance, compulsory inscriptions of "the human" and the gendered-racial-colonial structuring of its physiology and historical subjectivity, distensions of racial-colonial genocide and anti-Blackness as technologies of extermination and logics of social formation, and so forth.

The historicity of white supremacy's animus surfaces in the periodic and experimental harnessing, recalibration, and institutionalization of these vacillating, orbiting violences. If the stuff of the "historical" entails an alchemy of (white, racial) subjectivity, militarized and fortified collective bodily integrity, and moral amnesty from evil (which is both the pretense and outcome of the Manifest Destiny delusion), then the white supremacist animus can be traced in the historical archive as that which dynamically orders and enables proliferated violence in particular moments of apparent transition or contingency: in this case, the shift from racial chattel slavery to Southern apartheid, and genocidal racial-colonial conquest to neocolonial domination. The narrative force that tethers white supremacy's productive violence to its epochal civilizational ambitions may at times be disrupted or detached. Evidence of such rupture surfaces in the archive, enabling while compelling confrontation with the speculative self-narrations of White Being. Its archive/memoir anchors the logocentric aspirational ensemble of white supremacy, promiscuously blurring past/present, here/there, and human/inhuman.

I depart from the Thirteenth Amendment's recodification of slavery not only because it has been a primary cultural and legal technology for the modern anti-Black social formation of the United States, but also because it implicates and enables the abstracted authorial white subject that mediates the official archives of white supremacist statecraft. While the archives of the Freedmen's Bureau and U.S. colonialist pacification in the Philippines index disparate historical and geographic locations in White Being's documentary memoir, they are inseparably linked in the narrative regime of White Being's ascendancy.

An insurgent reading of the overlapping transitions from plantation slavery to apartheid segregation and genocidal colonialism to neocolonial national sovereignty exposes a primary narrative technology of White Being: In moments of social and state reform, the ascendancy of White Being remains the *assumptive* premise of (national) progressivist change; this ascendancy, in turn, permeates a generalized white/national disavowal and political rejection of the ethical imperatives of abolition, decolonization, reparation, and redistribution (and so on) in moments of transition from large-scale systems of racial-colonial dominance. The archival narratives of white (self-)reform thus work to reproduce anti-Blackness and racial-colonial power, in part through the exhibition of White Being's capacity to (momentarily, contingently) recognize other (non-white, extra-white, anti-white) racialities and thus discipline as it hails non-normative genres of human being.

As Glen Coulthard has persuasively argued, such forms of state and civil recognition work in the service of White Being and generally violate or undermine the integrity of Aboriginal and Indigenous peoplehood.

> Anyone familiar with the power dynamics that structure the Aboriginal rights movement in Canada should immediately see the applicability of Fanon's insights here. . . . [T]he liberal discourse of recognition has been limited and constrained by the state, the courts, corporate interests, and policy makers in ways that have helped preserve the colonial status quo. With respect to the law, for example . . . even though the courts have secured an unprecedented degree of protection for certain [Aboriginal] "cultural" practices within the state, they have nonetheless repeatedly refused to challenge the racist origin of Canada's assumed sovereign authority over Indigenous peoples and their territories.[19]

The archival self-narratives of White Being extend the liberal coercions of recognition, consistently performing a "reformist" narrative: That is, the white human's manifest violence is the constant subject of re-narration, re-institutionalization, and rearticulation (for example, the Thirteenth Amendment) in the face of other, insurgent humans' various modalities of life, being, resistance, rebellion, and revolt against logics of dehumanization. Its own archives illustrate how the authorial practice of White Being marshals discursive, militarized, institutional, juridical, and ontological violence against all other modalities of human being.

Yet it is in the very moments when White Being disavows and reforms white supremacist institutionalities that other humans are invited to participate in the liberal humanist ceremony: the conflation of *human* being with *White* human being, a pattern of Civilization that is rendered ever more sustainable with the announcement of an egalitarian openness to others formally joining and/or cosplaying *this perverse human genre*. This conflation echoes Du Bois's foundational assertion that "if we take . . . Genius as the savior of mankind, [sic] it is only possible for the white race to prove its own incontestable superiority by appointing both judge and jury and summoning only its own witnesses."[20]

As David Roediger and others have amply demonstrated in resonance with Du Bois's foundational explications of white raciality, common sense notions of whiteness change over time, in relation to specific cultural and political circumstances.[21] For the purposes of this chapter, "White Being" is the flesh-borne imagination of a worldly access to power that presides over—authorizes and authors—shifts in the social narrative. It is a fiction that is in many ways more powerful than social or juridical truth: Truth, in the cultural and legal sense, is offered as fathomable and immediate, with consequences that bear on the limits of a community (its borders, members, and normative conduct) as well as that community's interpretation of what is good, rational, and collectively life-sustaining. Subjected to the governing narratives of White Being, however, "truth" can never again be neutral, fair, or just: The archival memoir of its truth-making provides a species template for the modern white human that, as Sylvia Wynter exhaustively demonstrates, neither tolerates nor apprehends *any other genre of human being*.[22] In White Being, there is nothing less than an authoritarian universal—Civilization—a compulsory call to war that leverages neutralization, domestication, and extermination of other human species against the alternative of those same others' de-speciation and categorical inclusion (momentary or otherwise) in the only Human Family that thrives on the correct side of the Darwinian evolutionary chain. The archive beckons.

The Freedmen's Bureau and the Memorialization of White Terror

In the context of blooming white violence and political reaction in the aftermath of emancipation and civil war, the Freedmen's Bureau was an exercise of white governmentality that alleged to perform a feat of magic. It would, first, protect a fictive Black (male) civil subject whose inhabitation of citizenship and civil society was essentially and organically fragile, traumatic/traumatized, and terrorized; second, facilitate a national re-suturing that accommodated and placated Confederate treason and its postbellum survivals; and third, breathe civic life—"freedom"—into the social body of a population whose chattel racial enslavement had recently been recodified under the terms of racial carceral criminalization (per the Thirteenth Amendment). Du Bois's account of the Bureau's inception in a 1901 essay for *The Atlantic Monthly* is instructive to the extent that it reveals both a masculine longing for authentic Black civil subjectivity and the irreducibility of the (former) white master as the flesh-and-blood instantiation of an emergent modern sociality:

> Here, at a stroke of the pen, was erected a government of millions of men,—and not ordinary men, either, but black men emasculated by a peculiarly complete system of slavery, centuries old; and now, suddenly, violently, *they come into a new birthright*, at a time of war and passion, in the midst of the stricken, embittered population of their former masters.[23]

"Birthright," by classical definition, assigns certain entitlements and privileges as congenital inheritances: A person (under patriarchal normativity, a first-born son) carries/possesses certain rights by virtue of their birth, and these rights are not contingent on benevolent bestowal or recognition by a civil correlate, state or proto-state regime, or external authority. According to the *Oxford English Dictionary*, the term carries two meanings: "1. Right by birth; the rights, privileges, of possessions to which one is entitled by birth; inheritance, patrimony. (Specifically used of the special rights of the first-born.)"; and "2. Native right; lot to which birth entitles."[24] Du Bois's description of Black men as those who "*come into a new* birthright" suggests that emancipation reinscribes rather than resolves the gendered/masculinist position of Black male non-personhood: They who have heretofore existed outside of and in alienation from the cultural and legal structures of rights and inheritance are forced into a collective encounter with the liberal reformist violence of "humanization" that, following Fanon and Wynter, inaugurates the violence of *species/genre reclassification* via humanism and Man.[25]

Wynter considers how the ideological and narrative regime of Darwinian evolution and its teleological conceptions of Man shaped modern knowledge apparatuses during the latter nineteenth century, and thus confronted the same asymmetries of (non-)personhood and human being that were induced in emancipation's fabrication of the freed slave man's "birthright." She writes that during this period,

> [B]oth *Nigger* and its transformatively generated semanteme *native* . . . functioned at the level of empirical reality as the embodiment of the dysgenic Other . . . as the . . . that-which-is-in-itself that guarantees the . . . secular model of the absolute subject in its bourgeois conceptualization.[26]

Such white humanist violence is in ample evidence throughout the Freedmen's Bureau archive. A December 1, 1863 letter to Abraham Lincoln, composed by a conglomerate of northern Freedman's Aid Societies (the regional precursors of the Freedmen's Bureau), reveals the national and racial/white supremacist subjectivities that would preside over the civil shepherding of the Black population. Stipulating the moral, religious, political, and economic rationales for the establishment of a federally controlled Freedmen's Bureau, the missive offers a Christian-inflected humanist rendition of the white man's post-emancipation burden:

> The national instincts of self-preservation have precipitated a general, if not universal, emancipation upon us a century in advance of merely

human arrangement or hopes. With all the misery that attends and must attend the sudden liberation of millions of slaves, God shows that he prefers that misery, with its glorious cause and consequences, to all the ease, comfort, or content which ever accompanied a firmly established and prosperous slave society.[27]

Drawing from the rhetorical and cosmological apparatuses of Manifest Destiny, the letter describes a program that reforms the institutional and ideological infrastructures of Black subjection to white sociality. Aligning with the compulsory labors and obligations of the modern white national subject, the creation of a Freedman's Bureau indexed the availability of Black life for manipulation by a white master *telos*—a narrative protocol of recognition by White Being, an invasive solicitation that would be actualized through disciplinary, patriarchal access to the reconstructing white nation's regimes of masculinist civility and politicality.

Here, i am especially interested in the lived experience of White Being as it accesses entitlement to the (millennial) presumption of bodily integrity. This structure of presumption remains a somewhat underappreciated, undertheorized production of the long Civilization project, which continuously creates and reproduces the Wynterian positions of "Nigger" and "native" as the external definitions and physiological indicators of presumed vulnerability to bodily *dis*integration. In confrontation with the actuality of delimited Black freedom and the potentially transformative possibilities of Black Reconstruction (per Du Bois's periodization of Black mobilizations into and around the electoral and governing apparatuses of the Southern racial state after the Civil War), the white civil being conceived the Freedmen's Bureau amidst new feelings of bodily fragility and endangerment.[28]

The presumption of white bodily integrity was interrupted by the specter of the emancipated ex-slave's masculinist inhabitation of proper politicality as the materiality of Black "freedom," a position that implied the immanent possibilities of Black revenge, radical justice, and/or liberation—in other words, the end of presumptive white bodily integrity. The precursors to the Freedmen's Bureau responded to this moment of contingency and endangerment— the possibility of White Being's *non*-ascendancy—by cultivating a relation of self-protective guardianship with "negro life":

[T]here is a moral economy to be considered. . . . The honor, the dignity, the moral and religious character of this nation is at stake. Our duties to God and man are not to be sacrificed to any mere peculiar considerations. . . . *White life is not safe when negro life is held cheap.*[29]

Unsurprisingly, political defenses of slavery in the latter nineteenth century often embraced a "moral economy" similar to that of the Freedmen's Aid Societies' liberal guardianship: The anticipated physical defense of white life formed a common parameter for both pro-slavery advocates and the administrators of Black emancipation.

Considered in the context of this white affinity, Du Bois's lexical framing of post-emancipation Black male citizenship as a "new" birthright alludes to the transparent fraudulence of the White Reconstruction project in this historical moment: Not only would the Freedmen's Bureau proctor a fundamentally (that is, racially) illegitimate polity, but it would also be inhabited by white state subjects (many of them former Union army officers) whose labors of governing could neither comprehend nor operationalize the idea of Black citizenship in an emergent, reconstructing civil society formed and reproduced in anti-Black terror. Colonel O. Brown, an assistant commissioner of the Bureau, crystallizes this unsolvable dilemma in his 1865 report on Virginia:

> The problem to be solved was, how to provide for the protection, elevation, and government of nearly half a million of people suddenly freed from the bonds of a rigorous control, acquainted with no law but that of force, ignorant of the elementary principles of civil government and of the first duties of citizenship . . . and entertaining many false and extravagant notions in respect to the intentions of the government towards them.[30]

Locked in the conundrum of white civil modernity's confrontation with a paradigmatic Black alienation from both "government" and "civility," the Freedman's Bureau and its administrative antecedents are best understood as troubled *managerial* incarnations of white supremacist institutionality.

As a vehicle of national-political narrative, the Bureau was both the institutional author and inheritor of white racial melodrama. As a political-bureaucratic innovation, it reformed and extended the moral and ethical architectures of White Being. Whatever restrictions it encountered in the form of Southern resistance to external "Yankee" occupation were mitigated by an autonomy of governance over the public discourse, administration, and political parameters of Black welfare. It was this direct management, disciplining, and rhetorical production of a projected Black civil proto-human that animated the Bureau as a primary apparatus of Reconstruction:

> We have found the freedman easy to manage, beyond even our best hopes . . . docile, patient, affectionate, grateful, and although with a great tribal range of intellect from nearly infantile to nearly or quite

the best white intelligence, yet with an average mental capacity above the ordinary estimates of it.

We have no doubts of the aptitude of the slave for freedom under any fair circumstances. But we see that his circumstances must be inevitably unfair . . . and that, independently of a great and paternal care on the part of the government, they will be so bad as to wring cries of shame and indignation from the civilized world. . . . [31]

According to Paul S. Peirce's venerable 1904 study, the essential task of the Freedmen's Bureau, as decreed by Commissioner (and Union General) Oliver Howard, was to fulfill a racial client-relation, that is, "to supply the wants and guarantee the freedom of the negroes."[32] Consider, then, how a counter-reading of the Bureau's official archive might lay bare the conceptual premises and assumptive logics that enable this bureaucratic module of white civil agency, its institutional and narrative projection of "negro" desire ("wants"), and the political invention and reproduction of the racial client-relation at the heart of the "freedom" nexus.

As a memoir of White Being, this archive narrates the logics of reform and remaking that sustain the sociality of white supremacy in the face of its potentially radical disruption by the counter-statecraft of Black Reconstruction. Du Bois contextualizes the Freedmen's Bureau as a technology of state-managed emancipation while indicating its limitations as an administrative regime vulnerable to the toxic white supremacist camaraderie that continuously bonds state officials across the North-South divide:

> [T]he Freedmen's Bureau, which rose automatically as a result of the slaves' general strike during the war, and came directly out of the consolidation of the various army departments of Negro affairs, now loomed as the greatest plan of reasoned emancipation yet proposed. For this reason, the bill for its establishment met covert and open opposition. *It was opposed by all advocates of slavery, and all persons North and South who did not propose that emancipation should really free the slaves*; it was advocated by every element that wanted to achieve this vast social revolution by reasoned leadership, money and sacrifice. It was finally emasculated and abolished by those in the North who grudged its inevitable cost, and by that Southern sentiment which passed the black codes.[33]

Du Bois stresses how the Freedmen's Bureau was structurally undermined and politically weak from its moment of inception: In 1866, President Andrew Johnson twice vetoed Congressional bills intended to sustain the Freedmen's

Bureau beyond its first year (the second veto was overridden by Congress). In this historical context, the embryonic project of what Du Bois names "abolition democracy" can be apprehended as an aspirational—though ultimately brittle—(racial) nationalism that failed to defeat a layered, irreconcilable anti-Blackness that structured the institutional, juridical, and genealogical foundations of the nation-state. This modern nation-state could neither tolerate nor administer the juridical fact of Black emancipation or the social and geographic decarceration of Black life in the wake of the chattel plantation's demise.

As "the principal expression and extension of federal authority in the defeated South" that "embodied what the Union would have freedom mean—in constitutional, ideological, and practical terms," the Bureau's most prominent functions included legal advocacy and ostensible civil protection for emancipated Black people throughout the South, the construction of public schools for the newly freed population, and the mediation of "free labor" contracts between the formerly enslaved and their formerly slaveholding white employers.[34] Du Bois writes,

> The government of the un-reconstructed South was thus put very
> largely in the hands of the Freedmen's Bureau. . . . It made laws,
> executed them and interpreted them; it laid and collected taxes,
> defined and punished crime, maintained and used military force, and
> dictated such measures as it thought necessary and proper for the
> accomplishment of its varied ends.[35]

As widely noted by historians of the Reconstruction era, the Bureau's work was consistently undermined by a lack of clarity regarding the parameters of its charge and political scope of its executive authority. Randall M. Miller states that "the Bureau never was master of its own fate," describing its bureaucratic design as one that anticipated its own quick obsolescence; Peirce writes that by early 1870, "the bureau lived on, but its life grew ever narrower and more insignificant. . . . By July, 1870, the school funds were all expended or promised. The entire force employed by the bureau in October, 1870, did not exceed eighty-seven persons."[36]

Yet rather than characterizing the Freedmen's Bureau as a "failed" governmental effort or as evidence of the Reconstruction state's negligence and abandonment of a Black population that was acutely vulnerable to revivified economic exploitation, physical violence, and state-sanctioned racial terror, it is more useful to apprehend the Bureau's formation and implosion as a therapeutic moment in the memoir of White Being. Anchored in Du Bois's analytical framing, a counter-narration that reframes the Bureau's slow, systemic

collapse as a fulfillment rather than failure of post–Civil War (White) Reconstruction helps to radically, productively disarticulate the proctor-orientation
of White Being that lords over the official archive.

One of the Freedmen's Bureau's most lasting and impactful political labors
(alongside its attempted implementation of public schooling) may have been
its chronicling—more precisely, its liberal white nationalist storytelling—of
anti-Black violence and white racial terror.[37] Huntsville, Alabama agent John J.
Wagner provides a glimpse into the mundane mechanics of this chronicling/
narration in his 1871 congressional testimony:

> *Question:* Have you kept a memorandum of the outrages committed
> since you have come to this place—Huntsville?
> *Answer:* I have kept a kind of a memorandum when anybody came to
> me. I thought the best way to do, where the outrages were of a very
> serious nature, was to write their statements out and have them sworn
> to, either before Judge Douglass, probate judge, or the clerk of the cir-
> cuit court, and some copies of these I kept and gave to Mr. Lakin,
> and some copies I forwarded to General Crawford.[38]

Such accounts clarify how the Bureau's official compilation of "outrages" was
almost entirely conducted, interpreted, and mediated by *white* investigators
who were not only fundamentally unfamiliar with Black people's inhabitation
of such conditions, but whose information gathering methods were piecemeal
and fragmented at best. Let us consider the ad hoc scatteredness—the institutional sloppiness—of the white Reconstruction state's methodological approach
to Black Southern testimonials as an unintended invitation to reread the
temporality, geography, and frequency of anti-Black terror in the latent post-
emancipation Confederacy. What if we explicitly read the informational labors
of the Freedmen's Bureau as providing little more than a minor fragment—a
squinting white glimpse—of an anti-Black, post-emancipation totality?

An 1868 investigation of white racist violence in St. Bernard Parish (Louisiana) fractionally illustrates the normalized density of anti-Black terrorism that
permeated white reactions to emancipation. The investigator's rhetorical conflation of Black sociality with the contingent category of "freed people" magnifies the irreconcilability of the "free Black/negro" position with modern civil
subjectivity.

> At first I found the freed people hesitating and diffident in giving me
> information, and it was only under promise that they would not be
> brought into trouble by telling me facts of which they were personally
> cognizant.

This is manifestly the result of intimidation by the whites in the
parish, and there are but few of the freed people who do not live in
continual dread and fear of being abused and killed on the slightest
pretext.[39]

A close reading of congressional records leads to the unavoidable conclusion
that the Bureau's data gathering on post-emancipation, Reconstruction-era
white racial terror in the South culls but a minimal indication—and not a remotely comprehensive or empirically adequate account—of the frequency,
intensity, and geographic breadth of anti-Black violence in this period.[40]

As the institutional voice of postbellum, enlightened white civil society's
official outrage over the anti-Black terrorism waged by a projected feudal, pre-
modern, backward Southern whiteness, the Bureau's collected testimonial
and pseudo-ethnographic accounts of anti-Black violence echo a core argument advanced earlier in this chapter: that the intimate, physiological structuring of slavery's regimes of dominance and subjection both foreshadowed
and significantly facilitated the ritualized, systemic, gratuitous civil violence
(white mobbing, rioting, lynching, kidnapping, torture, murder) that was documented by the Freedmen's Bureau with woeful incompleteness. One official's
testimony in the 1868 report on Louisiana starkly summarizes the racist state's
repression of Black political power in deference to reinvigorated, weaponized
white Southern dominance:

The freedmen throughout [St. Landry] parish are disarming. The
whites are all armed. The colored population are at the mercy of the
whites, but those who remained at their homes during the late troubles
were not molested further than the taking of their arms. They are,
however, in great fear of being injured and cruelly dealt with.[41]

Given the fact that a dynamic and complex regime of anti-Black violence was
constitutive of the antebellum plantation South, the sedimentations and grassroots remobilizations of this regime were central to the dynamics of the late
nineteenth-century and early twentieth-century White Reconstruction. As
such, the work of the Freedmen's Bureau encompassed the vital discursive and
ideological labor of rationalizing and politically externalizing the obscene,
gruesome remnants of a Southern white supremacist premodern.

A December 1865 Congressional report submitted by Thomas Smith, a Bureau Chaplain and Sub-Commander, frames the immediate post-emancipation
period as a point of historical departure for renewed modalities of slavery's
foundational gendered racist violence. Dispatched to Shongalo, Mississippi,

to investigate "an alleged outrage committed by the citizens on freedmen at that place," Smith matter-of-factly describes an incident of white terrorism that held Black life—in fact, Black joy—as its target of fatal reaction:[42]

> On the evening of November 25 the colored people were having a party; first they had a quilting, then a dancing party; about ten or eleven o'clock, while (according to their statement) the people were enjoying themselves very pleasantly, a company of white men, supposed to number about twenty, came up suddenly, set fire to all the buildings, then, surrounding them, began, and for some time continued, to discharge fire-arms, also refusing to let the people come out at the doors. . . . A few persons escaped through the doors, the rest through the windows, taking with them such things as they were able to carry. The white men drove the colored people away, and went round picking up the bundles and other articles of property, throwing them all into the fire. They caught the poultry and threw them all into the fire. Then went to a hog-pen and shot one of several fat hogs in the pen. It was said that one man, a stranger in the place . . . hearing of the party, had gone to it, and when about to make his escape . . . several shots were fired at him; he fell, and his body was lifted up and thrown into the fire; was burned so, that when the inquest was held the jury was unable to distinguish either the race or sex, and called in a surgeon to decide those points.[43]

Such white mob violence—genocidal in its logic, localized and intimate in its scale—was catalyzed by the crisis of racial-national meaning wrought by the Thirteenth and Fourteenth Amendments (especially as the latter unilaterally imposed citizen status on formerly enslaved people born in the United States). Having surrendered its formal racial monopoly on both citizenship and "freedom," the Southern white world was on the cusp of implosion: Its long-running institutional capacities, carceral methods, and ceremonies of racial self-actualization and self-recognition—external expressions of the South's peculiar chattel-based activation of White Being as a lived, worldly narrative regime—were structurally displaced at the moment of formal abolition, emancipation, and delimited Black male citizenship.

What made this world intelligible to itself once again was its revitalization of Black bodily subjection to violent white will; as Fanon has described, white racial terror is a *sociogenic* practice that rewires White Being's circuits of cohesion and rewrites its narratives in the midst of "Black freedom": "society, unlike biochemical processes, does not escape human influence. Man [sic] is what brings society into being. The prognosis is in the hands of those who are prepared to shake the worm-eaten foundations of the edifice."[44] Reading the Freedman's Bureau archive alongside the thinking of Fanon and Du Bois clarifies how anti-Black terror is not only socially productive (in this case, reconstructive), but is also indispensable to the remaking and sustaining of White Being's ascendancy in historical periods of irruptive insurgency against its calcified regimes of institutionalized dominance.

Proliferating anti-Black violence unfolded through a revision of white terrorism's relation to the Reconstruction state, the electoral form and legislative substance of which were deeply contested by various political and popular blocs in the wake of civil war. The groundbreaking scholarship of John Hope Franklin and Evelyn Brooks Higginbotham (*From Slavery to Freedom*), Paula Giddings (*When and Where I Enter*), and Clyde Woods (*Development Arrested*), among many others, exhibit the impact of Black mobilizations for—and gendered, Black feminist-led debates over—electoral empowerment through the apparatus of voting rights in specific locales while illuminating the significance of "Blues Epistemology," which Woods frames as "a theory of social and economic development and change" that frames and guides collective Black creativity, community, and radicalism in the *longue dureé* of the Southern plantation society.[45] Woods writes,

> Attempts by working-class African Americans to establish social democracy within a plantation-dominated economy provided the material basis for an ethic of survival, subsistence, resistance, and affirmation from the antebellum period to the present. The kin, work, and community networks that arose from these efforts served as the foundations of thousands of conscious mobilizations designed to transform society.[46]

In the years following emancipation, the insurgent sociality and praxis of Blues Epistemology shaped Black Reconstruction, complicating and confounding the aspirational white supremacist conjuring of the postbellum national reunion. Under these conditions, it became clear that the Freedmen's Bureau's collected testimonials could not be organized into a progressive nationalist narrative of emancipation.

Rather, the Bureau's textual and data inventory formed an extended preface to the Tilden-Hayes Sellout of 1877, which resolved the deadlocked 1876 U.S. Presidential election by withdrawing federal proctorship and military occupation of the South, condoning the civil re-militarization of the surviving Confederate bloc and enabling the South's acceleration toward an apartheid socio-political order.[47] In the context of this repression of Black Reconstruction via empowerment of the plantation elite, Smith's characterization of Shon-galo's racial climate can be re-read as a period-specific enunciation of *white social truth*:

> Threats of burning out the colored people had been made at different times by the white people. The reason they assigned was that they would break up the free niggers.[48]

The political linking, violent affiliation, and discursive conflation of burned Black flesh with "free" Black bodies works within the sociogenic logic of anti-Blackness while situating the aspirational (anti-)sociality of white supremacy: Smith's pithy account suggests that subjection to systemic fear, physiological and psychic vulnerability, and violent fatality are the categorical condition of the emancipated Black being's civil existence as such. Put another way, if the semi-permanent threat of being "burned out" is the premise for "free nigger" existence, then it is the narrative (hence *political*) reification—the liberal rac-ist *taken-for-grantedness*—of white civil life's absolute unfamiliarity with and White Being's transcendence of the systemic fragility of Black bodily integrity that structures the Freedmen's Bureau's archival chronicling. In fact, the Bu-reau's ledgering of fatal and near-fatal anti-Black violence—its selective plot-ting of casualties onto rudimentary data/incident tables in a textual exhibition of empirical rigor—fictionalizes a white familiarity with Black death and sub-jection, recoding experiential terror through numerical abstraction and pseudo-scientific description (see Figure 3).[49]

The ritualized, culturally codified racist terror of the post-emancipation pe-riod was so mundane in its consistency and transparent in its social mandate that the Bureau's congressional reports and official testimonies assume the voice of ethnographic detachment: White racist violence and its layered pro-ductions of Black vulnerability to repression, bodily disintegration, and social terror are empirically and anecdotally catalogued under the rubric of "out-rages," often detailed through a month-by-month accounting of "notable in-cidents" in specific cities, counties, and regions. A portion of the 1868 report on "Freedmen's Affairs in Kentucky and Tennessee" is typical:

> On the 29th of January, at Frankfort, the capital of Kentucky, a mob of white citizens took a negro from the jail and hung him until he was dead. This negro had been arrested and placed in jail charged with raping a white girl. Sufficient information has been received since to establish the fact that the man was innocent. But whether he was or not, this enforcement of lynch law under the very shadow of the capitol of the State of Kentucky shows how little protection a colored

Recapitulation of casualties.

Name and designation.	Nature of casualty.	Date of casualty.	Remarks.
Felio Pablo*	Killed	Oct. 25, 1868	By Andy Mayo, Thompson Morgan, and other freedmen.†
One white man, (Dem. club.)	Wounded	do.	By Eugene Loch.†
Mike Curtis*	Killed	do.	By Syco John Reuf.
Eugene Loch†	do.	do.	By Vallvey Veillon.
Thompson Morgan †	do.	do.	Supposed by Pablo Felio, and body consumed in burning house.
Josiah Johnson†	Wounded	do.	By Pablo Felio.*
Little Jacob†	do.	do.	Do.
John Proctor †	do.	do.	Do.
Billy Smith †.	do.	do.	Do.
Henry Sterling†	do.	do.	By Democratic procession.
Spencer Jones, (aged 50 years,) †	do.	do.	By Vallvey Veillon.*
Pierre Golet†	Killed	Oct. 26, 1868	By Julian Serpas.*
Res Voltaire†.	do.	do.	By Fen io, Leone, Porter, & party.
Baptiste Clemer†	do.	do.	Do. do.
Emile Azenor†.	do.	do.	Do. do.
Francis ——— †.	do.	do.	Do. do.
Henry ——— †	do.	do.	Do. do.
Joseph Cole†	do.	do.	By Vallvey Veillon.*
Felix Thomas, (freed woman,)	Wounded	do.	By Alma Marshal *
William Froleck†.	do.	do.	By Philip Goodyear.*
David Jones†	do.	do.	Do.
——— Marshal †	do.	do.	By Julian Serpas.*
Alfred Les †	do.	do.	By parties unknown.
Two freedmen, Decro x place	do.	do.	Do.
Nelson ———, (aged 99 years,)†	Killed	Oct. 27, 1868	Do.
Sophia Marshal, (freedwoman,)	Wounded	do.	By Julian Serpas.*
Eugene Joseph†	do.	Nov. 1, 1868	By Sa:apio Yona.*
——— ——— Arnold †	Killed	Nov. 3, 1868	By parties unkown.

* White.   † Colored.

Designation.	Killed.	Wounded.	Total.
Whites	2	1	3
Freedmen	9	14	23
Freedwomen		2	2
Aggregate	11	17	28

NOTE.—One of whites killed by democratic procession ; Mike Curtis, the policeman.

Figure 3. "Recapitulation of casualties," printed in testimony of First Lieutenant J. M. Lee, October 4, 1868. (Sen. Ex. Doc. No. 15, 40th Congress, Session 3, page 34.)

man can expect from the civil authorities of this State. A colored man—name unknown—was shot and killed at Newton, Scott county, on the night of the—day of January. A colored woman named Betsey was unmercifully whipped at Georgetown, Kentucky.

On the 30th day of January, Wm. Scorggins, a small negro boy, was stabbed by Mr. Scroggins, (white,) while working in a hemp field. Two freedmen were shot and dangerously wounded at Central Furnace, western Kentucky. . . .

Two colored men were waylaid and shot in Henry county, Kentucky, near the Trimble line, by "regulators." Another colored man was also shot and dangerously wounded in the Louisville sub-district. . . .

A little girl, aged nine years, was, on the 17th day of January, brought to the freedmen's hospital by a man named Bull. Upon examination it was found that her hands and feet were frozen dreadfully. Her back was scarred all over, the stripes having probably been inflicted with a cowhide. Upon investigation it was ascertained that the whipping was done by the wife of Mr. Bull, and the child was frozen by being compelled by Mrs. Bull to sleep in the coal-house. All of the child's toes were amputated. *This happened in the law-abiding city of Louisville.*[50]

Such accounts pervade the Freedmen's Bureau archive. The sheer accumulation of scenarios exceeds summary characterization, and reads as a mind-numbing, fractured totality that radically demystifies liberal narratives of emancipation, U.S. nationhood, freedom, citizenship, enfranchisement, and the sociality of modern White Being. Archival testimonies and reports covering the states of Louisiana, Kentucky, Tennessee, Missouri, Arkansas, Mississippi, South Carolina, Georgia, Florida, and Virginia examined for this chapter make it clear that Freedmen's Bureau officials were under no illusions that such violence was anything other than a durable, consistent, overarching feature of the postbellum Southern social condition. To take the just-cited report on its own terms, anti-Black terrorism generally co-existed with, affirmed, and reproduced "law-abiding" white civil society. Anti-Blackness, in this sense, is *both* a precondition and primary method of white supremacy as a modality of social formation and futurity.

A critical genealogy of white raciality can and must read gendered racist atrocity against the grain of the racist state's official archival and other narrative discursive regimes. Here, i am less concerned with the journalistic *content* of such archival accounts and whether they accurately and adequately describe a period of proliferating racist terror: They certainly do not. Against such a positivist interpretive tendency, we might attempt an insurgent reading of the Freedmen's Bureau archive that explores the evidentiary indications of the "intra-species" struggle that defines the logic of White Reconstruction in specific historical conjunctures: How does the narrativity of White Being attempt to reproduce the presumptive integrity of white civil and biological life as the premise of social coherence and rational politicality in specific moments and places?

Freedman's Bureau administrators consistently juxtapose their apparatus of white racial-civil custodianship with the pathological, race warmongering reactionary social impulse they attribute to backward white Southerners. Matter-of-factly affirming the existence of "race war" while simultaneously disavowing the Bureau's obligation to ensure "safety for the negro," an 1868 report on Tennessee states,

> [T]hough in many counties a favorable state of things exists, yet there is really a war of races constantly going on. It is true that the war seems to be carried on by the whites, *or rather by the ruffianly portion of the white race*. There is much in the political condition of Tennessee to account for a state of disorder. It is my opinion that there will be no peace for Tennessee and no safety for the negro while the majority of property-holders and tax-payers and of the white men are disfranchised. *This, however, is not within my province either to condemn or cure*.[51]

The Bureau's post-emancipation white civil subject professes distance from an allegedly vestigial white racial terror (here misnamed "war") while consistently disidentifying with the figure of the "ruffian," "disfranchised" white Southerner. White Being, in such times, represents a transcendence of the gruesome casualties of white racial reformism, effacing anti-Black subjection as a taken-for-granted of its reconstructed claim to ascendancy. A December 1865 address to the "Freedmen of Kentucky" by a Bureau assistant commissioner provides a typical pronouncement of the nobility of White Being's remade, reformed ascendancy amidst anti-Black reaction:

Freedmen of Kentucky:
   . . . All the colored people . . . in the State of Kentucky, are free, and your friend, the assistant commissioner of the Freedmen's Bureau, desires to address you in a few plain words:
   . . . You should love Kentucky, for it is a noble old State—your native State, your home and the home of your children, and now a free State.
   I advise you to remain in your old homes, and that you enter into good contracts with your former owners and masters. You have been associated with them for many years; you are bound to the old home by many ties, and most of you I trust will be able to get on as well with your late masters as with any one else. . . .
   Let the past be forgotten. Treat all men with respect; avoid disputes; demonstrate to Kentucky and to the world, by your faithful observance of the laws, by your sobriety and good morals, and by your thrift, that you are not only qualified for the precious blessing of freedom, but for the high and responsible duties of citizens of the Commonwealth.[52]

The rhetoric of racial paternalism strives to supersede the mores of the Southern slave society: Such statements extrapolate the white nation-building project's premises of coherence in a crucial moment of reformist articulation, in which Black freedom becomes an *administrative* burden foisted on white politicality. The address invokes the political specter of Black citizenship as the negation of white racial terror, while subtly affirming a buzzing white panic over the immanence of Black revolt and retribution. What, after all, does it mean to attempt to entrap the unarmed Black "freedman" within the carceral—and potentially deadly—docility of a White Being cosplay via conformity to the "high and responsible duties of citizens of the Commonwealth?" Prescriptive statements such as "Let the past be forgotten," "avoid disputes," and "faithful observance of the laws" inscribe a vernacular of *white supremacist self-protection*, wherein the disciplinary funneling of Black "freedom" into the compliances of respectability naturalizes white terror as an unfortunate though unmovable fact of Black life.

Brigadier General C. H. Howard's rationale for expanding the administrative capacity of the Freedmen's Bureau is an exorcism of the omnipresent demons of Black resistance, insubordination, and insurrection. Positing that the Bureau must be strengthened "for the protection of the whites against any hostile combinations of the blacks," he contends,

> This will be needed as long as the present public sentiment of the whites continues, *insuring a corresponding distrust and hostility on the part of the blacks*. Our agents have done much to allay such ill-feeling; and however unreasoning and ignorant the freedmen may be in any community, and however much their number may preponderate over the resident whites, they will generally heed and be governed by the advice of United States officials.[53]

Numerous Bureau testimonies characterize anti-Black violence as a force of societal nature: It is inevitable, uncontrollable, unpredictable, irrational, and thus beyond the ethical or agential domains of an emergent postbellum white civil politicality. An 1866 Bureau missive reads,

> There is a place about nine miles from this called Meadeville [Kentucky], formerly a guerilla headquarters. At that place there has been a reign of terror for two weeks. The pretense of the rascals concerned in it is to expel all the freedmen. They have made the declaration that no one shall hire a negro, not even the former owners of them. . . .
>
> The family of a certain John Blant Shacklett . . . with cocked pistols, paraded several negroes about the street, and went in search of some

who had been in the army, and would undoubtedly have killed them if
they had been found. Some of us (very few) went into business about
this point, and they were soon cleaned out, two being badly wounded.
      I [learned] yesterday they were assembled in force at Meadeville.
No process of law can be served upon them. Now, what are we to do? I
cannot undertake the business, for I have been thumped to death
nearly heretofore.[54]

Throughout the archive, officials reiterate the generalized incapacity of white
Southerners to either politically apprehend or socially accept Black emancipation and civil freedom. In this narrative historical thread, an ethic of white
supremacist civil disobedience produces gendered bodily/sexual violence
and psychological warfare against Black humanity, a force of white sociality
that can neither be accessed nor prevented by the White Reconstruction
regime.

      This archive of anti-Black violence is White Being's memoir-in-progress—a
living curation of political rationalization, ideological brainstorm, and edito-
rialized *bildungsroman.* The Freedmen's Bureau documents, testimonials, and
other texts are not simply a compilation of "primary" and "secondary" evidence
of White Reconstruction's historicity, they are also a real-time recording of the
emergent modern white subject's (reluctant) proximity, familiarity, and tragic
coexistence with sustained Black suffering and death in the post-emancipation
moment. While the extensive testimonial accounts and correspondent chronicling of racist homicide, kidnapping/hostage-taking, and white supremacist
terrorism are dense, they nonetheless betray a sense of morbidly entitled dis-
interest in their tone and cadence. Brigadier General Howard's 1865 report for
South Carolina, Georgia, and Florida is typical:

A colored woman, after much maltreatment, made her escape. She
says her master insisted she was not free; that he cared nothing for
"Lincoln's proclamation;" and when she asked to be allowed to go
away and take her children, she was confined on bread and water, and
finally got away as best she could, leaving her children behind, but
promising to get help and come for them.[55]

. . . I became convinced that . . . in Florida . . . with the majority of the
people, there was the same unwillingness, or moral incapacity, to treat
them with fairness and as freemen. I was informed by a high military
official that, since the hanging of a citizen for murder at Tallahassee,
convicted by a military court, and the pending trial of another for
shooting a negro, he had received letters from parties declaring they

would not "live in a country where . . . a man must be tried for his life for shooting a nigger."[56]

Between such narratives of incorrigible white racial barbarism, there is a palpable sense of helplessness and non-accountability that threads throughout the Bureau reports:

> *It will be impossible* to secure to freedmen their just rights without the aid of a military force. Colored people are driven from their homes and their houses burned . . . I am powerless to accomplish anything without soldiers. . . . [57]

> While I remain in the position I desire the power to protect the poor, the weak, and the ignorant, who confidently look to this bureau for the protection which the State, made rich by their unrequited toil, yet fails to afford them.[58]

> Outrage and disorder is the rule. . . . The officers of the bureau in that district have been active and energetic, but they have met with but little success in their efforts.[59]

> I would but say that it has long been my conviction that for a freedman to attempt to have himself righted before the civil courts of this State, outside of a few of the principal cities, is a farce. Magistrates, constables, and attorneys dare not, if they were so inclined, do justice to a colored man where his opponent is white. On their lives they dare not.[60]

Such statements of resignation and bureaucratic, juridical, and martial impotency are not merely the lamentations of frustrated officials encountering the internal delimitations of Reconstruction's abortive attempts at modern liberal nation-building. They are also the collective articulation of a transformative moment in the memoir of White Being.

Freedmen's Bureau officials characterize their collective historical subjectivity as if it is ethically alienated from the peculiar unreformability of the Southern white racist reactionary. This suggests a conjunctural racial moment in which White Being renovates, reforms, and finally revivifies its (self-)narratives of ascendancy, power, and dominance. The premodern, plantation-attached Southern white Confederate subject is the biographical Other of the emergent liberal modern white national/Reconstruction subject that, throughout the Freedmen's Bureau archive, attempts to author as it proctors proper Black civil existence. Simultaneously, this White Reconstruction subject re-writes the story of white Americana as the revival of an enlightened democratic telos, over and against the Confederacy's premodern, savage whiteness. Assistant Commissioner Clinton B. Fisk devotes the closing lines of his 1866 report to precisely such an epitaph for a "barbaric" (and finally failed) white civilization: "It has fallen to my lot to officially stand by the death-bed of slavery in the United States. Kentucky's throes are but the aspiring agonies of the great barbarism."[61]

Notably, the work of the Freedmen's Bureau was largely undertaken by U.S. Army personnel. As such, the reformist nation-building with which the Bureau was engaged came to be known in most quarters as the martial statecraft of "pacification." In this sense, its charge deviated from the traditional wartime obligations of raising troops, organizing and training for battle, and waging conventional war. Instead, it was preoccupied with implementing the latter stages of counterinsurgency (see Chapter 1). The intensive focus on civil assimilation of and administrative service to a Black population presumably in need of close state proctorship was not merely an institutionalization of the delimited terms of emancipation, but was also a show of military and political force that preemptively (and actively) addressed the potentials and actuality of Black revolt *qua* Black human praxis (signified in part by the political-cultural labors of Black Reconstruction).

Beede's historicization of pacification describes its genesis in the Reconstruction period while gesturing to its spatial-temporal movement beyond the continental United States, across the Pacific Ocean, and into the Philippine archipelago via the Spanish-American War of 1898:

> "Pacification" was a term used more by the army than by the marines or the navy during the period examined in this volume. Between 1861 and 1898 the army received a good deal of experience with pacification; that is, noncombat assignments involving interaction with and services to the civilian population.[62]

The experimental work of constituting post-emancipation white politicality through the Freedmen's Bureau was, in this context, much more than a utilitarian state mobilization directed toward the reunification of the white nation. The labors of re-narrating White Being also fabricated a matrix through which to comprehend the animus of white civilizational/national ascendancy through the complex arrangement of genocidal and proto-genocidal enslavement, conquest, and colonialist regimes as well as the politically generative, socially productive venture of reformist nation-building.

Thus pacification, defined by the U.S. Army as "the process by which the government [asserts] its influence and control in an area beset by insurgents" by way of "local security efforts, programs to distribute food and medical supplies, and lasting reforms (like land redistribution)" is a versatile, dynamic tactic of White Reconstruction that bridges the seemingly distant and/or disparate (anti-)social formations and political geographies constituted in the ascendancy of White Being.[63] On the one hand, tracing the statecraft of pacification at the turn of the twentieth century, from the Reconstruction of the U.S. South to the U.S. colonialist occupation of the Philippines, stretches the geographic and theoretical parameters of anti-Blackness as a condition of modern nation-building and of white supremacy as an aspirational futurity. On the other hand, as a political and military technology of the modern (white) state, pacification reasserts the historical-archival *authorial* primacy of White Being in sites of war, crisis, and counter-Civilization insurgency.

Pacification, in its planning and (attempted) execution, projects modern white raciality as a global totality that abrogates frontiers and national borders at the very same time that it militarizes and wages war over them. White Reconstruction, as a historical logic of reform, rearticulation, adaptation, and revitalization that works through a changing ensemble of cultural and political projects, extrapolates pacification into the militarized ontological evisceration and geographic displacement of Other beings and life worlds. A trans-Pacific genealogy of pacification illuminates the globality of this extrapolation.

Philippine Pacification as Reimagination of (White) Civil Society

Pacification already implies the possibility of the alienated racial other's (newly or recently) historicized humanity and labored adequacy for civil subjectivity. At the same time, its processes unfold through the agency of a transparent white historical subject: This white subject—along with its (nonwhite) derivatives or correlates—is presumed to possesses the wisdom, rationality, and pragmatic wherewithal to *actually* pacify people/places/insurgencies while undertaking the perpetual, epochal duties of remaking civil society amidst the casualties of land conquest, enslavement, and colonialist domination. The case of Philippine pacification, as another moment of revelation for White Being, emerges through three broad, overlapping global-racial crises: 1) the putative culmination of Manifest Destiny's continental colonial frontier fantasy; 2) the explosive contradictions between emancipation, slavery's recodification, post-Tilden-Hayes Reconstruction, and post-civil war national re-suturing; and 3) the trans-Pacific, post-1898 extensions of U.S. racial colonialism.

What analytical, narrative, and conceptual tools might be developed and/or refined through a reading of the U.S. "emancipation" and "pacification" regimes' spread across the Confederate geographies of postbellum, genocidal anti-Black terror in the South into the racial-colonial rearticulations of anti-Blackness and Manifest Destiny conquest in the early twentieth-century Philippines? How might a theorized, speculative archival tracking of pacification across the geographies of white-proctored emancipation further enrich a genealogy of White Being as a relentless aspiration to worldliness? This stream of narrative archival interrogation considers the Freedmen's Bureau and Philippine colonial pacification as major components of a militarized political-cultural totality that indexes White Being's aspirational ascendancy during the early twentieth century.

The U.S. colonial conquest of the Philippines was genocidal in its conception and execution, instituting a panoply of systemic and ad hoc violences and fatalities that permeated "pacification campaigns" throughout the archipelago.[64] Here, i am less concerned with revisiting the human, ecological, epistemic, infrastructural casualties wrought by the conquest than i am with studying the archival narratives and disclosures of the US colonial project's foundational diagnosis of Filipinos as "infantile, immature subjects, unready yet for self-government of body or polity—as *formes frustes* [incomplete manifestations of disease] stalled on the trajectory from native to citizen," a concept amplified by Sen. Albert Beveridge's infamous 1900 statement on the floor of Congress that "the common people [of the Philippines] in their stupidity are like their caribou bulls. . . . They are incurably indolent. . . . They are like children playing at men's work."[65] Such clinical and metaphorical associations of Filipinos with childhood, adolescence, beasts of burden, and disease—a racial-colonial grammar that presumes and anticipates the innate maturity and healthfulness of the white subject—suggested the *racial* necessity of the cultural (civil society-building) work of "Americanization" as well as the compulsory pedagogical form of the U.S. colonialist nation-building regime in the aftermath of U.S. conquest.[66]

Philippine historian Renato Constantino's classic 1970 essay "The Miseducation of the Filipino" provides an acute analysis of the U.S. proctored transition from post-war colony to nominally independent neocolony.[67] Echoing Carter G. Woodson's paradigmatic 1933 text *The Miseducation of the Negro* (a book shaped by Woodson's encounters with colonialist white supremacy during his time as a high-level administrator of the U.S.-created public school system in the Philippines), Constantino succinctly outlines this phase of colonialist pacification:[68]

> The first and perhaps the master stroke in the plan to use education as an instrument of colonial policy was the decision to use English as the medium of instruction. . . . With American textbooks, Filipinos started

learning not only a new language but also a new way of life, alien to their traditions and yet a caricature of their model. This was the beginning of their education. At the same time, it was the beginning of their mis-education, for they learned no longer as Filipinos but as colonials.[69]

Colonial pacification in the Philippines (1904–1946) closely followed the sweeping militarized conquest of the "forgotten" Philippine-American War (1899–1902).[70] This geography of U.S. colonial occupation extended and elaborated the template of reformist white supremacist proctorship that defined the political work—and archival authorship—of the Freedmen's Bureau; in so doing, the conquest/pacification of the Philippines revised as it reproduced the political-discursive conflict between the "barbaric" feudal/chattel enactments of anti-Blackness and the emerging modern, civilized, reformist white supremacist national pedagogy of U.S. nationhood. Nerissa S. Balce considers the visual culture of racial-colonial violence in her study of "American imperial abjection" at the turn of the twentieth century. Her study demonstrates how the connections between the U.S. racist state's overlapping racial domestications of the Philippine archipelago and U.S. South were well understood by those who lived in intimacy with white racial terror:

> The conflation between [B]lack and Filipino images, seen as logical and entertaining by white audiences, would, unsurprisingly, harden opposition of [B]lack communities to the Philippine-American War, as it would serve to cement, for these communities, the connection between the brutal conduct of the war by Americans against Filipinos and the upsurge of lynchings committed by whites on [B]lack Americans.[71]

The ongoing confrontation between anti-Black, racial-colonial atrocity and paternalistic white modernization destabilized White Being's autobiographical equilibrium and political identity throughout the latter years of the nineteenth century. This antagonism was partly reconciled through the racial-colonialist project of imagining and materially constructing the "independent" modern Philippine nation-state/neocolony, an effort that facilitated a narrative disavowal of the savage "pre-modern" white supremacist violence of slavery, conquest, and colonization.

Focusing on the changing comportment of white supremacist animus brings rigorous attention to nuanced shifts in the self-articulation and self-comprehension of White Being. Sarita See's conceptualization of "the disarticulation of empire" is especially useful in this context:

> If one heeds what is happening in the shadows of the American empire, one starts to see the profound impact and unexpected consequences of

colonialism, the history of which irrupts in ordinary and extraordinary ways.[72]

Following See, a critical trans-Pacific framing of *both* Manifest Destiny and the emergent apartheid aftermath of racial chattel slavery allows for a re-contextualization of Beveridge's vision of White Being's ascendancy in the Philippine colonial context:

> The Philippines are ours forever, "territory belonging to the United States," as the Constitution calls them, . . . We will not repudiate our duty in the archipelago. . . . We will not renounce our part in the mission of our race, trustee, under God, of the civilization of the world. . . . He has marked us as His chosen people, henceforth to lead in the regeneration of the world. . . .
>
> [The Filipinos] are not capable of self-government. How could they be? They are not of a self-governing race. They are Orientals, Malays, instructed by Spaniards in the latter's worst estate.
>
> They know nothing of practical government except as they have witnessed the weak, corrupt, cruel, and capricious rule of Spain. . . . What alchemy will change the Oriental quality of their blood and set the self-governing currents of the American pouring through their Malay veins? How shall they, in the twinkling of an eye, be exalted to the heights of self-governing peoples which required a thousand years for us to reach, Anglo-Saxon though we are?
>
> Let men beware how they employ the term "self-government." It is a sacred term. It is the watchword at the door of the inner temple of liberty, for liberty does not always mean self-government. Self-government is a method of liberty—the highest, simplest, best—and it is acquired only after centuries of study and struggle and experiment and instruction and all the elements of the progress of man. Self-government is no base and common thing to be bestowed on the merely audacious. . . . Savage blood, Oriental blood, Malay blood, Spanish example—are these the elements of self-government?[73]

While Beveridge's oration is well-known as an enunciation of white national-ist patriarchal arrogance and is often read as primary documentation of clas-sical white supremacist colonial ideology, it has generally been conceptualized as a discursive *artifact* of a U.S. national-racial past.

Against this compartmentalizing analytical impulse, i would stipulate that Beveridge's discourse on Anglo-Saxon Civilization is better understood as, first, a trans-Pacific extension and re-imagination of the cultural geographies and political tropes of genocidal Manifest Destiny and its modalities of aggression against Indigenous and Native peoples; and, second, a paradigmatic, common-sense articulation of a *national epistemological* structure inseparable from its anti-Black ideological and institutional precedents and derivatives.[74] Here, the civil and pedagogical projects of colonialist pacification are directed toward conditions and peoples presumed to be restless, disorderly, wild, and immanently warlike. This, in part, is how the project of remaking White Being's ascendancy permeates the aftermath and active presence of militarized racial-colonial atrocity.

During the period of Philippine colonization, a statecraft of proctored national independence conceptualized and implemented colonialist occupation as a form of liberal white supremacist nation-building.[75] Central to this colonialist proctorship was a preemptive U.S. supervision of Philippine national independence (scripted for consummation on July 4, 1946) that would be administered through the Philippines Independence Act of 1934 (commonly known as the Tydings-McDuffie Act). This colonial legislation evidenced the reconstruction of a global racial protocol, traceable through the overlapping institutional formations of the Bureau of Indian Affairs, Freedmen's Bureau, and U.S. colonial administration of Philippine independence.

The Philippine colonial project must be understood as an early twentieth-century political offspring of the New World/Civilization project.[76] Rick Baldoz depicts the guiding political-ideological problematic of this period as a colonial debate steeped in projections of the epistemic and ontological ascendancy of White Being:

> Imperialists . . . used paternalistic racism to undercut Filipino demands for national self-determination in the aftermath of the [Spanish-American War] and to justify claims about the need for a protracted period of Anglo-Saxon discipline and tutelage in the islands. Anti-imperialists drew on a very different strand of racial ideology to frame their case. American society, they argued, was already beset by racial conflicts, and the annexation of the Philippines would only add to the nation's intractable "race problem."[77]

While the Reconstruction of the U.S. South entailed a remaking of White Being that disavowed its agency and complicity in the reproduction of post-emancipation anti-Black atrocity, the conquest of the Philippines induced an ethical crisis for white historical subjectivity in defining the racial logic of colonial administrative power.

We can read President Franklin D. Roosevelt's 1934 missive to Congress as an executive letter of recommendation attesting to the successful maturation

of the Filipino civil subject. The document performs a vernacular and historical revision (erasure?) of the historical facts of genocidal colonialist conquest,
obscuring four decades of U.S. racial-colonial dominance with a narrative of
global government of and for Philippine "sovereignty." Herein lies a vital moment in the memoir of White Being: a *transposition* between the mobilization of civil/social/biological death (chattel slavery, frontier conquest, and
colonialist occupation) and the proctoring of political sovereignty for racial subjects unfamiliar (and generally incompatible) with modern politicality (the
ongoing statecraft of Civilization).

> To the Congress:
> Over a third of a century ago the United States as a result of a war
> which had its origin in the Caribbean Sea acquired sovereignty over
> the Philippine Islands. . . . *Our Nation covets no territory; it desires to
> hold no people over whom it has gained sovereignty through war against
> their will.*
>
> In keeping with the principles of justice and in keeping with our
> traditions and aims, our Government for many years has been com-
> mitted by law to ultimate independence for the people of the Philip-
> pine Islands whenever they should establish a suitable government
> capable of maintaining that independence among the nations of the
> world.
>
> For 36 years the relations between the people of the Philippine
> Islands and the people of the United States have been friendly and of
> great mutual benefit. . . . After the attainment of actual independence
> by them, friendship and trust will live.[78]

Roosevelt's vacillation between reverence for sovereignty, valorization of violent colonialist occupation, and unilateral assertion of U.S.-Philippine "friendship" amounts to both a narrative grandstand and trans-Pacific racial protocol.
The movement of white politicality comports through a democratic capaciousness that is entwined with the *assumptive ethicality* of White Being.

This ethical self-immunization allows the colonialist authority to defer
meaningful accountability for its long, ongoing accumulation of casualties and
atrocities while delimiting the colonized subject's political recognition as a
proper civil being (via "independence"). Put another way, Roosevelt's letter of
racial recommendation positions the colonialist statecraft of white supremacy
as always having held dear the best interests of the racially colonized. The latter's political destiny, in turn, is contingent on the paternal civil pedagogy of
the white state figure and its multiple juridical, military, and bureaucratic embodiments. What unfolds in this and similar coterminous archival texts are

the narrative technologies of See's "disarticulation of empire," the longer consequences of which have deformed the national historical memory as well as
much of the scholarly historical record of the global imperial U.S. racist state:

> [T]he compulsive, organized nature of imperial forgetting has ren-
> dered inarticulate and incoherent the history of colonialism. Unlike
> other Western colonial projects, American imperialism traditionally
> does not recognize itself as such. To the extent that it has entered
> the national imagination, the transoceanic empire is perceived as a
> scattered, diffuse, almost nonterritorial entity. . . . The empire appears
> disembodied, simply expansive swaths of the Pacific Ocean littered
> with barely discernible bodies of islands.[79]

It was under these conditions that the presidentially appointed Philippine
Commission investigated social conditions, made executive recommendations,
and initiated a comprehensive governmental-juridical overhaul during the
early years of occupation (1900–1916). The Commission was charged with administering and managing Philippine state and civil society into a proper
modern existence: In its first four years, the Commission passed over 1200
pieces of legislation, including policies that covered the reorganization and
modernist streamlining of Philippine "municipalities," purchases of individual land tracts and buildings, rationalization of national coinage, creation of
public schools, and bureaucratic organization of tax collection.[80]

The work of the Philippine Commission suggests that the transposition between white supremacy's violent/fatal processes and benevolent/reformist
ventures is never quite complete, and that its unfinishedness is not evidence
of the colonial administration's failure, but is instead a *productive* expression
of the global-civilizational imperatives of white statecraft and civil life. The
endemic incompatibility between White Being (as well as white politicality)
and its racially "immature," "stalled," or otherwise under-evolved political
adoptees, assimilates, and wards induces a perpetuality of white proctored redress, reform, and racial pedantry. Read through this productive incompatibility, Roosevelt's discourse is not merely a facile (though no less effective and
powerful) rewriting of the facts of U.S. colonialist dominance, but is also an
assertion of white governmentality's ascendancy in the calibration of "sovereignty" as the logical narrative outcome of Philippine colonization.[81]

Racial colonialism is not reducible to its massive casualties, transgenerational
traumas, and genocidal violences, even as it can never be delinked from them.
Similarly, the legacies of white supremacist national modernities, including
notions of national independence and sovereignty, are not the unilateral and
singular production of white historical agents in a one-to-one correspondence

with the racial-colonial political apparatus. The protocols of wardship/assimi-
lation/neocolonialism compose uneven dialogical processes, often precipitat-
ing sudden lurches and shifts in identification, affect, and political
sentimentality.

In a refraction of Roosevelt's political mythology of Philippine-U.S. friendship, the 1935 gathering of the Liga Patriotica in Manila exhibits the racially
colonized subject's interpretative performances of modern sovereignty in and
through a pageantry that valorizes white ethicality and its correlate governmentality. The Liga Patriotica's archival texts illustrate a disciplinary contingency within the racial-colonial historical geography: The (militarized)
protocols and pedantic bureaucratic regimes of the racial-colonialist state demand that the colonized subject ritually acknowledge the *magnanimity* of a
white colonial politicality that is willing to (potentially) recognize the colonized's (potential) capacity to exercise modern political self-determination.
The Liga's "Resolution 1," dated May 16, 1935, reads at first gloss like a syco-
phantic valorization of the United States for graciously granting Philippine independence. Opening with a declaration of "the gratitude of the people of
the Philippine Islands toward the government and people of the United States
for the passage of the Tydings-McDuffie Law and certification of the Constitution of the Commonwealth," the document continues,

> [T]he Liga Patriotica . . . hereby extends its most sincere and profound
> gratitude to the Congress and people of the United States of America
> for the passage of the Tydings-McDuffie Law; to the illustrious Presi-
> dent of the United States of America, the Honorable Franklin Delano
> Roosevelt, for his approval of the Constitution of the Philippines . . .
> thus making the establishment of the Philippine Republic, the only
> Christian republic in the Far East, possible; and to our beloved Gover-
> nor General, the Honorable Frank Murphy, for his services for and his
> deep and abiding faith and interest in the Filipino people.[82]

On the one hand, the Liga Patriotica's memorialization of U.S. colonial pa-
tronage compresses the idea of Philippine "sovereignty" into a pledge of allegiance to the neocolonialist United States. Such a gesture erases the multiple,
coterminous revolutionary struggles for national democracy, indigenous self-
determination, and sovereignty that seek (to this day) the eradication of U.S.
empire as well as the overthrow of an emergent modern Philippine nation-
state. The resolution also effaces the dense layers of anti-colonialist resistance
against U.S. occupation articulated by the Philippine petit bourgeoisie,
intelligentsia, and local political leaders throughout the first two decades of
U.S. conquest. The Liga's rhetoric of gratitude instead locates the putative sov-

ereignty of Philippine civil life firmly within the narrative arc of Roosevelt's anti-colonialist neocolonialism. Yet, such performances of loyalty to the U.S. colonial and neocolonial order nonetheless failed to conceal vast, varied forms of insurrection against U.S. occupation and governance.

Organized resistance to the colonial civil government surfaces throughout the U.S. congressional archive of this period. A document from the 56th Congress dated February 27, 1901 includes facsimiles of Philippine authors' handwritten signatures (see Figure 4) and translations of protest missives from the municipal governments of the island of Cebu that cast doubt on the sincerity of the Liga Patriotica's (and many other civic groups') professions of Filipino loyalty to the U.S. colonialist (and incipient neocolonialist) order. The proceedings of the Danao municipal council are symptomatic of this political counter-tendency:

They sign this document of protest in order to make the facts known. Done in the town of Danao, September 25, 1900.

PROTEST.

Figure 4. U.S. Congress facsimile of signatures accompanying transcription of municipal protest against creation of U.S. colonial civil government (Danao, Cebu province, 1900). (Sen. 234, 56th Congress, Session 2, page 2.)

PROTEST.

The undersigned, members of the popular junta (municipal council) of Danao, of this province, declare that they objected to taking the required oath of allegiance to America. They state that for objecting to this they were thrown into prison and were obliged to work in an objectionable and mortifying way. . . . That they refused to take the oath at first because it was contrary to their inner belief. . . . But after great suffering and ill treatment they were obliged to take the oath under duress. . . .

Therefore, since the undersigned were forced to take the oath, they protest against the forces employed to compel them to do so, and declare that they forswear the oath, which was against their will and honest convictions.

They protest against these acts of violence, which they declare is contrary to all honor and right. They also affirm that they were compelled to leave their town to avoid the acts of violence committed by the soldiers under a despotic American captain stationed in that town.[83]

The continuities between colonialist political coercion and Filipino performances of allegiance to U.S. (neo)colonial power (Roosevelt's "friendship"), as well as the symbiotic linkages between genocidal colonialist violence and U.S. civil pacification, are constitutive of a modern Philippine political genealogy. A tension within these circuits of force and racial-colonial recognition tears at the archival seams of the U.S. pacification project.

The colonial statecraft of civil construction and modernization, initiated during the Philippine-American War (1899–1902) and continuing through the 1930s, was confronted by a vast constellation of resistance, encompassing Filipino *ilustrado* (formally educated Philippine petit bourgeoisie) claims to self-determination, provincial armed rebellion, and Indigenous peoples' anti-colonialist struggles. Close examination of the social and juridical infrastructure of U.S. colonial state-building, military and bureaucratic occupation, and political proctorship further reveals the *narrative* technologies of the neo-colonial undertaking as it confronts this spectrum of resistance across the archipelago.

The 1909 Philippine Commission Report details legislation, school and hospital development, and other colonialist infrastructure-building projects that reflect a cultural, economic, and sociopolitical conception of modern Philippine civil society and presumes the endemic necessity (and ultimately benevolence) of U.S. capitalist, state, and military occupation. The report's discursive movement between rhetorics of explanation and advocacy suggests deep concern over the feasibility of instituting modern economic development and political sovereignty in the archipelago. Criticizing the U.S. federal government's interference with the land-based expansion of private American business interests in the Philippines, the report subsumes colonized peoples' quality of life to the mandates of capital's mobility:

> The fact that no large tract of land has been purchased of the government, and that no single large enterprise has been undertaken for the development of agriculture, in our judgment proves conclusively that the limitations placed by [U.S.] Congress on the quantity of land which one corporation or individual may acquire from the public domain has had the deterrent effect of preventing capital from coming here, *which could not but prove beneficial, not only to the capitalist, but also to the Philippine Islands from the development of their latent resources and the opportunity for employment and better conditions of living which it would bring to the inhabitants.*[84]

Consider the U.S. racial-colonial project as a cultural formation that pivots on such narrativizations of expansion, possession, productivity, and capital mobility. This is to delicately resituate Edward Said's critical project within the early twentieth-century Philippine condition:

> [A]t the outset one can say that so far as the West was concerned during the nineteenth and twentieth centuries, an assumption had been made that the Orient and everything in it was, if not patently inferior to, then *in need of corrective study by the West.* The Orient was viewed as if framed by the classroom, the criminal court, the prison, the illustrated manual. Orientalism, then, is knowledge of the Orient that places things Oriental in class, court, prison, or manual for scrutiny, study, judgment, discipline, or governing.[85]

On the one hand, the archival texts of Philippine pacification demonstrate the strategic, bureaucratically managed conflation of the pathways toward U.S. proctored independence—production of viable civil society, facilitation and political-military protection of U.S. capital, construction of modern governmental apparatuses, and so on—with the global ambitions of the neocolonialist U.S. empire. On the other hand, this archive also *fictionalizes* pacification through the symbols and speculative imagination of white supremacist sociality. To clarify: i understand pacification's social imagination/fiction to be *constitutive* of its structural, institutional, and material (extra-discursive) mobilizations. The colonial narrative of pacification serves as both a primary inspirational text for

White Being in a specific historical moment and political geography of racial coloniality, and as direct political guidance for a peculiar conceptualization of U.S. racial-colonial power that, from its inception, was fixated on paternalistic protocols for conceding formal sovereignty to colonized populations.

The durable link between the social imagination/fictions of pacification and its substructure of racial-colonial violence becomes evident in archival moments that rupture the clinical sterility and descriptive tedium of conventional state recordkeeping. Departures from empirical tedium and narrative cleanliness are especially conspicuous in textual fragments that reveal the stubborn persistence of Philippine civil discord, particularly resistance to and armed insurrection against U.S. colonial occupation among Muslim and other non-Christian Indigenous populations, as well as the multiple pestering failures, insufficiencies, and lingering pathologies pocking the Philippine civilization-building infrastructure. In the latter case, the projected customs, culture, and physical comportment of the Filipino "native" are not merely the collective object of disciplinary reform for pacification's white supremacist proctorship and civil pedagogy, but also a primary focus of racial-colonialism's logic of reconstruction.

The tale of pacification collapses on its own flimsy fiction in a Commission report titled "Conditions as to Peace and Order." Extending a genealogy of genocidal continental conquest against Indigenous peoples in North America, the U.S. military radically expanded its operations in the Philippines after the Spanish-American War, permanently dislocating native cultural and political economies, killing 1–2 million people, and destroying an unknown mass of homes, villages, and sacred objects. In the immediate aftermath of this ecological, cultural, and human carnage, the persistence of Indigenous Philippine resistance to U.S. occupation disrupted pacification's white supremacist narrative of paternal benevolence. The archive of pacification builds a narrative arc of official silence around the casualties wrought by the first decade of the U.S. colonial invasion, compartmentalizing the latter phases of the colonial project into a narrative of racial modernization that isolates its conditions of operation from the fallout of genocidal conquest. It is as if the Commission's treatment of surviving Indigenous insurrectionists presumes the prior decade of genocidal violence as a natural, unavoidable, and/or ordinary feature of the social and historical span that is not worthy of substantive comment. In this storytelling of U.S. colonial conquest, the archival (and academic) silence enmeshing the "forgotten" U.S.-Philippine War is itself an epistemological project: The ongoing insurgencies against U.S. authority are not evidence of authentic anti-colonial war, but are textually dispersed as isolated *criminal* disruptions of a U.S. proctored civil peace. U.S. colonialist repression fictionalizes itself as civic policing for (but not *of*) the Filipino colonial/civil subject. Those who dare to disrupt this story are actively unnamed, with precious few exceptions:

> We believe it is safe to say that never before in the history of the islands has public order been as well preserved as it is to-day. With the exception of one fanatical agitator, who has committed no depredations, but seems to maintain an organization in the provinces immediately north of Manila, which purports to be religious in its character, *there is not one outlaw in the whole island of Luzon who is of sufficient note to be mentioned by name.* . . . the same condition prevails throughout the Visayan Islands, with the single exception of Samar, where one of the later chiefs among the polahans is still at large. . . .
>
>   This statement, however, does not hold good of the island of Mindanao, where during the year there have been several serious infractions of public order. The first of these resulted in the punitive expedition by the constabulary against certain Moros inhabiting the country between Lake Lanao and Cotabato Valley, known as the Buldong country. The second were depredations of a band of pirates under the leadership of a man by the name of Jikiri.[86]

Equally disruptive to the story of pacification is the racial incorrigibility of the Filipino, whose human praxis stubbornly fails (or refuses) the tutorship of a white supremacist cultural modernity. The Commission insists, for example, that the dismantling and reforming of Filipino eating habits must become a focal point of colonial social engineering:

> Another change toward which the energies of the government should be bent, but one fraught with much more difficulty and one in which any general progress can not be expected except during the lapse of a considerable number of years, is teaching the people to eat with knives and forks and to discontinue the present custom of eating with the fingers, which prevails among the lower classes throughout the archipelago.[87]

In addition to asserting that eating with the hands is a trait so ingrained that it will require "considerable years" of racial training to undo/correct/civilize, this passage gestures toward a generally undertheorized, speculative—though no less practical—dimension of colonialist white supremacy. The endemic failure of the colonial native to inhabit the *white raciality* of the modernist, civilizational *telos* sustains the social dream of pacification in perpetuity: White Being's ascendancy is affirmed in the native's endemic—that is, racial—failure to fulfill the expectations accompanying their (involuntary, coerced) residency within white civil society's political, cultural, and physiological architectures. It is not merely the native's "custom" of eating that disturbs and disrupts the disciplinary white supremacy of pacification; it is the native body's gestures, its epidermal and physiological unassimilability to white civilizational expectation, and finally its lurking susceptibility to racial regression to pre-tutorial mores that present a permanent threat of betrayal to the Civilization project.

To address the genealogy of pacification as both a narrative of Civilizational fulfillment and productively failed racial tutelage nourishes the theoretical conception of white supremacy as an aspirational social logic that crosses multiple registers. The aggressive, bureaucratic fabrication and management of Filipino civil society valorizes a certain surgical and procedural cleanliness— "It is fortunate that the Philippine people themselves appreciate the value of pure water. . . . This most encouraging feature of the work indicates that it will not be difficult to persuade the Filipino to make use of other sanitary facilities when offered"—that is nonetheless consistently sullied by the racial-colonial ward's ineptitude, stubborn disobedience, or phenotypic betrayal of white politicality and its civic template.[88]

The archival texts of Philippine national emancipation are simultaneously a rationalization of the "outcomes" of pacification and a re-scripting of white raciality that relies on a narrative foreclosure—what Said would call the colonizer's invasive "knowing"—of Filipino raciality. This epistemic compartmentalization of Philippine being attempts to selectively smooth over the discordances, incompatibilities, and incorrigibilities defining the post-conquest Philippines, simplifying a complex social and cultural geography that, according to the colonial archive's own account, is characterized by a multiplicity of tribal, ethnic, religious, linguistic, and phenotypic racial subjects rather than a singular "Filipino" raciality. The possibility of such a wild, epistemically disruptive, anti-national proliferation of tribal and linguistic modalities of human being is that which requires foreclosure, sacrificed to the modern white fictions of political independence and national sovereignty that reassert Civilization's trans-Pacific distension of Manifest Destiny.

Representative Millard E. Tydings's 1934 report "Philippine Independence" drafts a racial-colonial genealogy of the Philippines, situating "Moro," "Mohammedan," and "Pagan" difference as relatively inessential differentiations within an otherwise racially monolithic modern national Filipino subject.

Ninety-two percent of the approximately 13,500,000 inhabitants of the Philippine Islands are Christians. Four percent are Pagans and 4 percent Mohammedans. These Mohamedans are the so-called "Moros." The Mohammedan, the Pagan, and the Christian Filipinos are racially identical. Their history and tradition are the same. The Mohammedan and Pagan Filipinos have for a long time acquiesced in the government of the islands by the Christian majority. . . .

There is no substantial evidence that these Moros and others have protested against Christian preponderance in the government.[89]

Given the abundant, coterminous and archival evidence of revolt and armed insurrection in different parts of the archipelago during and beyond this period, Tydings and the Committee on Territories and Insular Affairs do not provide a remotely credible account of the Moro and non-Christian population's disposition toward the veritable governmental monopoly exercised by Christian Filipinos during this period.[90] Rather than providing a reasonably rigorous description of intergroup antagonisms across the archipelago's wide variance of political, topological, ecological, and cultural geographies, the report embraces the white supremacist statecraft of colonial narrativity: It harnesses the unruly humanity of the archipelago's many peoples—their vast differences of bodily presentation, cultural self-definition, social reproduction, political organization, and spiritual/religious practice—under a disciplinary story of modern raciality. In addition to rationalizing, erasing, and otherwise minimizing the evident, long-running, and persistent tensions, wars, and antagonisms among the peoples of the Philippines, the report unfurls superficial explanations of religious, tribal, and regional difference, clumsily conflating the archipelago's "inhabitants" into a racial, historical, and traditional "sameness." This narrative act is vital to the conceptual apparatus of proctored sovereignty: Addressing the period preceding the U.S. colonial presence, the report assesses Filipinos' alleged preparedness for modern white racial mentorship:

> *The Filipino people are the beneficiaries of several centuries of civilization.* Long before the Spanish conquest of the islands in the latter half of the sixteenth century, the inhabitants possessed a certain degree of culture, including written languages, characteristic arts, and industries. . . . This civilization and culture were, like the people themselves, of Malay origin, but with Indonesian and Mongolian elements.
>
> Spanish occupation of the islands for more than 3 centuries introduced and established Christianity, European jurisprudence, language, and customs. It centralized authority and tended thereby to unify the country.[91]

The vindication of White Reconstruction in this instance entails an extended affirmation of the pacification project as an ethical success, determined by whether the racial proctorship of colonized wards results in their capacity to assimilate *just enough* of the rituals, rhetorics, and institutional forms of white politicality to justify the white gift of emancipation.

As the U.S. racial-colonial state unfurled the fiction of white supremacist benevolence as "a practical apprenticeship in self-government" for the proper Filipino racial-national subject, the pacification project also instituted a conjunctural audit of White Being's ascendancy in a new political habitus, under changed conditions of racial embodiment.[92] In the wake of genocidal conquest, White Being was entangled in a Civilization project that simply could not shake its commitment to world deforming violence even while it formulated a colonial template for *racial capaciousness* that extended the institutional geographies and politicalities of modern (white) state and civil society to the very peoples it diagnosed as racially alien, sociologically and economically underdeveloped, and physiologically and culturally incorrigible.

In this context, Tydings's report (an almost identical version of which was submitted to the Senate by Senator John McDuffie) marks a definitive moment in the memoir of White Being.[93] The text offers a story of White Being as an enactment of ethical racial ascendancy that rests on a divinely ordained and rationally cultivated capacity to arbitrate the (un)tamed native's access to sovereign governmentality. This grandiose racial-political generosity becomes the narrative keystone of Philippine emancipation:

> The people of the islands are not unmindful of our efforts at the cost of our blood and large expenditures of our public funds for their progress and development, and to give them their place in the sun. . . . From a standpoint of education, the administration of justice, and a capacity to maintain their economic progress, it is not doubted that the Filipino people are fully competent to set up and maintain a free and independent government. . . .
>
> Every step taken by the United States since the inception of American sovereignty over the Philippines has been to prepare the Filipino people for independence. As a result, they are now ready for independence politically, socially, and economically.[94]

White supremacist pedagogical agency forms a global, epochal spatial-temporal bridge that spans entry to the privileged reaches of the free and self-determining world (that is, the world of White Being), while defining the proper parameters of civic life. This form of racial-coloniality posits decisive departure from the genocidal violence that subjects the native—across its Indigenous genres of human being—to both political-military subordination and the immanent threat of cultural-to-biological extinction. Philippine independence is a definitive achievement of white supremacist modernity, in a manner that demystifies the universalizing terms of "modernity" as such.

> Their educational and economic standards are higher than those of other countries in that part of the world. Under our inspiration and tutoring they have come to understand and prize and covet democracy. They recognize their debt of gratitude to the American people.
>
> . . . We owe it not only to the Filipino people, but also to our own to name the day and the way of Philippine independence.[95]

If such archival statements compose White Being's autobiographical movements and nuances—its positivist assertions of historical identity as well as its melodramas of tragedy, violence, victory, and self-actualization—then we might also depart from instances in the archive when the colonized native becomes the active (and often compromised or vulnerable) *biographer* of the white supremacist animus. (Recall that this is the epistemological and methodological position advocated by this book.)

Against the state protocols, ideological regime, and white colonial proctorship of Philippine emancipation, we can read a characteristically Filipino sarcasm, irony, and performative contradiction in Philippine Senate President (and later President of the Philippine Republic) Manuel Quezon's 1934 performance of Americanist sycophantism:

> Because the Filipino people cannot, consistent with their national dignity and love of freedom, decline to accept the independence that the [Tydings-McDuffie] act grants;
>
> *Resolved*, That the Philippine Legislature, in its own behalf and in behalf of the Filipino people, express, and does hereby express, its appreciation and everlasting gratitude to the President and the Congress of the United States and the American people.[96]

I am suggesting, by way of this example, that an archival re-reading of white supremacist animus critically foregrounds a critical praxis of "life" and "dignity" that haunts Quezon's superficial gratitude for the benevolent productions of white supremacist reformism (in all its varieties). Within Quezon's pronouncements of Filipino non-agency ("the Filipino cannot . . . decline to accept . . ."), there is a lurking resentment over the coercive conditions of emancipation as a colonial and neocolonial imposition—in fact, as a nonchoice that already usurps the capacity of the modern Filipino civil subject to act as a "self-determined" political being. Echoing the Danao council's condemnation of being "obliged to take the oath under duress," Quezon's "everlasting gratitude" can and must be read to echo the casualties of colonial violence through the diplomatic terms of intercourse between two asymmetrically sovereign and "independent" state bodies. Such is a critical historical reading practice that privileges severe analysis and disarticulation of White Being's narrative integrity, which is to say, a demystification and disintegration of the presumed epistemic subject of white supremacy's archival texts.[97] Such a political and theoretical practice may enable a broader critical praxis of human being that articulates through scholarly activist labors against the archival and other discursive regimes that reproduce the fatal dominance of Wynter's "millennium of Man."[98]

Conclusion: A Problem of Definition

The global permutations of White Being's narratives shape conceptions of modern politicality across different political and cultural geographies. Contestations over the means and principles through which social formations ought to be organized and "ruled" (in Gramsci's sense of the protracted labors of generating popular "consent") are shaped by the political productions of the white Civilizational animus, from bourgeois republicanism and militarist fascism to derivative "democracies" and European socialist governmentalities.[99] Iterations of white politicality—as they encompass notions of proper and legitimate political subjectivity, rights, government, statecraft, reform, and even revolution—constitute the disciplinary premise of modern political discourse as well as the institutional prototypes through which such political discourse manifests in processes of rule, change, and transformation.

The archival re-narrations presented in this chapter attempt to contextualize another key theoretical question for the study of White Reconstruction and the longer archive of White Being's ascendancy: What are the conceptual (including epistemic) premises of coherence and grammars of articulation through which Civilizational narratives and their institutional mobilizations obtain their generalized currency, common accessibility, and ethical acceptability *within and beyond historically situated "white" audiences?*

At stake in this chapter's reflections on the Freedmen's Bureau and Philippine pacification/emancipation archives is a reconsideration of white supremacy's flexibility and durability as an aspirational historical telos of racial progress, as well as a critical reflection on the violence of White Being that persists across the specificities of institutional mobilizations, rhetorical shifts, and transformations of white social subjectivities.

A few points of departure can sustain critical discussion of the historically situated and politically contextualized logics of anti-Blackness and racial-colonial power that condition the narrative and institutional genealogies of White Being. Moving from the archival work of this chapter, there appear to be at least three overarching registers of white supremacist animus that cohere across various moments and geographies:

1. The ascendancy of White Being constitutes a *narrative indelibility* that shapes the political-cultural discourses and material social worlds that it invades, occupies, and otherwise produces; within this narrative structure, white supremacy serves as a logic for assessing and administering other peoples' gendered racial fitness for nation building, citizenship, rationality, Civilization, and inclusion in the protocols and institutional regimes of Man across different times and places. Such mobilizations elaborate (and naturalize) White Being as a narrative of human being that is "structured in dominance."[100] When discursive regimes and institutionalizations of existing narratives fail to make sense of White Being's (disavowed) violence, they become subject to processes of erosion, external challenge (See's notion of "irruption"), and reform/reconfiguration.

2. White supremacy's intertwined logics of historicity, sociality, and (human) subjectivity assemble a pre-conception of proper politicality that forms the historical and institutional framework through which struggles over social power—and not merely state power— are disciplined, articulated, and rendered intelligible by dominant (if not actually "hegemonic") regimes of racial-colonial order. The ascendancy and fabricated transparency of the normative white political subject, for example, compose the matrix against which the comportment, fashioning, and self-enunciation of Other political actors are punitively apprehended, judged, and measured. Such calibrations of "the political" are often so inherent to the social form—akin to the genotype of the organic political body that it nourishes—that white supremacist politicality effectively escapes the parameters of critical engagement: Put differently, this politicality becomes densely, gravely taken-for-granted.

3. White supremacy's aspirational—though no less social and material—logics of remaking, reform, and futurity "haunt" as they guide and follow the movements and transitions of White Being across historical moments: The ascendancy of White Being, as both a Civilizational imperative and affective structure (that is itself not exclusive to "white people"), is preceded and accompanied by its deep entanglement in systems of coordinated human subjection,

misery, and fatality.[101] This is how the death, violation, displacement, expropriation, and subjection of all Other humans become symbiotic with the white archival subject's socially produced—and generally militarized—presumption of entitlement to physiological and spiritual integrity. The narrative consequence of this long historical condition is that Others' deaths are rendered tolerable in their tragedy, reliably reproducing the sanctity of White Being as the earthly Civilizational project of transcending unexpected fatality. The animus of white supremacy seems to constantly invoke and reinvent this relation of tolerance, acceptance, and comfort with Other peoples' disintegration and degradation.

In the context of this provisional framing, the ascendancy of White Being is not a problem to be decisively solved or escaped. Rather, it is a condition of sustained antagonism—a social-historical state of emergency—that can and must be constantly, critically, and radically confronted and opposed rather than obscured or reified. In his famous reflection on the "darker races of the world" in *Darkwater*, Du Bois centers the genealogy of Black radicalism in a counter-vision of global futurity that levels White Being. This speculative, collective, insurgent labor generates a narrative praxis against ascendancy:

> If the Negro could speak for himself in the South instead of being spoken for, if he [sic] could defend himself instead of having to depend on the chance sympathy of white citizens, how much healthier a growth of democracy the South would have. So, too, with the darker races of the world. No federation of the world, no true inter-nation— can exclude the black and brown and yellow races from its counsels. They must equally and according to number act and be heard at the world's council.[102]

Departing from Du Bois's gesture toward a counter-archive of globality, it is possible to construct radical labors of critical reading and re-narration that utilize official archives against their assumptive epistemic and political structures. This is part of a larger collective praxis through which autonomous, liberated, and speculative politicalities can (and must) organically emerge: a praxis that envisions as it acts on White Being's abolition, that is, a work of imagination that requires extended theorization as it is mobilized into creative scholarly activist practices of every possible kind. What i have offered in this chapter is but a limited, narrow example of such an effort.

3

Goldwater's Tribal Tattoo

On Origins and Deletions of Post-Raciality

Introduction: From "Post-Racial" to Post-Raciality

Post-racial discourse rests on the allegation of an undoing. Borrowing heavily from the malleable (and often densely neoconservative) rubrics of "colorblindness," post-racialism quietly endorses the mundane continuities of racist, anti-Black, and racial-colonial state and extra-state violence even as it stipulates the dissipation and obsolescence of overt, official, and brutally direct forms of racial dominance.[1] There is almost nothing empirically credible about the post-racial narrative. Yet, as a field of knowledge production, the post-racial discursive regime is formidable and far-ranging, leaking into and beyond the U.S. presidential administrations of Barack Obama (on whom post-racialism relies for its discursive traction) and Donald Trump (whose white supremacist and white nationalist positions frequently appropriate post-racial vernaculars and political logics). Contrary to some dismissive characterizations, post-racial discourse is a complex formation of knowledge and culture: As it steadily creeps into the ensemble of a period-specific cultural and political common sense, it accumulates gravity as an explanatory device for dynamic, persistent proliferations of anti-Black and racial-colonial state and state-condoned dominance.

This chapter reimagines as it studies the archive of *post-raciality*, understood as the epistemological, affective, and practical precedent of that which has been more recently named and identified as post-racial discourse.[2] Denise Ferreira da Silva's conception of "raciality" in *Toward a Global Idea of Race* situates race as a historical regime of meaning, power, and subject formation that cannot be adequately addressed by conventional sociological notions of race relations and racial population/identity categories, nor by the variety of race-as-epiphenomenon theses that permeate many Marxist-influenced an-alytics.[3] Silva's framing inflects the work of Gilles Deleuze and Félix Guat-tari, facilitating a conception of "post-raciality" as a *problematic of immanence* that, in turn, resituates the epistemological and ideological origins of early twenty-first-century post-racial discourse in White Being's vast reservoir of his-torical and autobiographical fictions.[4]

Post-raciality is a furtive presence in the archive of White Being, surfacing in allegations of subjectivity, sociality, political empowerment, and (self-)remak-ing that refine anti-Blackness and racial-colonial power by way of disavowing implication in their casualties, violences, and mundane evil. To expropriate and resituate Deleuze and Guattari's notion of immanence, we might under-stand post-raciality as that which

> . . . assumes its immanent concrete existence only in the subsequent forms that cause it to return under other guises and conditions. Being the common horizon for what comes before and what comes after, it conditions universal history only provided it is not on the outside, but always off to the side, the cold monster that represents the way in which history is in the "head," in the "brain" . . . [5]

This is to say, post-raciality is internal to the aspirational logics of White Re-construction, shaping its narratives while often remaining inchoate, textually incoherent, and detectable only through disloyal and invasive re-readings of White Being's long archival memoir.

A critical genealogy of post-raciality calls for an archival, historically rigor-ous critical engagement with the conditions of discursive, political, and insti-tutional possibility for contemporary post-racial discourse. Such an approach attempts to generate a deeper understanding of the epistemic, political, and symbolic (that is, archival) roots of post-racialism's national and global antici-pation/diagnosis of the disappearance of racism (and even "race") within worldly expressions of White Being's ascendancy.[6] A qualification is therefore in order: A critical summation of post-racialism's early twenty-first century mo-ment of cultural-ideological legitimation in the election of Obama—and sub-sequent disarticulation at the hands of resurgent post-2016 white supremacy, anti-Black state and extra-state terror, colonialist ecocide and cultural geno-cide, and white nationalist reaction—is not the primary concern of this chap-ter. Rather, i am interested in how post-raciality induces two simultaneous tendencies in the ongoing contemporary half century of White Reconstruc-tion: the affixation of logics and imaginaries of carceral anti-Blackness and racial-colonial extermination to narratives of White Being in overwhelming synchrony with a changing, reforming racial/racist state, while blurring and/

or disavowing White Being's complicity and agency in the regimes, relations, and systemic violences that define the social conditions and institutional entitlements of racial subject-formations ("white" and otherwise). The following pages unpack these intertwined, dense tendencies.

Post-raciality enables re-narrations of white raciality within changing conditions of white supremacist social formation. The subjects of white supremacy's aspirational sociality—including those whom Sylvia Wynter references as the "nonwhite"—aspire to live and thrive in these changing conditions as ostensibly ethical, rational (racial) beings who access ontological and epistemic coherence through their assumptive freedom from implication in the systemic and widespread terror, suffering, fatality, displacement, war, and insurgency that constitute the (anti-)socialities of "dysselected" peoples and communities. Wynter argues that this order of violence emerged with acute momentum in the eighteenth century, marking a convergence of the Darwinian evolutionary paradigm with the militarized dominance of Western cultural knowledge structures fixated on a transatlantic chattel colonial racial order:

> To sum up: it is in this context that a new principle of nonhomogeneity, that of DuBois's Color Line in its white/nonwhite, Men/Natives form (i.e., as drawn between the lighter and darker races), will now be discursively and institutionally deployed as a "space of Otherness" on which to project an imagined and extrahumanly (because ostensibly bio-evolutionarily) determined nonhomogeneity of genetic substance between the category of those selected-by-Evolution and the category of those dysselected-by-Evolution. The Color (cum Colonial) line would, therefore, be made to reoccupy the places earlier occupied by Heaven/Earth, supralunar/sublunar, and by the rational humans/ irrational animals premises of nonhomogeneity in order to enable the selected/dysselected, and thus deserving/undeserving status organizing principle that it encoded to function for the nation-state as well as the imperial orders of the Western bourgeoisie . . . [7]

Following the contours of Wynter's "white/nonwhite, Men/Natives" schema, post-raciality is embedded in both episteme and affect (forming thought and feeling), while marking the peculiar ontological status of the ascendant White Being that thrives in conditions of anti-Black and racial-colonial violence/ terror while imagining (and constantly re-narrating) its innocent distance from such atrocity and fallout. Post-raciality is, in this sense, a whispered narrative of coming-into-sociality. It is significantly extra-discursive, as its aspirational narratives of ethically liberated subjectivity are often unarticulated or under-articulated, lingering in the realm of an identifiable though only semi-coherent (white/multiculturalist) racial sentimentality.

Post-raciality thus suggests the liberation of the present- and future-tense of White Being from ethical and political accountability for the planning, supervision, and construction of Civilizational edifices that materialize the logics of anti-Black ontological evisceration and racial-colonial genocide. In other words, post-raciality (in its immanence) enables a *sovereign* inhabitation of (anti-Black, racial-colonial) sociality that permanently averts historical responsibility for the deadly making of this very same sociality. This aversion is structured in delusional and ahistorical denials of the accrued entitlements (protected life, entitlement to the assumption of bodily integrity, recognized subjectivity and personhood, militarized land occupation, and so on) that facilitate white raciality's "sovereignty" in the first instance. In this way, post-raciality implies the vindication and (continued) social ascendancy of those (white and "nonwhite") historical subjects who, in their identifications with and performances of White Being, thrive on such violences as the premises of their systemic (though sometimes contingent) entitlement to bodily integrity and self-making as citizens, national subjects, and juridically recognized "free" beings (that is, as makers of properly recognized socialities). In the racial lurch of the early twenty-first century, the curricula and official archives of post-raciality tuck the long historical casualties of racial chattel, genocide, land conquest, and asymmetrical domestic warfare into the folds of an alienated and unaccountable past tense.

The rest of this chapter attempts a creative genealogy of post-raciality, undertaken in provisional case study form through a reflection on the intimate and public makings of a prominent white racial state figure: 1964 "law and order" Republican Presidential candidate and longtime U.S. Senator Barry Goldwater. This tracing, or counter-narrative, attempts to demystify the recent emergence of post-racial discourse while situating it within the logics of White Reconstruction, including its iterations through counterinsurgency and civil rights.

Archiving White Reconstruction: Narrative and Methodology

The national and global relations of anti-Blackness and racial-colonial violence remain in distended continuity with the contemporary period, continually surfacing in regimes of policing, criminalization, (domestic) warfare, property relations, popular cultural production, and so forth.[8] Such global formations of state, ecological, and economic violence are determined by a complex of forces, including resurgent reactionary (hegemonic and non-

hegemonic) nationalisms, hierarchically produced gender and sexual vulnerabilities, environmental and land expropriations, and various globalities of
racial capitalism, including but not limited to neoliberalism. Simultaneously
shaped by and autonomous of this ensemble of determinations, the aspirational
logics of white supremacy permeate changing regimes of racial subjection. A
critical problem for the contemporary moment entails the prevailing *periodizations* of epochal racial power/violence that reify the past tense as the
temporal container of history's severest forms of systemic racism. Such archival manipulations have the effect of narratively sterilizing the contemporary
ongoing period of White Reconstruction as if it is a comparatively more enlightened, benign, or simply less violent globality of racial power. Howard Winant and Michael Omi, in their paradigmatic text *Racial Formation in the
United States*, construct a historical schema that typifies this telos of racial
power and violence:

> Racial rule can be understood as a slow and uneven historical process
> which *has moved from dictatorship to democracy, from domination to
> hegemony.* In this transition, hegemonic forms of racial rule—those
> based on consent—eventually came *to supplant those based on
> coercion.* Of course, before this assertion can be accepted, it must be
> qualified in important ways. By no means has the U.S. established
> racial democracy at the end of the century, and by no means is
> coercion a thing of the past. But the sheer complexity of the racial
> questions U.S. society confronts today . . . suggests that hegemony is a
> useful and appropriate term with which to characterize contemporary
> racial rule.[9]

The narrative and theoretical structures of this and similar scholarly works also
imply that the social logic of white supremacy and the structuring presence of
anti-Black and racial-colonial violence (in their institutionalized, extralegal,
and ad hoc forms) are, by historical definition, less severe or pervasive in the
post-1960s period. Such progressivist historical depictions are analytically
misled and overly optimistic in their depiction of the sociopolitical aftermath
of successful insurgencies against large-scale, state-centered systems of anti-
Blackness and racial-colonial domination during the twentieth century. Further, because the crux of Omi and Winant's schema rests on an undertheorized
conceptualization of racial "hegemony" that posits its definitive "displacement" of "coercive" regimes of racial dominance, its contemporary analytical
applicability is at best highly contingent, and at worst entirely illusory—by way
of example, the proliferation of the U.S. criminalization, policing, and carceral
regime as a new and primary modality of systemic racist state violence *accelerated*

during the very decade in which the authors published and eventually re-issued *Racial Formation* (the mid-1980s to mid-1990s).

The contemporaneous expansion of anti-Black, racial-colonial carceral war amounts to a living archival rebuttal of Omi and Winant's "coercion-to-hegemony" narrative and further suggests that new formations of state violence (that is, coercion) are not only structuring features of the contemporary period, but are also the systemic and discursive rearticulations of the logics of "racial dictatorship" and "domination" that permanently undermine the possibility of racial hegemony. Omi and Winant seem to reify the racial teleology of dictatorship-to-democracy and domination-to-hegemony in their sociological framing of racial power. An adequate rejoinder (and possible corrective) to such thinking requires creative and critical theoretical, archival, and narrative practices that demystify this racial telos.

As a counter-periodization of the "post-Civil Rights" period of emergent racial "hegemony," the notion of White Reconstruction strategically amplifies the symbiosis between what Clyde Woods describes as the "resilient relations" of densely structured, long historical carceral anti-Black and racist violences as well as the significant sociopolitical and cultural shifts in the racial social text that have unfolded since the 1960s.[10] Omi and Winant's text exemplifies how many scholarly, journalistic, and popular cultural narratives of this ongoing half century have relied on a strange fiction: that the operational logics of anti-Blackness and racial-colonial violence have been decisively displaced from their sturdy and readily identifiable housing in official state and juridical regimes—for example, formal segregation and apartheid/colonial juridical orders—and remobilized, reconfigured, and rearticulated via other covert, subtle, indirect rhetorics and institutional strategies. A critical archiving of White Reconstruction's conditions of emergence can facilitate a more rigorous understanding of how such racial fictions are imagined and acted upon through the overlapping protocols of racial statecraft, governance, and (white) biography. This approach can also reveal the durable, dynamic *continuities* of anti-Blackness and racial-colonial violence as they adhere to the logics and narratives of post-raciality.

"With malice towards none, with charity for all": Encountering the Goldwater Archive

The Arizona Historical Foundation's collection of Senator Barry Goldwater's personal and political papers (spanning over 100 years of documents) provides a rich archival source through which to examine the logics, rhetorics, and narratives of White Reconstruction and post-raciality. Given Goldwater's centrality to the ideological and political framework of "law and order" that crystallized white supremacist reaction to the abolition of Jim Crow segregation, my analytical motivation for visiting the AHF archive was to find a body of primary historical materials that might reveal some of the foundational schemas, social imaginations, and institutional protocols of post-1960s White Reconstruction. I anticipated that Goldwater's archive would illustrate the complex entanglements between emergent state mandates of racial-national reform, the policing and governance of radical antiracist, anticolonial, and domestic revolutionary/liberation movements (including those that permeated the civil rights–focused streams of the Black freedom movement), and the reactionary re-scripting of white supremacist social desire and imaginary in the aftermath of American apartheid's imminent eradication.[11]

The encounter with Goldwater's papers was unsettling, intimate, and morbidly comedic. I perused seemingly endless (auto)biographical inscriptions of white statecraft, reaction, and self-making that coursed through his public papers, photos, and private correspondence. One typical journal entry, written on the day of John F. Kennedy's inauguration, betrays Goldwater's regretful reflections on the Republican Party's political mistakes during the preceding two terms of the Eisenhower presidency:

> The power of the unions, inflation, the plight of gold, the louder voices of diminishing minorities—*these chickens should have been destroyed before reaching the roost*, and it was our failure to do this that will haunt the memory of these past eight years.[12]

For many readers, Goldwater's private thoughts will read as a time-twisted white echo of Malcolm X's 1963 reflection on JFK's assassination: "I said what I honestly felt—that it was, as I saw it, a case of 'the chickens coming home to roost.' I said that the hate in white men had not stopped with the killing of defenseless black people, but that hate, allowed to spread unchecked, finally had struck down this country's Chief of State."[13] Lodged in Goldwater's aforementioned January 1961 lament is the internal struggle of an aging white subject of the racist state confronting the inevitability of their own obsolescence. The defensive language of collective obliteration is markedly grave to the point of melodrama ("our failure . . . will haunt . . ."), and the future of this particular modality of white existence appears to be in question, if not in doubt.

Reading Goldwater's papers in the basement of the Arizona State University library, i began to suspect that such archival betrayals of White Being's fragility were also quiet confessions of susceptibility to Other beings' renarrations, counter- and defensive violences, and insurgent socialities—that which "should have been destroyed before reaching the roost." I did not anticipate the glimmers of post-raciality—generally under-articulated, though periodically pronounced—that repeatedly surfaced across the public and private registers of Goldwater's archive. Such a presence was unexpected, given Goldwater's well-earned historical standing as the "Father of Modern Conservatism" and his lasting notoriety as a major catalyst of the reinvigorated anti-Black "law and order" state via his presidential nomination speech at the 1964 Republican National Convention.

Guided by the methodological approach refined by Macarena Gómez-Barris and Herman Gray, this interaction with Goldwater's archive focuses on "traces and inscriptions, things often absent from the purview of disciplinary knowledge, not simply because we do not have the tools to see them but because imprints of power do not easily slide into proscriptive categories that definitively and indefinitely measure social inequality."[14] This study, re-reading, and re-narration of Goldwater's (textual) gestures, ephemera, and evidentiary corporeality are further informed by the capacious counter- and anti-disciplinary model of archival study exemplified by Lisa Lowe in her "unsettling genealogy of modern liberalism."[15] Departing from Walter Benjamin's well-known encouragement (in "Theses on the Philosophy of History") to read official histories "against the grain" and philosopher Michel Foucault's formulation of genealogy as a "history of the present," Lowe argues for an engagement with the colonial, chattel historical archive that "[makes] legible the forcible encounters, removals, and entanglements omitted in liberal accounts of abolition, emancipation, and independence."[16] She constructs a method of archival reading that empowers a deeper understanding of "the processes through which the forgetting of violent encounter is naturalized, both by the archive, and in the subsequent narrative histories."[17] Here, it is worth foregrounding how this queering of the archival/archiving method is an utter necessity for scholars who confront such materials with a deep sense of discomfort, a feeling engendered by creepy proximity to the textual materiality and temporal promiscuities of White Being.

Among the most conspicuous and unexpected archival indications of Goldwater's strange congruence with the ethical and ideological structures of post-raciality is a campaign pamphlet from his exploratory campaign for the 1960 Republican Presidential nomination. The Goldwater for President Committee's visual and narrative framing of the conjunctural shift in the institutional ensemble of U.S. racial power suggests post-raciality's proximity to modern state power as such. The seemingly incongruous pairing of Lincoln and Goldwater (see Figure 5) prefaces the logic of White Reconstruction. Despite Goldwater's unwavering opposition to both desegregation and the 1964

1860   1960

"In loneliness sublime
He dared confront the time
and speak the Truth"

On this centennial anniversary of the first election of ABRAHAM LINCOLN, let us scan the political philosophy and ideals of a great American who loved the men he fought against as much as he loved the nation he fought for. At his second inauguration, with his own great heart bleeding, he spoke words that will live forever: "With malice towards none, with charity for all." Then let us ponder the words of another great American who faces the crisis of our times with the strength, wisdom and humility that mark all men of destiny whom God raises up in times of great trial.

Figure 5. Pamphlet from Barry Goldwater for President Committee, circa 1960 (photo provided by author). (Barry Goldwater for President Committee 1960, Pamphlet, Personal and Political Papers of Senator Barry M. Goldwater [1909–98], FM MSS #1, Arizona Historical Foundation, Series I, Alpha files, box 95, folder 1.)

Civil Rights Act, the pamphlet tethers Goldwater's presidential ambitions to the centenary of Lincoln's election (1860) while invoking the vindicating national-historical memory of slavery's nominal abolition as well as the inaugural moments of late nineteenth-century Reconstruction. On the one hand, Goldwater's aspiring candidacy suggests White Being's confrontation with another epochal abolition a century after Lincoln's issuance of the Emancipation Proclamation. On the other hand, Goldwater personifies white reaction to the *speculative sociality* of an incipient civil rights regime—a state regime that would formally eliminate the juridical endorsement and enforcement of white supremacist, anti-Black apartheid.

The pamphlet funnels a banal white humanism that refracts and elaborates the ideological and philosophical structures of post-raciality. Its cover text reads,

> On this centennial anniversary of the first election of ABRAHAM
> LINCOLN, let us scan the political philosophy and ideals of a great
> American who loved the men he fought against as much as he loved
> the nation he fought for. At his second inauguration, with his own
> great heart bleeding, he spoke words that will live forever: "With
> malice towards none, with charity for all." Then let us ponder the
> words of another great American who faces the crisis of our times with
> the strength, wisdom and humility that mark all men of destiny whom
> God raises up in times of great trial.[18]

In such archival moments, the planners and organic intellectuals of White Reconstruction magically tether a white supremacist social imaginary to the imperatives of post-segregation racial-national reform: Goldwater-as-neo-Lincoln institutes a speculative, working blueprint for the remaking of White Being's ascendancy in a moment of vulnerability. Here, the visioning of a refurbished white nationalism obliterates the casualties, antagonisms, and unfinished labors enmeshing slavery's (non-) abolition while claiming an ahistorical ethical high ground for its accomplishment in and through a historical white raciality.

Such nationalist storytelling reproduces a patriarchal ethical ascendancy that coheres White Being in moments of acute crisis: Undifferentiated white "men of destiny" must always negotiate "times of great trial" in the service of God and nation. It is in such archival moments that the architects of White Reconstruction begin to conceptualize their labors: the pamphlet's visual and pseudo-historical text *demands another reconstruction*, guided by a colonial, anti-Black, and aspirational white supremacist post-raciality that subsumes the liberationist insurgencies of the racially oppressed to the violently flattening universalisms mandated by White Being's rearticulated ascendancy.

This opening encounter with Goldwater's papers encourages a counterdisciplinary methodology that re-narrates the archival interaction with white subjectivities. Such interactions with white raciality intimate a form of intellectual and epistemic solidarity with Mohawk scholar Audra Simpson's praxis of "ethnographic refusal." Simpson's work moves from the premise that "no situation such as the one we all inherit and live within is 'innocent' of a

violence of form, if not content, in narrating a history or a present for ourselves."[19] Arguing for a method predicated on modalities of Indigenous refusal
that intertwine with practices of sovereignty (epistemic, territorial, political,
and otherwise), Simpson clarifies the stakes of her scholarship as a form of
counter-disciplinary and anti-disciplinary praxis:

> . . . I knew that there were limits to what I could ask—and then what
> I could say—within the scope of my project on Mohawk nationhood,
> and those limits extended beyond any statement on ethical forms of
> research that either the American Anthropological Association or the
> Social Sciences and Humanities Research Council of Canada . . .
> required. And so it was that I wrote an ethnography that pivoted
> upon refusal(s). I was interested in the larger picture, in the discur-
> sive, material and moral territory that was simultaneously historical
> and contemporary (this "national" space) and the ways in which
> *Kahnawakero:non*, the "people of Kahnawake," had *refused* the
> authority of the state at almost every turn. The ways in which their
> formation of the initial membership code (now replaced by a lineage
> code and board of elders to implement the code and determine
> cases) was refused; the ways in which their interactions with border
> guards at the international boundary line were predicated upon a
> refusal; how refusal worked in everyday encounters to enunciate
> repeatedly to ourselves and to outsiders that "this is who we are, this
> who you are, these are my rights."[20]

Emboldened by Simpson's approach to epistemic and methodological sovereignty, i contend that a similar intellectual disposition—anti-colonial, liberation oriented, self-determining, methodologically and theoretically rigorous,
and creatively disloyal to disciplinary scripts and dominant historiographies—
can and must inform encounters with the ascendancy of White Being in every
possible archival site. That is, if White Being is in significant part a (self-)nar-
rative and/or toxic memoir through which mind-boggling mobilizations of
dominance and violence are consistently marshaled, it is entirely ethical and
necessary to build creative methodological and theoretical measures that contribute to the *leveling* of White Being, the exposure of its evil and world-
deforming fictions, and thus the re-narration of White Being as an ongoing
story that temporalizes, signifies, and institutes a coercively universalist aspiration for normative human life in the "millennium of Man."

Building such a genealogy of post-raciality—and of White Being generally—
demands critical creativity and methodological experimentation, in large part
because in its immanence, post-raciality is insidious white magic. It is usually

not simply in evidence nor easily retrieved, and its furtive appearances tease, escape, and dazzle the apprehension of its historicity and cultural continuities. The genealogy of post-raciality must be *found, assembled, and narrated* in the process of the archival encounter with White Being and its nonwhite correlates.

Such an approach pivots on a unique set of evidentiary questions: How does post-raciality surface in archival texts that well precede the early twenty-first-century mobilizations of "post-racial" discourse? Is it possible to identify how post-raciality constitutes the historical (white) subjects of the racial/racist state, particularly in archival texts and artifacts that show such subjects to be actively engaged in the complex, dynamic aspirational statecraft of white supremacy? How can a radical genealogy (and active re-archiving) of post-raciality provide analytical, theoretical, and political tools for pedagogically addressing (and productively dismantling) the resilient common sense regimes of colorblindness and post-racialism? How does such a genealogy and archiving of post-raciality reveal the discursive and narrative architectures of an emergent (and unevenly developing) post-racial anti-Black and racial-colonial state?

Such a praxis of genealogy may require strategic departure from traditional, disciplinary forms of academic loyalty to the archival text and subject.[21] Such disloyalty is guided by a radical intellectual mandate to find and read the animus that lies beneath and within the archival source and its assumptive subject—this is to actively, radically inhabit and demystify what Simpson identifies as the violence of form/content that permeates and conditions the narration of the historical present tense. The archival encounter can induce creative and productively intrusive conversations with—and counter-narrations of—the formative (and therefore vulnerable) white subject that is intimately available for interpretation via their personal journals, photographs, private correspondence, and so forth. Goldwater's archive offers a significant opportunity for reflection and counter-narration, particularly because it is replete with examples of white racial animus permeating the logics and discursive allegations of post-raciality.

Racial Deletions: Post-Raciality in the Pencil Mark

I have begun to argue that a still-emergent twenty-first-century post-racial discourse must be situated within a longer archive of post-raciality that is entangled in the historical continuities of anti-Blackness and racial-colonial violence. Post-raciality is a tendency in White Being, surfacing in acts of revision and remaking that aspire to restore a position of ascendancy while disavowing White Being's ethical implication in the relations of fatality and violence that render such an aspiration conceivable, articulable, and achievable. Perhaps counter-intuitively, this work requires an intimacy with the deletion. Avery Gordon's work on ghosts and haunting invokes a version of such intimacy:

> The ghost is not simply a dead or a missing person, but a social figure, and investigating it can lead to that dense site where history and subjectivity make social life. The ghost or the apparition is one form by which something lost, or barely visible, or seemingly not there to our supposedly well-trained eyes, makes itself known or apparent to us, in its own way, of course. The way of the ghost is haunting, and haunting is a very particular way of knowing what has happened or is happening. Being haunted draws us affectively, sometimes against our will and always a bit magically, into the structure of feeling of a reality we come to experience, not as cold knowledge, but as a transformative recognition.[22]

Departing from Gordon's speculative sociological and historiographical insight, i am considering the act of racial deletion as a signature (non-)marking of post-raciality. The racial deletion offers an inadvertent mode of entry into the "dense sites" of anti-Blackness and racial-colonial violence—that is, the archival scenes that always seem to be postponed in the official and public social scripts of racial discourse (including some critical scholarly studies of race and racial power).

The deletion of which i am writing is dissimilar from Gordon's "way of the ghost" because it encompasses an ensemble of political-cultural decisions that fabricate non-visibility; the generalized effect of the deletion is often the inverse of haunting, as it allows for a (potentially permanent) avoidance of recognition and affective confrontation with histories of violence. In this sense, tracing the racial deletion may help demystify the systemic productions of White Being's ethical distance from (or dysfunctional intimacy with) genealogies of anti-Black, racial-colonial violence. Let us force the deletion into appearance, in order to account for its contribution to these long archives of violence.

Distinguished from the declarative public discourse of twenty-first-century post-racialism, the longer genealogy of post-raciality indexes an affective modality and ontological privilege in which particular social (racial) subjects live and thrive through conditions of racial dominance while simultaneously performing their pretensions of ethical alienation from (and personal unaccountability for) those very same conditions. In post-raciality, the subjects of White Being imagine their agential centrality to a *futurity liberated from racial animus,* as if the anticipated abolition of racial domination facilitates the perpetuity, rather than the radical disruption, of White Being's starring (that is, oppressive and mundanely violent) role in the theater of modern historical agency. (While it is not my intent to elaborate such an implication in this chapter, this schema suggests that post-raciality is not exclusive to the domain of white racial subjects, although it does entail the absolute, permanent preservation and protection of white racial subjects, even and especially in the post-racial imaginary of nonwhite and ostensibly anti-racist subjects.) While recent articulations of post-racial discourse openly denounce racism, white supremacy, and racial "extremism" (often through moralizing opposition to figures of "hate"), post-raciality can both coexist with and facilitate the proliferation of those very systems of dominance. This apparent contradiction (which i will argue is closer to a symbiosis) surfaces throughout the Goldwater archive.

It may be useful to recall the more commonly circulated historical memory of Barry Goldwater: He is known as the "father of modern conservatism" to many, and as the harbinger of a new chapter in the Republican Party's reactionary anti-Black politics to others, due in large part to his widely publicized vote against the 1964 Civil Rights Act, the right-wing populist militancy of his 1964 presidential campaign platform (see Figure 6), and the long-term ideological-electoral traction of his "law and order" Republican presidential nomination speech (a pronouncement that significantly framed the forthcoming renaissance of racial criminalization, carceral jurisprudence, militarized policing, and racist state violence).[23]

Figure 6. 1964 campaign button. Unidentified artist, Pin 1964, Smithsonian Institution. (From the National Portrait Gallery, Smithsonian Institution website: http://face2face.si.edu/my _weblog/2009/12/portrait-of -barry-goldwater-by-burton -philip-silverman.html.)

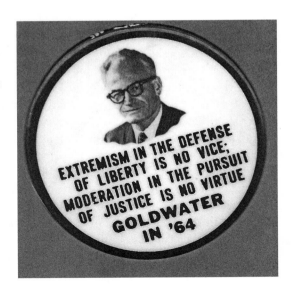

Goldwater infamously supported Joseph McCarthy until the bitter end of the latter's political career, accepted public political endorsement from the white nationalist John Birch Society, and was a nationally prominent anti-union and anti-labor legislator. Goldwater's articulation of an orthodox "states' rights" argument in opposition to the Civil Rights Act served as a prototype for what would later become the Republican Party's anti-Black "Southern Strategy," which transformed electoral campaigns and platforms from the 1980s onward. Goldwater vigorously defended school segregation in his denunciation of the U.S. Supreme Court's 1954 *Brown v. Board of Education* decision, wherein he asserted the primacy of the U.S. Constitution's protection of state sovereignty over the impositions of federal government.

Despite a landslide defeat at the hands of Lyndon B. Johnson in the 1964 presidential election, Goldwater remained a prominent national figure, serving as a U.S. Senator (Arizona) from 1952 to 1986, with a short hiatus from 1964 to 1968. In his latter Senate days, he criticized the expanding presence of the Christian Right in the Republican Party and went so far in 1996 (two years before his death) as to rebrand Senator (and Republican presidential nominee) Bob Dole and himself the "new liberals" of the Republican Party. Such is the Barry Goldwater who befits recognition as a primary public/organic intellectual of the post-1960s White Reconstruction.[24]

Some of Goldwater's personal papers reveal a less familiar figure. The archive of the white father of modern conservatism is fractured by a complicated relationship to post-raciality, post–civil rights racial liberalism, and multiculturalist white supremacy (see Chapter 1), exhibiting the scattered, urgent, and crisis-driven movements of a white subject struggling to re-assemble itself in the context of apartheid's abolition. At times, his papers inscribe post-raciality in casual acts of deletion. A pencil-drawn mark, flowing from Goldwater's hand not long after his retirement from the U.S. Senate, appears in an otherwise unremarkable, personally edited draft of a letter dated August 11, 1989. The short correspondence congratulates General Colin Powell on his nomination as the next Chair of the Joint Chiefs of Staff by President George H. W. Bush and includes a crossed-out line that was eventually excluded from the final version of the letter.

After offering Powell his hearty commendations, Goldwater relates—and partially retracts—his own alleged biographical affinity to Reagan's newest appointee by recounting the context of his 1930 appointment to the Army Reserve's 25th Infantry (see Figure 7).

Similar examples of Goldwater's racial goodwill and colorblind intentionality are scattered throughout his personal papers, including numerous accounts of his role in desegregating the Goldwater family drug store's employment

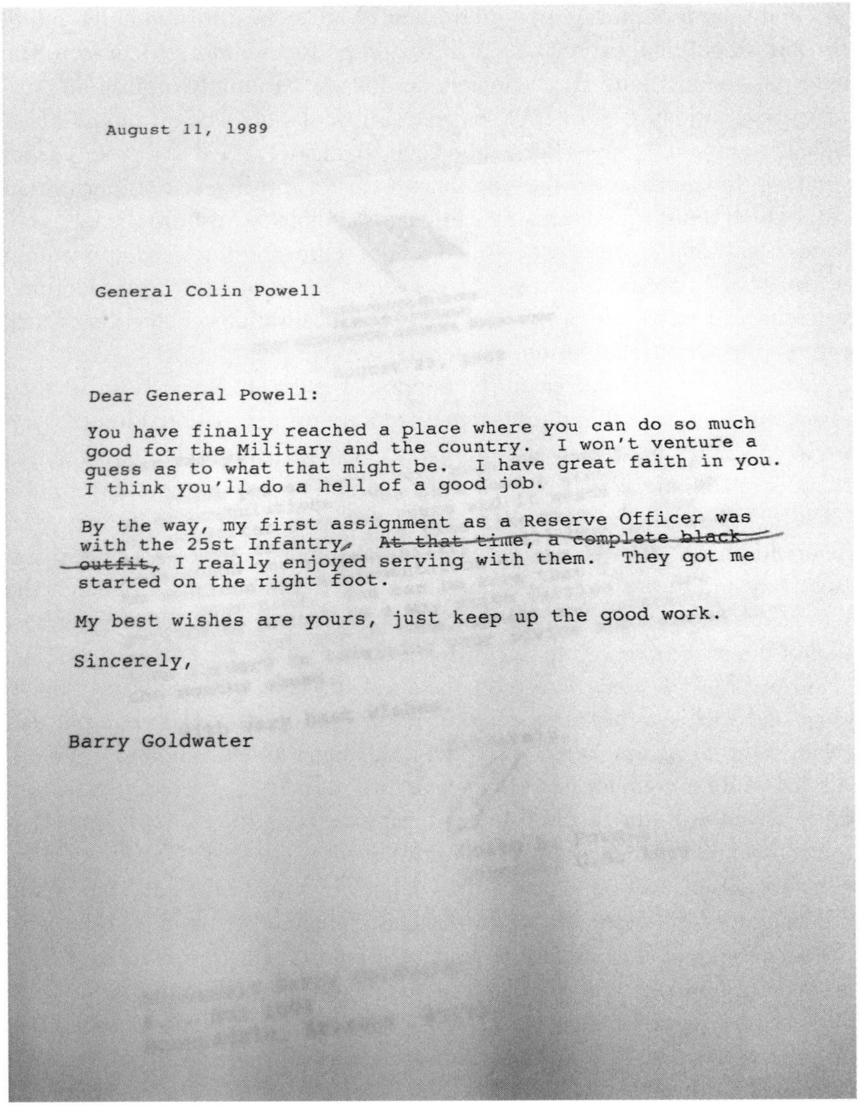

August 11, 1989

General Colin Powell

Dear General Powell:

You have finally reached a place where you can do so much good for the Military and the country. I won't venture a guess as to what that might be. I have great faith in you. I think you'll do a hell of a good job.

By the way, my first assignment as a Reserve Officer was with the 25st Infantry. ~~At that time, a complete black outfit,~~ I really enjoyed serving with them. They got me started on the right foot.

My best wishes are yours, just keep up the good work.

Sincerely,

Barry Goldwater

Figure 7. Deleted line from Powell correspondence. (Barry M. Goldwater, Draft of Correspondence to Gen. Colin Powell, August 11, 1989, Personal and Political Papers of Senator Barry M. Goldwater [1909–1998], photo by the author. FM MSS #1, Arizona Historical Foundation, Series I, Alpha files, Colin Powell, 1988–1997, box 17, folder 9.)

practices and dozens of instances proclaiming his centrality to the integration of the Arizona National Guard. In the draft correspondence to Powell, Goldwater proudly cites his membership in a previously segregated all-Black regiment in order to locate his white biography within the broader racial-national telos of which Powell's appointment is a crowning moment. Refraining from overt reference to the Blackness of his compatriots, the pencil mark reflects Goldwater's performance of racial familiarity with Powell as a proto-post-racial figure; in this context, Powell's appointment *requires* Goldwater's deletion of explicit racial referents.

This minor and otherwise ignorable archival fragment exposes an otherwise privatized post-raciality: It is an intimate moment of self-redaction in which the white state subject gratuitously identifies with Blackness in the act of erasing it. The logic of this editorial act, and the manner of Blackness's deletion, not only displaces open acknowledgment of the fact of U.S. military apartheid, but also pre-emptively denies the possibility of ethical accountability, reparation, or redress. Such deletion and denial are primary characteristics of post-raciality and consistently resurface in the contemporary discourses of post-racialism.

This chapter has referenced vital work on ghosts, traces, and specters in the critical humanities and interdisciplinary fields.[25] Here, i stretch the parameters of such critical labors to consider the importance of deletions—particularly, racial deletions. What animates such acts of erasure? What new political-archival texts and readings do such deletions *create* through their attempted, incomplete, and failed revisions of White Being's memoir/archive? How do such deletions contribute to the making of White Reconstruction's racial state subjects?

When Goldwater crossed through this sentence (Linda Whitaker, chief archivist of the Goldwater papers, assured me that the pencil mark came from Goldwater's own hand), how was he self-narrating his relation to Blackness and/or (military) segregation and its aftermath? What does such an editorial elimination suggest about the contingency—the flimsiness—of Powell's racial state subjectivity? Does Goldwater fear that Powell will be offended by the deleted remark, and if so, how does he perceive the nature of the offense? How does Goldwater's casual reference to and deletion of his biographical intersection with military segregation reveal a primary logic of post-raciality: the capacity of the white archival subject to engulf relations of racial dominance in self-indulgent proclamations of affinity with and physical proximity to a racial/Black Other?

Such archival minutiae catalyze a labor of critical genealogy that is animated by a creative praxis of textual and narrative assembly; the work of assembly in this instance may occur through exercises of informed, willful speculation and imagination (in fact, such creative intellectual labor is already performed in the act of noticing and addressing the minutiae). This candid, minor editorial moment in Goldwater's personal papers indicates how the narrative structure of post-raciality is not only a precursor for White Reconstruction's social and epistemic architectures but is also a reinscription of White Being's ascendancy. The draft of Goldwater's 1989 correspondence evidences a post-racial sensibility that is emergent, if not fully articulated, at a historical moment when (neo)conservatism, the economic regimes of neoliberalism, and the cultural apparatuses of multiculturalism are in convergence: In the mark of the pencil, it is possible to excavate a fragment of White Being's flailing attempts to stretch and re-narrate its relation to Black racial positionality (via Powell and the 25th Infantry) within the changing significations and inclusionist maneuvers of the racist, anti-Black state.

Such deletions not only create opportunities for speculative counternarrative against the white archival subject's privatizations of racial anxiety, but also call for interpretive reading practices that undermine the generalized, assumptive integrity—ethical, epistemic, and otherwise—of White Being's authorship of the historical script. Goldwater's pencil maps the convergence of multiculturalist statecraft and the "post-civil rights" racist state's organic subject formations, both of which are inseparable from durable and dynamic regimes of state violence. At play in this example is the hierarchical raciality of the U.S. military and national security configuration, rearticulated through Powell's landmark appointment. There are stories lurking in Goldwater's editorial strike.

By way of this encounter with Goldwater's racial archive, and in continuity with the arguments introduced in prior chapters, i am suggesting that the logics of post-raciality are embedded in the long genealogy of White Being. To the extent that the ethically self-assured white state/social subject cannot accommodate its implication in and complex, ongoing cultivation of the violences of historical and coterminous systems of anti-Blackness and racial-colonial dominance, the narratives of White Being's social ascendancy are structured in denials of the terms, conditions, and existence of the state *as an anti-Black, racial-colonial state*. Post-raciality forms the perverse grounds for White Being's asymmetrical ethicality, building on two interwoven narratives: first, that the modern, sovereign white human is *not essentially responsible* for the historical and still-prevailing regimes of anti-Black, racial-colonial dominance and terror through which modern political, economic, and cultural systems continuously (re)form; and second, that the liberal white racial subject of the modern Civilizational project is always on the verge of sharing the humanist fruits of recognition (civil, sovereign, human, and otherwise) with its racial antagonists so long as the terms of recognition (including definitions of freedom, self-determination, nationhood, and personhood) do not displace or otherwise threaten to obliterate the logic of ascendancy.

Post-raciality structures and saturates the discursive and narrative channeling of an imagined post-animus racial future into the historical present tense of socialities structured in the ascendancy of White Being, often generating rhetorics and political practices that suggest ethical commitment to anti-racism, feminism, and class-based social justice. (For example, nineteenth-century white abolitionists, white women's suffragists, and the early twenty-first-century Occupy movement all feature elements of post-raciality in their organizing schemas, political lexicon, and historical imaginaries.) Goldwater's deletion opens toward a critical consideration of how such channelings might be speculatively traced, particularly when they are apprehended as archival marks of White Being that affirm rather than erase implication in Others' conditions of subjection to state violence.

Goldwater's Left Hand: Indian Land and the "Smoki People"

The archiving of White Reconstruction's organic intellectuals induces an ethnographic account of white fantasy and self-making, particularly as the latter processes interact with genealogies of genocidal and proto-genocidal racial-colonial violence. It is a peculiar privilege of white political subjectivity that it can periodically claim to intellectually comprehend and affectively identify with the social and historical positionalities of survivors, social inheritors, historical targets, and political dissidents of racial-colonialism, all while inhabiting none of the conditions instituted by such deep historical violences.

Such a privileged mobility of identification and imagination is signified in a bodily marking that Goldwater wore for most of his adult life: a tattoo on the base of his left hand that identified him as a member of an Arizona white men's group called the "Smoki People." In fact, Goldwater's archive contains extensive descriptions and personalized contextualizations of his Smoki skin ink: One conspicuous example is his 1975 letter to Spider Webb, president of the Tattoo Club of America. Webb spotted an obstructed, partial image of the hand tattoo in a news photo and immediately wrote to Goldwater to inquire as to its meaning. Goldwater's response to Webb reads,

> Dear Mr. Webb:
> The tattoo I wear on my lefthand [sic] is that worn by the Smoki people, a non-Indian group in Prescott, Arizona, whose purpose is to perpetuate the dances and songs of the Southwestern Indian.[26]

Elaborating on the tattoo's intended symbolism, Goldwater continues,

> The first two dots are given after the first dance and depict the bite of
> the snake. The Next two dots are given after the next two dances, so
> all that a man ever wears are four dots and these depict three dances.
>
> If he is made a member of the Council he gets a quarter circle and
> if he is ever made Chief he gets a half circle. I am the only Honorary
> Chief they have so I put my half circle at the other end to where it is
> customarily worn.[27]

Founded in Goldwater's hometown of Prescott, Arizona, in 1921 by a group of
white businessmen and politicos, the Smoki People were best known for an
annual public spectacle they dubbed the "Snake Dance," a performance ostensibly intended to honor a sacred Hopi tradition. Goldwater describes this
practice in a 1980 letter to one of his constituents: "Every year on the Saturday
nearest the full moon of August, we put on an Indian ceremonial in which
we dress ourselves as Indians, and sing and dance the Indian songs and ceremonials as best we can."[28] Active for more than seventy years, the Smoki People
disbanded in the early 1990s after an extended period of protests by Hopi representatives who objected to the white fraternity's desecration of their religious and spiritual practices.

Philip J. Deloria's (Dakota) historical study of the white American tradition
of "playing Indian" suggests that the Smoki, like other "object hobbyists" driven
by the "impulse to preserve vanishing Indian culture," exemplify how "playing Indian has been central to efforts to imagine and materialize distinctive
American identities."[29] Goldwater's involvement with the group appears to have
played a central role in his lifelong fascination with Indigenous peoples of the
southwestern United States, and firmly locates his biography within a broader
striving for white masculine national identity that postscripted the period of
continental land conquest.[30] Deloria writes,

> At the turn of the century, Indian play helped preserve a sense of
> frontier toughness, communal warmth, and connection to the conti-
> nent often figured around the idea of the authentic. . . . [A] diverse set
> of [white] hobbyists sought authenticity and identity in America's
> original signifier of unique selfhood—the Indian.[31]

Resonating with Goldwater's description of the Smoki as "a non-Indian
group," Deloria differentiates their costuming and performance from pro-
totypical redfacing: "while the Smokis played Indian on a regular basis,
they felt strongly about not being mistaken for real Indians." This differentiation is worth closer analytical attention for its reflection of a peculiar

racial-colonial sentimentality that anticipates latter twentieth- and early twenty-first-century notions of (liberal-to-neoconservative) colorblindness, multiculturalism, and post-racialism.

Aside from its evident racial creepiness (a major characteristic of such object hobbyists and other Indian fetishists throughout the U.S. settler colonial epoch), the Smoki People were a synthetic expression of modern white post-raciality: As an alchemy of white men's social club, post-conquest cultural expropriation, anti-Indian sacrilege, and colonialist frontier theater, the Smoki understood themselves to be engaged in respectful, accurate, dignified preservationist performances of Southwest and Plains Indian cultural-religious ceremonies (particularly those of the Hopi and Navajo).[32] Per Goldwater, "The Smoki is an honorary group of white men who are committed to the preservation of traditional Indian dances."[33] Some visual artifacts of the Smoki People provide further illustration (see Figures 8 and 9).

Such expropriations, desecrations, and distortions are the cultural material of whitefacing, understood here as the historical tradition of white racial subjects performing racial-colonial fantasy through modifications of skin, body,

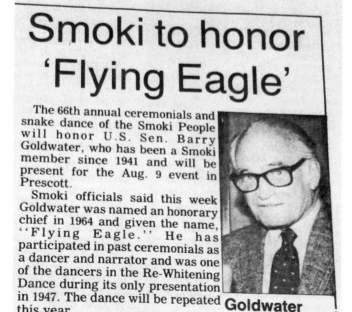

Figure 8. Scan of article from The Courier (Arizona), May 2, 1986, page 1b. (provided by author)

Smoki to honor 'Flying Eagle'

The 66th annual ceremonials and snake dance of the Smoki People will honor U.S. Sen. Barry Goldwater, who has been a Smoki member since 1941 and will be present for the Aug. 9 event in Prescott.

Smoki officials said this week Goldwater was named an honorary chief in 1964 and given the name, ''Flying Eagle.'' He has participated in past ceremonials as a dancer and narrator and was one of the dancers in the Re-Whitening Dance during its only presentation in 1947. The dance will be repeated this year.

Goldwater

The Smoki People is made up of non-Indians living in Prescott. It was organized in 1921 by a group of

Figure 9. Arizona Governor Howard Pyle (left), a Smoki dancer, and Barry Goldwater hold a bull snake used in the annual Smoki ceremonies at the Prescott Fairground (photographed by Lloyd Clark), August 9, 1952. (History and Archives Division, Arizona State Library, Archives and Public Records.)

fashion, comportment, and vernacular that project mastery over other non-white humans. Whitefacing is the performative obverse of redfacing, which Michelle Raheja (Seneca) defines as

> . . . a series of acts performed by Native Americans that draw upon Indigenous performance contexts and spiritual traditions but are staged under conditions controlled, more often than not, by white filmmakers using new technologies and often in conflict with Indigenous self-representations. At the same time, the term redfacing signals the ways in which the work of Indigenous performers, like that of the trickster, is always in motion and therefore creates acts that operate ambiguously, acts that open themselves up for further reading and interpretation. Redfacing also provides a means of protection as a kind of virtual, visual prophylactic that keeps Native American cultural and spiritual practices somewhat sacrosanct, or at least hidden from the white tourist gaze.[34]

As a period-specific exemplar of whitefacing, the Smoki signify a colonial white supremacist reaction to redfacing's complex lineage of Indigenous performativity: a performative spectacle of white (male) settler bodies that undermines the sanctity and integrity of Indigenous traditions, a communing of White Being that publicly iterates the entitlements of racial transparency (its presumption of access to other modalities of being, its epistemological self-positioning as authority and expert in matters Indigenous, and so on), and a denaturing of durable, coterminous and ongoing Indigenous performativities (including and beyond Raheja's exhaustive genealogy of redfacing) that reproduces the logics of Native elimination and cultural genocide.[35]

The invention of the Smoki can also be understood as a modern white settler response to what J. Kēhaulani Kauanui (Kanaka Maoli) calls "enduring indigeneity":

> I use ["enduring indigeneity"] in two senses: first, that indigeneity itself is enduring—that the operative logic of settler colonialism may be to "eliminate the native," as the late English scholar Patrick Wolfe brilliantly theorized, but that indigenous peoples exist, resist, and persist; and second, that settler colonialism is a structure that endures indigeneity, as it holds out against it.[36]

The white men of the Smoki were no dilettantes in their mobilization of White Being against the vexing, post-frontier problem of enduring indigeneity: Their immersion in the performative project of white frontier indigeneity was enabled by a hoarding of Native (Hopi) objects, tanning of pale epidermis, and, crucially, an articulation of post-raciality that framed their mutilating labors of cultural-spiritual violence and unintentional self-satire as an ethical gesture that honored the Native peoples of the region. The Smoki People understood themselves *as* white men, *for* white men, identifying with a white man's burden to honor and protect "the Indian."

This post-conquest whiteface troupe bestowed the title of honorary Smoki chief on Goldwater in 1964, renaming him "Flying Eagle" in reference to his enthusiasm for piloting small aircraft.[37] It seems clear that members of the Smoki harbored no illusion that they were anything but white men, and their performative frontier indigeneity was a visceral inhabitation of White Being in the form of civil communion. Goldwater's whiteface conveys the power of post-raciality as a form of white self-delusion that labors to deny the fact of enduring Indigenous presence. Here, post-raciality vacillates between a (delusional) presupposition of and active insistence on the *finality* of colonialist conquest and genocide: the peculiar Smoki hallucination is sustained through its performance of tribute, cultural apology, and ludic reparation for Manifest Destiny and its long present tense.

Moving with the work of Native and Indigenous studies thinkers such as the aforementioned Raheja, Simpson, Deloria, Coulthard, and Kauanui, as well as Mishuana Goeman (Seneca), Keith Camacho (Chamorro), Jodi Byrd (Chickasaw), Scott Lyons (Ojibwe/Dakota), Scott Morgensen, Patrick Wolfe, and others, it is possible to mobilize a historicized narrative labor that exposes the archives of post-conquest White Being to decolonial and anti-colonial epistemes, creative re-tellings, and critical retheorizations.[38] Such a narrative labor might treat Goldwater and his Smoki brethren as ancestral figures of contemporary multiculturalist (and emergent post-racial) cultural and political regimes within which the traces of historical genocidal colonial logics are clearly in evidence: Within these settler and slave master archives, the privileged inhabitants of White Being enact their imperial entitlement to expropriate, play with, and exhibit the most intimate and sacred elements of targeted peoples' communal existence.

Goldwater stakes precisely such a claim in a 1986 letter to *The Prescott Sun*, righteously defending the existence of the Smoki People in its waning years:

> The Smoki people, in my mind, are as justified in doing what they are doing as any group whose purpose is to collect and preserve items of custom and culture, whether they be Indian, Mexican, Polish, German, etc. I think what the Smoki have always done has calmed the objections of the Hopi whose dances we use more than any other.[39]

Goldwater's archive provides a partial biography of post-raciality that (somewhat unexpectedly) anticipates the aspirational ideological labors of early twenty-first-century post-racial discourse. The social imagination of post-raciality entangles the ascendancy of White Being with the social-historical logics of racial-colonial genocide (see Chapter 4). While these logics have been historically inseparable from the productions of white social life and white racial-settler subjectivities since the Enlightenment, and have been apocalyptically proliferated throughout Western modernity's reign of global terror, this archival re-narration challenges the historiographic (and deeply political/ideological) presumption that the long violences of racial-colonial genocide can be apprehended as if they are containable, periodized historical isolates—that is, as past tense "events."[40] Within this critical archival encounter, it becomes possible to identify how the coherence of white sociality and the assumptive futurity of White Being are mutually grounded in a distended relation to the processes, stories, and long consequences of land, cultural, and ecological conquest.

Goldwater's attachment to genealogies of settler colonialist displacement and evisceration reached a denouement near the end of his life, when he literally claimed a swath of Indigenous land as his own. In 1989, three years after the death of his spouse, Goldwater successfully petitioned the U.S. Board on Geographic Names to designate a natural rock formation in Navajo territory as the "Margaret Arch." After extended debate and resistance, the Navajo consented to the indulgent ritual of white mourning. A series of archival images depict Goldwater dedicating the Margaret Arch from a Navajo podium (see Figure 10). (Notably, the Navajo electoral vote played a crucial role in Goldwater's elections to the Senate until the early 1970s, when he had a falling out with tribal chairperson Peter MacDonald.)

Barry Goldwater's deletions, private letters, tattoos, and mournings provide an opportunity to trace post-raciality within the memoir of White Being. Creative, critical, and promiscuous adaptations of this historical, theoretical, and narrative approach—when focused on white state subjects like Goldwater— may provide critical insight into the robust conditions of possibility for the emergence of White Reconstruction.

Counter-Tracing: "Post-Racial" Irruptions

The narrative archiving of white raciality is a critical praxis that situates the long genealogies of racial-colonial and anti-Black power as formative of the present and future tense. At stake is an epistemological project that subjugates White Being to irruptive re-tellings of its inhabitants' origins, intentions, and desires as well as their deep, collective implication in other humans' casualties. Enacting such irruption, the tracing of racial deletions—here manifest in Goldwater's pencil-to-paper edits, but evident in other archives as discarded photos, ignored pleas, disappeared records, unpublished writings, or any other manner of (attempted) ephemeral exclusion from official historical records—reassembles fragmented, fleeting archival moments. This reassembly, in turn, enables sundering re-narrations of such erasures as *reproductions* of racial-colonial violence. Sharon Luk's study of letter correspondence by Chinese, Japanese, and Black captives in the context of California's racist carceral history opens into a durable methodological framing of the critical praxis proposed by this chapter:

What vitalizes human relationships to the letter when the human embodies the crisis rather than cultivation of man and the mortal stakes of the problem of representation?

. . . [T]he production and circulation of letters open real and imaginative possibilities, both engrained in the letter and in excess of

Figure 10. Barry Goldwater at dedication of "Margaret Arch" on Navajo land, March 19, 1988. (Personal and Political Papers of Senator Barry M. Goldwater [1909–1998], FM MSS #1, Arizona Historical Foundation, Series I, Alpha files, Boards and Memberships, Smoki People, 1967–1996, box 46, folder 6. Image provided by author.)

it. . . . [T]hese forms of connection—structural, physical, ideological, and affective labor internalized in the letter—create alternative conditions that both ground and animate endeavors to reinvent people's own means of living.[41]

What possibilities for insurgent, speculative, narrative reimagination of history, futurity, and sociality might emerge if Luk's approach were adapted to the problem of White Being's epistolary authorship, in all its forms?

Goldwater's records awaken suspicion that the early twenty-first-century emergence of "post-racial" discourses and popular vernaculars is linked to a longer genealogy of white subject-formation(s) that exhibits two of the foundational discursive elements of post-raciality: first, the simultaneous denial and re-narration of anti-Black, racial-colonial violence in the formation of a white national modernity, accompanied by a labored compartmentalization of the affective and epistemic parameters through which that violence can be historically articulated and experienced *in the present tense*; and second, the constant gesturing toward an aspirational social and ontological condition of *consummated* post-raciality, that is, a condition wherein anti-Blackness and racial-colonial dominance are magically divested of their continuities in socialities present and future, and thus definitively normalized in their inscription as non-racial, non-colonial formations of power.

The archival work i have attempted in this chapter embraces a precarious methodology, an experimental narrative approach to primary research that does not rely on (much less prescribe) a formulaic way of engaging/building/re-narrating the archive. What i have offered is as much a creative fiction of knowledge production as it is a descriptive accounting of the Goldwater archive's "contents." As a critical genealogical method, this examination attempts to prey on the historical evidence of what Silva terms the "transparency thesis" of white raciality, that is, the allegation of the white human as a self-evident, self-knowing being whose capacity for agency is unaffected by the vagrancies and external stimuli of nature and the material world, including alien human/racial others.[42] In this case, to visit and counter-narrate White Being's archival memoir is to momentarily irrupt white racial transparency, and to subject the rhetorical and cultural production, as well as the public policy and state-making activities of the racist state's architects to a creative, disloyal, and at times undeservedly generous scrutiny and theoretical meditation.

In fact, it is already an act of undeserved generosity to render such care and seriousness to the archive of someone like Goldwater, whose political work was responsible for incurring vast damage in marshaling the logics of anti-Blackness and racial criminalization through the wave of white supremacist reaction that followed the overthrowal of American apartheid. I and others can perhaps be accused of a fleeting, nonequivalent inversion of the traditional racial structuring of the archival and ethnographic engagement: for a brief moment, it is the powerful white man, a principal figure of the racist state, whose life is appropriated as the raw material for a critical agenda.

Those of us aspiring to participate in some combination of critical intellectual labor and radical praxis are not only entitled to creatively read and irruptively re-narrate the archive of White Reconstruction's organic intellectuals, state-building figures, ideological architects, and social visionaries, but are *obligated* to use such archives disloyally, treasonously, and against their own racial and political grain. In some ways, what i am proposing in this chapter amounts to a visit with white racial paranoia, an engagement with a white raciality that always seems to be at war with its own obsolescence, especially in the face of uprising Black, queer, Indigenous, colonized, displaced, captive peoples. We search for the indelible inscriptions of anti-Black, racial-colonial violence in the movements and ephemera of the white human, precisely because its conditions of existence are stubbornly tied to the conception, remaking, periodic invigoration, and constant distension of a global order that must *remain* a deadly, chattel, carceral, colonial global order, even and especially within moments of racial reform and post-racial optimism.

Post-racial discourse is mutually reinforced by the proliferation of protogenocidal logics of gendered racial criminalization/incarceration and the expanding apparatuses of anti-Black, anti-colonial domestic and global warfare.[43] These logics of violence and dominance will be addressed in the following two chapters in order to extend and enrich this critical genealogy of White Reconstruction.

4

"Civilization in Its Reddened Waters"

*Anti-Black, Racial-Colonial Genocide and the
Logic of Evisceration*

Introduction: "... and they hide the truth from themselves"

While the capacity to destroy and/or eliminate populations, geographies, ecologies, and ways of life constitutes global white modernity and its long historical present tense, the modern concept of genocide provides a morbidly incomplete accounting of gendered anti-Black, racial-colonial violence.[1] This chapter focuses on the cultural, political, and juridical consequences of the institutionalization of the genocide concept after World War II, in and beyond the establishment of the 1948 UN Convention on the Prevention and Punishment of the Crime of Genocide. Situated within the global genealogies of anti-Blackness and racial-colonial dominance, "genocide" is a discursive regime that attempts to fold an alleged extremity of modern power into an accessible conceptual-juridical artifact. In this sense, "genocide" invokes, but cannot fully engage, a deep tracing of the violences, exterminations, and fatalities encompassed by the long preceding processes of the global Civilizational project.

I place "genocide" in quotations throughout this chapter when i am critically addressing the conditions of its constitution as a modern discursive regime, centrally though not exclusively through its institutionalization in the jurisprudence of the UN Convention on the Prevention and Punishment of the Crime of Genocide (hereafter the UN Genocide Convention), the creation of the academic field of Genocide Studies, and the term "genocide's" canonization in specific historical instances of atrocity. By offsetting the term in such textual moments, i hope the reader will be attentive to the hegemonic humanist (and thus anti-Black, racial-colonial, juridical and epistemological) assumptions that structure its circulation within the modern global text. My use of "genocide" in this way enunciates the term as contradictory and contested, rather than self-evident and settled.

A qualification on the limits of this discussion is in order: i am not interested in conducting a critical review of the dense academic and legal quarrels over the juridical and scholarly definitions, historical parameters, juridical and methodological effectiveness, and conceptual singularity of "genocide" as a production and projection of the modern human rights and Western academic knowledge regimes.[2] Rather, i will dwell on the forms of dehumanization, ontological negation, and Civilizational violence that are insufficiently invoked, marginally referenced, and pragmatically compartmentalized by hegemonic genocide discourses, even as "genocide" intends to definitively name them as such.

Anti-colonial theorist and revolutionary Aimé Césaire, writing at the moment of genocide discourse's emergence, exposes the racist parochialism of the concept's origins:

> And they wait, and they hope; and they hide the truth from themselves, that it is barbarism, the supreme barbarism, the crowning barbarism that sums up all the daily barbarisms; that it is Nazism, yes, but that before they were its victims, they were its accomplices; that they tolerated that Nazism before it was inflicted on them, that they absolved it, shut their eyes to it, legitimized it, because, until then, it had been applied only to non-European peoples; that they have cultivated that Nazism, that they are responsible for it, and that before engulfing the whole edifice of Western, Christian civilization in its reddened waters, it oozes, seeps, and trickles from every crack.[3]

In Césaire's meditation, the emergence of Western genocide discourse is animated by a narrative privileging of white death as the instance through which Other peoples' encounters with Western modernity's logics of racial extermination and terror are to be apprehended, calibrated, and conceptually qualified. Despite Nazism's orchestration of a sophisticated racist Aryan regime and its targeting of ostensibly inferior racial stock for social and physical liquidation, Césaire reminds us that the scandal of its ascendancy for white modernity was borne in its infraracialization and industrialized killing of millions of (non-African, non-Arab, non-Asian descended) Europeans.[4]

Césaire's poetics anticipate the retroactive racialization of Jewish subjection to Nazi-administered genocide as a *white* human apocalypse and, in turn, its narrative resonance—as The Holocaust, and not merely another holocaust—with the ascendancy of White Being.[5] Norman Finkelstein argues that "a subtext of the Holocaust uniqueness claim is that The Holocaust was uniquely evil. However terrible, the suffering of others simply does not compare."[6] Put another way, the discursive structuring of The Holocaust serves as the canonical point of reference for "genocide," while (retroactively) constituting it as mind-boggling white Jewish death. In this way, the racial canonization of genocidal scandal works in the service of White Being's ascendancy and is central to the creation of the state of Israel as a settler-colonial, apartheid state that inscribes opposition to the occupation, displacement, and militarized-carceral denigration and normalized social neutralization of Palestinians as "anti-Semitism" (itself a transparent cipher for claims of anti-whiteness when directed at nonwhite critics of Israel).[7]

Israeli historian Ilan Pappé builds a case for implicating the UN-facilitated, Zionist creation of the state of Israel within a longer history of Western colonial conquest situating Israel's militarized land seizures within the contemporary juridical rubrics of ethnic cleansing. Pappé's historical schema highlights the narrative and ethical contradictions of the Zionist discursive-political regime while also provoking an interrogation of "genocide" as a modern concept that is structured in the temporal, carceral, militarized relations of racial coloniality:

> For Israelis, to recognize the Palestinians as the victims of Israeli actions is deeply distressing, in at least two ways. As this form of acknowledgement means facing up to the historical injustice of which Israel is incriminated through the ethnic cleansing of Palestine in 1948, it calls into question the very foundational myths of the State of Israel, and it raises a host of ethical questions that have inescapable implications for the future of the state. Recognizing Palestinian victimhood ties in with deeply rooted psychological fears because it demands that Israelis question their self perceptions of what "went on" in 1948. . . .
>
> The inability of Israelis to acknowledge the trauma the Palestinians suffered stands out even more sharply when set against the way the Palestinian national narrative tells the story of the Nakba, a trauma they continue to live with to the present.[8]

Pappé's account closely aligns with Steven Salaita's meditation on the historical continuities between U.S. and Israeli nation-building via settler-colonialist conquest and the harnessing of a white supremacist Civilizational imaginary. Here i call attention to Salaita's foregrounding of Israeli "exceptionalism" as a racial nationalist claim of historical and ethical entitlement to settler-colonial violence. For Salaita, this entitlement rests on a valorization of the active, state-sanctioned and state-executed neutralization and/or pacification of a savage, backward Indigenous present tense:

> I think Israel's sense of exceptionalism is quite similar to the one in the United States. They don't use the term Manifest Destiny, but the concept is very much at play. They are affecting modernity in Palestine the same way the United States did. In other words, they're taking "pre-civilized" societies and they're either removing them and clearing a space for civilization, or they're undergoing a process of civilizing them and bringing them into modernity.[9]

Pappé's and Salaita's critical appraisals of modern Zionist nation-and-state-building discourses accentuate an irreconcilable contradiction between the canonical status of The Holocaust in the inscription of the modern conceptualization of genocide, and the centrality of the Israeli settler state to a politics, statecraft, and ethical articulation of reparation for this canonized genocide. This apartheid-inducing reparation simultaneously subjects Palestinians to colonial displacement, apartheid state violence, and what Loubna Qutami describes as a Palestinian ontology of *Nakba*.

> Nakba has come to be a persistent condition for Palestinians across time and space. It has come to be a definitive feature of Palestinian insecurity and lack of permanence. It has become a constant experience of displacement, exodus, siege, imprisonment, and death across generations. . . . In the end, the Palestinian ontology of Nakba(at) is caused by multiple dimensions of enclosure and annihilation.[10]

Qutami, Pappé, and Salaita radically challenge the conceptual roots of genocide discourse and jurisprudence, instigating a theoretical examination of its juridical, scholarly, and ontological origins. Following Qutami, the Palestinian ontology of Nakba catalyzes a productive, potentially creative *epistemological* disruption of modern genocide discourse that decenters the (generally unacknowledged) white juridical-academic raciality of its hegemonic authorship.

It is in part from within this brutal ontological, epistemological, and historiographic white chauvinism—a keystone of racial modernity—that Frantz Fanon writes his famous essay "The Fact of Blackness." Echoing Césaire, Fanon demystifies the condition of the white-on-white Holocaust by revisiting the permanence of Black ontological subjection to the modern racial order:

> Simple enough, one has only not to be a nigger. Granted, the Jews are harassed—what am I thinking of? They are hunted down, exterminated,

cremated. But these are little family quarrels. The Jew is disliked from the moment he is tracked down. But in my case everything takes on a *new* guise. I am given no chance. I am overdetermined from without. I am the slave not of the "idea" that others have of me but of my own appearance.[11]

Fanon's thought provokes a longer elaboration of the systemic logics and dense, collective experiences of humiliation, degradation, terror, and death to which Black (non-)being is subjected in excess of its physiological destruction. To be "hunted down, exterminated, cremated" is the historical condition for Black life and its insurgent socialities in confrontation with the anti-Black racial chattel/carceral power that coheres modern Western social formations. For Fanon, such methods of attack compose the latter stages of an exterminating logic of violence that both precedes the physical acts of brutalization and killing and provides an external temporal (as well as bodily/racial) limit to the historical spectacle of the Nazi-conducted white/Jewish holocaust. While the (seemingly) exceptional, acute, and temporally discrete character of the Nazi-administered genocide is incommensurate with the epochal violence that structures the formation of Black and Indigenous being in the Civilizational period, the Nazis nonetheless relied on such precedents and coterminous examples of racial-colonial violence to conceive, plan, and actualize their modernist innovations of industrialized killing.[12]

"Genocide" as Impasse of the Racial

This chapter extrapolates Fanon's recapitulation of the dominant genocide narrative as a white European "family quarrel." "Genocide," as a modern conceptual and jurisprudential formulation, is the impasse of the racial: To invoke its terms already suggests exceptionality and absolute abnormality, yet the making of racial power, in all its iterations, rests on logics of the genocidal that collapse into regimes of normalcy/normativity, universality/humanism, and sociality/civil society. Racialization—that is, the characterization and discursive marking of human bodies and groups within hierarchical valuations of life and being—structures and permeates virtually every form of social differentiation, external identification, military-police mobilization, jurisprudence, national development, and environmental intervention (from the destructive to the allegedly protective) in modern globality as well as its precedents in the conquest period.

The *logics* of genocide, shaped in the material-historical domains of global racialization, thus paradoxically precede the inauguration of "genocide" as a formal lexicon—in this sense, anti-Blackness and racial-colonial power are the unspoken, illegible *preconditions* for the term's articulation as a meaningful referent to the intra-racial nadir of (white) modernity (The Holocaust). Following Joy James, prima facie evidence of racism's "logical culmination in genocide" surfaces throughout the long, multiple, and often overlapping genealogies of anti-Blackness, racism and racial-colonial dominance in the Wynterian "millennium of Man."[13]

The logic of genocide surfaces in the dispersal of human beings across what Wynter identifies as modernity's fatal racial continuum, characterized by the devastating binary distinction between the "selected" and the "dysselected" (the latter, for Wynter, traverses "the category of 'natives' and 'niggers'"):

> By placing human origins *totally* in evolution and natural selection . . . [the bourgeois/white thinkers of the modern West] map the structuring principle of their now bourgeois social structure, that of the *selected* versus *dysselected*, the *evolved* versus *non-evolved*, on the only still extra-humanly determined order of difference which was left available in the wake of the rise of the physical and, after Darwin, of the biological, sciences. This is the difference that was provided by the human hereditary variations which we classify as *races*. This is where DuBois's colour line comes in.[14]

Wynter's (and Du Bois's) conception of racial modernity focuses on the emergence of the overlapping Western scientific and humanistic epistemes as knowledge forms that symbiotically intertwine the (rationalist) production of racial difference (via the biological, social, and natural sciences) with the discursive-ideological, and thus broadly cultural installation of global white ascendancy. Modern raciality produces the latter discursivity through fluctuating notions of historical telos, aesthetic-cultural supremacy, and the white human's "transparency" as a meta-symbiosis of power/dominance that aspires to apprehend, shape, and anticipate human destinies—generally, globally, and permanently.[15]

In resonance with Wynter, Said delineates the epochal distinction drawn by modern Empire between those who know (the West as "Knowledge") and that which is to be known (Egypt, the Orient, and so on, as "the object[s] of such knowledge"): "To have such knowledge of such a thing is to dominate it, to have authority over it."[16] In confrontation with racial-colonial power, Said's analytic can be stretched to address the generational, flesh-and-bone, ontological, and cultural consequences of an anti-Black, racial-colonial modernity that has *always* linked the epistemic supremacy of White Being (in its transparency and allegedly inherent rationality) to the physiological destruction, denigration, and/or violent compartmentalization of its racial antagonists (objects of external study/knowledge/classification, dispersed along spectra of nonrationality-to-nonbeing). To rephrase Said, there are those who know and must live, and those who *are to be known in their proximity to death/ obsolescence.*

There are few instances in which Civilizational modernity's—and by extension white academic raciality's—logic of epistemological bureaucratization has graver consequences than in the conceptualization and theorization of "genocide." Here, i wish to attend to a theoretically aggressive rearticulation of genocide that focuses principally on targeted peoples' poetic responses to formations of anti-Blackness and racial-colonial violence.[17] How do involuntary conditions of collective evisceration and ontological negation become the historical terms through which threatened peoples articulate counter-genocidal forms of radical, collective genius?

Contrary to many scholarly and activist approaches to the topic, this chapter refrains from recitation of historical body counts and other empirical indicators of a global hierarchy of life and death. Such data have been readily available for many years, and i am unconvinced that positivist recollections of this historical archive will meaningfully alter the conditions to which it testifies. Rather, i am interested in building a praxis of creative and rigorous political-theoretical *literacy* around the stakes of anti-Blackness and racial-colonial power while embracing the various forms of creative insurgency that resist, interrupt, abolish, and transform the historical-material terrains of those historical violences.

The modern (post–World War II) institutionalization of "genocide" is stalked and disrupted by the world-making, Civilization-building, socially productive technologies of dominance that have made possible the consolidation of the very units of sociality—humanity, the Civilized world, mankind, nation-state, and modern jurisprudence—on which the UN Genocide Convention (and hegemonic genocide discourses more generally) depends for its epistemic and juridical cogency. Hence, it is less important to consider whether "genocide" provides an *adequate* rubric through which to render particular forms of power and violence legible to "mankind and the civilized world" (in the words of the UN Genocide Convention) than it is to rigorously examine how the field of genocide discourse creates a largely unintended opportunity for a *radical decentering* of the very same Civilized (white) humanity it implicitly defends and valorizes.[18]

"Genocide" as Juridical and Academic Regime

There are two hegemonic apparatuses through which "genocide" has been institutionalized and implemented as a technology of modern knowledge and
jurisprudence. On the one hand, there is a *legal regime on genocide* that has
been structured by the overlapping United Nations human rights and international juridical infrastructures. The field of genocide jurisprudence moves
from the common understanding that the UN Convention on the Prevention
and Punishment of the Crime of Genocide (ratified in 1951) forms the essential
basis for any viable engagement with genocide.[19] Expectedly, this juridical
regime privileges "law" and "rights" as the political, cultural, and institutional registers through which genocide is to be defined, arbitrated, and otherwise interrupted and engaged.[20] On the other hand, there is an *academic
regime on genocide* dominated by the field of "Genocide Studies," encompassing a professional scholarly discourse that began to crystallize in the 1980s and
which has since yielded an identifiable set of academic journals, anthologies,
conferences, and circuits of scholarly debate.[21] The legal and academic regimes
are mutually entangled in what J. Sebastian names the "ontological construction of universal rights" as a gendered racial production of a colonial and anti-
Black modernity.[22]

Across these two hegemonic fields of genocide discourse there is broad
consensus on two foundational points. The first area of general agreement
concerns the paradigmatic role of Polish legal scholar and Nazi Holocaust survivor Rafaël Lemkin as the conceptual innovator of the term "genocide."
Lemkin participated in (and was eventually expelled from) the UN committee
that authored preliminary drafts of the Genocide Convention, and his lengthy
1944 text *Axis Rule in Occupied Europe* builds a sweeping historical definition of genocide that foregrounds Nazi Germany as its principal case study.[23]
Counterintuitively, the second point of consensus entails the Genocide Convention's endemic weakness as a legal and conceptual framework for purposes
of rigorous academic definition and research, policy-based intervention, and
effective prosecution of alleged perpetrators.

Central to its structural flimsiness is the convention's formulation of the
prosecutorial burden of proving genocidal "intent" regardless of the magni-
tude of evidence of damage and human casualty. Samuel Totten, William S.
Parsons, and Robert K. Hitchcock address this problem in relation to Indigenous and Aboriginal peoples:

> Cases claiming genocide of [I]ndigenous peoples have been brought
> before the United Nations, but generally they have brought little
> result, in part because government representatives *claimed that there*

had been no intent to destroy indigenous peoples as such, and that the groups were never eliminated "as an ethnic or cultural group." Governments and other agencies usually state that the deaths of indigenous people were an "unintended consequence" of certain actions, such as colonizing remote areas, and that there were no planned efforts to destroy people on the basis of who they were.[24]

The Genocide Convention's "intent clause" has played a rather extraordinary, even singular, role in undermining the legal feasibility of potential criminal cases against national governments of the First and Second Worlds as well as the more recent Global North, including the United States, the former Soviet Union, France, Canada, and Great Britain.

Beyond these two major points of consensus, the legal and academic regimes on genocide are in constant flux, and the debates therein are expectedly contentious and often unsettled. While a comprehensive diagnosis and critique of these hegemonic discursive regimes will not be undertaken here, it is nonetheless possible to characterize some of the defining elements of their overlapping problematics as a premise for this chapter's critical departure.

The legal regime on genocide is characterized by five structuring concerns: legal definition, juridical criminalization, presumption of a perpetrator/victim dyad, conceptualization of proof of "intent," and clarification of the legal parameters of the UN's jurisdiction. These formative elements of the legal regime attempt to construct a sufficiently stable legal standard through which alleged genocides can be addressed, prosecuted, and (ostensibly) remediated through the apparatuses of international jurisprudence. Crucially, these five concerns define a field of political struggles within genocide discourse that unfold through the institutions, epistemological frameworks, and punitive logics of criminal law. In this sense, "genocide" tends to be framed within a narrow cultural-political grammar—allegations of genocide are made legible through a peculiar politics of representation—that compartmentalize world-altering violences as deviant, anti-social, and relatively isolatable *criminal* acts committed by discretely identifiable people or groups of people (whether individuals, governments, militaries, or other collectives/organizations).

While such a conception of "genocide" as an isolatable crime may be well-suited for international criminal justice proceedings, it fails to account for the possibility that particular forms of anti-Black and racial-colonial genocide are un-isolatable, dynamic, proliferating historical forces that organically emerge from the normative economic, cultural, legal, and epistemic formations of given socialities, including but not limited to modern and post-colonial nation-states.

The academic regime on genocide has been defined through the emergence of Genocide Studies since the late-1980s. While the academic regime replicates or significantly overlaps with many of the conceptual, empirical, and methodological elements of the legal regime, it significantly expands the parameters of the hegemonic jurisprudential discourse through (largely social scientific and historical) case studies; philosophical and theoretical debate over key ethical, definitional, and methodological issues; and critical examination of the limits of jurisprudence for apprehending or intervening on genocides. The crucial point of symbiosis between the academic and legal regimes on genocide is in their generalized acceptance of the causal assumption that *criminalizing* genocide is a sound and (potentially) effective way to prevent or deter its future occurrence. Consequently, the academic regime's methodological and narrative concerns largely reproduce the legal regime's dichotomous "perpetrator"/"victim" narration of genocide as a criminal act.[25]

This binary frame has enabled a widespread academic fixation on reductive—if not altogether simplistic—conceptions of individualized and identifiable perpetrators, largely displacing sustained analysis and theorization of how genocides may be produced through the normalized (rather than exceptional) operation of social, political, economic, and military systems regardless of the autonomous or self-determined actions of their agents, administrators, and leaders. Echoing Eduardo Bonilla-Silva's notion of a "racism without racists," the academic regime's generally voluntaristic conception of the genocide perpetrator creates the paradox of "genocides without killers."[26]

Arguably the most insidious aspect of the hegemonic academic regime on genocide is its largely undertheorized adherence to the assumptions, epistemic traditions, and conceptual structures of (white) Western humanism. The major methodological, archival, and conceptual streams within the academic regime, including those concerned with the protocols of legal testimony and criminal accountability, project an idealized human victim-subject of "genocide," namely, they who are sufficient to the task of legitimating and empowering the preventative and punitive capacities of the academic and legal apparatuses by exemplifying/performing/embodying notions of the credible victim, testifier, truth-teller, survivor, and advocate.[27] Genocide Studies scholar David H. Jones, for example, proposes a "model" of social subjectivity that encompasses the "civic conscientiousness" and "moral exemplariness" that is necessary for "the prevention of genocide":

> While this conception includes the ordinary altruistic virtues such as the capacity to feel love, affection and disinterested benevolence for others, it denies that these are sufficient to provide the kind of civic

and political motivation needed in citizens. In order for persons to be moral exemplars, they must also have [other] virtues: practical wisdom, autonomy, and civic virtue generally. In addition, *and most importantly*, the civic virtues are *assumed to emerge from, and to be largely dependent upon*, participation in liberal institutions and democratic culture. . . . [C]ivic virtues are defined *in terms of citizenship*, thus, they are *inherently* social, institutional, political, and communal.[28]

The pre-conceptual apparatus of the academic regime on genocide tends to fabricate the ideal subject of (human) rights/citizenship/law as a projection of the legal and philosophical genealogies of Western white liberal humanism: This subject's rational, self-determining sociality unfolds outside of and alienated from the conditions of acute and perpetual vulnerability to the (physiologically, culturally, spiritually, and subjectively) disintegrating, degrading, terrorizing, and exterminating violence of the New World Civilizational racial text and its modern Western ensemble. In fact, such forms of disruption and disintegration generally produce various forms of systemic alienation between particular peoples, geographies, and oppressed tribes/nations and the formalized structures of political modernity that are so casually reified in Jones's (and others') philosophical discourse: citizenship, "civic virtues," "autonomy," "liberal institutions," and so on.

As Randall Williams has persuasively argued, the "moral" problematic of hegemonic genocide discourse "insists on the centrality of Western Man as the guarantor and protector of rights and humanity."[29] A white supremacist humanist universalism courses through presumptive conceptualizations of the legally apprehensible victim-subject, a form of human being that is self-determined in its peculiar, rational capacity for providing a testimonial that can transcend the assumptively distorting and perverting traumas of genocidal violence. Compounding this discursive apartheid and conceptual coloniality, the legal and academic discourses on genocide betray a generalized undertheorization—if not a gaping ignorance—of at least five interrelated dynamics:

  The inextricability between the violences explicitly invoked by
    hegemonic notions of "genocide" and the specificities of anti-
    Blackness and racial-colonial violence as distinct and overlapping
    global forms of gendered, physiological violence and (anti-) social
    dominance.
  The methodological inadequacies of disciplinary social scientific
    empiricism and juridical calculation in accounting for the complex
    genealogies of violence that are invoked by "genocide"; to the extent
    that such violences irreparably interrupt, disrupt, and otherwise

alter the cultural, affective, biophysical, ecological, and institutional terms of various peoples' capacity for cultural and social reproduction across historical moments and generations, such positivist and litigious approaches to the problem of "genocide" are intellectually and ethically inadequate.

As a discursive regime that emerges through a crisis of white Western modernity and is cohered through the modern jurisprudence of human rights, "genocide" incompletely addresses the *generalized* conditions of historical existence for peoples subjected to anti-Black, racial-colonial regimes of violence, displacement, and disruption.

The peoples inhabiting what João Costa Vargas identifies as the historical conditions of an anti-Black "genocide continuum" are not merely victims of oppression and targets of commodification and ontological destruction; against the violence and terror of dehumanization and extermination, they constantly generate new forms of thought, sociality, survival, collective life-making, freedom, and human relationality that are constituted by (and not fraudulently transcendent of) genocidal conditions.[30]

The creative, collective genius that emerges from such conditions (chattel enslavement, settler-colonialism, militarized conquest, land displacement/occupation, domestic warfare, and otherwise) produces urgent insights into the complexities of genocide as a social and historical logic, while producing forms of praxis that seek to abolish the social conditions produced and cultivated by this logic.

The last point establishes a point of departure for the rest of this chapter. How do people act, create, commune, and produce insurgent modalities of human being under conditions of actual and threatened extermination and massive, collective terror? How are genocidal conditions complexly inhabited, resisted, and survived? How do the creative acts, scholarly labors, and collective movements that have been vital to defending endangered life worlds and cultural genealogies under conditions of deadly and massive duress provoke a radical rethinking of the genocide concept? Such questions confront "genocide" as a post–World War II bureaucratization and professionalization of academic and juridical knowledge, and therefore suggest that the knowledge-hegemony of human rights law and the Western academy is as much a part of genocidal power as its military, ideological, economic, and other institutional dimensions.

Following the critical work of Saidiya Hartman, Alyosha Goldstein, Andrew Woolford, Frank B. Wilderson, Zakiyyah Iman Jackson, Calvin Warren, and others who stress the ontological violence of gendered anti-Black and racial-colonial power, it is possible to identify a historical logic of genocide that dynamically, selectively targets particular peoples for collective subjection to mourning, grieving, loss, terror, and irreparability as primary lived and transgenerational (inherited) conditions of community and being.[31] Such inhabitations of genocidal historical logics significantly preclude, or altogether preempt, particular peoples' capacity (and willingness) to fulfill the academic regime's standards as proper "(potential) victim" subjects of "genocide" as defined by the UN Genocide Convention and the primary streams of Genocide Studies.

To the extent that the white humanist fantasy tacitly underwrites the coherence of academic-juridical discourses on genocide, the capacity to engage the problem of genocide *as an anti-Black and racial-colonial problem* will remain delimited by a white supremacist epistemological circuit.

Toward a Black Radical, Racial-Colonial Poetics: We Charge Genocide Redux

Given the severity of "genocide's" epistemological, political, and jurisprudential limitations, it is necessary to study how and why movements and collectives struggling against various forms of anti-Blackness and racial-colonial dominance utilize the term as a political rhetoric and engage its legal regime as a tactic for radically confronting white humanism. The classic accusation of anti-Black genocide lodged against the U.S. government in the 1951 *We Charge Genocide* petition and the devastating global diagnosis of the 2007 UN Declaration of the Rights of Indigenous Peoples (UN DRIP) exemplify the possibilities of such strategic work.[32] Rather than reading such overtly state-directed and public-facing critical labors as exceptional, one-off interventions on the human rights juridical apparatus, it is more useful to read and narrate them as contributions to a continuum of radical challenges to the ascendancy of White Being.

How do such collective mobilizations of a de-provincialized genocide concept burst the discursive seams of prevailing languages that avert direct and substantive reference to conditions of normalized, broadly unrecognized forms of systemically induced suffering and degradation? The lexicon of genocide, when repurposed as a tactical description of anti-Black and racial-colonial violence, can potentially erode or obliterate the edifices of liberal-progressive pretension that generally prescribe state and societal reforms as the practical-and-realistic interventions on socialities and state formations structured in racial dominance.[33]

By way of example, Chicago's intergenerational grassroots organization We Charge Genocide (WCG, also discussed in Chapter 5) radically demystified the tacit liberal premises of conventional police accountability and anti-police brutality rhetorics during an intensive three years of activity from 2014 to 2016. Linking its organizational origins to a specific historical tradition of Black radicalism, WCG cited the 1951 UN petition filed by the Black communist-led Civil Rights Congress as the primary inspiration for its mission. In this sense, the organization's genesis and collective, public labors signified an early twenty-first-century accusation against a (proto-) genocidal U.S. racist state. Its 2014 report to the UN Committee Against Torture, *Police Violence against Chicago's Youth of Color*, offers a highly accessible (online) archival, testimonial, and analytical document that illustrates a condition of police terror/violence for Chicago's Black and Latinx youth:

> The prevalence of harassment, involuntary searches, and verbal abuse are not the result of unusual transgressions by select, individual [Chicago Police Department] officers. Rather, they are illustrative of institutional racial bias and systemic endorsement of targeting and harassment of young people of color. . . . This cruel and degrading treatment of Chicago's youth of color serves to silence, traumatize, and control entire communities. It creates a climate where youth of color feel unsafe and learn that they always are suspects and that their lives are not valued in the eyes of the state.[34]

The report's citations of police torture and violence include, but are far from limited to, killings of unarmed Black and Brown children and young adults, officer sexual assault/rape, racially targeted mass arrests, and thick descriptions of a citywide culture of state-sanctioned impunity for Chicago Police Department officers.[35] WCG builds a present tense archive, addressing a climate of comprehensive, systemic vulnerability to everyday, normally functioning, non-scandalous racist state violence. The report's archival and testimonial analysis exposes the limitations of liberal-progressive journalistic and activist tendencies that compartmentalize police violence into compilations of isolatable incidents that reify the notion that policing is somehow separable from its systemic practices, and thus suggest that its endemic, persistent violence is reformable or otherwise correctable.[36] (During its short organizational existence, We Charge Genocide selectively supported localized efforts for police reform and accountability while consistently challenging the limitations of reformism as a political paradigm.)[37]

Police Violence against Chicago's Youth of Color patiently creates a rigorous definition of "police violence" across its fifteen pages, with sections titled, "Chicago Police Violence: Harassment and Abuse," "Chicago Police Violence: Use of Deadly Force," "Chicago Police Violence: Sexual Assaults," and so on. Infused with statements from survivors of police harassment, police street terror, and police torture, the report composes a lucid rejoinder to the underlying assumptions of Michel Foucault's well-known conception of the disciplinary society and Giorgio Agamben's conceptualization of the state of exception, both of which fail to account for anti-Black, racial-colonial state violence as unexceptional, physiologically and trans-generationally violent, systemic and sustained conditions of modern socialities.[38]

We Charge Genocide's abolitionist analytical accounting of Chicago's historical geography clarifies how the city's regime of police violence cannot be adequately described through the terms of "police brutality," in part because the explanatory integrity of the latter concept rests on two categorical premises: first, that the identified police actions and behaviors are, in fact, violations of law or institutional policy—"police brutality" suggests an abrogation of the police officer's law-sanctified entitlement to exercise state-legitimated violence, whereas WCG's notion of "police violence" addresses the totality of domestic warfare's protocols, tactics, and casualties; and second, that such police actions and behaviors can be discretely, reasonably, and adequately grieved, redressed, and/or corrected through existing juridical and institutional/state procedures (for example, citizen complaints, whistleblower grievances, internal and grand jury investigations, and potential criminal prosecutions).[39] We Charge Genocide challenges and displaces prevalent discourses of police brutality by building a rigorous analytical narrative of police violence as systemic, institutionalized, juridically condoned police torture, cruelty, inhumane and degrading treatment, murder, harassment, and unjustified detention.[40]

Further, by challenging the exceptionalist narratives that tend to individualize the police and state-condoned assassination of Black men and boys (for example, Oscar Grant, Trayvon Martin, Michael Brown, Eric Garner, Tamir Rice, George Floyd, Ahmaud Arbery, et al.), WCG amplifies a radical feminist, trans, and queer critique of anti-Black, racist police violence that begins to address its complexity as a gendered, sexualized regime of coercive (hence neither "disciplinary" nor "exceptional") power.

Reports received through the PEL ["Police Encounter Line," We Charge Genocide's resource for facilitating confidential reports from youth on "negative experiences with the police"] and other youth-focused NGOs in Chicago offer evidence that rape, sexual assault, and sexual harassment of women—including transgender women, as well as transgender and gender non-conforming individuals who do not identify as women—is committed with alarming frequency by the [Chicago Police Department].[41]

Rather than fixating on bringing individually identified "bad cops" to criminal trial for the purposes of prosecution by the very same racist state apparatus that equips the police with deadly impunity in the first place, WCG argues for abolitionist forms of justice and accountability that are compatible with specific forms of short-term institutional change, specifically those that facilitate the growth of community-based self-determination and/or subordinate police authority to the collective will and oversight of ordinary (poor, working-class, criminalized Black, Latinx) Chicagoans (see Figure 11).

We Charge Genocide's critical abolitionist praxis significantly departs from approaches to police reform that reproduce episodic narratives of police brutality and fail to apprehend the historical continuities of anti-Black state power as a primary foundation and sustained demonstration of modern U.S. sovereignty.[42] As a scholarly abolitionist text, *Police Violence Against Chicago's Youth of Color* radically rethinks the institutionality of policing, flowing from a present-tense testimonial archive that amplifies the collective

Figure 11. PPL's Response Team (@ChiCopWatch). (Twitter, November 13, 2014, https://twitter.com /ChiCopWatch/status /532927362183483392.)

 **PPL's Response Team** @ChiCopWatch   (Follow)

We stood in protest of police violence & the perpetual hypocrisy of US laws & policies silencing our torture #WCGtoUN

8:05 AM - 13 Nov 2014

imperatives of survival, communal bodily integrity, radical social and economic justice, and self-defense against police terror and potentially deadly state violence.

We Charge Genocide exemplifies a form of creative, collective narrative genius that recognizes the long historical present tense of ordinary peoples' normalized encounters with state-facilitated and state-condoned social evisceration. In tension with the UN Genocide Convention's pronounced mission to "to liberate mankind from such an odious scourge," We Charge Genocide refutes such pretentious universalisms and instead engages in the immediate and militant defense of a localized Black and Brown humanity.[43] As this insurgency against the police power of the racist state is animated by a Black radical genealogy, it patterns its organizational practices within a sober, grounded analysis of a climate of intensive, systemic, numbingly normal racist terror, invasiveness, and physiological vulnerability.

WCG's critical praxis provides an constructive point of departure for the larger argument of this chapter: Against the hegemonic legal and academic institutionalizations of genocide discourse, the tactical appropriations and rearticulations of "genocide" in counter-narrations of anti-Black and racial-colonial power indicate the radical insufficiency of existing critical/activist arsenals in communicating the gravity of surrounding (and long historical) conditions of existence for peoples on the underside of the Civilization project. These counter-narratives further demonstrate how the hegemonic terms of "genocide" as an institutionalized global human rights rhetoric were/are not intended to be purposed toward an indictment of the U.S. government, police, military, or civil society.

The violence, casualties, and devastations that "genocide" attempts to discursively access constantly escape the term's epistemic parameters because the collective inhabitations of anti-Blackness and racial-colonial dominance are *constitutive of* rather than exceptional to the foundations of Civilization and white Western, euroamerican modernity. Flourishing debates within and between Black studies, Native and Indigenous studies, settler-colonial studies, and critical ethnic studies are constantly reshaping theoretical and pedagogical approaches to historicized notions of race, colonialism, political ontology, and social movement.[44] Of interest here are the possibilities and pitfalls of considering "genocide" as another keyword in the unfolding critical discourses of anti-Blackness and racial-colonial power. If we concede, for now, that the term cannot be fully disinterred from its foundations in modern human rights jurisprudence and the epistemic regimes of Western liberal humanism, it seems doubtful that *hegemonic* genocide discourse can be effectively appropriated and refashioned for other kinds of radical praxis.

Yet, as signaled by the work of We Charge Genocide, there is possibility for a deeper consideration of how a *poetics* of anti-Black, racial-colonial genocide lives and moves on the underside and disavowed edges of the dominant juridical and academic regimes. What would it mean to sustain a critical engagement with the counter-epistemes and mobilizing affect/effect of the genocide poetics that signify the constitutive excess of the term's established definitional and legal formalities? How do such insurgent, disloyal rearticulations and remobilizations of "genocide" complicate and contribute to different forms of radical praxis against the modern Civilizational order?

The disruptive political audacity and transformative power mustered by groups like We Charge Genocide emerge from the fact that their conditions of urgency override the question of whether their use of the term "genocide" is abiding by proper legal standards or academic definitions. WCG enacts a poetics of genocide as pure accusation, a dense incitement of collective knowledge buttressed by rigorous methods of testimonial truth-telling and grassroots archiving. Such scholarly activist insurgencies are counter-salvos against the buzzing cultural significations and accumulating casualties of undeclared gendered racist domestic warfare waged by the state and generally endorsed by a popular white/multiculturalist common sense.[45] Mobilizations of a poetic lexicon of genocide, in these and other geographies and historical moments of liberationist opposition to anti-Blackness and racial-colonial state violence, do not pivot on the juridical feasibility of the accusation and charge, nor do they rely on the term's (incomplete) capacity to bring definitive legibility to the suffering and casualties of populations and bodies targeted for systemic vulnerability. Rather, these mobilizations enrich and proliferate different peoples' praxis of artistry and creativity, wherein "genocide" is repurposed as a keyword in a morbid and weaponized poetry of insurrection, an irruptive announcement of emergency within a state of normalcy that echoes Raphaël Lemkin's paradigmatic (though stubbornly under-engaged) definition of genocide as "a problem not only of war but also of peace."[46]

To consider the insurgent poetics of genocide in its full artistry is to grasp other epistemic, (extra-)ontological, and collective physiological positions—that is, to consider how the genocide accusation, as affirmation of a shared shedding of blood, collectively resistant life, and resilient being, is also a capacious and deindividualized explication of Frantz Fanon's meditation on epidermalization: "As a result, the body schema, attacked in several places, collapsed, giving way to an epidermal racial schema."[47] When genocide becomes the chosen vernacular for those inhabiting the most acutely repressive and coercive geographies of the carceral, chattel, settler state, there is a laceration of the societal-institutional skin that binds anti-Blackness, racial-colonial power, and institutionalized dehumanization to societal normalcy. In such moments, the critical labors of interpretation and re-narration socialize the obligations of radical (abolitionist) praxis by calling on surrounding communities of loved ones, solidarity activists, scholars, artists, journalists, and others to deeply engage— that is, *read*—the poetics of genocide in real time. It is toward two recent examples of such narrative-interpretive possibility that i now turn.

Freedom Non-Demands: The Georgia (2010) and California (2011) Prison Strikes

Anti-Blackness and racial-colonial power are structured in perpetuity, crossing while reconfiguring temporalities and geographies, permeating history, social experience, and the struggle toward human being for those subjected to their changing regimes of dominance. Here, i follow Wynter's lead in conceptualizing *human being* as a lived and suffered verb (as praxis) rather than a Western humanist or coercively universalized white supremacist noun.[48] Writing in the aftermath of the 1992 Los Angeles rebellions, Wynter meditates at length on the mundane police jargon of "NHI" (no humans involved)—an abbreviation frequently used in LAPD phone and radio communications to describe incidents involving Black people—as a reference to both the fundamental precarity (hence foundational impossibility) of Black civil existence and the institutional implications of normalized social liquidation:

> For the social effects to which this acronym [NHI], and its placing outside the 'sanctified universe of obligation,' of the category of young Black males to which it refers . . . whilst not overtly genocidal, *are clearly having genocidal effects* with the incarceration and elimination of young Black males by ostensibly normal, and everyday means.[49]

For those whose humanity is perpetually held in question or preemptively denied, the praxis of human being already requires revolt against the technologies of elimination, social liquidation, and terror that evidence "genocidal effects." Anti-Blackness and racial-colonial power are not only produced in the formation of Western modernity but are the conditions of modernity's material and philosophical emergence as such.

The carceral-chattel anti-Blackness and racial-colonial displacements of modern sociality are lucidly, critically re-narrated and disrupted in the theoretical and political texts generated by the 2010 Georgia prisoners' strike and the 2011 Pelican Bay Prison (and California prison-wide) hunger strike. (While the Pelican Bay strike launched a second phase in 2013, i focus on its inaugural moments here.) Organized by thousands of (overwhelmingly Black) people incarcerated in prisons across the state, the Georgia prisoners' strike began as a one-day action on December 9, 2010, continued for about one week, and quickly grew to become the largest prison strike in U.S. history. The strike organizers' press release brought attention to the inhumane practices of the Georgia Department of Corrections (DOC) and called for public support to force the DOC to "stop treating [imprisoned people] like animals and slaves and institute programs that address their basic human rights."[50] Utilizing contraband cell phones, the strike assumed a variety of nonviolent resistance tactics across Georgia state prisons, including work stoppages, a refusal to exit cells, and hunger strikes. While it was largely neglected and underreported by mainstream and leftist media outlets alike (with the notable exceptions of online venues *Black Agenda Report* and *Facing South*), the Georgia strike nonetheless galvanized a contingency of national support among incarcerated and non-incarcerated people.

The strikers' political language and organizing strategies encouraged a deeper reflection and historicized analysis of militarized racist carceral state power in at least three ways. First, their commitment to nonviolent tactics and strategic use of public appeals likely prevented Georgia state authorities from following the paradigmatically homicidal examples of state officials and prison guards in the deadly 1971 San Quentin (CA) and Attica (NY) Rebellions (among many others). It cannot be overstated that a central dimension of the strikers' political success was their detailed analytical attention to the state's historical predisposition to inflict massive, gratuitous bodily violence and juridical-corporeal punishment on captive Black people during such moments of carceral insurgency. Nonetheless, the DOC and other Georgia officials engaged in semi-contained, strategic, and violent repression of organizers, participants, and other imprisoned people during and after the strike. Such a state response is theoretically significant because it attempts to dissipate the radical *extra*-carceral politicizations that might unfold in response to the strike (this point will be elaborated shortly).

Second, the Georgia prisoners' strike used the language of *racial chattel slavery* to convey the historical and experiential dimensions of carceral state violence in its everyday institutional form:[51]

> The prisoners fault the [Georgia DOC] for having prisoners work for free "in violation of the 13th Amendment to the Constitution prohibiting slavery and involuntary servitude."[52]

Testimonial and investigative accounts reveal that, across racial subjectivities, the Georgia strikers assembled common political ground through a collective re-narration of the degrading conditions of incarceration as affixations of the historical power structures of anti-Black domination.[53]

Third, the vernacular of the Georgia prisoners' strike (particularly in its formal demands, outlined later in this section) complicate notions of "labor" and "work" as they tend to be used in contemporary progressive critiques of neoliberalism, while bringing acute attention to the extra-capitalist economies of the gendered racist policing-carceral regime. The strikers narrated themselves as simultaneously inhabiting the categories of civil death (convicted people), slavery, and captive labor.

On the heels of the Georgia strike, the 2011 Pelican Bay hunger strike was similarly remarkable for having been conceived and led by people (overwhelmingly Latinx, Chicanx, and Black) incarcerated in California's security housing units (SHU), high-designation forms of incarceration in which people are segregated from the mainline prison population, locked in small cells for at least twenty-three hours per day, and disallowed any in-person human interaction beyond encounters with correctional officers. Organized through a variety of illicit and creative means (an open discussion of which will not be included in this chapter in order to avoid risk to strike organizers), the strikers communed around collective, long-running grievances against the punitive practices and administrative protocols of the California Department of Corrections and Rehabilitation (CDCR), which included arbitrary (and often indefinite) assignation of incarcerated people to the SHU, subjection to sustained sensory deprivation, malign medical neglect, unannounced and unjustified "cell extractions," invasive body searches, and various forms of low-intensity torture and physiological punishment (sleep deprivation, inedible/spoiled/non-nutritious foods, lack of outdoor access, exposure to constant noise and fluorescent light, and so on).[54]

The hunger strike commenced on July 1, 2011 and immediately sparked solidarity actions among some 6,500 other incarcerated people across the California state system. The Pelican Bay strikers garnered the attention of a broad community of anti-prison, prison reform, prisoners' rights, and carceral abolitionist activists and advocates. Within days, there were allied prison and jail strikes across the United States, including mobilizations by incarcerated people at Ohio State Penitentiary, Red Onion State Prison (VA), Marion Communication Management Unit (IL), and Collins Bay Institution (Ontario, Canada).[55] The Prisoner Hunger Strike Solidarity coalition became the primary civil society/"free world" correlate of the Pelican Bay movement and was supported by a spectrum of high-profile prison and criminal justice reform, incarcerated peoples' rights, and abolitionist organizations such as Legal Services for

Prisoners with Children, All of Us or None, Campaign to End the Death Penalty, California Prison Focus, Prison Activist Resource Center, Critical Resistance, California Coalition for Women Prisoners, and American Friends Service Committee.[56]

The first phase of the Pelican Bay strike lasted three weeks, after which the CDCR promised a thorough review of its policies. Dissatisfied with the CDCR's failure to respond to the movement's five core demands, the hunger strike initiated a second phase on September 26, 2011, inspiring an even wider network of about 12,000 incarcerated people to take solidarity actions in California, Arizona, Mississippi, and Oklahoma (notably, the latter three states incarcerate people transported from California state prisons). The second phase of the Pelican Bay strike lasted several weeks and was followed by similar actions throughout California for months thereafter. Due to its efficacy as a widely supported, public-facing mobilization of incarcerated people that also created a practical paradigm and mobile method for movement-building under repressive conditions, the Pelican Bay mobilization of 2011 has been acknowledged as a watershed moment in the history of carceral political rebellions.[57]

A gendered organization of political labor characterized both movements' grassroots geographies and organizing infrastructures. While the strikes were initiated by people incarcerated in men's prisons, an overwhelming amount of on-the-ground mobilizing, public discursive production, and other activist-intellectual work (hand-to-hand circulation of petitions, social media organizing, press conferences, community teach-ins and workshops, college campus lectures, and so on) was carried out by women who identified as loved ones and (immediate as well as extended) family members of the imprisoned strikers. Angelica Camacho's research on the Pelican Bay hunger strike details this critical facet of the struggle's conceptualization of gendered racist state violence while also rethinking the assumptive terms often used to describe those who create and sustain such movements. Reflecting on the work of California Families Against Solitary Confinement (CFASC), Camacho writes,

> At the forefront of organizing and mobilizing attention for the hunger strike in Southern California were prisoners' mothers, wives, family, and loved ones who were predominately women and often had no prior experience in "political activism."
>
> . . . It was the mobilization of common everyday people, often with no prior experience organizing a rally or even comfortable and familiar with the word revolution, radical, and/or activist, that helped gain a large part of the public's attention.[58]

Their familial understanding and knowledge of prison terror accompanied by a refusal to allow the continual dehumanization of their loved ones in prison brought them together. They were ready to turn their burning despair into hope and possibility.[59]

[CFASC organizer] Dolores Canales . . . framed her commentary as a mother, hoping that others with children would be able to comprehend, and ultimately open their mind, heart, and ears to the idea of shutting down the SHU. . . . In part, her decision to share her daily haunting as a mother was a public call to view the men in the SHU beyond the label of a prisoner—to perceive them as family.[60]

Such articulations of labor, mobility, voice, and institutional position refract the gendered conditions of anti-Black, racial-colonial violence that emanate from geographical sites of incarceration like Pelican Bay: At a student-organized public event at the University of California, Riverside in late 2011, several women who bore leadership responsibilities in the Prisoner Hunger Strike Solidarity coalition discussed how their imprisoned loved ones' experiences in the SHU shaped and deformed their own "free-world" existence in proximity to the racist carceral state. Their testimonial analysis not only educated faculty members, students, staff, and non-university affiliated attendees about the short-term sociopolitical stakes of the strike, but also demonstrated how the regime of carceral state violence is not isolated to discrete, seemingly faraway steel-and-concrete sites of incarcerated people's institutionalized suffering. For the coalition leaders, Pelican Bay (and the criminalization/carceral apparatus writ large) was not "somewhere else." Rather, the SHU represented a center of gravity for a carceral regime that produced deeply personal forms of domination, demoralization, and everyday terror.[61]

The complex gendering of the carceral regime's multiple layers of violence thus structures and haunts the generally masculinist representation of the prison strikes' political culture and symbolic apparatus and directs attention toward the extended aftermath of both strikes as a condition that is borne by both imprisoned (cisgender, queer, and trans) men and their distended, disrupted relations with children, elders, loved ones, and others in the so-called free world.[62] In this way, the Pelican Bay hunger strike critically elaborates radical feminist abolitionist framings of the prison industrial complex and its expansive, extra-carceral technologies of domination.[63]

The Georgia and California carceral strikes are living archival examples of a human praxis that disrupts the naturalized authorial subject of the international human rights regime: They who are presumed to be free, propertied, citizenship-bearing, and generally white or white-proximate (with varying access to the rights regime across classed cisgender, trans, queer, heteronormative, and homonormative social positions).[64] In what follows, i offer a close reading of a crucial portion of the strikes' living archive: Their respective public demands, which served as the movements' primary public texts. I begin by offering both sets of demands in their unedited entirety:

Georgia Prison Strike Demands
(issued December 8, 2010)

A *Living Wage for Work:* In violation of the 13th Amendment to the Constitution prohibiting slavery and involuntary servitude, the DOC demands prisoners work for free.

Educational Opportunities: For the great majority of prisoners, the DOC denies all opportunities for education beyond the GED, despite the benefit to both prisoners and society.

Decent Health Care: In violation of the 8th Amendment prohibition against cruel and unusual punishments, the DOC denies adequate medical care to prisoners, charges excessive fees for the most minimal care and is responsible for extraordinary pain and suffering.

An *End to Cruel and Unusual Punishments:* In further violation of the 8th Amendment, the DOC is responsible for cruel prisoner punishments for minor infractions of rules.

Decent Living Conditions: Georgia prisoners are confined in overcrowded, substandard conditions, with little heat in winter and oppressive heat in summer.

Nutritional Meals: Vegetables and fruit are in short supply in DOC facilities while starches and fatty foods are plentiful.

Vocational and Self-Improvement Opportunities: The DOC has stripped its facilities of all opportunities for skills training, self-improvement and proper exercise.

Access to Families: The DOC has disconnected thousands of prisoners from their families by imposing excessive telephone charges and innumerable barriers to visitation.

Just Parole Decisions: The Parole Board capriciously and regularly denies parole to the majority of prisoners despite evidence of eligibility.[65]

Pelican Bay Hunger Strike Demands
(written April 3, 2011, widely issued July 1, 2011)

1. *End Group Punishment and Administrative Abuse*—This is in response to PBSP's [Pelican Bay State Prison's] application of "group punishment" as a means to address individual inmates' rule

violations. This includes the administration's abusive, pretextual use of "safety and concern" to justify what are unnecessary punitive acts. This policy has been applied in the context of justifying indefinite SHU status, and progressively restricting our programming and privileges.

2. *Abolish the Debriefing Policy, and Modify Active/Inactive Gang Status Criteria—*

   Perceived gang membership is one of the leading reasons for placement in solitary confinement.

   The practice of "debriefing," or offering up information about fellow prisoners particularly regarding gang status, is often demanded in return for better food or release from the SHU. Debriefing puts the safety of prisoners and their families at risk, because they are then viewed as "snitches."

   The validation procedure used by the California Department of Corrections and Rehabilitation (CDCR) employs such criteria as tattoos, reading materials, and associations with other prisoners (which can amount to as little as greeting) to identify gang members.

   Many prisoners report that they are validated as gang members with evidence that is clearly false or using procedures that do not follow the *Castillo v. Alameida* settlement, which restricted the use of photographs to prove association.

3. *Comply with the US Commission on Safety and Abuse in America's Prisons 2006 Recommendations Regarding an End to Long-Term Solitary Confinement—*CDCR shall implement the findings and recommendations of the US Commission on Safety and Abuse in America's Prisons final 2006 report regarding CDCR SHU facilities as follows:

   End Conditions of Isolation. Ensure that prisoners in SHU and Ad-Seg (Administrative Segregation) have regular meaningful contact and freedom from extreme physical deprivations that are known to cause lasting harm.

   Make Segregation a Last Resort. Create a more productive form of confinement in the areas of allowing inmates in SHU and Ad-Seg [Administrative Segregation] the opportunity to engage in meaningful self-help treatment, work, education, religious, and other productive activities relating to having a sense of being a part of the community.

End Long-Term Solitary Confinement. Release inmates to
general prison population who have been warehoused
indefinitely in SHU for the last 10 to 40 years (and counting).

Provide SHU Inmates Immediate Meaningful Access to: i)
adequate natural sunlight, ii) quality health care and treatment, including the mandate of transferring all PBSP- SHU
inmates with chronic health care problems to the New
Folsom Medical SHU facility.

4. *Provide Adequate and Nutritious Food*—Cease the practice of
denying adequate food, and provide wholesome nutritional meals
including special diet meals, and allow inmates to purchase
additional vitamin supplements.

PBSP staff must cease their use of food as a tool to punish SHU
inmates.

Provide a sergeant/lieutenant to independently observe the
serving of each meal, and ensure each tray has the complete
issue of food on it.

Feed the inmates whose job it is to serve SHU meals with meals
that are separate from the pans of food sent from kitchen for
SHU meals.

5. *Expand and Provide Constructive Programming and Privileges for
Indefinite SHU Status Inmates.*

Examples include:

Expand visiting regarding amount of time and adding one day
per week.

Allow one photo per year.

Allow a weekly phone call.

Allow two (2) annual packages per year. A 30 lb. package based
on "item" weight and not packaging and box weight.

Expand canteen and package items allowed. Allow us to have
the items in their original packaging [the cost for cosmetics,
stationary, envelopes, should not count towards the max draw
limit].

More TV channels.

Allow TV/Radio combinations, or TV and small battery operated
radio

Allow Hobby Craft Items—art paper, colored pens, small pieces
of colored pencils, watercolors, chalk, etc.

Allow sweat suits and watch caps.

Allow wall calendars.

Install pull-up/dip bars on SHU yards.
Allow correspondence courses that require proctored exams.[66]

Activist organizations, academic scholars, and investigative media outlets, including those previously cited, have carefully documented and thoroughly analyzed the administrative and state responses to the Georgia and California demands.[67] Rather than summarize this informative journalistic and analytical work, however, i wish to critically address the generally reductive public interpretation of the strikers' demands as articulations of incarcerated people's collective desire to be *recognized*—by the state and public alike—as subjects of the state and modern jurisprudence worthy of accessing the modern regimes of (civil and human) rights as well as the rudimentary protective and caretaking capacities of the modern liberal state.

A simplistic reading of their public appeals might elicit the conclusion that the Georgia and California strikers merely sought accessible, immediate reforms of their carceral conditions—that is, piecemeal though urgent carceral harm reduction—and that prison administrators and state officials could have met their demands without remotely compromising the cultural ascendancy or punitive logic of the carceral and criminalization regimes. Put differently, the strike demands did not appear to challenge the fact of incarceration, and to the contrary, seemed only to seek improved conditions of incarceration that might render the prisons more sustainable, "humane," and dignified.

On the other hand, if we learn from the archival, activist ethnographic, and historiographic work of Orisanmi Burton, Joy James, Dan Berger, Toussaint Losier, and others, the Georgia and California strikes can and must be situated within a longer genealogy of hemispheric carceral uprisings. Read and re-narrated within this rich and deeply textual tradition, the strikes can be more fully apprehended and analyzed as complex forms of collective, radical narrative praxis that confront the most severe forms of censorship, politically animated punishment, and militarized state coercion.[68] Further, an abolitionist pre-reading of the *conditions of carceral repression* facilitates a critical interpretive method—that is, a creative, speculative *reading practice* that engages the writing, art, correspondence, and other forms of radical (counter- and anti-) carceral cultural production as involuntarily delimited discursive labors. Such a generative (rather than traditionally empiricist or positivist) method can retell the story of the demands as, in part, an obliteration of the presumed authorial position of liberal modern rights-bearing civil subjects—those who are generally entitled to make demands on the state—that in turn enlivens the captive, chattel, rights-eviscerated being as a primary critic and (re)maker of politicality, sociality, and historical subjectivity.

Perhaps it is necessary to study the Georgia and California strikers' public-facing platforms in the context of what Stephen Best and Saidiya Hartman magnify as "the extralinguistic mode of black noise that exists outside the parameters of any strategy or plan for remedy." To consider the strike demands as carceral creations of Black noise—that is, as insurgent, ambient, irruptive gestures toward (Black) liberation in excess of the written and circulated political text—is to rethink their politicality as such:

> Black noise represents the kinds of political aspirations that are
> inaudible and illegible within the prevailing formulas of political
> rationality; these yearnings are illegible because they are so wildly
> utopian and derelict to capitalism (for example, "'forty acres and a
> mule,'" the end of commodity production and restoration of the
> commons, the realization of "'the sublime ideal of freedom,'" the
> resuscitation of the socially dead). Black noise is always already barred
> from the court.[69]

Reading the strike demands as a poetics of impasse and production of Black noise brings focused attention to the incarcerated strikers' collective and perpetual confrontation with a logic of evisceration. This logic encompasses the proliferating, cross-generational, trans-geographic, and often non-fatal forms of (carceral) state violence that exceed the hegemonic conceptual apparatus of "genocide." To articulate demands from within a collectively politicized *inhabitation* of this logic of evisceration is to perform (that is, write) a poetry of emergency that foments carceral—and extra-carceral—insurrection against the systemic and discursive production of incarcerated people as a socially liquidated (and formally civilly dead) population.

Incarcerated people are subjected to a generalized legal and cultural status of chattel fungibility that reflects the 13th Amendment's centrality to the emergence of the contemporary criminalization-policing-carceral regime. The Amendment's enunciation of a re-scripted, proto-modern continuity of carceral racial chattel dominance (see Chapter 2) is to consider the centrality of the anti-Black state to the innovation of modern civil "freedom" (and for that matter Black "emancipation") as well as to the creation of eviscerating, proto-genocidal and genocidal institutionalizations of state and extra-state violence: "Neither slavery nor involuntary servitude, except as a punishment for crime whereof the party shall have been duly convicted, shall exist within the United States." The Georgia and California strikers re-inhabited this geography of domination as a collective, complexly political and creative act—as a *carceral praxis of human being*—embracing what João Costa Vargas calls the "urgency imperative" formed in anti-Black state and social formations.[70]

Re-read through a speculative interpretive method, the Georgia and California demands expose how extra- and supra-genocidal violence—that is, violence that exceeds as it anticipates physiological extermination by subjecting targeted people to distended, eviscerating forms of physiological domination—shape the everyday sociality that is cohered through systems of policing, criminalization, and state capture (the essential institutional expressions of Lemkin's "peace," as it were). In such a context, it seems puzzling that the strikers refrained from staking a logical, rudimentary demand: *They made no call for "freedom," just clemency, or fair release.* What is to be made of this absent demand? Does the non-demand for freedom/release imply a collective resignation to the legal fate of conviction? Was this silence a strategic concession to a seemingly indelible, punitive national consensus that reifies the status of those duly convicted, rendering their captive status beyond the realm of reasonable political questioning? Did the absence of the freedom demand intend to enhance the more immediate possibilities of securing better nutrition, medical care, family visits, and fairer parole protocols? On the other hand, was the non-demand part of an attempt to navigate the punitive political climate within which the strikes were organized, in which the prospect of prisoners striking for "freedom" might be met with brutal repression from a racist state that would not hesitate to treat the strikers as incarcerated domestic terrorists?

In addition to provoking such questions, the strike demands also constitute credible, reflexive, and historically lacerating statements about the social and cultural condition—the "peace"—within which they are being articulated. Following Fred Moten and Stefano Harney, it is necessary to apprehend the strike demands as fugitive, creative texts authored and embodied by people who are surrounded by the symbols, weapons, protocols, and carceral furnishings of a sociality structured in genocidal and proto-genocidal dominance.[71] Reflecting on the work of the Black Panther Party, Moten and Harney write,

> Their twinned commitment to revolution and self-defense emerged
> from the recognition that the preservation of black social life is
> articulated in and with the violence of innovation. This is not a
> contradiction if the new thing, always calling for itself, already lives
> around and below the forts, the police stations, the patrolled highways
> and the prison towers.[72]

The Georgia and California strikers offer a living text of demand that flows in historical continuity with the Panthers' praxis. The demands are gifts of radical narrative possibility that—if well-cultivated and curated by their readers, including their fugitive publics—irrupt the places of normalized evisceration and racist state violence from which they have been conceived. The political languages and practical agendas of the strikes confront the substructure of the carceral regime—the brutal, perverse constitution of Lemkin's "peace"—and disrupt the political common sense that produces and is produced by that regime.

On the other hand, the demands are also political statements issued by people inhabiting carceral sites of formal civil death and contemporary social death, exposing how the prison is a *condition of existence*, not merely a fleeting blip in one's civil biography.[73] How else to make sense of the fact that the strikers are forced to demand the figments of nourishment that might otherwise differentiate them from racially configured, twenty-first-century bare life?[74] Nutrition, human touch, personal communication, bodily heat, medical care, freedom from cruelty, and a couple photographs—to be forced to mobilize for such things, at the risk of further vulnerability to the technologies of evisceration, is to articulate another kind of accusation that exceeds the gesture of the militant demand.

Omer Bartov convincingly argues in *Murder in Our Midst* that genocide is a logical derivative and synthetic expression of Western modernity rather than a corruption of or aberration from it. His work in this vein is analytically useful and its insight is in many ways indispensable, particularly because the text offers a historicized analysis that carefully delineates how the modernist logics of rationality, productivity, and social development were central to the architectures and methods of the Nazi-administered genocide in Germany. Most notably, Bartov installs the notion of "industrial killing" as a technology of modernity that blurs distinctions between war, sociality, (human) labor, and (human) death.[75] Yet, Bartov's theoretical approach does not suffice in addressing the peculiar modern logics of *anti-Black and racial-colonial* genocide, especially as they are obliquely invoked by the California and Georgia prison strikers.

Anti-Blackness and racial-colonial power—including their genocidal and proto-genocidal forms—are as much defined by irrational, gratuitous, non- or dysfunctional, anti-modern and/or "pre-modern" expressions of violence—physiological and otherwise—as they are by the clinical, precise, systemic emergence of industrial killing. The constitutive violence of these formations of power consistently befuddle the logics of rationality and industry, and cross into the realms of perpetual ontological disruption and cultural degradation, laboriously induced and long-sustained racial terror, multi-generational regimes of physiological disarticulation (including gratuitous violence against the body, mind, and spirit), and so forth. Not only are such anti-modern and pre-modern (one is tempted to say, savagely European) dimensions of anti-Black and racial-colonial genocide not addressed by the rubrics of industrial killing and modernist rationality, many of them are *not actually about "kill-ing" at all*—rather, they are about the production of conditions of terror and death that intend to shape targeted peoples' everyday lives.

The historical forms of Aboriginal and Indigenous genocide, by way of par-adigmatic example, are replete with supra-rational/extra-rational exercises in systemic degradation, dehumanization, and collective deracination (in the dual sense of forcible separation from one's roots in a certain cultural geogra-phy and subjection to colonial violence that attempts to foster one's alienation from their own historical indigenous/tribal identity). These genocidal forms mutually shape—and do not merely supplement—the clinical, brutal genocidal violence that derives from the systems and logics of modernist rationality (Bar-tov's "industrial killing"). Norbert Finzsch, among several others, provides a comparative genealogy of genocide discourse that disrupts the modernist theoretical-historical prejudices of Genocide Studies, interrupting the mod-ern genocide telos by bringing attention to how "Darwinian thinking was pre-ceded by and overlapped with an archaic racism with genocidal potential, constituted by the visual othering of indigenous populations in [eighteenth- and nineteenth century] America and Australia."[76] Such a coupling of premod-ern racism with genocide, conceived as both a precedent of and foundation for the modern onto-epistemic scientific regime, ruptures Nazi Germany's (and Europe's) privileged analytical status within hegemonic genocide discourses.

A poetics of genocide has been creatively, collectively voiced by peoples in-habiting, resisting, repulsing, and surviving the conquests, human fungibili-ties, land and cultural displacements, and violent expropriations (cultural, ecological, bodily, and otherwise) of the New World Civilizational order, with the effect of strategically de-centering and displacing the canonical status of the Nazis' scandalous weaponization of modernity. This is to suggest that the experiences of various Black and Indigenous peoples in the New World, Af-rica, and elsewhere compose the foundational matrices through which *all mod-ern "genocides" have emerged*, including and especially the Nazi atrocity. Racial chattel, land conquest, and racial coloniality produce a genocidal *logic of evisceration* that permeates the totality of the premodern to modern eras of Civilization. To critically acknowledge and engage with this logic is to re-narrate genocide's historical foundations while reconsidering the premises and implications of such theoretical structures as Foucault's biopolitics, Agam-ben's *nomos* of the modern, Achille Mbembe's necropolitics, and so forth.[77]

Anti-Blackness and racial-colonial violence, as the global expressions of what Cedric Robinson identifies as Civilizational, intra-European "racialism" (see Chapter 1), are the conditions of modernity's material and epistemic co-herence as such.[78] The overlapping, contradictory, divergent, asymmetrical, and complexly simultaneous violences of anti-Blackness and racial-colonial dominance are the animating fields of power that enable the emergence and sustenance of modern institutionalities. What, then, is the *productive violence* of such power, once such violences are understood as the precursor, production, and perpetual condition of modernity?

The vast majority of those who organized and participated in the Georgia and California strikes (as well as the extended solidarity strikes) were serving finite sentences and were scheduled for eventual release. Yet they clearly understood that the delimited liberty of decarceration was only tantamount to a *recalibration* of their criminalized status from "prisoner" to convicted felon/former prisoner. The strike demands, as narratives of a carceral historical present tense, could not presume a social futurity based on the assumptive entitlements of rights-bearing, free civil subjecthood. Strikers (and many of their non-incarcerated supporters) clearly understood that, once released, their nominal access to civil liberty would be preemptively evacuated by the relative permanence of their subjection to the distended, extra-institutional carceral power relations of criminalization, policing, and state surveillance (via parole, criminal record, and so on).

Few groups have more clearly illustrated the structuring anti-sociality of the U.S. carceral regime than All of Us or None, formed in 2003 and continuously led by formerly and currently incarcerated people. All of Us or None has built multiple local and national advocacy campaigns based on a supple analysis of how the institutional and material logics of carceral criminalization do not evaporate upon release from incarceration:

> [A] whole system of discrimination has built up based on arrests, convictions, and incarceration. This discrimination is a mask for race discrimination because the majority of people being targeted for arrest and imprisonment in the US today are people of color, in numbers far exceeding their proportion of our population. It's also a form of discrimination that is widespread . . . [79]

While All of Us or None is committed to building "a powerful political movement to win full restoration of our human and civil rights," its praxis is intentionally mobile, deprovincializing, and conducive to rearticulations.[80] The organization's campaign-oriented work, which has been taken up by chapters in numerous U.S. states including Texas, Oklahoma, Michigan, North Carolina, and California, reflects a tactical commitment to post-incarceration civil rights: Its most prominent campaigns include "Ban the Box" (a "nationally-recognized effort to eliminate questions relating to a person's arrest or convic-

tion history from all applications—for housing, employment, benefits, etc.")
and "Voting Rights for All."[81]

A dynamic reading of All of Us or None's organizing rhetoric, which includes
extended tributes to recently deceased incarcerated activists, radical educators,
(unrecognized) US political prisoners, and revolutionaries, calls attention to
what is arguably its fundamental mission: the imagining, narrating, convening, and claiming of a collective *political subjectivity* among people whose
criminalized and post-incarcerated status not only renders them vulnerable to
permanent marginalization from the modern rights regime, but also subjects
them to systemic housing insecurity, economic instability, and deprivation of
the capacity to access basic needs (including rudimentary security from state
violence). Further, given its prominent public solidarity with the Pelican Bay
hunger strike, All of Us or None can be seen as working in harmony with the
fugitive gestures of demand that issue from carceral sites in and beyond Georgia and California, disrupting a post-civil rights racial telos of liberal futurity
even as its public work places tactical emphasis on civil/human rights for incarcerated and formerly incarcerated people.[82]

Guided in part by the radical conception of political community convened
by All of Us or None, an abolitionist and Black radical rereading of the Georgia and California strikers' demands illuminates how the incarcerated organizers publicly refused to presume their own biographical and physiological
futures outside the time and space of the prison. The strikes were a radically
collective acknowledgment that anti-Black, racial-colonial criminalization and
incarceration are simultaneously points of ontological *origin* and (anti)social
destination. As such, the strikers' demands on the state were a coded, though
no less transparent meditation on the fact that nominal release from prison is
only a transitional stage within the carceral regime's structure of perpetuity.
The demands, read as lasting meditations on the scope and temporal totality
of a carceral present tense, refuse to dignify the notion of post-release civil
freedom—or of "peace" free of state violence—and thus radically delink from
any universalized notion of a social future. To the contrary, the Georgia and
California strikers lay claim to the notion that beyond prison there is *nowhere
and no time to go*, nurturing a politics of possibility that embraces an ethic of
militant, radical political creativity: a shattering of the "peace" of carceral
chattel/genocide.

The Georgia and California prison strikes clarify how an insurgent, radical poetics of (carceral) genocide may inhabit the impasse between the modern juridical-academic regime and the logic of evisceration that permeates
anti-Blackness and racial-colonial power.

A Logic of Evisceration

This closing section critically departs from the work of settler colonial studies scholar Patrick Wolfe, stretching the historical and theoretical parameters of his widely cited historical theorization of settler colonialism's "logic of elimination." Wolfe's work focuses on the conditions of duress constituting Indigenous socialities within the geographies of Civilization, opening toward radical analysis of the enmeshing anti-social formations that permeate post-conquest settler-colonial political and cultural geographies.[83] The logic of elimination, for Wolfe, reflects the perpetuity of a historical process in which Indigenous being—and their projected figurations in the settler imaginary—is subjected to physical, discursive, biological, and legal technologies of mitigation, displacement, and erasure: Thus, "settler colonialism destroys to replace."[84] Following this critical historical schema, the logic of Indigenous elimination is central to the construction and reproduction of modern state and juridical orders, as well as their constituting cultural orders. Thus, the Indian/Aboriginal/Native—that is, the figure of the Indian/Aboriginal/Native, the remnants of Indigenous being and life modalities, and the persistent and haunting presences of Indigenous peoples within and beneath the modern global cultural-political order—must always be subjected to technologies of elimination, even and especially in the aftermath of their large-scale physical, ecological, and cultural liquidation.

Distinguishing "elimination" from "genocide," Wolfe provides a durable and non-teleological framework through which to examine the different global permutations of the settler colonial relation, which flourishes through symbiotically complex forms of racial-colonial power; he argues persuasively, for example, that "assimilation [of Indigenous people] should not be seen as an invariable concomitant of settler colonialism. Rather, assimilation is one of a range of strategies of elimination that become favored in particular historical circumstances."[85] Wolfe's logic of elimination enables a theory of gendered racial-colonial power that centers a relational, dynamic conception of world-altering violence—such a theoretical approach radically challenges the exceptionalist terms of "genocide" that characterize its formalized, hegemonic juridical-academic uses.

It is precisely through Wolfe's dynamic apprehension of Indigenous inhabitations of (and insurgencies against) the settler colonial logic of elimination that we might subtly depart from the otherwise delimited understanding of "genocide" that marks his and other scholars' critical projects. Elsewhere, i have discussed what i understand to be Wolfe's mis-estimation of the historical applicability of the category of genocide to African and Africa-derived peoples'

experiences with the genocidal capacities of chattel enslavement and apartheid.[86] Here, i am more interested in attending to the conceptual and theoretical openings created by his consistent attention to the historical present
tense(s) of epochal, world-altering violences via the perpetuity of "elimination."
Iyko Day facilitates such an approach in her extrapolative reading of Wolfe's
work, particularly through her argument that "mixing alien labor with Indigenous land to expand white property was the basis and objective of settler colonialism."[87] Day's careful distinction between the positionalities (and, by
extension, the ontological formations) of alien labor further clarifies "the divergent historical and economic contexts of Asian and African labor" and highlights "the heterogeneity contained within an alien position."[88] In collegial
engagement with Day's reframing of Wolfe's thesis, i am interested in how a
privileging of the (often simultaneously) productive and destructive, supra/
extra-rational and coldly rationalistic logics of racial-colonial violence might
sustain a rethinking of the constitutive features of modernity, (racial) capitalism, empire, and radical politicalities.

Tiffany Lethabo King embraces such a critical agenda through a rigorous
reconsideration of the deep analytic gaps characterizing much materialist and
Marxist thought. Meditating on Julie Dash's classic film *Daughters of the Dust*,
King considers how "the regime of colonial visuality . . . hides aspects of conquest like genocide. Specifically, the colonial regime of visuality obscures and
invisibilizes the genocide of the Cherokee people of the Sea Islands through
the rubric of labor."[89]

To read the genealogies of (modern) racialization alongside Wolfe's logic
of elimination, Day's historical materialist analysis of the "overarching economic rationale of settler colonialism," and King's retheorization of colonial
(visual) cultural regimes is to again consider the acute inadequacy of hegemonic genocide discourses for apprehending and explaining the constitutive
violences of the Civilizational order.[90] If "genocide" is not sufficient for the
work of deep, radical historical conceptualization of these foundational epochal violences, how do the critical poetics of We Charge Genocide and the
Georgia and California prison strikers (among others) exemplify and actively
create an alternate lexical field that may be more conducive to differentiating
the lowest common denominators of gendered racial-colonial power from
other forms of ordering, hierarchy, and subjection, including (but not limited
to) anti-Blackness? How might such forms of collective thought *renarrate* the
historical present tense that we differently inherit and inhabit?

I close this chapter with a counter-thesis that departs from Wolfe's logic of
elimination: that abolitionist, Black radical, de-/anti-colonial, and other radically insurgent inhabitations of chattel, carceral, and colonial geographies of

perpetual violence wage self-defensive combat against a Civilizational logic of evisceration that is complex, dynamic, and asymmetrical in its material and discursive consequences. This conceptualization of Civilizational violence emerges through sustained, speculative interpretations of radical genocide poetics within and against the epistemic, definitional, and historical limitations of hegemonic juridical-academic genocide discourses. Here i will provide seven cursory elaborations of this counter-thesis, with the qualification that they are offered as provisional rather than definitive contributions to the living archive of radical and abolitionist praxis referenced throughout this book.

First, the concept of evisceration—with etymological roots in the Latin word for disembowelment or the removal of the viscera—can be projected to encompass violence exerted on the complex totality of physiology, across the individual and collective scales.[91] The notion of a logic of evisceration alludes to the unbreakable connection between spiritual, psychic, affective, and physical-biological experiences that include cross-generational, epigenetic inheritances of world-deforming systems of dominance, displacement, and terror. Such systems exert drastic physiological consequences (depression, suicide, paranoia, cancer, and so on), even in the absence of direct physical brutality.[92] A 2007 symposium organized by The Academies of Arts, Humanities and Sciences of Canada, for example, included research that addressed the causal relation between social conditions and human genetic expressions, indicating the need for further research on how "[t]he boundaries of gene expressions, behaviour, and the social fabric are . . . shaped by the impacts at the organism level of epigenetic regulations, within which environmental factors play a . . . causal role."[93] Dorothy Roberts pointedly clarifies how transgenerational epigenetic factors shape Black people's susceptibilities to socially induced disease, illness, and early death:

> Through epigenetics . . . the effects of racism on parents might be transmitted to their children, perpetuating inequalities across generations. These pathways may explain, for example, why African Americans have higher rates of both low birth weight and adult cardiovascular disease. . . . Epigenetic influences on children's health may have fooled some scientists into seeing genetic causes for health disparities that do not exist. Epigenetics may masquerade as genetic difference, but its biological effects stem from the environment, not mutations of the genetic code. . . . [94]

Crucially, Roberts warns that the implications of such scientific insight should not lead to simply "consign[ing] another generation to the biological fallout of past discrimination," in a reiteration of anti-Black scientific racial determinism. Rather, she contends that the "hopeful message" of this research "is that epigenetic changes are caused by the environment and therefore can be environmentally interrupted so that future generations can enjoy better health."[95] Following Roberts, the eviscerating violences of the New World Civilizational project endanger and violate different peoples' ontological, psychic, spiritual, and cultural integrity as such. Such endangerment and violation indelibly deform and damage targeted peoples' physiological health, collective capacities for biological and social reproduction, and shared ability to sustain themselves as coherent and self-aware groups, tribes, and peoples. In this context, the historical and multigenerational experiences of the logic of evisceration can be differentiated from notions of social, civil, or biological death, as well as from "genocide," biopower, necropolitics, and eurocentric states of exception.

Second, the logic of evisceration illuminates how the production of "race" as a global physiological signification has formed a complex technology of violence and terror *sui generis*. Here, the conceptual is also already the visceral (and the eviscerating). The processes of racialization inaugurate hierarchies of life and death, producing a global assemblage that both anticipates and is the precondition for modernity's global imaginary.[96] By producing (i.e., inventing and fabricating) the categorical objects of its discourses of knowledge/degradation, racial power is already a life-or-death antagonism between those who embody the positionality of self-determined racial knowing and those whose bodies/beings are deformed and otherwise dominated by the regimes of racial knowledge.

Third, a deeper focus on racial power as a gendered technology of evisceration helpfully displaces some of the hegemonic gender narratives enmeshing "genocide" and genocidal violence. Adam Jones, for example, claims in his widely referenced article "Gendercide and Genocide" that the targeted killing of *men* makes up the primary gendering force in the history of mass murder, war, and genocide. Referencing several examples from the 1980s and 1990s, Jones contends, "Regardless, and crucially, the most vulnerable and consistently targeted population group, through time and around the world today, is noncombatant men of a 'battle age,' roughly 15–55 years old."[97] Jones's claim becomes far less credible, however, when accounting for the long genealogies of eviscerating (and arguably genocidal) anti-Black, racial-colonial violence.[98] Within the living archives of evisceration, the categories and abstracted classifications of gender and sexuality are destabilized and disrupted, subjected to various forms of distortion, transgression, and manipulation/mutilation within the infrastructural emergence of the "world" to which Jones refers. Cultural and juridical attacks on the biologically and discursively essentialized female womb, colonialist and chattel constructions of birth status inheritance (free/unfree, citizen/noncitizen), and discursive constructions of women and gender-queer people as objects of specific forms of genocidal violence reflect the logic of evisceration as an *actively gendering* form of power. Such violence does not merely come to bear on already existing, statically gendered bodies but is itself engaged in processes of forcefully (re)defining and remaking gender and gendered sexuality as primary expressions of world-deforming power. Radical feminist and queer conceptions of bodily/sexual violence, for example, challenge the notion that rape and sexual brutality are merely tactical or preparatory elements of racializing regimes; rather, as forms of collective evisceration, such gendered sexual violences are ends within themselves, enacting anti-Blackness and racial-colonial dominance as conditions of both intimate and systemic bodily subjection.[99]

Fourth, a rigorous conceptualization of the logic of evisceration can enrich a speculative narrative praxis that positions racial terror, collective experiences of physiological vulnerability, and the gendered disruption (if not almost complete destruction) of peoples' life worlds as the normalized conditions of Civilization and modernity. While the hegemonic legal and academic genocide regimes betray an overwhelming tendency to privilege notions of the scandalous and exceptional, a narrative centering of the experiences of evisceration induced by gendered anti-Blackness and racial-colonial power de-centers the historical and political canonization of the Nazi-administered holocaust and undermines its status as the assumptive, unchallenged paradigmatic calibration of the outer extremes of modern (state) power. This narrative and theoretical maneuver directly challenges the installation of a reified category/figure of *vulnerable White Being* as the primary reference point for genocide's—and modern power's—most egregious casualties (for example, Primo Levi's autobiographical and Agamben's ethnographic and historical conceptualizations of the *Muselmann*).[100] Alex Weheliye spurs such a reframing in his incisive rejoinder to Agamben's furtive attempts to install the figure of the *Muselmann* as the "transcendence of race, and therefore politics, via the sublatory powers of a radical post-Holocaust ethics." Arguing that "racialization . . . operates simultaneously as the *nomos* and matrix of modern politics," Weheliye enables a theoretical approach to evisceration that rigorously apprehends its systemic, martial institutionalization as a primary technology of racialization, foregrounding the latter as the condition of possibility for genocidal and proto-genocidal violence.[101] Those who create a poetics of genocide from within a radical recognition of this condition of possibility are re-telling the story of Civilization/modernity.

Fifth, a historicized conceptualization of the logic of evisceration brings attention to the proliferating, socially productive forms of violence that constitute modern social formations, during and beyond the institutional existence of apartheid, land expropriation, racial chattel slavery, and militarized conquest. That is, the logic of evisceration may significantly outlast a specific anti-Black state system or discrete militarized mobilization of racial-colonial dominance, to the extent that it permeates the normative sociality of the succeeding order (Lemkin's "peace"). Conceptualized as a determination of the social and not merely its antithesis or obliteration, the logic of evisceration can be understood as a complex, dynamic form of power/dominance that is central to everyday social intercourses.

Sixth, a theorization of the logic of evisceration compels rigorous reconsideration of scholarly activist and academic notions of social determination and material substructure, reigniting critical dialog with a variety of Marxist and historical materialist traditions. A host of old and new questions follow: What analytical and theoretical insights—and, for that matter, what collective political practices—are catalyzed by locating the eviscerating violences of Civilizational power at the conceptual center of social and economic determinations at the local, regional, and global scales? How does the logic of evisceration compose an economic circuit of its own, that is, an interstice of labor, commodification, expropriation, and alienation that overlaps with but is not reducible to conventional notions of economy and economic exchange?

Seventh, a rigorous conceptualization of the logic of evisceration concentrates historiographic and theoretical attention on different peoples' actively insurgent, fugitive, and liberationist inhabitations of gendered anti-Blackness and racial-colonial violence. Such inhabitations constitute an impasse of power within which critical, abolitionist, anti- and de-colonial, and radical creativities constantly emerge. This impasse reveals the scandal of racialization as a long-historical formation of dominance: Despite racial power's inclination to obliterate, capture, and violate its targets, irruptions of liberation and self-determination persistently inhabit the logic of evisceration *as the destabilization of racialization's lowest common denominator.* To embrace the political creativities of such inhabitations is to accept the invitation to envision futurity, justice, reparation, human freedom, and peace against their devastating conditions of historical possibility. Given the historical circumstances of our pedagogical and intellectual labors, this may amount to an uneven inheritance of the bottom line. The next chapter examines another significant expression of that inheritance.

Coda: June 2020

There is a wave of familiar misery, albeit unfamiliar in form, that releases to variations of flourishing. Some of the thriving is destined for bad endings—white militia bros cosplaying fantasies of coup and restoration, elected officials juggling self-implicating conspiracy stories with absurdist rehearsals of states-manship. Much of the flourishing—really, the only kind that matters beyond itself—remakes the next five minutes, crafting a tomorrow that has never been anything but contingent.

I am rushing through final revisions of this book while the United States is on fucking fire. They killed Breonna Taylor, Ahmaud Arbery, George Floyd, and many more Black people over the last few weeks. Floyd's merciless video-recorded murder by a white Minneapolis police officer—who kneeled on Floyd's neck for 8 minutes and 46 seconds—was the tipping point. There are, of course, thousands of tipping points—the only question is whether and when one of them will trip righteous outrage and incite collective rebellion in their multiple, overlapping, simultaneous forms. I must admit that it seems profane to be writing of these police killings *in the moment*, as if they are somehow unique and separable from anti-Black genocide as a fact of hemispheric American life.

I humbly but unapologetically contend that the street protests and mass insurgencies thriving across the United States as i write these words cannot be attributed to these three incidents, or even a hundred other such recent incidents of anti-Black police violence. Such casualties at the hands of state power are a systemic, institutionalized fact of American life that are experienced differently—radically so—by people inhabiting the (anti-Black) genocidal impasse of which this chapter speaks. I work mere blocks from the scene of Tyisha Miller's killing at the hands of Riverside Police Department officers in 1998—a trauma that has continued to define many Black students' and coworkers' collective experiences of UC Riverside and Inland Empire Southern California more generally. Despite what RPD did to her, she will never be gone, and her subjection to the American bottom line will perpetually present justified cause for insurrection and revolt against the thick anti-Blackness of this local world.

Demonstrating alongside loved ones and family in the streets of downtown Riverside on June 1, 2020, it was ever clear that the poetics of which i write in this chapter proliferate when shit gets hot. "Genocide" forms one of the primary languages through which (in this case, overwhelmingly Black) people communicate a collective commitment to intensified insurgency against the juridical-cultural tolerance/justification/celebration of Black death as essential functions and outcomes of policing. To my eyes, white people were the ones who leaned on the old phrase "police brutality" while others drew from graver vocabularies of anti-Blackness, colonialism, and absolute exposure to state violence and white civil society's entitlement to kill, destroy, humiliate, and terrorize. The terms of genocide appeared on handmade signs carried by children, elders, and everyone in between. In this crowd, policing and genocide were unified systems of violence, inseparable from the early twenty-first-century U.S. nation-building project.

I offer this coda in honor of those who are continually working to confront and abolish this condition of anti-Black genocide, many of whom are referenced in this book, and far many more of whom are not.

"Mass Incarceration" as Misnomer

Domestic War and the Narratives of Carceral Reform

"Morality, Common Sense, Decency":
The Normativity of "Mass Incarceration" Reform

"Mass incarceration," "police brutality," "school-to-prison pipeline," and other such terms have emerged as keywords of an invigorated early twenty-first-century liberal-to-progressive critique of U.S. anti-Black and racial-colonial state violence. A process of institutionalization pushes such critical terms into a popular lexicon as vernaculars of coalition that convene various communities and publics, from academic scholars and policy reform advocates to nonprofit organizations, philanthropic foundations, and grassroots movements. The ascendance of a national discourse on "mass incarceration" requires specific critical attention not only because it has become a widely circulated rhetoric of reformist mobilization, but also because its political and ideological traction relies on a pervasive narrative structure that tells a troubling story.

The tale goes something like this: First, there is an uneven, though spreading, lamentation that a contemporary, half-century U.S. statecraft of carcerality has intensified an institutional-cultural capacity and will to criminalize, police, prosecute, incarcerate, and culturally denigrate targeted bodies, places, and populations (often, though not always explicitly acknowledged as Black geographies). This liberal confession does not identify these developments as evidence of expanding infrastructures and juridical protocols of gendered anti-Black, racial-colonial domestic war (against "drugs," "gangs," undocumented migrants/"illegal aliens," queer people, "terrorists," and so on). Rather, the reformist framing of mass incarceration suggests that both criminal law and law enforcement have been infiltrated by corrupt, mean-spirited, ignorant, racist, or otherwise misdirected agents of the state with disastrous outcomes for structurally vulnerable, historically disfranchised, systemically oppressed, overwhelmingly Black populations, communities, and geographies.

In the echo of this lamentation, an ensemble of alarmed accounts and wrenching testimonials by journalists, activists, social scientists, legal advocates, survivors, and other witnesses endorse the notion that otherwise well-intentioned law-and-order state projects (including but not limited to the aforementioned domestic wars on drugs, gangs, and so on) have exceeded or "failed" their operational objectives and mutated into institutionalized forms of large-scale, systemic racial discrimination, including though not limited to the emergence of an anti-Black "New Jim Crow."[1] In this ensemble of accounts and testimonials, there is an underlying assertion that such juridically sanctioned, culturally normalized state violence is a *betrayal of American values* as well as a violation of the egalitarian ethos that allegedly constitutes the U.S. national project.[2] Legal scholar and former President of the John Jay College of Criminal Justice Jeremy Travis crystallizes this reformist *bildungsroman* in a 2015 address to the National Forum on Criminal Justice:

> [T]he unifying theme that we must keep in mind is this: we live in an era of mass incarceration because we have chosen, through policy choices, to dramatically expand the use of prison as a response to crime. There is a corollary to this finding: If our democracy got us here, it is our democracy that must get us out of here.[3]

In this version of the story, the tyranny of a (white/multiculturalist) "we" animates a sense of patriotic outrage. This mystified reform-oriented subject, in turn, is the subject of a universalized ("unifying") call to national accountability that bypasses the long historical facts of particular peoples' foundational alienation from—and violent subjection to—U.S. nation-building. This tyrannical "we" engages in broad, public discussion of the possibility that the juridically sanctioned statecraft of human dysselection has produced an unnamed "mass" of unintended casualties.

The story of "mass incarceration" then spreads into dense accounts of degradation and suffering that traverse articulations of individualized tragedy and collectively, communally voiced, insurgent outrage. (It becomes clear, however, that many of the most incisive testimonials of carceral damage significantly preceded the widespread acknowledgment of this period of crisis.) The most privileged publics—those cohered through the social-historical entitlements generated by anti-Blackness, white supremacy, racial-colonial power, and their post-apartheid, multiculturalist variations—consume the righteous patriotic outrage and belch it up as a newfound revelation of national scandal; "mass incarceration" was unfolding, flourishing, and metastasizing under their oblivious noses, and *now "we" must deal with it.* The Others, that is, those long subjected to the violence and casualties of domestic carceral war, openly wonder what alternate reality their privileged counterparts must have inhabited for all these years and debate whether and how to coalesce with these liberal-progressive protagonists of entitled outrage.

A protracted discursive skirmish ensues as media pundits, elected officials, social scientists, policy think tanks, liberal philanthropic and advocacy organizations, and emergent grassroots and virtual/social media collectives attempt to make sense of—that is, to definitively narrate—this turmoil. Entering the fray (at the same time that they are formed by it) are multiple coalitions of organic and professional intellectuals—of the racial state, nonprofit/foundation regimes, and liberal cultural industry, including think tank- and corporate-commissioned academics, writers, and artists—who strive to rejuvenate a paradigmatic liberal and moral faith in the possibilities of righteous national reforms that ameliorate the asymmetries of the carceral state. Symptomatically, the likes of Van Jones, Kim Kardashian, and Jared Kushner join in the skirmish, side by side.[4] Jones (among the most visible liberal Black pundits in U.S. broadcast media) personifies an opportunism characteristic of such reformist periods: His 2018 CNN special on "prison reform" and apparent behind-the-scenes role in the Trump administration's 2020 executive order on "police reform" appropriate the momentum and vernaculars of (Black-led) rebellions and collective organizing against the anti-Black, racial-colonial state (see Figure 12). Such maneuvers effectively commodify these mobilizations and movements in a manner that services the pundit's media profile and professional network (a pattern of behavior Jones has consistently exhibited since the 1990s), reifying reform while implicitly re-criminalizing those deemed unworthy of the reformists' goodwill.[5] From an April 2016 *New York Times* op-ed: "Reform is imperative, not just for its economic or budgetary benefits, but for individuals who deserve a second chance and the families and communities who stand beside them."[6]

Liberal humanist alarm soon yields to a sense of shared national grievance: *The New Yorker* asserts that "[t]he scale and the brutality of our prisons are the moral scandal of American life," while the Open Society Foundation announces a $50 million grant to the American Civil Liberties Union by proclaiming "America's bloated prisons are an appalling and expensive failure, the politics of fear overwhelming common sense and human decency."[7]

"Morality," "common sense," and "decency" re-narrate generations of police terror and carceral displacement as if they are the unintended, atrocious conse-

CNN ✓
@CNN

CNN political commentator @VanJones68 interviews
Senior White House advisor Jared Kushner to discuss
prison reform #CITIZENCNN

Watch live: CNN.com/watchCITIZEN
Follow live updates: cnn.it/2EzLlJC

7:06 AM · Oct 22, 2018 · SocialFlow

Figure 12. CNN (@CNN),
"CNN's @VanJones68
will discuss prison reform
with senior White House
adviser Jared Kushner
at CITIZEN by CNN."
(Twitter, October 21,
2018, https://twitter.com
/CNN/status/1054057248
065011714.)

quences of a tragically "misled" War on Drugs culminating in 2.3 million people
held captive by the state. (This number reflects the comprehensive research of
the Prison Policy Initiative, and includes incarcerated children, undocumented
people, and people detained under the exceptionalist auspices of the post-2001
U.S. "War on Terror." The most frequently cited incarceration figures drawn
from the U.S. Bureau of Justice Statistics fail to account for the latter carceral
populations.)[8] This storytelling reframes carceral domestic war in liberal reformist terms as a compendium of discrete, mistaken excesses of state power that
largely derive from criminological error, electoral opportunism, and vague
"moral" failure; thus, in this political narrative, *"mass incarceration" can be redressed and reformed within the existing systems of law, policy, and justice.*

Throughout this chapter, the specific phrase "mass incarceration" will be
framed with scare quotes in order to indicate its ideological and rhetorical
functions. Other phrases such as "mass incarceration narrativity," "mass incarceration reformism," and "mass incarceration discourse," on the other hand,
will henceforth appear without quotations because they explicitly reference
"mass incarceration" as a discursive production rather than a sociological or
criminological matter-of-fact.

The logical schema of mass incarceration reformism leverages the narrative structure of White Reconstruction:

"Mass incarceration" is a national crisis.

"Mass incarceration" is a result of the state's momentary dysfunction, economic wastefulness, and juridical irrationality (and not its constitutive logics of racial-colonial power).

"Reform" is the compulsory ("mandatory") response to this crisis.

Some human casualties of "mass incarceration" deserve a "second chance," and others do not.

Reconstitution of (heteronormative, patriarchal, economically productive) "families" and "communities" forms the moral imperative for "mass incarceration" reform.

"Mass incarceration" requires another iteration of White Reconstruction's historical narrative structure (see Chapter 2).

This schema produces a *mass incarceration narrativity* that occludes the systemic atrocities of carceral domestic war by reducing them to symptoms of a reformable nationalist malfunction. The projected, liberal-progressive white/multiculturalist "we" reveals its inner monologue:

> *If there is such a massive problem, it can be fixed; if "we" bring rational heart to mind in another adventure of liberal (white/multiculturalist) humanist reform, and if we follow these stories of carceral atrocity into the tragedy and insist over-and-over-again that such harrowing details are not the intended outcome of this state or its marshaling of police and punitive legal force, then solutions are imminent; there is nothing fundamentally wrong with national culture, policy, or law that cannot be reformed; in such reform, the threads of an exceptionalist U.S. racial modernity may once again be pulled taut around the jagged, always-disarticulating edges of the civil underside, where the statecraft of terror unfolds on intimate geographies of the flesh.*
>
> *The story of "mass incarceration" continues, open to optimistic revision as reform reproduces fundamental relations of dominance, violence, and systemic vulnerability.*

Mass incarceration narrativity attempts to discipline and harness an epochal fallout. Yet a radical tracing of this fallout yields to another kind of insurgent account: The ongoing half-century of White Reconstruction is a marshaling of police power, criminal justice policy, and anti-Black, racial-colonial national culture that sustains transgenerational damage on the capacities of targeted communities and people to reproduce themselves as such. The logics and protocols of anti-Black carceral war serve as the premises and templates for the criminalization, policing, and incarceration of (non-Black) Other peoples. The totality of this fallout cannot be triaged or redressed through liberal promises of futurity, redeemed citizenship, revalued civil life, or a vigorously reformed state because its violences are indelible and are constantly inhabited and carried by their differently positioned inheritors. Mark Neocleous brings this point home:

> . . . liberalism has from its inception been a political philosophy of war, has been fully conscious of this and, as a consequence, has sought to bury this fact under various banners: "peace and security"; "law and order"; "police."[9]

The depth and reach of the carceral state's systemically induced, targeted casualties are a permanent rebuttal to mass incarceration narrativity's militant reformist optimism.

Craig Willse's counter-disciplinary approach to the study of the racially criminalized condition of "homelessness" provides tools for a critical disarticulation of mass incarceration narrativity. His material and conceptual analysis clearly demonstrates how the ideological and discursive formation of "mass incarceration" expands rather than challenges the punitive common sense of policing, criminalization, and human capture. For Willse, common notions of "homelessness" not only reify and naturalize the systemic outcomes of complex economic, cultural, and juridical processes, but also constitute a violently *normative* discursive and institutional regime that actively produces and naturalizes the condition of violence it putatively names:

> [T]he construction of "homelessness" as a problem has in fact obscured the material conditions that produce housing deprivation, proliferating expertise and management techniques while allowing housing insecurity to expand. . . . [I]n fact housing systems and their inhabitants are conformed through relations of capital and sociolegal regulation. In other words, the life organized by systems of housing insecurity and deprivation does not precede those systems. Rather, housing systems produce the lives contained within, shaping, for example, vulnerability to living without shelter as an expression and

experience of racialized subordination in labor market and consumer economies.[10]

Following Willse's analytical and theoretical method, i am concerned with addressing how and why "mass incarceration" has become a strangely generic term of twenty-first-century liberal-progressive coalescence, hailing a broadly reformist consensus even as it is invoked at the expense of more incisive, radical terms that demystify the convergences of anti-Black and racist state violence, gendered racial criminalization, and logics of asymmetrical social liquidation. How does the discourse of "mass incarceration" spread the absurdities of a multiculturalist, post-racial liberal agenda by subsuming the casualties of the anti-Black, racial-colonial carceral state under the terms of a "mass?" What are the extended consequences of a mass incarceration narrativity that rests on the premise that the criminal justice regime is *not* functioning as its founders and most fair-minded administrators intend(ed) it to function?

On the one hand, "mass incarceration" reinscribes and amplifies the cultural and political logics of White Reconstruction by descriptively subsuming incarcerated people under the notion of an undifferentiated "mass." On the other, the militarized juridical (policing) protocols of domestic war simultaneously reshape and exploit the social topographies and political geographies constituted by racial capitalism, anti-Blackness, and racial-colonial power, creating acute and sustained—as well as paradigmatic and incomparable—*differentiations* of suffering, casualty, vulnerability, and carceral criminalization across gendered and racialized social profiles.

By domestic war, i am referencing the dynamic ensemble of state technologies that attempt to discipline, contain, and socially/politically neutralize the creative, insurgent (and often criminalized) socialities enabled by ongoing liberation and self-determination struggles of oppressed, colonized, and displaced (incarcerated, segregated, colonized) peoples (see Chapters 1, 3, and 4). Domestic war unfolds continuously, across the overlapping historical and geographic conditions of deindustrialization and racial capitalism's uneven abandonments of poor and working class people, the rise and imminent decline of neoliberal/global capitalism, persistent resurgences of white nationalisms (including their respectable, liberal variations), and the persistence of collective, creative human praxis that challenges the ascendancy and armed dominance of White Being.[11]

The rhetoric of "mass incarceration" not only fraudulently universalizes the fallout of carceral domestic war, but also serves to "label" this complex totality in the most reductive possible terms. Following Stuart Hall, Chas Critcher,

Tony Jefferson, John Clarke, and Brian Roberts's classic study of moral panic and "mugging" in *Policing the Crisis*, "mass incarceration" emerges in the vernacular of White Reconstruction as a fabrication of a field of meanings, assumptions, and conclusions:

> Labels are important, especially when applied to dramatic public events. They not only place and identify those events; they assign events to a context. Thereafter the use of the label is likely to mobilize *this whole referential context*, with all its associated meanings and connotations.[12]

By conjuring a notion of national crisis within a specific referential context, "mass incarceration" coalesces a reformist response to—and compulsory narration of—an epochal cultural-political fallout induced over a period of decades by an anti-Black, racial-colonial state. Contrary to the implicit guarantees of mass incarceration reformism, however, this damage cannot be reversed or repaired by promises of universal civic futurity or redemptive access to normative social life.

Dean Spade forcefully addresses a version of this irreconcilable contradiction in his conceptualization of critical trans praxis. Foregrounding the endemic violence of gender normativities that "impact—and extinguish—the lives of trans people," Spade focuses on how "norms like these *become part of the resistance itself*," (emphasis added) spurring a trans politics "that tirelessly interrogates processes of normalization by analyzing their impacts and revising its resistance strategies as it observes their unintended consequences."[13] Building on a genealogy of abolitionist praxis, Spade's critical trans analytic clarifies how contemporary reformist discourses are assembled through an ensemble of interactions between the racist state, non-profit industrial complex, corporate mass media, and academic research agendas.[14] The next sections utilize Spade's methodological and analytical approach by attempting to construct a working genealogy of "mass incarceration" as an institutionalization and emergent statecraft of carceral reformist normativity: a field of ethical assumptions, diagnostic questions, policy parameters, and state protocols that structure the narration of alleged criminological "crisis" while delimiting the scope of potential and proposed "solutions."

Mass Incarceration Narrativity: Origins and (Failed) Analogues

While similar criminological terms surfaced as early as the 1970s and 1980s, the work of the thirty-four-member National Criminal Justice Commission

(NCJC) during the mid-1990s is significantly responsible for the emergence of "mass incarceration" as an early twenty-first-century political problematic.[15] Funded by numerous non-governmental agencies, the NCJC included well-known progressive and anti-racist public intellectuals, critical race theory scholars, and radical criminologists such as Nils Christie, Derrick Bell, Charles Ogletree, Vincent Schiraldi, Eddie Ellis, and others. From 1994 to 1996, the NCJC developed a broad, incisive analysis of the U.S. criminal justice regime that included comprehensive policy recommendations for what it described as "the largest and most frenetic correctional buildup of any country in the history of the world."[16] The NCJC's labors were far-reaching and global in scope, and its research labors culminated in the publication of *The Real War on Crime*, a widely cited text published by trade press HarperCollins in 1996. This report, among other widely circulated (print and online) publications by such organizations as Justice Policy Institute and Prison Activist Resource Center, played a significant role in framing progressive reformist and emergent radical anti-carceral/abolitionist analyses of the U.S. criminal justice infrastructure over the next decade or so.[17]

Between the late 1990s and early 2000s, a groundswell of public scholars, grassroots and (formerly) incarcerated activists and organizers, legal/civil/human rights advocates, academic researchers, and activist attorneys both expanded and challenged the discursive-political limits of criminal justice reform advocacy, fostering complex interactions between radical anti-prison, carceral and penal abolitionist, prison moratorium, and human rights critiques. Encompassing such organizations as Legal Services for Prisoners with Children (founded 1978), The Sentencing Project (1986), Critical Resistance (1997), Prison Moratorium Project (1998), and Justice Now (2000), this vibrant and often internally contentious activist discourse addressed the astronomical growth, unprecedented scale, and vast social consequences of the U.S. prison industrial complex, while periodically addressing the global expansion of carceral state power. The term "mass incarceration" attained its initial rhetorical traction during this period, surfacing in academic, activist, and progressive think tank analyses and prominently appearing in such influential texts as David Garland's *Mass Imprisonment: Social Causes and Consequences* (2001), Marc Mauer and Meda Chesney-Lind's *Invisible Punishment: The Collateral Consequences of Mass Imprisonment* (2002), and Michelle Alexander's widely read *The New Jim Crow: Mass Incarceration in the Age of Colorblindness* (2010).[18]

Notably, anti-racist, Black radical, feminist, queer, trans, immigrant rights, and abolitionist activists, scholars, and creative practitioners have periodically used modified versions of "mass incarceration" throughout this period, including such rephrasings as "Black mass incarceration," "racist mass incarceration," and "mass (immigrant) detention."[19] In its full discursive historical context, "mass incarceration" indexes a range of critical political interventions across moments, places, and collective labors. Yet while the term's full etymology escapes reductive or monolithic ideological characterization, it is nonetheless possible to identify how its *institutionalization* during the first two decades of the twenty-first century mobilizes a form of carceral statecraft that pivots on the narrative logics of White Reconstruction.

Given the wide circulation and popular influence of Alexander's *The New Jim Crow* across multiple communities and publics, it is necessary to closely examine how the book's narrative arc crystallizes many of the key plot points and political implications of mass incarceration narrativity. As numerous scholars have rigorously addressed the book's analytical and methodological shortcomings, i will refrain from reiterating their critiques here.[20] Rather, i will offer a concise reflection on the text's significance as a *liberal managerial* narrative that galvanizes a counter-abolitionist, militantly reformist approach to analyzing and addressing the asymmetrical casualties of contemporary carceral domestic warfare. (To be fair, it should also be acknowledged that Alexander's own analysis and political position on the U.S. carceral regime has moved closer to an abolitionist perspective since the publication of this book.)[21]

Alexander presents her central thesis through a devastating depiction of the post-1970s United States as a period defined by anti-Black criminalization and large-scale racist incarceration. Introducing the potentially radical historical analogy of a "New Jim Crow," she characterizes the rise of the contemporary carceral-policing regime as a rearticulation and re-institutionalization of anti-Black segregation. Alexander's accessible prose, fluid storytelling, and lucid (though sometimes inaccurate) re-narration of empirical data and legal tedium into satisfying explanatory modules accomplishes the difficult intellectual task of bridging multiple specialized and non-specialized (academic and extra-academic) readerships. In this sense, the text's insurgent scholarly activist potential rests on the author's willingness and capacity to fulfill the analytical and speculative possibilities of developing the concept of a New Jim Crow beyond (or even against) its initial narrative presentation as a provocative *analogical* tool. Unfortunately, the book undermines the radical potential of its own analogical framework in the final chapters when Alexander stipulates that the contemporary carceral condition cannot and should not be conceptualized in substantial institutional continuity with the (old) Jim Crow order. She contends that while "the parallels between the two systems of control are striking . . . there are important differences" that not only disrupt their comparability but also delineate their significant opposition to each other as anti-Black, racial socialities.[22]

Cataloguing the institutional, cultural, and political divergences between the racist state regimes of Jim Crow segregation and post–Jim Crow racial incarceration, Alexander compartmentalizes carceral anti-Blackness into discretely periodized historical segments, with barely a gesture toward the possibility of temporal, institutional, and cultural ebb-and-flow across their geographies and histories: "[The] list of the differences between slavery and Jim Crow . . . might well be longer than the list of similarities. The same goes for Jim Crow and mass incarceration."[23] In its penultimate chapter, *The New Jim Crow* makes a declarative narrative gesture toward an optimistic racial-historical telos that is jarringly incompatible with the empirical and testimonial evidence outlined in the book's previous two hundred–plus pages.

Alleging that the recent historical period (and onset of the Obama presidency) is marked by an "absence of racial hostility in the public discourse" as well as a paucity of "overt racial hostility among politicians . . . and . . . law enforcement officials," the book unwittingly reveals how mass incarceration narrativity reiterates the aspirations of post-raciality (see Chapter 3).[24] Alexander continues,

> [E]ven granting that some African Americans may fear the police today as much as their grandparents feared the Klan . . . and that the penal system may be as brutal in many respects as Jim Crow (or slavery), the absence of racial hostility in the public discourse and the steep decline in vigilante racial violence is no small matter. It is also significant that the "whites only" signs are gone and that children of all colors can drink from the same water fountains, swim in the same pools, and play on the same playgrounds. Black children today can even dream of being president of the United States.
>
> Those who claim that mass incarceration is "just like" Jim Crow make a serious mistake. Things have changed.[25]

Alexander's unsupported assertion that the emergence of "mass incarceration" has been accompanied by a generalized cultural-political decline in racist (anti-Black) discourse and reactionary racist mobilization is distressing for both its historical inaccuracy and potentially dangerous cultural, policy, and activist implications. On the one hand, this narrative grossly obscures the reawakening and expansion of organized white supremacist and far-right white reactionary movements in the immediate post–Civil Rights (post-1965) period as well as in the years following Obama's first presidential inauguration, evidenced by the near tripling of Ku Klux Klan membership during the decade of the 1970s, multiplication of white reactionary "hate groups" in the 2010s,

and accelerated mainstreaming of white nationalism and overtly white supremacist and far right wing/Alt-Right ideologues during and after the 2016 U.S.
presidential election.[26]

On the other hand, the text provokes the deeper question of whether the
Jim Crow narrative analogy can potentially provide a useful critical prism
through which to apprehend the formation of the U.S. carceral regime in the
time of White Reconstruction. Here, Alexander's failure to substantively engage an extensive body of prior and contemporaneous *abolitionist* scholarly activist thinking and writing extends beyond citational negligence and leaks
into complicity with a peculiar historical-analytical distortion—specifically, the
failure to contextualize, theorize, and narrate the formation of the contemporary carceral-criminalization regime in historical and institutional continuity with overlapping and foundational carceral genealogies of anti-Black
statecraft, racial-colonial bodily violence, state-induced (land and geographic)
displacement, and subjection to relations of chattel dominance. Symptomatically, mass incarceration narrativity's reliance on the rhetorical and analytical
ploy of (forfeifed) analogy facilitates a strange presentism premised on a refusal to engage with the long archives of critical praxis that rigorously explicate the deep, dynamic continuities of the very same anti-Black, racial-colonial
carceral forms that compose the conditions of material-historical possibility
for "mass incarceration."[27] As *The New Jim Crow* has become a canonical text
for activists, pundits, students, academics, policymakers, elected officials, faith
community leaders, and other critics of the U.S. carceral regime, its omnipresent citation—having sold well over a million copies in its first decade of
circulation—evidences the broad institutionalization of mass incarceration
narrativity.[28]

Brennan Center Blue Ribbons: The Fallout of "Unintended Consequences"

Aside from Alexander's text, few efforts to institutionalize mass incarceration
narrativity have been more influential than those undertaken by New York
University Law School's influential Brennan Center for Justice, a nonprofit
and nonpartisan policy think tank founded in 1995 by the family and former
clerks of Supreme Court Justice William J. Brennan to serve the mission of
"[holding] our political institutions and laws accountable to the twin American ideals of democracy and equal justice for all."[29] Responding to a broad
spectrum of public demand (in and beyond New York City) for police accountability and criminal justice reform, the Brennan Center hosted a 2014

conference titled "Shifting Law Enforcement Goals to Reduce Mass Incarceration." Headlined by U.S. Attorney General Eric Holder, the event featured an array of federal prosecutors (from New Jersey, Maryland, Kansas, Alabama, Louisiana, and the U.S. Department of Justice, among others), police officials, a former president of the National Rifle Association, and a former chair of the American Conservative Union.[30] The conference mission statement foregrounds the criminological *policing logic* that shapes the emergence of a mass incarceration reform bloc:

> This conference offers an opportunity to assess the way federal prosecutors can shift priorities. It will allow us to hear how state and local law enforcement can innovate so that safety does not come with the high costs of unnecessary incarceration. And it will gather the nations' top budget experts to explore how economic incentives can steer policy—wisely or unwisely—throughout the system.
>
> We are deeply grateful to US Attorney General Eric Holder for his encouragement for this work and his presence today. We are appreciative, as well, to the law enforcement leaders who will speak out in this conference. . . .
>
> The Brennan Center works to reform the systems of democracy and justice. We seek to ensure that American institutions follow core values. *Thus we are committed to ending mass incarceration as a mission for our organization.*[31]

This conference served as the basis for the "Blue Ribbon" Brennan Center report *Federal Prosecution for the 21st Century* (foreword by former U.S. Attorney General Janet Reno), a far-reaching document that recommends "concrete reforms to federal prosecution practices to support 21st century criminal justice policies." Echoing and revising the conference mission statement, the report suggests a criminal justice approach that "would reorient prosecutor incentives and practices toward the twin goals of reducing crime and reducing mass incarceration."[32] While the report reneges on the conference's commitment to "ending" mass incarceration in exchange for merely "reducing" it, the authors provide no clarifying remarks.

Federal Prosecution for the 21st Century reproduces the seemingly canonical liberal criminological assumption that the astronomical expansion and militarization of gendered anti-Black, racist incarceration is in fact and unquestionably an "unintended" outcome of U.S. criminal justice statecraft. Mass incarceration narrativity, in this sense, thrives on the earnest political belief that the casualties of a half-century of domestic war—carceral and otherwise—

have somehow accumulated outside of and isolated from the infrastructure-building, policymaking, and ideological mobilizations of the state and its planners, constituents, and administrators.

> It is truly remarkable how much safer the country has become since the crime wave of the 1980s and 1990s. . . . *But the policy response to the crime epidemic has yielded an unintended consequence.* The United States has more than tripled its incarceration rate over the past four decades.[33]

The report is devoid of any substantive evidence or argumentation that affirmatively demonstrates the presumed unintentionality of "mass incarceration." To the contrary, the notion of unintended consequence tacitly relies on a series of methodological and epistemological assumptions (mostly derived from mainstream criminology) that abstract the carceral-policing regime from its operational protocols and histories in gendered anti-Black, racial-colonial domestic war. This foundational historical abstraction enables a self-fulfilling idealization of liberal-conservative coalition that anchors the pragmatic agenda of mass incarceration narrativity.

Federal Prosecution for the 21st Century seamlessly cites criticisms of mass incarceration from prominent right-wing figures like Senator Rand Paul and New Jersey Governor Chris Christie while referencing California Attorney General Kamala Harris's advocacy for "a third way forward: smart on crime" and New York City Police Department Commissioner William Bratton's 2014 pledge (borne of a laughable deficit of self-awareness) to engage in "collaborative problem-solving with the community."[34] On the momentum of these endorsements, the Blue Ribbon report urges prosecutors to "address the root causes of violence or unethical behavior . . . [and] focus on prevention strategies . . . in an attempt to prevent crimes rather than just punish offenders after they commit them."[35] Crucially, the report's composition, rhetoric, recommendations, and analytical framework signify ambitions toward "bipartisan" consensus that rest on a centering of *prosecutors* as the principal architects and organic intellectuals of the reformist carceral state: Of the fifteen Blue Ribbon panelists, eleven were current or former district attorneys, one a former Associate Deputy Attorney General at the U.S. Department of Justice, and another a Deputy Director of the Executive Office for U.S. Attorneys.

The reformist premises of the Brennan Center's work rest on the liberal belief that anti-Black and racial-colonial state violence are *not* fundamental and systemic (or otherwise "intended") productions of the criminal justice, carceral, and policing regimes. This premise founds the Brennan Center's primary strategy for mass incarceration reform: a methodological revision and bureaucratic invigoration of *criminal prosecution* that heavily invests in the prospect of a more balanced symbiosis of preemptive policing, preventative criminology, and focused, punitive incarceration within the statecraft of sustained, rationalized domestic carceral war. In this instance, the stated objective of "ending mass incarceration" is tantamount to endorsing an expanded policing regime guided by neoliberal managerial methods and personnel assessments.

The Brennan Center plan proposes a corporate approach to "organizational change," replicating a vernacular of bureaucratic leanness, institutional agility, efficient management of organizational waste, and punitive disciplining of personnel deemed ineffective or underachieving.[36] By way of example, the Brennan Center report advocates "Success-Oriented Funding," in which government resources and grants are tied to a prescriptive vision of prosecutors as the leaders of state-led criminal justice reform.[37] The report envisions a reinvigoration of the mission and method of criminal prosecution in the new millennium, heavily investing in the prospect of a more balanced (hence lean, nimble, and agile) symbiosis of pre-emptive policing, preventative criminology, and punitive incarceration.

The report's advocacy of Success-Oriented Funding for prosecutors rearticulates the neoliberal cultural-disciplinary structure that inflates notions of individual responsibility as a salve for shrinking state capacity. This funding structure fixates on the rituals and performance metrics of personnel reviews as the primary mechanisms for rationalizing the criminal justice apparatus:

> As noted by the Blue Ribbon Panel, US Attorneys can help move the country away from overreliance on punishment and incarceration. They should begin with implementing Success-Oriented Funding in their own offices, turning inward to evaluate their own policies and their staff's performance.[38]

> Grounded in basic principles of economics and management, Success-Oriented Funding provides incentives to achieve . . . priorities, thereby changing practices and outcomes. It can be applied to all criminal justice agencies, actors, and funding streams.[39]

By fetishizing U.S. Attorneys as autocratic bureaucratic figures, the reformist telos privileges the federal prosecutor as the primary historical agent of momentous institutional change.

The figure of the U.S. Attorney becomes the narrative approximation of a law-and-order superhero: This figure is not only charged with the grave responsibilities of protecting civil society and swiftly enforcing (criminal) justice but is also vested with a dense *moral* gravity. As a valorized state figure, the U.S. Attorney's public performances shape the hegemonic common sense of the martial racist state:

> Federal prosecutors play a distinct and significant role in combating crime . . . [they] are the protectors of federal criminal and civil law, charged with investigating cases and seeking justice in challenging circumstances. They handle cases large and small, complex and simple, violent and petty . . . they ensure that offenders are held accountable for crimes committed. They are charged with serving justice and keeping the public safe.[40]

> Members of the Blue Ribbon Panel overwhelmingly believed prosecutors could play a leading role in rethinking prisons as the central tool for fighting crime, *either through the bully pulpit* or through other means such as alternatives to incarceration.[41]

We should be clear: The context and substance of the Brennan Center's convening of police, district attorneys, and liberal academics is structured in a collective state of denial. There is no acknowledgment in either the conference proceedings or *Federal Prosecution for the 21st Century* that the prior and contemporaneous half-century of carceral-juridical planning resulted in relatively well-anticipated, systemically predictable, and paradigmatically asymmetrical casualties, including and beyond the condition described as "mass incarceration."

The reform measures proposed by the Brennan Center report would undoubtedly institute a shift in criminal justice culture, protocols, electoral platforms, and "intentional" prosecutorial outcomes: If the prosecutorial paradigms and methods inducing "mass incarceration" are akin to criminal justice saturation bombing, *Federal Prosecution for the 21st Century* argues for the sociological and criminological merits of high-yield prosecutorial precision strikes, focusing policing, juridical, and carceral state capacities "on fewer but more significant cases, as opposed to fixating on sheer volume."[42] Yet the Blue Ribbon report can also be read (via Louis Althusser's critique of ideology) as the preliminary outline of a *carceral-policing problematic*: a formulation of the problem of "mass incarceration" that presupposes the procedural framework and criminological methodology through which the statecraft of reform might proceed.[43]

This problematic presumes that the crisis of "mass incarceration" unfolds through the linked causalities of discrete, mendable symptoms of institutional dysfunction—economic wastefulness, bureaucratic inefficiency, governmental bloat, juridical irrationality, ill-conceived or poorly applied policy, and so on—none of which "intentionally" induce systemic asymmetrical, gendered racist criminalization/incarceration. Based on this vast field of presupposition, vigorous reform and managerial redirection of jurisprudence, bureaucracy, and policy toward the goals of criminological precision (of which fractional decarceration is one part) and maximum prosecutorial operativity can presumably recalibrate the protocols and outcomes of the criminal justice apparatus. In this manner, mass incarceration narrativity forms the rhetorical and logical conditions of legibility for a reform of the carceral racist state that attempts to *manage the casualties* of unacknowledged domestic war.

The Brennan Center demonstrates how research, policy, and advocacy institutions play a vital role in establishing certain phrases and keywords as properly recognized significations of both crisis and crisis response. As forms of narrative institutionalization, such cultural-political productions create disciplinary—and periodically repressive—discursive regimes that attempt to define the parameters of "askable questions" while delimiting the horizons of social-historical imagination for activists, researchers, legal advocates, teachers, and other critical practitioners engaged in challenging anti-Black and racial-colonial (state) power. Further, when such narratives gain traction among various publics—and demonstrate the potential to become hegemonic—it becomes ever more likely that the organic intellectuals of the ("post-racial") racist state will appropriate and/or rearticulate the plot points of such discursive regimes. The next section briefly considers three prominent examples of such carceral statecraft spanning ten months in 2014–2015.

Law-and-Order in the Obama Era: Three Speeches

U.S. Attorney General Eric Holder's keynote address for the Brennan Center's 2014 conference provides an early indication of a reformist shift in the carceral state paradigm. Holder opens the speech by making his intentions clear:

> Clearly, criminal justice reform is an idea whose time has come. And thanks to a robust and growing national consensus . . . we are bringing about a paradigm shift, and witnessing a historic sea change, in the way our nation approaches these issues.[44]

Holder repeats the well-worn criminological critique of punitive, poorly managed, large-scale incarceration as a sociological engine for unproductive anti-sociality, recidivism, and criminality rather than authentic "public safety." In so doing, he throws a half-century of U.S. criminal law and carceral expansion into the trash bin of American ill-repute and liberal shame. Invoking terms gleaned from anthropologist Oscar Lewis's classically racist and colonial formulation of a "cycle of poverty" as well as Daniel Patrick Moynihan's era-defining concept of a "tangle of [Black] pathology," Holder situates "over-incarceration" as a primary institutional cause of racial disparity in the post-apartheid United States:[45]

> [F]or far too long—under well-intentioned policies designed to be "tough" on criminals—our system has perpetuated a destructive cycle of poverty, criminality, and incarceration that has trapped countless people and weakened entire communities—particularly communities of color. . . .
>
> [T]his astonishing rise in incarceration—and the escalating costs it has imposed on our country, in terms both economic and human—have not measurably benefited our society. We can *all* be proud of the progress that's been made at reducing the crime rate over the past two decades—*thanks to the tireless work of prosecutors and the bravery of law enforcement officials across America.*[46]

Guided by the mandates of institutional sustainability and liberal-centrist political respectability, Holder's unqualified praising of police and prosecutorial power suggests a symbiotic relationship between the reform of "mass incarceration" and the enhancement of the racist state's capacity to surveil, patrol, repress, discipline and contain—that is, to socially and geographically incarcerate—criminalized populations beyond the brick-mortar-and-steel sites of the jail, prison, or detention center. In this way, Holder tethers the rationalization and downsizing of an allegedly flawed criminal justice *carceral* regime to an expansion of the criminal justice *policing and domestic war* regime. Through the joined figures of the prosecutor and the (non-racist, community-grounded) police officer, his address adapts elements of the classical law-and-order paradigm articulated by Barry Goldwater in 1964 (see Chapter 3) and couches them in a reformist vernacular custom-fitted to the aspirational post-racialism of the Obama era.

Holder's vision of carceral reform not only leverages influence on the re-planning of the state's carceral and criminal justice infrastructure but also—inseparably—shapes the public discourse of police reform in the context of contemporaneous national protests and grass roots uprisings in response to the police killing of Michael Brown in Ferguson (Missouri):

> As we saw all too clearly last month—as the eyes of the nation turned to events in Ferguson, Missouri—whenever discord, mistrust, and

roiling tensions fester just under the surface, interactions between law enforcement and local residents can quickly escalate into confrontation, unrest, and even violence. These tensions simmer every day in far too many communities across the country. And it's incumbent upon *all* of America's law enforcement officers and leaders to work with the communities they serve to defuse these charged situations by forging close bonds, establishing deep trust, and fostering robust engagement.[47]

Holder's embodied, racialized public positioning as the U.S. Attorney General, that is, as a rare Black figure of juridical authority and state-ordained respectability, is paramount to the public performance and racial (sub)text of his address. His reformist rhetoric reproduces fraudulent mythologies of police vulnerability (anticipating the right wing, Fraternal Order of Police–fueled notion of a "War on the Police") even as he calls on the biographical authenticity of (Black, male) experience to identify himself with those subjected to the street-level exercises of the racist state:[48]

> [W]e must never lose sight of the immense and unyielding difficulties inherent in the law enforcement profession—from the training they receive to the risks these brave men and women incur every time they put on their uniforms; from the dangers they face . . . to the anguish of family members who awaken at night to the sound of a ringing telephone—hoping for the best, but fearing tragic news about a loved one out walking the beat.
>
> . . . As the brother of a retired law enforcement officer, I understand well how challenging—and how thankless—their vital work can be. As our nation's Attorney General, I will *always* be proud—and steadfast— in my support for law enforcement personnel. . . . And as an African-American man . . . I also carry with me an understanding of the mistrust that some citizens harbor for those who wear the badge.
>
> . . . It's time to build on the outstanding leadership that so many local police are providing—and the reform efforts that are underway in St. Louis County and elsewhere—by making this work a focused, national priority.[49]

Read in the political context of a growing national movement against anti-Black, misogynist, trans and queer phobic, and colonial police violence, it is almost impossible not to apprehend Holder's address as a liberal state response to a spreading popular discourse on the seemingly intractable problem of legitimated, legally condoned (and fatal) racist state power.

While the bulk of the speech is devoted to prosecutorial reform—"for these [proposed] changes to become permanent, we'll need to rely on the dedication—and the leadership—of federal prosecutors in Washington and in all 94 of our United States Attorney's Offices"—it also builds a narrative logic through which to tell an updated national story of police reform:[50]

> [W]e must take into account the preconceived notions that certain people may bring to interactions with police—preconceptions that may be informed by generations of experience; by the totality of what it has meant to be a person of color in the United States. We must consider corresponding notions that police may bring to interactions with certain communities and individuals. . . . [51]

Holder echoes the scripts of post-raciality by falsely equating "certain people's" long-formed communal knowledge of anti-Black, racist policing—a living archive of testimonial, archival, and grassroots evidence that is fundamentally oriented toward collective self-defense against predatory, systemic state terror— with the "corresponding" knowledge that police bring to bear on "certain communities and individuals." Central to this state narrative is the insistence on a fraudulent correspondence—a false ethical equivalence—between anti-Black, racial-colonial carceral state violence and collective resistance/revolt/ organized movements against it. Mass incarceration narrativity, in particular, relies on a sanitization of the historical breadth and systemic permutations of the terror, inflicted suffering, and violent fatality that constitutes anti-Black policing as the primary operational and infrastructural paradigm for modern police protocols; these permutations include the complex ensemble of jurisprudence, policy, and cultural production that meshes the constant threat of predatory law enforcement with the sanctioning role of district attorneys (including federal prosecutors) in effectively decriminalizing and generally valorizing fatal, terrorizing, and maiming police violence.

Holder's keynote address can be read as a draft platform for a statecraft of "mass incarceration" reform that grows police presence in a period of burgeoning grassroots movements and rebellions that (radically) question the fundamental legitimacy of police power.

> . . . [T]he Justice Department is working with major police associations to conduct a broad review of policing tactics, techniques, and training—so we can help the field swiftly confront emerging threats, better address persistent challenges, and thoroughly examine the latest tools and technologies to enhance the safety, and the effectiveness, of law enforcement. Going forward, I will support not only continuing

this timely review, but expanding it—to consider the profession in a comprehensive way—and to provide strong, national direction on a scale not seen since President Lyndon Johnson's Commission on Law Enforcement nearly half a century ago.[52]

Holder's address ends with a pledge to "seize this important moment [and] renew our determination to combat crime," suggesting that the principle problem to be addressed is not actually "mass incarceration," but the ineffectuality of a domestic war regime that catalyzes its own forced obsolescence.[53]

Around the time of Holder's resignation as U.S. Attorney General in Spring 2015, newly declared Presidential candidate Hillary Clinton made a similar call for national criminal justice and police reform at the David Dinkins Leadership and Public Policy Forum at Columbia University. Foregrounding the "era of mass incarceration" in her platform speech, Clinton urges increased use of police body cameras while decrying how "far too many people believe they are considered guilty simply because of the color of their skin."[54] Clinton clings to one of the structuring, mystified, and disciplinary ambitions of white multiculturalist civil society: the fostering of affective connections between the militarized police and their implicitly Black subjects of occupation and coercive exchange.

> We have to come to terms with some hard truths about race and justice in America. There is something profoundly wrong when African-American men are far more likely to be stopped by the police and charged with crimes and given longer prison terms than their white counterparts. . . . There is something wrong when trust between law enforcement and the communities they serve breaks down. . . . We must urgently begin to rebuild bonds of trust and respect among American between police and citizens.[55]

Clinton's subsequent Twitter post further inscribes the key plot points of mass incarceration narrativity in shorthand: "End mass incarceration. Address inequality. Restore trust between law enforcement & communities."[56] While Clinton's rhetorical turnabout on the politics of anti-Black criminalization was widely noted during her campaign, it must be emphasized that her 2015–2016 campaign platform did not substantially contradict the substance of her mid-1990s grandstanding on the scourge of Black youth "superpredators" in endorsement of President Bill Clinton's 1994 crime bill. In fact, there are substantial narrative and policy continuities between her now-infamous 1996 speech at Keene State University (New Hampshire) and the pro-police tenets driving the mass incarceration reform narrative. The prefatory remarks to Clinton's bestial demand to "bring [superpredators] to heel" can be read as a durable, long-resonating premise for the carceral reformist wager offered to more recent electoral generations: Here, *policing is itself a form of sociality*, within which safety, community, and "progress" are institutionalized and expanded through domestic militarism:[57]

> We have actually been making progress . . . as a nation, because of what local law enforcement officials are doing, because of citizens and neighborhood patrols are doing. . . . because we have finally gotten [sic] more police officers on the street. . . . If we have more police interacting with people, having them on the streets, we can prevent crimes, we can prevent petty crimes from turning into something worse.[58]

Holder and Clinton exemplify how the most prominent representatives and spokespeople of the carceral racist state appropriate, distort, and redirect activist vernaculars that might otherwise be purposed toward radical and abolitionist critiques of domestic warfare, including but not limited to the policing and carceral regimes.

President Barack Obama's July 2015 address to the NAACP National Convention in Philadelphia builds on the Holder-Clinton message, drawing from a classical civil rights lexicon while positing a primary rationale for "mass incarceration's" reform: the compulsory need for Black and Latino boys and men (and to a secondary extent, girls and women) to attain heteronormative racial respectability by way of proper parenting (fathering), gainful employment, and good citizenship.

> The bottom line is that in too many places, [B]lack boys and [B]lack men, Latino boys and Latino men experience being treated differently under the law.
>
>   . . . This is not just barbershop talk. A growing body of research shows that people of color are more likely to be stopped, frisked, questioned, charged, detained. African Americans are more likely to be arrested. They are more likely to be sentenced to more time for the same crime.
>
>   What is that doing to our communities? What's that doing to those children? Our nation is being robbed of men and women who could be workers and taxpayers, could be more actively involved in their children's lives, could be role models, could be community leaders, and right now they're locked up for a non-violent offense.

So our criminal justice system isn't as smart as it should be. It's not keeping us as safe as it should be. It is not as fair as it should be. Mass incarceration makes our country worse off, and we need to do something about it.[59]

Obama's NAACP speech reifies "mass incarceration" by refraining from a substantive analysis (in fact, from even a superficial acknowledgement) of its complex institutional, discursive, and juridical origins in multiple infrastructures, practices, policies, and protocols of the anti-Black, racial-colonial state. "Mass incarceration" is largely reduced to a liberal catchphrase that vaguely acknowledges racial disparities in the administration of criminal justice while obscuring the carceral logic that permeates the long historical statecraft of U.S. nation-building. This discursive isolation of "mass incarceration" allows Obama to fictionalize anti-Black state violence through a rather alarming act of historical revisionism:

> [I]t is important for us to recognize that violence in our communities is serious and that historically, in fact, the African American community oftentimes was under-policed rather than over-policed. Folks were very interested in containing the African American community so it couldn't leave segregated areas, *but within those areas there wasn't enough police presence.*[60]

It is worth noting that Obama's alternative historical fact-making attracts thunderous applause from the NAACP audience, suggesting that his call for greater police presence in Black communities complements rather than contradicts his demand for carceral racial reform. In places, the speech seems to draw directly from the law-and-order populist rhetoric of Goldwater's ill-fated 1960 presidential campaign. To read Obama's and Goldwater's parallel enunciations of the mandate for domestic warfare is to illuminate the continuities of gendered racist moral panic across multiple generations and publics:

OBAMA
There are a lot of folks who belong in prison. [Applause.] If we're going to deal with this problem and the inequities involved then we also have to speak honestly. There are some folks who need to be in jail. They may have had terrible things happen to them in their lives. We hold out the hope for redemption, but they've done some bad things. Murderers, predators, rapists, gang leaders, drug kingpins—we need some of those folks behind bars. Our communities are safer, thanks to brave police officers and hardworking prosecutors who put those violent criminals in jail.[61]

GOLDWATER

We must, and we shall, set the tide running again in the cause of freedom. . . . [F]reedom—balanced so that liberty lacking order will not become the slavery of the prison cell; balanced so that liberty lacking order will not become the license of the mob and of the jungle.

. . . The growing menace in our country tonight, to personal safety, to life, to limb and property, in homes, in churches, on the playgrounds, and places of business, particularly in our great cities, is the mounting concern, or should be, of every thoughtful citizen in the United States.

. . . History . . . demonstrates that nothing—nothing prepares the way for tyranny more than the failure of public officials to keep the streets from bullies and marauders.[62]

As Obama builds the case for a reform of the carceral racist state that strengthens and rationalizes the statecraft of law-and-order, it becomes increasingly clear that "mass incarceration" holds little integrity as either an explanatory or analytical term.

Rather than serving any significant definitional purpose, "mass incarceration" inaugurates a political coalescence of academics, journalists, nonprofit organizers, philanthropic institutes, think tanks, elected officials, and well-intentioned grassroots organizers in a reformist venture that attempts to address the asymmetrical casualties of domestic war by calling for improved (and thus "fairer") technologies of criminalization, policing, and incarceration. Put another way, the prospective reform of "mass incarceration" strengthens and sustains the logic and institutional coherence of the *carceral regime*, reconstructing its juridical and administrative apparatuses to conform with respectable liberal-progressive (post-racial) sensibilities; at the same time, mass incarceration narrativity cultivates a refurbishing and revivification of the *policing regime* amidst intense, widespread revolt against its widely evidenced modus operandi of anti-Blackness and gendered racist violence.

The Brennan Center's Blue Ribbon paper, the discourse of the Obama-Holder-Clinton bloc, *The New Jim Crow*, and other such policy documents, speeches, tweets, texts, and media statements constitute the broad parameters of mass incarceration narrativity. These political labors must be read and analyzed in their totality *as cultural texts* that shape the common sense of an actively "reforming" criminal justice regime by delimiting thinkable alternatives to the legal, policing, and incarceration infrastructures of U.S. domestic war. Mass incarceration narrativity endorses (and is ultimately complicit with) a statecraft of policing that skillfully links liberal post–Civil Rights racial sympathy and the long historical fact of anti-Black, racial-colonial state repression to adamant demands for criminal justice rationality and a kinder, gentler, though expanded cultural and martial infrastructure of domestic war. Departing from the examples cited thus far, it is worth considering several questions regarding the substance, significations, and sociogenic consequences (per Frantz Fanon's and Sylvia Wynter's discourses on sociogeny) of the mass incarceration narrative:[63]

> How does the narrative of "mass incarceration" obscure rather than clarify the origins, casualties, and structuring logics of carceral power?
>
> What are the policy implications of a reformist diagnosis that views asymmetrical carceral casualties as a largely unintended—and ultimately fixable—outcome of systemic unfairness, poorly conceived and/or maladministered laws, class/racial/gender/religious/ citizenship bias, and/or jurisprudential dysfunction?
>
> How does "mass incarceration" reform, as conceived by liberal-to-progressive think tanks, pundits, activists, elected officials, academics, and state agents, rely on a reinvigoration, refinement, and expansion of policing and criminal prosecution?
>
> Who are the "mass" of "mass incarceration?" What *work* does this undifferentiated naming of the "mass" do, across the fields of critical/activist discourse, policy and legal reform, and racial state planning?
>
> If decarceration is part of the carceral reform agenda, what criteria determine who is worthy of release from state captivity?
>
> Who are the presumed subjects (historical agents) and anticipated/ assumed constituencies of the "mass incarceration" reform narrative?
>
> What if the politically canonized, common sense assumption that "mass incarceration" is an "unintended consequence" of the state's planning, administration, and normative operation is false?

In Defense of White Being: "Mass Incarceration" Reform as Domestic War Remix

The discourse of "mass incarceration" surfaces in the highest executive offices of the anti-Black, racial-colonial state as a matter of broad public engagement. This chapter has considered a series of symptomatic texts that exhibit two paradigmatic tendencies of mass incarceration narrativity: First, mass incarceration reformism endorses an expansion of the anti-Black, racial-colonial state's policing power as a condition for rationalizing and reforming state carceral power. The expansion of policing power, in turn, further mobilizes the logics of carceral state violence beyond the discrete physical sites of prisons, jails, detention centers, and juvenile facilities. As reformist approaches to "mass incarceration" condone—or explicitly call for—enhanced regimes of social control, spatial containment, state surveillance and focused policing of particular profiled beings (inclusive of bodies, geographies, and communities), the logic of carcerality thrives and expands through modalities of state-sanctioned restriction, criminalization, and/or immobilization of human movement, resonating with histories of border rangers, frontier warfare, colonial occupation, slave patrols, and punitive industrial and agricultural labor discipline.

Second, the cultural-political assessment of "mass incarceration" as a national crisis rests on overlapping narrative-analytic insistences: That the primary consequences of the "mass incarceration" epoch—that is, the rigorous institutional and cultural militarization of law, civil society, and carceral state against Black life and futurity generally, and against Brown, Indigenous, queer, and non-normative being and futurity in specific geographies—may be morally reprehensible and historically tragic, but are ultimately the unintended outcome of an isolated moment in the life of U.S. criminal justice policy and carceral domestic war; and following the logic of this narrative, the reform of "mass incarceration"—including "ending" or "reducing" it—requires the fortification of police, criminal jurisprudence, and *properly administered* incarceration as permanent conditions of sociality, statecraft, nation-building, citizenship, "public safety," and "democracy." To end/reduce "mass incarceration," in this reformist telos, is to strategically refine the technologies of criminal justice rather than to address their roots in dynamic, historical regimes of anti-Black surveillance, punishment, displacement, and carceral state violence.

The constitution of White Being (in its North American and global formations) is, from its foundations, materially and symbolically dependent on a militarized-carceral order of freedom that subsumes other forms of life/sociality to various anti-social formations of displacement, evisceration, and vulnerability to extinction. As a matter of jurisprudence, national culture, and epistemic normativity, it is long established that the multiple fatal dichotomies of freedom/unfreedom (freedom/slavery, self-determination/colonization) mutually constitute the nation-building project. Yet these violent couplings are not abstracted from, but rather formed within coterminous, epochal conceptions of Civilization and White Being (forms of human self-making/community/

subjectivity that signify and embody Godfulness, scientific rationality, evo-lutionary development, and economic productivity, to echo the Wynterian schema of "Man") that cohere in gendered anti-Blackness and racial-colonial orderings of body, land, ecology, and ontology.[64]

Put another way, a logic of carcerality shapes notions of (state and extra-state) institutionality in the making of Western Civilization and its peculiar form of modernity. This logic of carcerality shapes institutions such as the jail, prison, concentration camp, and reservation as well as the presumptively non-carceral sites of the school, housing project, nuclear household, assembly line, call center, strawberry field, and asylum (etc.). In this sense, anti-Black and racial-colonial technologies of incarceration (particularly state-formed re-gimes and systems of capture and spatial confinement, not limited to jailing and imprisonment) constitute the "free world."[65]

In the shadow of this looming archive of carceral statecraft and nation-building, the narratives of "mass incarceration" attempt to re-signify the his-torical facts of targeted, proto-genocidal-to-genocidal anti-Black incarceration as reformable criminal justice malfunctions and a fixable national moral problem, the gradualist execution of which is already accompanied by vindi-cating present tense parables of post-racial Americanist triumph over the "new Jim Crow." (This triumphalism was perhaps most conspicuously exem-plified by President Donald Trump's boastful, self-aggrandizing signing of the Step Act in 2018.)[66] Persistently challenging this aspirational reformist common sense is the well-worn recognition, supported by the potent and frequent convergence of cross-generational wisdom of experience and inci-sive historical scholarly activist analysis, that the evident asymmetries of fatality and misery—which is to say the flesh-borne facts of asymmetrical domestic war—reflect the paradigmatic (hence unreformable) anti-Black and racial-colonial logics of U.S. statecraft in all of their dynamic, nuanced complexities. To be clear: the specifically criminalized profiles and popula-tion categories identified by geography, gendered-racialized physiology, reli-gion, gendered-sexual presentation, citizenship status, and social subjectivity compose the peculiar and asymmetrical targets of a half-century carceral domestic war that *has never come close to targeting the "mass" of the U.S. population.*

This period-defining carceral war illuminates another irreconcilable con-tradiction: While the rhetorics of "mass incarceration" shape a moment in the life of U.S. political culture, they also tacitly reify the long historical facts of *white* decriminalization, decarceration, and constitutive "innocence." Who is the alleged "mass" of "mass incarceration?" Who is named or hailed into co-

Figure 13. Image from *San Francisco Bay View*, February 17, 2015. (From an article by Anthony Robinson, Jr., "The Value of Black Life in America, Part 1," *San Francisco Bay View*, February 17, 2015, http://sfbayview.com /2015/02/the-value-of -black-life-in-america-part -1/. Used with permission of *San Francisco Bay View*.)

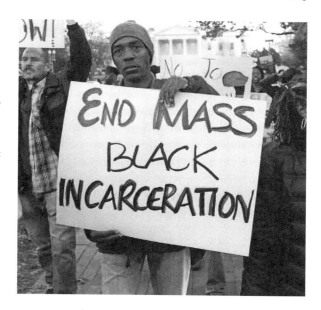

alescence by this vernacular of reform? How does the common usage of "mass incarceration" reproduce a white supremacist assumptive structure of casual and official white innocence while affirming the normativity of white bodily entitlement to physiological integrity and civil mobility?

Mass incarceration narrativity deforms, displaces, and obscures other analytical, theoretical, and insurgent (scholarly activist) languages of revolt, including those that invoke as they re-invent the feminist, queer, anti-racist, Black radical, abolitionist, anti-colonial, and Indigenous decolonial languages of domestic warfare, state violence, anti-Black genocide, police terror, and settler colonial occupation, among others. To be clear, i am not arguing that the emergent *lingua franca* of "mass incarceration" is simply an opportunistic theft of terms and concepts originating in radical, revolutionary, abolitionist, and/ or anti-colonialist movements. To the contrary, keywords like "mass incarceration" are discursive sites of cultural and political struggle. While often appropriated in bad faith by the statecraft and cultural politics of White Reconstruction, such terms are also subject to radical rearticulations of concept, theoretical structure, and praxis, ranging from carceral abolition and Black Lives Matter to the Georgia Prison Strike (see Chapter 4), Standing Rock, and Idle No More.[67] The notion of "mass incarceration," in particular, has been rearticulated by abolitionist, anti-racist, and Black radical practitioners as "Mass Black Incarceration" (see Figure 13).

Utilized by people in radical revolt against anti-Blackness and racial-colonial power, such keywords can be mobilized in excess of reformist agendas and against liberal ideological assumptions, extending a global genealogy of creative uprisings that expose the anti-Black, racist-colonialist state's unsustainability. Such radical analytics, methods, and collective knowledges identify the dense complexities of historical racial terror and significantly predate the early twenty-first-century crystallization of "mass incarceration" reformism.

Read alongside the archives of insurgent praxis, mass incarceration narrativity can be understood as a liberal multiculturalist and post-racialist *reaction* to genealogies of radical and liberationist struggle that embody, envision, and collectively plan redistribution of vital resources and social wealth, reparation for historical atrocities, abolition of carceral state violence, and liberation from anti-Blackness and racial-colonial power. The movement to reform "mass incarceration" is guided by a reflexive aversion to abolitionist, Black radical, feminist, Indigenous, decolonial, queer, and critical trans frameworks that conceptualize the evident dysfunction, negligence, brokenness, irrationality, and cruelty of the carceral state *as its paradigmatic form*. Such insurgent, abolitionist critiques identify how the historical rhythms of U.S. nation-building vacillate between genocidal anti-Black state violence, militarized (genocidal) racial-colonial domination, liberal reform, and developmental narratives of racial progress. Indebted to these critical genealogies, the closing section of this chapter offers a counter-definition of "incarceration" that liberates the term from its reified positioning within the early twenty-first-century liberal-progressive rhetoric of "mass incarceration."

"Slavery has been fruitful in giving itself names": Toward an Abolitionist Genealogy of Incarceration

Consider the storytelling implications of a radical racial chattel genealogy of the contemporary carceral regime, premised on the narrative techniques of historical continuity, transgenerational knowledge/wisdom, and the inhabitation of activated conditions of insurgency against U.S. slave coloniality (in and beyond western Africa, the Caribbean, and North America). The racial chattel relation forms as it facilitates the condition of Western (white) modernity as well as modern paradigms of (state) institutionality; the very coherence and preconceptual premises of modern institutions as socially stabilizing, rational bureaucratic structures—constituted in notions of positivist order, administrative/labor hierarchy, disciplinarity/compliance, stability, normative white subjectivity—are inseparable from the global power relations of racial chattel slavery and the transatlantic trafficking of incarcerated Africans. The long historical construction of racial chattel and its emancipated rearticulation in anti-Black, gendered racial criminalization radically disarticulates any allegation of a New World "mass": *there is no mass, there are only differentiations of places, people, physiologies, subjectivities, and futurities.*

A significant and growing community of scholars, including Sarah Haley, João Costa Vargas, Dennis Childs, Stephanie Smallwood, Angela Y. Davis, Colin Dayan, Marcus Rediker, Alex Lichtenstein, Sally Hadden, David Oshinsky, Douglas A. Blackmon, Matthew J. Mancini, Khalil Muhammad, and numerous others, definitively refutes the simplistic notion that the carceral continuities of the anti-Black chattel relation are exclusively or primarily characterized by the expropriation of prison (slave) labor.[68] Rather, this living archive traces the formation of the modern U.S. carceral regime as a revision and long revelation of slavery's anti-Black statecraft, cultural production, and (anti-)sociality. To read this body of work closely is to apprehend how the historical ensemble of anti-Black racial chattel violence has been persistently reformed (and not abolished) to fit the changing mandates of the "post-slavery," "post-civil rights," and recent "post-racial" and multiculturalist iterations of the American nation-building project. The roots of this changing reformist ensemble are entangled in the rise of the modern U.S. penitentiary as an institutional expression of the Thirteenth Amendment's juridical translation of slavery from a racial chattel institution to a criminal justice function. As discussed in Chapter 2, under the terms of emancipation, the slave relation was not abolished, but reconstructed through an emergent statecraft of criminal justice carcerality: Recall, "Neither slavery nor involuntary servitude, *except as a punishment for crime whereof the party shall have been duly convicted,* shall exist within the United States, or any place subject to their jurisdiction."[69]

The post-emancipation carceral chattel state proliferates anti-Blackness as a formation of violence and (anti-)sociality that potentially engulfs non-Black beings into its order. In this sense, the continuity of the chattel relation does not pivot on the reproduction of "involuntary servitude" as prison slave labor, but rather on the subjection of targeted, criminalized beings to a carceral logic of anti-Blackness that renders them *available* as fungible chattel. It is the terror of this availability that primarily defines the aftermath of U.S. slavery's (non)abolition. Mere months after Congress passed the Thirteenth Amendment, Frederick Douglass publicly anticipated that the carceral power of the slave relation would survive the (non)abolition of the plantation chattel regime: "I take this ground: whether this Constitutional Amendment is law [or] not . . . *I hold that the work of Abolitionists is not done. . . .*"[70] He elaborates:

> Slavery has been fruitful in giving itself names. It has been called "the peculiar institution," "the social system," and the "impediment". . . . It has been called a great many names, and it will call itself by yet another name; and you and I and all of us had better wait and see what new form this old monster will assume, in what new skin this old snake will come forth next. . . . [71]

Douglass's pronouncement of the undone, still-urgent work of abolition echoes throughout the history of scholarly activist abolitionist thought. In addition to consistently explicating how the terms of the Thirteenth Amendment form the "new skin" of the racial chattel power relation, recent contributions to this body of critical intellectual labor create a radical historicization that locates contemporary regimes of criminalization, policing, and incarceration within a longer national tradition of anti-Black nation-building and racist-colonial statecraft.[72] This abolitionist genealogy shows how the symbiosis of gendered racist criminalization with carceral "involuntary servitude" composes the durable premises of U.S. state formation and national (racial) culture across periods of crisis, reform, and reaction.

How, then, might the historical force of (anti-Black) carceral state violence, framed as a primary expression of the perpetual power relations of (transatlantic, hemispheric, and U.S.) racial chattel slavery, be re-narrated as point of origin for critically (that is, radically) studying and engaging the modern U.S. racist state, including its contemporary criminalization, policing, and carceral apparatuses?

During an intensely creative and productive two years of activity that included unprecedented testimony to the United Nations (UN) Committee Against Torture, the Chicago-based grassroots collective We Charge Genocide (see Chapter 4) authored a story of the historical present tense that serves as a living model of critical, radical departure from the political telos of mass incarceration narrativity.[73] Founded in 2014, We Charge Genocide defined itself as "an intergenerational effort to center the voices of the young people most impacted by police violence," articulating its mission within a Black radical and Black feminist radical tradition that drew on the legacies of Ida B. Wells and the Civil Rights Congress.[74] Exemplifying its commitment to generating radical narrative praxis, We Charge Genocide excoriated the American Civil Liberties Union in 2015 for failing to consult with local Black organizations and Black community leadership in its negotiations with the Chicago Police Department over the latter's notoriously racist "stop-and-frisk" policies.[75] The group resoundingly corrected the ACLU's reductive understanding of Chicago police practices:

We understand police violence to be rooted in historical and systemic anti-blackness that seeks to control, contain, and repress Black bodies through acts of repeated violence. Stop and frisk should be understood as a tool police use to punish Black people just for *being*. Police violence is always state-sanctioned violence, and further strengthening narrow supervision of police action by elites will never address that. This is why any legislative or law-based campaign to address police violence requires not just policy change, but an actual transformation of power relations between communities of color and the police.[76]

We Charge Genocide's narrative praxis exemplifies a form of creative, collective critique that disrupts and transforms the common lexicon of "police brutality" while bringing urgent, incisive attention to the historical present tense of ordinary peoples' normalized encounters with state-facilitated and state-condoned social evisceration. This radical genius emanates from a shared, complex comprehension of the United States as an accumulation of multiple generations of institutionalized dehumanization and ontological negation.

Before there was "mass incarceration," there was already *incarceration*, which is to say, when we engage in critical scholarly activist work that addresses "mass incarceration," we are obligated to offer a clear definition of the primary term. To learn from the critical analysis of We Charge Genocide is to embrace another narrative task, to be undertaken for the sake of disarticulating the assumptive terms of "mass incarceration" and nurturing other forms of insurgent storytelling against Civilization: that is, to radically define "incarceration" as a historical condition of gendered anti-Blackness and racial-colonial war, and to conceptualize the carceral regime against its juridical-cultural coherence as such. I undertake this task of definition in two parts, with each followed by a concise elaboration.

> I. Defined in the context of the modern U.S. nation-state, *incarceration* is legitimated state violence, mobilizing the power of law, policing, and (gendered racial) common sense to produce, fortify, and/or militarize the geographic isolation and (collective) bodily immobilization of targeted human groups.

Virtually all available empirical and archival accounts indicate that the institutional capacity, racialized asymmetries, geographic scale, multi-generational impact, and punitive longevity of U.S. carceral institutions stand alone in recorded human history. Few national peers in the modern period remotely approach the United States' late twentieth- and early twenty-first-century scales of jailing and imprisonment; in the last century, the rates of only a handful of nation-states exceed or are otherwise statistically comparable to U.S. rates of criminal justice incarceration (which peaked at 1000 per 100,000 people in 2008), among them apartheid South Africa, Gulag-era Soviet Union, and the Russian Federation during the immediate post–Soviet Union years.[77] Marc Mauer, writing in a 1994 report for The Sentencing Project, notes that "Black males in the US are incarcerated at more than four times the rate of black males in [apartheid] South Africa—3,822 per 100,000 versus 851 per 100,000."[78]

Comparisons to peer European First World/Global North nation-states further indicate that the contemporary U.S. carceral regime may require its own singular category of historicized analysis. Criminologist Franklin Zimring writes, "The rate of imprisonment achieved by 2007 in the United States was three times that of any fully developed nation at any point in the post World War II era," while a 2018 report by the Prison Policy Initiative (PPI) notes that the United States imprisons and jails at a rate 500 percent (United Kingdom) to 1800 percent (Iceland) higher than any of the other founding NATO member nations.[79] According to the Bureau of Justice Statistics, the United States has retained a population of more than 2,000,000 incarcerated people since the early 2000s.[80] As mentioned in the opening part of this chapter, this official calculation does not include the U.S. state's criminal justice captivity of children, mentally ill and disabled people, and undocumented migrants, nor does it encompass the (extrajudicial) incarceration of military prisoners in extraterritorial carceral (including "dark") sites. Further, the astronomical growth of the U.S. carceral regime since the 1970s cannot be attributed to any growth in "crime rates" (which have declined over the period in question).[81]

A vast archive of criminological data consistently demonstrates that U.S. criminal justice incarceration is structured in gendered anti-Blackness and racist state violence. The Sentencing Project has recently summarized the vast asymmetries in lifetime likelihood of imprisonment for U.S. residents born in 2001: 1 out of 17 for white men, 1 out of 6 for Latino men, and 1 out of 3 for Black men; 1 out of 111 for white women, 1 out of 45 for Latina women, and 1 out of 18 for Black women.[82] Hispanics are incarcerated under state jurisdiction at a rate 170 percent higher than whites, while "[t]hirty-six states had overrepresentation of Native Americans in prisons, ranging from 1.2 times the rate for Whites in Missouri and Tennessee to 14.5 times the rate for Whites in Nevada."[83] While rates of incarceration in the United States have slightly declined over the last decade or so and the Black-white gap in raw numbers of incarcerated people is slightly shrinking, the Pew Research Center reports that as of 2016, Black people are subjected to state captivity at a rate more than 500 percent greater than whites.[84]

By any historical measure, the institutional formation of incarceration within the purviews of U.S. criminal justice statecraft has produced a juridical, cultural, and militarized policing ensemble that naturalizes the condition of state captivity for criminalized people, populations, and geographies.[85] This is to suggest, conversely, that in any given historical moment there are also *generally decriminalized* people, populations, and geographies whose incarceration—however temporary—may seem dissonant, scandalous, and inherently unjust, hence unnatural. In fact, the dynamic reproduction of this circuit of criminalization-decriminalization—a state-governed and extra-state process that relies on multiple methods of incarceration as the physiological and symbolic executions of an alleged social order—is precisely what coheres the normative cultural legibility of such "American" notions as freedom, citizenship, peace, safety, respectability, nation, and community. Such commonsense notions are generally presumed to require institutionalizations of incarceration as the lowest common denominator of state-secured social order. This is at the roots of what this book has been referencing as "domestic war."

The United States provides a globally instructive case study of incarceration as a complex, dynamic symbiosis of modern nation building, criminological statecraft, domestic militarization, gendered racialization, and civil and social death. A strategically narrowed focus on the institutional formation of jails, prisons, and detention centers in the late twentieth- and early twenty-first-century United States may also facilitate a supple understanding of incarceration that can be useful across different historical conditions and sociopolitical/cultural contexts. While this geography-specific conceptualization requires revisions, corrections, elaborations, and translations if it is to be made useful to other sites of analysis, close attention to the U.S. example can nonetheless provide a useful genealogy of incarceration as a *Civilizational* power relation and paradigmatic feature of modern societies structured in racial colonial dominance.[86]

> II. Incarceration is a systemic logic and institutional methodology that produces and sustains spatial, cultural, and juridical structures of violence and dominance within different historical social and state formations.

Incarceration takes the form of narrative, juridical, spatial, and sociopolitical processes through which criminalized or otherwise (ontologically and socioculturally) pathologized populations are rendered collective targets of state-sanctioned social liquidation and political neutralization. This process may or may not involve premature physiological death and militarized killing. The immediate and accumulated individual and collective experiences of incarceration, however, are consistently articulated by captive populations in the vernaculars of warfare, survival, and involuntary intimacy with constant bodily and spiritual vulnerabilities to violence and degradation.[87] As such, incarceration is simultaneously repressive and productive power, a method of normalized (legally ordained) dominance and violence over particular targeted peoples' physiologies and environments. It is a technology of social order and a cohering of peace, lawfulness, and security through war, violence, and punishment. Incarceration, understood as a systemic logic and institutional methodology, materializes through numerous historically specific regimes of dominance, from slavery, apartheid, military occupation, imprisonment, and compulsory schooling to Native American reservations, environmental racism, and normative (colonial) sexual categorizations.[88]

Such a capacious and distended conception of incarceration indicates its inseparability from the emergence of Western modernity and the architectures of the peculiar Civilizational project—Civilization as a global colonial and racial chattel formation—that forms its historical condition of possibility. Incarceration facilitates protracted and immediate, spectacular and fatal forms of oppressive violence through the power relations of race, gender, class, sexuality, (dis)ability, nation, religion, and citizenship, among other socially ascribed differentiations of human beings.

Contrary to being a scandalous excess of the anti-Black, racial-colonial state in the post–Civil Rights Period, incarceration is more accurately understood as a paradigmatic—that is, fundamental, indispensable, and structuring—modality of what Fanon and Wynter call "sociogeny": the complex, changing processes through which external sociocultural "codes" produce notions of life, (human) being, identity/self, and historicity, within which "difference is psychically lived, fantasized, [and] contested."[89] Incarceration—which is to say, carceral statecraft and the logics of carceral power/dominance—is a form of warfare against those (human) beings that embody the symbolic orders of death, pathology, and unassimilability into the order of Civilization, an order that thrives in the long historical disordering, immobilization, and/or (attempted) destruction of other human socialities.

Contemporary journalistic, academic, artistic, activist, and popular cultural discourses of U.S. incarceration have overwhelmingly (and appropriately) focused on jails, prisons, and detention centers as the focal points of this contemporary criminal justice regime. An increasingly vast field of scholarship and advocacy addresses the collateral consequences of incarceration, including the damage and trauma inflicted on children, systemic (as well as informal, culturally sanctioned) impediments to post-release access to housing and employment, and the inability to participate in civil society or electoral politics on the same terms as other citizens.[90] The latter body of work suggests that "incarceration" is not a self-contained or historically isolated practice of legitimated state violence. Rather, incarceration is a logic and method of dominance that cannot be reduced to the discrete institutional forms of jails, prisons, and detention centers.

Incarceration has constituted—and been constituted by—the complex interaction of gendered relations of chattel and colonial power in their long, overlapping genealogies. It has emerged as a particular global formation through the historical technologies of captivity that structured the Transatlantic Middle Passage and the hemispheric racial chattel enslavement of African-descended peoples; and the geographic-ecological production of the Western Civilizational project via the Treaty of Tordesillas, Manifest Destiny, and the manifold forms of colonial conquest and occupation that have produced the (continuing and continuous) carceral subjection of Indigenous and Aboriginal peoples via reservations, nation-state borders, notions of "the frontier," and other incarcerating measures.

Far from accomplishing the actual dehumanization of its captives, these epochal forms of carceral violence have formed sites of origin for insurgent genealogies of rebellion and liberationist struggle, encompassing slave and prisoner revolts, Indigenous and anticolonial revolutions, artistic movements, anti-apartheid, and other forms of collective (carceral abolitionist) genius.[91] Any attempt to conceptualize the ongoing formation and geographic metastasizing of incarcerating regimes thus requires that the labors of dynamic critical theorization and conceptual reflection be situated in the radical possibility that the historical targets of incarceration are also the complex embodiment of its imminent undoing, hence its abolition as such.

The "Mass" (Then and Now): Other Terms

"Mass incarceration" pours into a global racial narrative—words, phrases, and concepts are emptied into an opening allegation of suffocating universality, a lie that speaks of a vaguely common subjection to suffering, of a "mass" that in its very imagination rescripts and amplifies the logics of intimate and global white supremacist life orderings. It is the unshakeable force of this narrative that drives some toward obsessive opposition to a liberal multiculturalist common sense, a hegemony that is no less vile and violent in its diverse embodiments, whether in Obama, Holder, Clinton, or otherwise. Given the density and breadth of systemic, institutionalized, state-sanctioned, and culturally normalized (if not valorized) violence that constitutes incarceration in direct continuity with the history of racial chattel, it seems clear that the historical technologies of incarceration have never targeted an undifferentiated "mass," but have consistently pivoted on the gendered racial profiling and criminalization of Black, Indigenous, queer, poor, and colonized (or colonially displaced) peoples.[92]

The ongoing present tense of normalized and legally sanctioned carceral terror (violence against the physiological, psychic, and cultural integrity of incarcerated people), directly and obliquely reflected in the public demands issued by the Pelican Bay (CA) and Georgia prison strikes (see Chapter 4), is the cumulative fulfillment of the anti-Black, racist state terror enabled by the Thirteenth Amendment's judicial rearticulation and distention of the racial chattel relation. As numerous abolitionist scholars have noted, the rise of the contemporary prison industrial complex is a direct outcome of the liberal-progressive "prison-reform" successes of the 1970s.[93] The political convergence between liberals, progressives, and "law-and-order" conservatives/reactionaries, located within the accelerating political and geographical displacements of globalization, generated a host of material transformations and institutional shifts that reorganized the scale and reach of the state's carceral capacities—prisons and jails—in direct, intensified relation to hegemonic political, cultural, and economic institutions, including public policy and legislative bodies, electoral and lobbying apparatuses, the medical and architectural/construction industries, corporate news media, and various other institutional forms.[94]

As widely discussed by critical scholars of carcerality across the fields of radical criminology, history, gender studies, and Black studies (among others), the reform of US criminal justice and carceral regimes has consistently resulted in the expansion and bureaucratic multiplication of carceral institutions. Dorothy Roberts provides a succinct outline of this carceral contradiction as part of an innovative argument for "abolition constitutionalism":

> [A]bolitionist philosophy is defined in contradistinction to reform: reforming prisons is diametrically opposed to abolishing them. Efforts to improve the fairness of carceral systems and to increase their efficiency or legitimacy only strengthen those systems and divert attention from eradicating them.[95]

Historical examples of this self-reproducing liberal carcerality saturate the last century of U.S. criminological modernity: For example, the reform of prison overcrowding through the 1970s and 1980s facilitated an astronomical growth in new prison construction (rather than decarceration and release), the reformist outrage against preventable deaths and severe physiological suffering from (communicable, congenital, and mental) illnesses yielded the piecemeal incorporation of medical facilities and staff into prison administration (as opposed to addressing the fact that massive incarceration inherently creates and circulates sickness), and reformist recognition of carceral state violence against emotionally disordered, mentally ill, and disabled captives led to the creation of new prisons and pharmaceutical regimens for the "criminally insane," and so on.[96] Following the historical trajectory of Angela Y. Davis's concise and accurate assessment that "during the [American] revolutionary period, the penitentiary was generally viewed as a progressive reform, linked to the larger campaign for the rights of citizens," it is crucial to recognize that the post-1970s emergence of the prison industrial complex is one of the most significant "reformist" achievements in US history, and is not simply the perverse social project of reactionaries and conservatives.[97] The contemporary carceral regime's roots and sustenance are fundamentally located in the American liberal-progressive impulse to reform institutionalized state violence rather than abolish it. Legal scholar Paul Butler, a former prosecutor, thus reaches a proto-abolitionist conclusion in 2016, suggesting that "attempts to reform the system might actually hinder the more substantial transformation American criminal justice needs."[98]

Such reformist approaches to "mass incarceration" fail to critically address incarceration, as it has been extensively defined here. Abolitionist and Black radical feminist scholar, activist, and grassroots organizer Mariame Kaba echoes the necessity for such a critical reframing:

> What a strange moment we're in . . . Prison "reform" is in vogue. . . .
>
> As someone who has devoted years of her life to the work of first reforming and then later abolishing prisons, one might think that I would be excited about recent developments. In fact, my natural skepticism is now at its peak mainly because I am a student of history. The prison itself was born out of a reform movement and since its inception in the US in the late 18th century, we have been tinkering towards imperfection. With every successive call for "reform," the prison has remained stubbornly brutal, violent and inhumane.[99]

Following Kaba's lead, consider what it might mean to work *against* a present tense liberal-progressive commonsense that seems inseparable from the anti-Black logics and white supremacist aspirations of the modern (carceral) humanist project. Against this commonsense, it may be possible to thrive in a refusal to surrender radical terms, a thriving that may in turn enable other radical possibilities, including the insurgent futurities already present in collective analysis, art, research, scholarship, and praxis. This is the dense reality of what some have begun to call "abolition" in the climate of twenty-first-century gendered anti-Black and racial-colonial state violence, within and beyond the United States.

Epilogue
Abolitionist Imperatives

A venal race of scholars, profiteering pander[er]s to national vanity,
have conspired to obscure the truth about abolition.

—C. L. R. JAMES[1]

Abolition as Historical Mandate

The revitalization of abolitionist praxis since the turn of the twentieth century
exposes the inadequacy of liberal-to-progressive reformist approaches to the
violence and terror wrought by a carceral anti-Black, racial-colonial state and
social formation.[2] Abolitionist (political, cultural, and classroom) education,
grassroots organizing and movement building, scholarly research, and creative
and performing arts have focused on the asymmetrical casualties of carceral
domestic war as foundational, systemic, and "normal" productions of an anti-
Black, racial-colonial sociality. Catalyzed and sustained by feminist, queer,
trans, diasporic Black radical, (formerly) incarcerated, Indigenous anti- and
decolonial, and other liberationist, revolutionary, militantly anti-carceral traditions, contemporary abolitionist practitioners have enlivened a foundational critique of the long Civilization project: that its institutions and state
formations cannot be reformed or "fixed" against their constitutive logics of
power, violence, negation, displacement, immobilization, and genocide.[3]

A historical mandate emerges from within this irreconcilable reformist contradiction, cultivating abolition as an imaginative, speculative collective
labor: While liberal-to-progressive reformism attempts to protect and reproduce the institutional and cultural-political coherence of existing state and
extra-state carceral/policing systems by adjusting, fixing, and/or refurbishing

them, abolitionist praxis addresses the historical roots of those systems in rela-tion to oppressive, continuous, targeted violence (war), and radically questions whether and how those relations might be uprooted and/or transformed (rather than reformed or fixed) for the sake of vulnerable peoples' existence, survival, and thriving as such.[4]

In the preceding chapters, i have conceptualized White Reconstruction as an ensemble of cultural and political projects, narrative structures, ideologi-cal tendencies, and state formations that exhibit the resilient, reformist quali-ties of white supremacy as an aspirational logic of sociality (Civilization) while reproducing the distinct and dense national, hemispheric, and global violences of anti-Blackness and racial-colonial power. As a contemporary ensemble, White Reconstruction attempts to rescue and fortify the ascendancy of White Being in response to persistent, thriving late twentieth- and early twenty-first-century liberationist insurgencies that not only seek to extinguish and/or radi-cally transform discrete institutionalizations of gendered anti-Blackness and racial-colonial violence, but also envision and plan the abolition of White Being as such. Such expressive, collective movements of autonomy, radical communal integrity, bodily defense, and cultural assertion—from the long historical genealogies of Black freedom struggle and Indigenous decoloniza-tion to the concentrated geographical antagonisms of prison hunger strikes and police abolition—pose the potential of undermining and potentially obliterating White Being's ascendancy as the coercively normative paradigm of human being within the globality of Wynter's "millennium of Man."[5] The period of White Reconstruction is yet another iteration of White Being as the militarized template for a Civilizational modernity that rests on the ca-pacity to expropriate, assimilate, liquidate, and alienate *all other beings* as the premise for its peculiar renditions of progress, reform, social coherence, ra-tionality, and order.

What would it mean to displace and level the ascendancy of White Being—to abolish its Civilization as such—while thrilling in the creative possibilities of insurgently thriving as descendants and inheritors of particular, differen-tiated conditions of historical vulnerability to its world-altering, systemic violences? On the one hand, in resonance with the epigraph from C. L. R. James that opens this epilogue, i am increasingly troubled by misappropria-tions and (seemingly calculated) political misinterpretations of "abolition-ist" critical praxis that either tolerate or actively reproduce White Being's ascendancy by relying on methods, institutions, and vernaculars of power that replicate the modalities of anti-Black and racial-colonial systems, from the settler nation-state and modern criminal jurisprudence to capitalist property relations and compulsory heteronormativity. On the other hand, the long, radical genealogy of abolitionist praxis—founded in hemispheric and transatlantic Black radicalism as organized movement, community creation, guerilla war, and cultural production—is far too significant and ethically demanding to be so easily distorted by mere opportunism or rhetorical extravagance.

Guided by a commitment to theoretical meditation and political counter-narrative, i offer this epilogue as a situated reflection on the obligation, risk, beauty, and liberationist power of abolitionist praxis in the early twenty-first century. I write these words while acknowledging my intellectual indebtedness and political accountability to a dynamic, constantly changing, often expanding community of practitioners who think, write, talk, and act in defiance of a prevailing political common sense that delimits the horizons of activist imagination to simplistic notions of "what is practical," "what is realistic," "what 'the people' will understand/accept/do," or even "what must be reformed first/now/soon."

This epilogue attempts to critically honor the praxis of current and recent collectives such as Critical Resistance, the Abolition Collective, Black Youth Project 100, We Charge Genocide, Idle No More, and #NoDAPL and the Standing Rock Sioux.[6] Abolition reflects these and other forms of collective, creative revolt against a carceral world; to contextualize abolitionist praxis within the vibrant traditions signified by these and other movements is to challenge teleological or formulaic notions of revolution and/or social transformation while also intervening on patriarchal and masculinist constructions of freedom/self-determination and shattering liberal-optimistic paradigms of incremental, reformist "social justice."

The Long Abolitionist Project

What are the historical conditions and political imperatives of abolition as a contemporary praxis? How does abolitionist praxis facilitate notions of freedom, justice, security, autonomy, self-determination, and community that do not rely on systems of carceral state power, including but not limited to criminal justice, policing, and (domestic) militarization/war? These working questions invite engagement with abolition as a practice of futurity that emerges through insurgent, counter-Civilizational histories—genealogies of collective genius that *perform* liberated human being under conditions of duress.[7]

The late Black liberation warrior, organizer, and Vice President of the Provisional Government of the Republic of New Afrika Safiya Bukhari wrote, in characteristically crystallized terms, that "[b]y definition, security means the freedom from danger, fear, and anxiety."[8] Security and freedom, for peoples subjected to the normalized state and extra-state violence of (global) U.S. nation-building, require a decisive departure from typical demands for policy reform, formal equality, and amped-up electoral participation. Throughout this book, i have focused on mobilizations of collective voice that abrogate while raising the political discourse of "demand" (see Chapter 4).[9] To consider the fullest implications of Bukhari's statement, in this context, is to embrace the imperative of abolition—understood in part as collective liberation from systemic, institutionalized, and transgenerational "danger, fear, and anxiety"—as a *minimal condition of sociality* for those subjected to the violence of gendered anti-Blackness and racial-colonial logics of dominance. This is also to suggest that abolition is better understood as a collective form of cultural and social creativity than as an accomplished, definitive outcome.[10]

Consider abolition as a long historical accumulation and future planning of acts, performed by and in the name of peoples and communities relentlessly struggling for their collective integrity as such. Embrace the obligation that accompanies affinity and identification with abolitionist praxis, understood as the complex, dynamic, and deeply historical collective labors of remaking sociality, politicality, ecology, place, and (human) being against the duress that some call dehumanization, others name colonialism, and still others identify as ontological subjection, racial slavery, and chattel incarceration. Abolition is constituted by acts long overlapping, dispersed across geographies and moments that reveal the underside of the New World and its descendant forms—the police, jail, prison, criminal court, detention center, plantation, reservation, and "border."

Untethered from nationally vindicating, liberal narratives of late nineteenth-century (and disproportionately white) abolitionists seeking redemption of the American project against its own constitutional anti-Black chattel carcerality, and in critical dialog with early twenty-first-century articulations of abolition, another conceptualization of the term becomes possible. Now and long before, abolition is a Black radical practice and analytical method that converses with anti- and decolonial Indigenous visioning. Growing from diasporic Black radicalism, abolition is a queer infrastructure in the making, a creative project, a collective performance, a feminist counterwar, an ideological struggle, a pedagogy and curriculum, an alleged social impossibility that is furtively present, pulsing, produced in persistent insurgencies of human being that undermine the totalizing logics of empire, chattel, occupation, heteropatriarchy, genocide, and Civilization as a juridical-narrative epoch.

The historical parameters of abolitionist praxis are (and must be) subject to rigorous scrutiny and collegial contestation: Beyond simplistic debates about what forms of radical and revolutionary movement "count" as abolitionist, it is necessary to generate sustainable, creative forms of ethical accountability to the genealogies of abolitionist struggle that emerge through the hemispheric and transatlantic Black liberation movement and periodically intersect with, diverge from, and contradict Indigenous anti-colonial, radical sovereignty and decolonial praxis; border and migrant decriminalization/decarceration; radical and revolutionary workers' movements; feminist, queer, and trans insurgencies against racialized intersections of patriarchy, misogyny, and heteronormativity; and other attempts to cultivate the possibility of collective futurities that actively detonate the millennium of Man to create joy and beauty in the ashes of its obsolescence.

Abolition, in its radical totality, consists of constant, critical assessment of the economic, ecological, political, cultural, and spiritual conditions for the security and liberation of oppressed peoples' fullest collective being, and posits that revolutions of material, economic, and political systems compose the necessary but still inadequate conditions for abolitionist praxis under the protracted violence of White Being's resilient ascendancy. Consider abolition, further, as a counter-Civilizational practice of freedom that defies the modern disciplinary (and generally militarized) orders of the citizen, the nation-state, jurisprudence, politicality, and—most importantly—the gendered racial ascendancy of the white human and its deadly regimes of normalized physiological and cultural-epistemic integrity. (The latter, to review, encompasses the rigorously reproduced, coercive *worldliness* of White Being in a relation of power/dominance with other life, including nonhuman life; this violent worldliness includes the toxic political, affective, and discursive differentiation of white life from the long asymmetries of Indigenous death, queer death, Black death, Third World death, and so on. This is the formation of historical dominance that Katherine McKittrick and Sylvia Wynter term "white radiance.")[11]

The substance of a long abolitionist project is already evident in the creations of the people, communities, and collectives referenced throughout this book. One significant lineage within this body of critical work traces and narrates the institutional transitions and juridical-cultural translations of racial chattel power from the carceral Middle Passage and the rise of plantation slavery to Jim Crow apartheid and the emergence of post-1960s carceral domestic war. Such tracings and (re-)narrations, in turn, evince the racial chattel relation as a dangerously durable, "reformable" paradigm of social, juridical, and cultural power that structures U.S. (global) statecraft and social formation in historical continuity.[12] This abolitionist analytic facilitates critical theorization of how the most concrete, everyday historical technologies of slave-state dominance—including but not limited to the slave ship, coffle, auction block, slave patrol, lash, and slave-hunting animals—are reflected in post-emancipation, modern, and post-American apartheid logics of policing, criminalization,

and incarceration. From Douglas Blackmon's account of the "industrial slavery," "slave farms," and "slave mines" of the immediate post-emancipation
period and Erica Meiners's examination of the racialized cultural-juridical
figure of "the child" as "a key technology of a shifting carceral regime," to
Damien Sojoyner's ethnographic conceptualization of (predominantly or plu-
rality Black) public schools as sites of "enclosure" in continuity with prisons and
historical anti-Black structures of state captivity, there is an ample and growing body of study that explicates the roots of the contemporary U.S. carceral
regime in the paradigmatic national power relation of racial chattel.[13]

As a living archive of counter-narrations that traverse scales of geography
and collectivity, the long historical praxis of abolition reflects, honors, and extends the creative genealogies of Black radicalism. In this sense, abolition is
not merely a practice of negation—a collective attempt to eliminate specific
forms of institutionalized dominance over targeted peoples and populations—
but is also a radically imaginative, generative, and socially productive communal (and community-building) practice. Echoing Bukhari's terms, abolition
envisions as it performs a radical reconfiguration of justice, collective spiritual
and physiological integrity, and social formation that does not rely on the paradigms and methods of institutionality, self-determination and governance,
power, and community that have long been coercively universalized through
the regimes of White Being and the specific formations of anti-Blackness and
racial-colonial institutionality/statecraft. As a Black radical expression, abolition comprehends the foundational gendered violence of racial chattel as constitutive of modern and contemporary regimes of spatial organization,
physiological discipline, necropolitical and biopolitical power, state power, war,
capital accumulation and property relations, criminalization, and labor exploi-
tation/expropriation.[14]

Heeding the continued relevance of Frederick Douglass's warning to his
contemporaries that they must remain vigilant to the continuities of slavery—that they "had better wait and see what new form this old monster
will assume, in what new skin this old snake will come forth next" (see Chapter 5)—contemporary abolitionist praxis magnifies how emancipation, freedom, and liberation from anti-Blackness and racial-colonial violence remain
unfinished projects precisely because the racial chattel relation has never
been abolished, and is constantly reanimated through changing regimes of
carceral domestic war.[15] In this context, the radical futurity of abolitionist
praxis is characterized by theoretical and analytical concerns that emerge
through a historical totality of cultural, organizing, artistic, (self-defensive)
paramilitary, educational, community-building, and anti-colonial/decolonial

practices that are inseparable from the (sometimes unacknowledged) specificities of abolitionism via Black radicalism.

Abolitionist Futurities

As a radical pedagogical and curricular project that crosses as it transforms
scholarly disciplines, intellectual traditions, activist practices, and counter-
Civilizational epistemologies, abolitionist praxis encompasses creative labors
of speculative futurity for those peoples who cannot presume an individual
(or collective) tomorrow in the long historical presence of gendered racist
state violence structured in domestic war: militarism, policing, occupation,
and incarceration.[16] Such futurities of liberation convene creative forces that
are, in part, interruptive and destructive in form and method.

For example: To demystify and fracture the proto-theological (and always
white supremacist) sanctification of police as suprahuman and supralegal embodiments of normative justice, safety, and communal (white bodily) integrity signifies the impact of abolitionist tactics, vernaculars, and organizing
strategies in disrupting the cultural narratives of White Reconstruction (recall
discussions in Chapters 1, 4, and 5). Thus, when reactionary blocs fabricate
moral panic by marshaling fearful, defensive white/multiculturalist reactions
to a fabricated "war on cops," screaming and whispering that "blue life matters"
in bad faith rebuttal to the activation of grass roots movements responding
to Black life's institutionalized subjection to police/state terror, there is a grain
of truth buried in their cynical posturing: Those in revolt against the normality, mundaneness, and always-indelible denigrations of the racist state *are*, in
fact, engaged in a struggle for liberation and safety that requires the abolition
of the police as a secular higher power that is systemically empowered to destroy, intimidate, ruin, torment, and kill. Abolition, as a practice of speculative futurity, is simultaneously a historicized acknowledgment and dynamic
diagnosis of Civilization as a condition and geography of war that necessi-
tates a guerilla response from those inhabiting its logics of liquidation and
demoralization.

What ethical and historical responsibilities structure potential engagements
in abolitionist praxis? How does such praxis encompass dynamic, reflexive,
consistent (auto-)critique as well as specific organizing methods, political strategies, and theoretical frameworks? If abolition is a creative—and not merely a
negating or destructive—praxis, then how can it be understood within Wynter's poetic, artistic, experimental conception of "human being" that disarticulates the hegemony of the Western, white genre of "Man?"[17]

The complexities (and multiple interpretations) of abolitionist genealogy arc toward a complete recreation of the social-cultural form as the minimal prerequisite for a liberation of (human) being from a global totality of chattel-colonial carceral violence. In concert with this foundational responsibility, i would emphasize that such work must be undertaken with a deeply historical, critical appreciation of how (feminist, queer) Black radicalism and Indigenous anti-/de-colonial praxis have long identified militarized, misogynist, anti-Black and racist-colonial carcerality as both the spatial method and preferred conceptual apparatus for the distended, ongoing New World/Civilizational project and its preeminent modern iteration in U.S. nation-building. In resonance with these traditions, Bukhari illuminates how insurgent modalities of human being can form the premises for large-scale, historically driven abolitionist social change. Her conception of Black liberation in this instance provides a preliminary directive for those who place themselves in the historical service of abolitionist projects:

> We must exorcise those characteristics of ourselves and traits of the oppressor nation in order to carry out that most important revolution—the internal revolution. This is the revolution that creates a new being capable of taking us to freedom and liberation. As we are creating this new being, we must simultaneously be struggling to defeat racism, capitalism, and imperialism—and liberate the Black Nation.[18]

Extrapolating Bukhari's rejoinder, Martha Escobar's work provides nourishing lessons in abolitionist praxis and scholarship.[19] Reflecting on the complexities of migrant women's experiences with U.S.-Mexico border-crossing, Escobar's text has significant implications for abolitionist organizing methodologies and strategies: By rigorously analyzing the connections between the anti-Black chattel-carceral state and the gendered racial criminalization of undocumented Mexican, Central American, and other racialized Brown migrants that spur the "expansion of the carceral society beyond the territorial boundaries of the US nation-state," she argues for a strategic retheorization and rethinking of activist and scholarly methods that foregrounds critical dialog between the liberal-progressive mainstream of the early twenty-first-century immigrant-rights movement and the constantly unfolding work of prison and carceral abolitionists.[20] Perhaps the most incisive contribution of Escobar's project is its analysis of the territorializing constructions of political interest that often isolate reformist, "rights"-based activisms from abolitionist praxis and thus undermine the possibility of productive activist confrontations with the root causes of suffering, misery, and interpersonal violence for criminalized Latina/x migrant women.[21] I invoke Bukhari and Escobar in this instance as examples of abolitionist praxis that are neither exceptional nor singular, but rather are symptomatic of the thoughtful, self-critical, radically collective sensibilities that have historically guided abolitionist thought and organizing methods.

There is a frightening beauty to historical abolitionist praxis, to the extent that it hinges on assertions of collective forms of human being as (criminalized, systemically pathologized) acts of insurgent self-determination, security, and communal reproduction—although without the sturdy guarantees, epistemological presumptions, and material entitlements of social futurity that characterize Western and Euroamerican (white) civil subjectivities.[22] *Insurgent abolitionist futurity*—as a collective, vulnerable, experimental, speculative imagination/performance/practice of liberation from carceral-Civilizational violence—constitutes a radical challenge to the fraudulent universality of liberal (read: white, humanist) social futurity.[23]

The fraud of liberal white futurity is nestled in the reformist narratives critically examined throughout this book. Such narratives reproduce a stubborn tautology: While the "American" past may be structured in multiple, mind-boggling, systemic eviscerations of human populations and their ways of life, and while these eviscerations may have been undeniably anti-Black and racial-colonial in their origins, administration, and rationalization, such serial atrocities of targeted suffering and demise nonetheless form ideal staging points for serial, dramatic national reforms and institutional reconfigurations that exhibit the exceptionality of American futurity and vindicate its imperial optimism; once undertaken, these reforms and reconfigurations sustain and remobilize the long historical logics of evisceration while subsuming past atrocity into a compartmentalized, alienated, ethically irrelevant temporality. In the reach of this narrative arc, reforms of the anti-Black, racial-colonial state amount to an intensive, historically specific remapping, reimagination, and rearticulation of the aspirational white supremacist entitlement of liberal futurity.

Under such a logic, White Reconstruction amounts to a contemporary Civilizational mandate to plan, manage, and reimagine liberal white futurity against the duress of Other beings' insurgencies. In confrontation with both liberation-directed insurgencies and the resilience of insurgent modalities of (human) being, such developments as the juridical abolition of official apartheid and the formal elimination of certain forms of gendered racial colonialism can be understood as White Being's maneuvers of self-sustainability. More precisely, White Reconstruction is a period-specific turn toward a flexibility of racial power—one that momentarily privileges a suppleness of racialized relations of dominance—that endorses state and social reform precisely because the presumptive citizen-subject, proctor, and administrator of that reform— White Being—is already vested with the entitlements of social futurity.

Within the popularized cultural politics and delimited upward socioeconomic mobilities endorsed by contemporary White Reconstruction (which both relies on and despises "affirmative action" and "diversity" as mechanisms for reordering the epidermal layers of generally but-not-always white-dominant institutionalities), there are renewed possibilities for attachment, allegiance, and affinity to the universalist ("colorblind"-to-"multicultural"-to-"diverse"-to-"people of color"-to-"post-racial") fraud of liberal futurity. There is an invitation to thrill in this compulsory fiction, to fantasize an authentically universal humanist future within the reconstructed ascendancy of White Being even as changed conditions continually yield palimpsests of degradation and humiliation.

If Survival Is Not Enough: Abolition as Creativity Imperative

On the other hand, it is possible to inhabit abolitionist futurity through already existing human praxis—which is to say, following Wynter, that the totality of what i have been referencing as a global abolitionist genealogy is available to those who are both willing and able to attempt a (collective, critically reflective) praxis of human being against the alienated, coercive universalization of white/Western/Civilizational human being. Wynter references the latter as "Man2," the "uniquely secular liberal monohumanist *conception* of the human—Man-as-*homo oeconomicus*."[24] In turn, she argues that this "genre" of human being narrates itself through the Western humanist ("monohumanist") episteme as the singular and exclusive physiological and ontological embodiment of an evolved, eugenic, Civilization-embodying humanity.[25] The primary epoch-shaping fallout of this "genre-specific" articulation of (white/Western/Civilizational) human being is its self-rendition as *universal Man*, the abstracted normative subject of modern rights/jurisprudence/rational knowledge, which by its very existence (as well as through its violent epistemic and academic practices) asserts the variously "dysselected" (pathological, under- or dys-evolved, culturally/genetically defective and inferior) status of *all other genres of human being* (the Afro-descended, the aboriginal, the unassimilable, the irrational, the subhuman, and so on).

> [T]he West, over the last five hundred years, has brought the *whole* human species into its *hegemonic*, now purely secular . . . model of being *human*. . . . This is a model that *supposedly* preexists—rather than *coexists* with—all the models of other human societies *and* their religions / cultures. . . . This is the enacting of a uniquely secular liberal monohumanist *conception* of the human—Man-as-*homo*

oeconomicus—as well as of its rhetorical overrepresenting of that member-class conception of being human (as if it is the *class of classes* of being human itself).[26]

While Wynter references the Masai people as the counterpoint to Man2 in the subsequent section of her essay, it is no less feasible (and necessary) to recognize and embrace the counter-Civilizational human praxis of other ordinary and extraordinary people in the belly of the Western, Euroamerican beast. Such people inherit and inhabit a state of intimate, proximate, permanent conflict (war) with the militarized, standardized, canonical genre of (white) humanity of which Wynter writes.[27]

Put another way, the foundations for abolitionist creativities rest in the complex mess of human praxis engaged by the peoples incarcerated by the geography, episteme, and (U.S.) nation-state form of the Civilization project. These creativities—in, from, and of the mess—flourish and potentially grow into fully articulated revolt against Civilizational carcerality, epistemology, normativity, and the violent/violating normality of (white/Western/Civilizational) human being.[28] *Such assertions of insurgent being are abolitionist acts:* The peoples inhabiting the layered undersides of modern citizenship and civil society—those who systemically, regularly experience the disciplinary, violent, punitive policing of civility and sociality—are actively inventing, sustaining, and otherwise performing modalities of social life (crucially, methods of survival if not collective thriving) that fundamentally challenge the assumptive coherence and humanist universality of "civility" and "the citizen" (Man, Man2, and so on).

The insurgency of abolitionist futurity is its politicization of this *underside position* and its re-narration of the terror that often subsumes those who can neither materially presume nor find existential entitlement in the futurity of their (individual and collective) bodily coordinates, spiritual life, and repressed, colonized, incarcerated, enslaved, and otherwise non-normative "genres" of human being. Here again is the frightfully beautiful abolitionist present and future tense: At stake is an ongoing, necessary confrontation with the life-deforming algorithms of a Civilization project that rests on the intersecting and entwined logics of chattel incarceration (enslavement) and racial-colonial genocide (cultural, biological, ecological, and otherwise). Abolitionist praxis is thus a radical acknowledgment that universalizing notions of (white) humanity are artifacts of dominance that are always immiserating and fatal in their militarized enforcement and juridical reproduction of gendered racial normativities.

Now consider abolition as an art form, the kind of creative truth that mixes the stuff of history into memory, survival, and breath, as well as resilient, resurgent, internally vexed, and often-nourishing formations of community that constantly escape the guarantees of any self-assured organizing plan. In some ways, this is not the time to insist on the renewed urgency of a radical abolitionist struggle because such a time preceded all of this, and its messengers have already presented themselves to us in the poetry, letters, manifestos, collect phone calls, and never-quite-private conspiratorial conversations shared with each other sometimes, but really, *all the damn time*. More than just a synonym or rhetorical cipher for revolutionary change or radical social transformation, abolition is an artful disruption of Civilization's—and White Being's—presumed, privileged futurity.

Abolition, as Ruthie Gilmore reminds, is a *creative* force: "it's about making things," even and especially in those rare historical moments when a definitive destruction of oppressive structures and power relations appears possible, practical, and capable of catalyzing a (potentially) radically different social form.[29] Within the last half millennium, such periods of creative destruction and creativity through destruction have flourished through multiple genealogies of confrontation with the hemispheric and ultimately global Civilization-form, resulting in the downfall of multiple apartheid orders, expulsion of colonial occupations, redistribution of life-sustaining wealth and resources, and periodic liberation of chattel-captive populations. Such moments of victory can and must be honored as contradictory, imperfect, and flawed accomplishments of abolitionist struggle that generate utterly human historical outcomes in the most counter-humanist, anti-Civilizational sense of the human (that is, the human as contradictory, imperfect, flawed, and wild—the demystification of Manz's fraud of self-mastery, rationality, and selectedness).

It is equally imperative to study, teach, theorize, and narrate such historical moments as revelations of radical possibility that obliterate the cultural tendency to reify existing systems of state violence, geographic displacement and capture, economic evisceration, and institutionalized dehumanization as if they are permanent, immovable, and natural facets of a universal order.[30] Such creative destruction and creativity of thought-within-destruction are primary pedagogical methods for abolitionist praxis now and in the foreseeable future; these creativities must be seized as they are imagined.[31]

The horizon of the possible is an abstraction of the political imaginary, enabling radical audacities of collective purpose while stoking anticipation of that which lurks beyond the horizon. Situated within a long and living history of liberation movements—that is, insurgent practices of human being that remake conditions of collective life, defend the integrity of physiology and peoplehood, and periodically reimagine ontology and futurity alike—abolitionist praxis is one important strain in a continuous unfurling of *radical* horizons.

To gaze at—while approaching—any abolitionist horizon as it moves, changes, and shifts is to subject oneself to interrogation by a significant political-historical question, at once deeply personal and powerfully collective in the implicit demands it exerts on inheritors of a dense genealogy of abolitionist labors: What historical responsibilities and ethical obligations does one embrace when identifying with and actively attempting abolitionist praxis?

While i do not find it useful to prescribe examples of "proper" or authentic abolitionist thinking, pedagogy, or collective labor given the range of relations and contingencies that shape the substance and possibilities of such work, i feel compelled to reiterate that *rigorous* (that is, critically researched and deliberately theorized) experimentation and radical creativity are the soul of this praxis. There is, in the end, no final fulfillment of the abolitionist social vision; there is only a collective, emergent desire that surges from the unshakeable ethical imperative to fight those forms of violence, negation, and terror that are the most culturally and politically sanctioned, valorized, and taken for granted within a particular historical moment. To resist, refuse, or disavow this desire is to be unaccountable to the historical truth of one's involuntarily inherited moment, in which the anti-Black, racial-colonial logics and accelerating institutional and military technologies of social liquidation have merged with history's greatest experiment in punitive human captivity, a linkage that increasingly lays bare racism's logical outcome in genocide.[32]

Let us provisionally conceptualize and engage with abolition as a praxis of liberation that is creative and experimental rather than formulaic and rigidly programmatic. Abolition is a "radical" political position, as well as a perpetually creative and experimental pedagogy. Formulaic approaches cannot adequately apprehend the biopolitics, dynamic statecraft, and internalized violence of genocidal, proto-genocidal, and ontologically exterminating systems of human domination. As a productive and creative praxis, this conception of abolition posits the material possibility and historical necessity of a social capacity for human freedom that centers, defends, and embraces insurgent life in the displacement of social, civil, and premature biological death. In this sense, abolitionist praxis does not exclusively concern itself with overthrowing the policing and carceral regimes, although it may strategically prioritize the police/jail/prison/detention center as central sites for catalyzing broader, radical social transformations. This is to extrapolate Angela Y. Davis's conceptualization of abolition as "a constellation of alternative strategies and institutions, with the ultimate aim of removing the prison from the social and ideological landscape of our society."[33]

Given the historical conditions each of us differently inherits—and which we continue to create—it is imperative to teach and generate critical and radical knowledges within the living present of multiple, overlapping racist (proto) genocides, formations of anti-Blackness, and reinscriptions of racial-colonial dominance. Abolitionist praxis inhabits—lives, breathes, and speaks—a pair of inseparable social truths: First, that liberation from gendered anti-Blackness and racial-colonial power, including state violence and related systemic logics of collective suffering, demoralization, and death, is entirely *practical* (though not always *pragmatic*), precisely because overturning and transforming such relations of dominance is a perpetual process of collective remaking (of self, sociality, politics, economy, culture, aesthetics, and so on); abolitionist freedom is not simply an end that is finally and securely achieved, but is a condition of being that resonates historically oppressed peoples' vast capacities to create, sustain, love, govern, and nourish under changing states of duress; and second, that the abolition of White Being and its genocidal logics of existence is the only ethical horizon toward which a collective liberation can strive if bare survival is not enough.

Notes

Introduction. "The Cause Is Effect": Inhabiting White Reconstruction

1. Sylvia Wynter, "Columbus, the Ocean Blue, and Fables That Stir the Mind: To Reinvent the Study of Letters," in *Poetics of the Americas: Race, Founding, and Textuality*, ed. Bainard Cowan and Jefferson Humphries (Baton Rouge: Louisiana State University Press, 1997), 151.

2. On anti-Blackness, João Costa Vargas and Moon-Kie Jung offer the following heuristic conception: "Heuristically . . . we understand antiblackness as structured, ubiquitous, and perduring disadvantages for Black people and structured advantages for nonblacks. Such articulated disadvantages and advantages take place in the realms of ontology (how individuals constitute and define themselves as such), sociability (lived social experience), and access to resources. Antiblackness helps us grasp the types of symbolic and actual forms of violence one is subjected to. The likelihood of social and physical death is a direct function of antiblackness." See João Costa Vargas and Moon-Kie Jung, Introduction to *Antiblackness* (João Costa Vargas and Moon-Kie Jung, eds.) (Durham, N.C.: Duke University Press, forthcoming). Calvin Warren's philosophical conceptualization provides a complementary framing: "*antiblackness*: an accretion of practices, knowledge systems, and institutions designed to impose nothing onto blackness and the unending domination/eradication of black presence as nothing incarnated. Put differently, antiblackness is anti-nothing. What is hated about blacks is this nothing, the ontological terror, they must embody for the metaphysical world." See Calvin Warren, *Ontological Terror: Blackness, Nihilism, and Emancipation* (Durham, N.C.: Duke University Press, 2018), 9.

3. Haunani-Kay Trask, *From a Native Daughter: Colonialism and Sovereignty in Hawai'i* (1993) (Honolulu: University of Hawai'i Press, 1999), 18

4. Frantz Fanon, *The Wretched of the Earth*, trans. Richard Philcox (1961; repr., New York: Grove Press, 2004), 5.

5. On White Being, see "Policing and the Violence of White Being: an Interview with Dylan Rodríguez" (commissioned interview with Casey Goonan), *Propter Nos* 1, no. 1 (Fall 2016): 8–18.

6. While the phrase permeates academic, journalistic, legal, and popular cultural texts, a few choice examples exemplify the spectrum of references to "post–civil rights" as a temporal and political moment. Eddie S. Glaude, Jr. reflects one of the primary assumptive premises of "post–civil rights" rhetoric in a *Time Magazine* op-ed, writing that "Trump broke the post–civil rights consensus that America would keep its racism quiet . . . I am convinced that, if we are to imagine the country as a genuinely multiracial democracy, we have to tell ourselves a better story about who we are, how we ended up here and why we keep returning to this hell." See Glaude, "Don't Let the Loud Bigots Distract You: America's Real Problem with Race Cuts Far Deeper" (op-ed), *Time Magazine*, September 6, 2018, https://time.com/5388356/our-racist-soul/.

Ta-Nehisi Coates offers a synthesis that largely adjoins with Glaude's, suggesting that: "The post-civil-rights consensus aims for the termination of injury. Remedy is beyond our field of vision. When old wounds fester, quackery is prescribed and hoary old fears and insidious old concepts burble to the surface—'matriarchy'; 'super-predators'; 'bio-underclass.'" See Coates, "The Black Family in the Age of Mass Incarceration," *The Atlantic*, October 2015, https://www.theatlantic.com /magazine/archive/2015/10/the-black-family-in-the-age-of-mass-incarceration/403246/.

Other interpretations of "post–civil rights" are readily evident across the ideological and political spectrum. See, for example, David Gergen and Jeremy Licht, "Politics, Post–Civil Rights," *U.S. News & World Report*, April 24, 2006, vol. 140, no. 15, p. 40; Terence Samuel, "Young, Black, and Post–Civil Rights," *The American Prospect* 18, no. 8 (September 2007), http://prospect.org/article/young -black-and-post-civil-rights; Eduardo Bonilla-Silva, *White Supremacy and Racism in the Post–Civil Rights Era* (Boulder, Colo.: Lynne Rienner, 2001); Eric K. Yamamoto, *Interracial Justice: Conflict and Reconciliation in Post–Civil Rights America* (New York: NYU Press, 1999); Matthew Frye Jacobson, *Roots Too: White Ethnic Revival in Post–Civil Rights America* (Cambridge: Harvard University Press, 2006).

7. Robert L. Allen, *Black Awakening in Capitalist America: An Analytic History* (1970; repr., Trenton, N.J.: Africa World Press, 1990), 17.

8. Dylan Rodríguez, "The Political Logic of the Non-Profit Industrial Complex," in *The Revolution Will Not Be Funded: Beyond the Non-Profit Industrial Complex*, ed. INCITE! Women of Color Against Violence (Cambridge, Mass.: South End Press, 2007), 21–40. See also Karen Ferguson's indispensable study *Top Down: The Ford Foundation, Black Power, and the Reinvention of Racial Liberalism* (Philadelphia: University of Pennsylvania, 2013).

9. Allen, *Black Awakening in Capitalist America*, 17.

10. See Nikki Giovanni, *Black Feeling, Black Talk, Black Judgement* (New York: William Morrow, 1970), 83; and Manning Marable, *Race, Reform, and Rebellion:*

The Second Reconstruction and Beyond in Black America, 1945–2006, 3rd ed. (1984; repr., Jackson: University Press of Mississippi, 2007).

11. See Cedric Robinson, *Black Marxism: The Making of the Black Radical Tradition* (1983; repr., Chapel Hill: University of North Carolina Press, 2000).

12. Noliwe Rooks, *White Money, Black Power: The Surprising History of African American Studies and the Crisis of Race in Higher Education* (Boston: Beacon Press, 2006).

13. Douglas S. Massey and Nancy A. Denton, *American Apartheid: Segregation and the Making of the Underclass* (Cambridge: Harvard University Press, 1993).

14. Stuart Hall, "Race, Articulation and Societies Structured in Dominance," *Sociological Theories: Race and Colonialism*, ed. UNESCO (Paris: UNESCO, 1980), 305–45.

15. See also Dylan Rodríguez, "White Supremacy," in *The Wiley-Blackwell Encyclopedia of Social Theory*, ed. Bryan S. Turner, Chang Kyung-Sup, Cynthia F. Epstein, Peter Kivisto, J. Michael Ryan, and William Outhwaite (Hoboken: Wiley-Blackwell, 2017).

16. Sylvia Wynter, "Unsettling the Coloniality of Being/power/truth/freedom: Towards the Human, After Man, Its Overrepresentation—An Argument," *CR: the New Centennial Review* 3, no. 3 (2003): 319.

17. Fanon, *The Wretched of the Earth*, 5 (emphasis added).

18. David Scott, "The Re-Enchantment of Humanism: An Interview with Sylvia Wynter," *Small Axe* 8 (2000): 131–32; Jasbir Puar, *Terrorist Assemblages: Homonationalism in Queer Times* (2007; repr., Durham, N.C.: Duke University Press, 2017), 3; and Rey Chow *The Protestant Ethnic and the Spirit of Capitalism* (New York: Columbia University Press, 2002), 3. For an overview of the discourses through which white supremacy and the ascendancy of White Being articulate across different historical and discursive contexts, see generally Tania Da Gupta, Carl E. James, Roger C. A. Maaka, Grace-Edward Galabuzi, and Chris Anderson, eds., *Race and Racialization: Essential Readings* (Toronto: Canadian Scholars' Press, 2007); Sylvia Wynter, "The Ceremony Must Be Found: After Humanism." *Boundary* 2 (1984): 19–70; Alexander G. Weheliye, *Habeas Viscus: Racializing Assemblages, Biopolitics, and Black Feminist Theories of the Human* (Durham, N.C.: Duke University Press, 2014); Tomás Almaguer, *Racial Fault Lines: The Historical Origins of White Supremacy in California* (Berkeley: University of California Press, 2009); David Lloyd, *Under Representation: The Racial Regime of Aesthetics* (New York: Fordham University Press, 2018).

19. See Scott, "The Re-Enchantment of Humanism: An Interview with Sylvia Wynter," 118–207 (emphasis in the original).

20. A full definition of white supremacy appears in Dylan Rodríguez, "White Supremacy," in *The Wiley-Blackwell Encyclopedia of Social Theory*, ed. Bryan S. Turner, Chang Kyung-Sup, Cynthia F. Epstein, Peter Kivisto, J. Michael Ryan, and William Outhwaite (Hoboken: Wiley-Blackwell, 2017).

21. On the continued relevance of apartheid logics, including "hypersegregation," to the United States in the decades following the official abolition of Jim Crow segregation, see generally João Helion Costa Vargas, *Never Meant to Survive: Genocide and Utopias in Black Diaspora Communities* (Lanham, Md.: Rowman & Littlefield, 2008); Traci Burch, "The Old Jim Crow: Racial Residential Segregation and Neighborhood Imprisonment," *Law & Policy* 36, no. 3 (2014): 223–55; Chenoa A. Flippen, "The More Things Change the More They Stay the Same: the Future of Residential Segregation in America," *City & Community* 15, no. 1 (2016): 14–17; Ron Johnston, Michael Poulsen, and James Forrest, "Ethnic and Racial Segregation in U.S. Metropolitan Areas, 1980–2000: the Dimensions of Segregation Revisited," *Urban Affairs Review* 42, no. 4 (2007): 479–504; Douglas S. Massey and Nancy A. Denton. "Hypersegregation in U.S. Metropolitan Areas: Black and Hispanic Segregation Along Five Dimensions," *Demography* 26, no. 3 (1989): 373; Douglas S. Massey and Nancy A. Denton, *American Apartheid: Segregation and the Making of the Underclass* (Cambridge: Harvard University Press, 1993); Douglas S. Massey and Jonathan Tannen, "A Research Note on Trends in Black Hypersegregation," *Demography* 52, no. 3 (2015): 1025–34.

On U.S. settler colonialism, see Alyosha Goldstein and Alex Lubin, eds., "Settler Colonialism," *South Atlantic Quarterly* 107, no. 4 (Fall 2008) (Durham, N.C.: Duke University Press, 2008); Glen S. Coulthard, *Red Skin, White Masks: Rejecting the Colonial Politics of Recognition* (Minneapolis: University of Minnesota Press, 2014); Ikuko Asaka, *Tropical Freedom: Climate, Settler Colonialism, and Black Exclusion in the Age of Emancipation* (Durham, N.C.: Duke University Press, 2017); Mark Rifkin, *Settler Common Sense: Queerness and Everyday Colonialism in the American Renaissance* (Minneapolis: University of Minnesota Press, 2014); Audra Simpson, *Mohawk Interruptus: Political Life Across the Borders of Settler States* (Durham, N.C.: Duke University Press, 2014); Iyko Day, *Alien Capital: Asian Racialization and the Logic of Settler Colonial Capitalism* (Durham, N.C.: Duke University Press, 2016); and Alyosha Goldstein, ed., *Formations of United States Colonialism* (Durham, N.C.: Duke University Press, 2014).

22. Antonio Gramsci provides a well-circulated outlining of hegemony and historical blocs in "The Modern Prince," in *Selections from the Prison Notebooks of Antonio Gramsci*, ed. Quintin Hoare and Geoffrey Nowell-Smith (New York: International Publishers, 1971), 123–205.

23. Stuart Hall, "Gramsci's Relevance for the Study of Race and Ethnicity," *Journal of Communication Inquiry* 10, no. 2 (1986): 15.

24. Ibid., 16–17.

25. Ibid.

26. See generally Luana Ross, *Inventing the Savage: The Social Construction of Native American Criminality* (Austin: University of Texas Press, 1998); Ibram X. Kendi, *Stamped from the Beginning: The Definitive History of Racist Ideas in America* (New York: Nation Books, 2016); Winthrop D. Jordan *The White Man's Burden: Historical Origins of Racism in the United States* (New York: Oxford

University Press, 1974); Laura E. Gómez, *Manifest Destinies: The Making of the Mexican American Race* (New York: NYU Press, 2008); Lon Kurashige, *Two Faces of Exclusion: The Untold History of Anti-Asian Racism in the United States* (Chapel Hill: University of North Carolina Press, 2016); and Reginald Horsman, *Race and Manifest Destiny: The Origins of American Racial Anglo-Saxonism* (Cambridge: Harvard University Press, 1981).

27. In addition to previously cited texts, see generally, Sarah Haley, *No Mercy Here: Gender, Punishment, and the Making of Jim Crow Modernity* (Durham, N.C.: University of North Carolina Press, 2016); David M. Oshinsky, *Worse Than Slavery: Parchman Farm and the Ordeal of Jim Crow Justice* (New York: Free Press, 1996); Joy James, *Warfare in the American Homeland: Policing and Prison in a Penal Democracy* (Durham, N.C.: Duke University Press, 2007); and Micol Seigel, *Violence Work: State Power and the Limits of Police* (Durham, N.C.: Duke University Press, 2018).

28. See generally, David R. Roediger, *The Wages of Whiteness: Race and the Making of the American Working Class* (London: Verso, 1991); and Joel Olson, *The Abolition of White Democracy* (Minneapolis: University of Minnesota Press, 2004).

29. Numerous works cited in this Introduction and succeeding chapters illuminate the racial-colonial violence of the United States as a conquest-based settler society. In addition to the Native and Indigenous thinkers cited throughout this book, see Gerald Horne, *The Apocalypse of Settler Colonialism: The Roots of Slavery, White Supremacy, and Capitalism in Seventeenth-Century North America and the Caribbean* (New York: Monthly Review Press, 2017); Patrick Wolfe, *Settler Colonialism and the Transformation of Anthropology: The Politics and Poetics of an Ethnographic Event* (London: Cassell, 1999); Candace Fujikane and Jonathan Y. Okamura, *Asian Settler Colonialism: From Local Governance to the Habits of Everyday Life in Hawai'i* (Honolulu: University of Hawai'i Press, 2008); and Scott L. Morgensen, *Spaces Between Us: Queer Settler Colonialism and Indigenous Decolonization* (Minneapolis: University of Minnesota Press, 2011).

30. Haunani-Kay Trask, "The New World Order," in *From a Native Daughter: Colonialism and Sovereignty in Hawai'i* (1993; repr., Honolulu: University of Hawai'i Press, 1999), 59–60.

31. In addition to texts mentioned previously, see David E. Stannard, *American Holocaust: Columbus and the Conquest of the New World* (New York: Oxford University Press, 1992).

32. Jodi Melamed, *Represent and Destroy: Rationalizing Violence in the New Racial Capitalism* (Minneapolis: University of Minnesota Press, 2011), 1.

33. Ibid., xv, 1.

34. Michael Omi and Howard Winant, *Racial Formation in the United States*, 3rd ed. (1986; repr., New York: Routledge 2015).

35. Howard Winant, *The World Is a Ghetto: Race and Democracy since World War II* (New York: Basic Books, 2001); and Howard Winant, *The New Politics of Race: Globalism, Difference, Justice* (Minneapolis: University of Minnesota Press, 2004).

36. Melamed, *Represent and Destroy*, 4–7.

37. See Dean Spade, *Normal Life: Administrative Violence, Critical Trans Politics, and the Limits of Law* (Brooklyn: South End Press, 2011); Nick Mitchell, *Disciplinary Matters: Black Studies, Women's Studies, and the Neoliberal University* (Durham, N.C.: Duke University Press, 2020); and Roderick A. Ferguson, *The Reorder of Things: The University and Its Pedagogies of Minority Difference* (Minneapolis: University Of Minnesota Press, 2012).

38. Melamed, *Represent and Destroy*, 5.

39. Ibid., 25.

40. Ibid., 139.

41. Jodi Kim, *Ends of Empire: Asian American Critique and the Cold War* (Minneapolis: University of Minnesota Press, 2010), 3.

42. Melamed, *Represent and Destroy*, 139.

43. Ibid., 4.

44. Omi and Winant, *Racial Formation in the United States*, 132 (emphasis in the original).

45. Ibid.

46. Melamed, *Represent and Destroy*, 6.

47. Manning Marable, "Preface," in *Race, Reform and Rebellion: The Second Reconstruction in Black America, 1945–1982* (London: Macmillan Press, 1984), xii.

48. Ibid., 169.

49. Ibid., 190.

50. Glen Sean Coulthard, *Red Skin, White Masks: Rejecting the Colonial Politics of Recognition*, 3 (emphasis in the original).

51. See Sara Ahmed, *On Being Included: Racism and Diversity in Institutional Life* (Durham, N.C.: Duke University Press, 2012).

52. Michel Foucault, "Truth and Power," in *Power/Knowledge: Selected Interviews and Other Writings, 1972–1977*, ed. Colin Gordon (New York: Pantheon Press, 1980), 117.

53. See Stuart Hall, "Race, Articulation, and Societies Structured in Dominance," in *Black British Cultural Studies: A Reader*, ed. Houston A. Baker, Jr., Manthia Diawara, and Ruth H. Lindeborg (1980; repr., Chicago: University of Chicago Press, 1996), 16–60.

54. Michel Foucault, "7 January 1976," in *"Society Must Be Defended": Lectures at the Collége de France, 1975–1976*, trans. David Macey (New York: Picador, 1997), 8–10.

55. See Dylan Rodríguez, "Disrupted Foucault: Los Angeles' Coalition Against Police Abuse (CAPA) and the Obsolescence of White Academic Raciality," in *Active Intolerance: Michel Foucault, the Prisons Information Group, and the Future of Abolition*, ed. Perry Zurn and Andrew Dilts (New York: Palgrave Macmillan, 2016), 145–68.

56. Denise Ferreira da Silva, *Toward a Global Idea of Race* (Minneapolis: University of Minnesota Press, 2007), 4.

57. In addition to Silva, *Toward a Global Idea of Race*, see Wynter, "Unsettling the Coloniality."

58. Denise Ferreira da Silva wages a largely underappreciated and devastating critique of Foucault along these very (racial) lines, a move that i read as a proxy for a far broader interrogation of white academic raciality *sui generis*:

> Foucault's excavations do not reach the place where European particularity is but an effect of the strategies of this productive ruler. For this reason, though a crucial contribution to the critique of modern representation, his own deployments of the thesis of productivity remain within its limits because he does challenge the ontological prerogative of interiority that guides accounts that locate man in transparency. (Silva, *Toward a Global Idea of Race*, 25)

59. Ashon Crawley, "University," in *Keywords for African American Studies*, ed. Erica R. Edwards, Roderick A. Ferguson, and Jeffrey O. G. Ogbar (New York: NYU Press, 2018), 214.

60. Rodríguez, "Disrupted Foucault." A number of works inform this engagement with the regime of white academic raciality, including Joy James, *Transcending the Talented Tenth: Black Leaders and American Intellectuals* (New York: Routledge, 1997); Lewis R. Gorson, *Fanon and the Crisis of European Man: An Essay on Philosophy and the Human Sciences* (New York: Routledge, 1995); Haunani-Kay Trask, *From a Native Daughter: Colonialism and Sovereignty in Hawai'i* (Monroe, Maine: Common Courage Press, 1993); Mitchell, *Disciplinary Matters*; Ferguson, *The Reorder of Things*; and Ashon Crawley, "University."

61. Dian Million, "Felt Theory: An Indigenous Feminist Approach to Affect and History," *Wicazo Sa Review* 24, no. 2 (Fall 2009): 54.

62. See generally, Cedric Robinson, *Black Marxism: The Making of the Black Radical Tradition* (1983; repr., Chapel Hill: University of North Carolina Press, 2000); Clyde A. Woods, *Development Arrested: The Blues and Plantation Power in the Mississippi Delta* (London: Verso, 1998); Joy James, *Shadowboxing: Representations of Black Feminist Politics* (New York: St. Martin's Press, 1999); Patricia Hill Collins, *Black Feminist Thought: Knowledge, Consciousness, and the Politics of Empowerment*, 10th Anniversary edition (New York: Routledge, 2000); Chela Sandoval, *Methodology of the Oppressed* (Minneapolis: University of Minnesota Press, 2000).

63. On the matter of premature death as a logic of racial power, see Ruth Wilson Gilmore's short definition of "racism" in "Race and Globalization," in *Geographies of Global Change: Remapping the World*, 2nd. ed., ed. R. J. Johnston, Peter J. Taylor, and Michael J. Watts (Oxford: Blackwell Publishing, 2002), 261: "Racism is the state-sanctioned and/or extra-legal production and exploitation of group-differentiated vulnerabilities to premature death, in distinct yet densely interconnected political geographies."

64. David Lloyd, *Under Representation: The Racial Regime of Aesthetics* (New York: Fordham University Press, 2019), 3.

65. Nicole Fleetwood, *Troubling Vision: Performance, Visuality, and Blackness* (Chicago: University of Chicago Press, 2011), 7.

66. Ibid., 6.

67. Katherine McKittrick, *Demonic Grounds: Black Women and the Cartographies of Struggle* (Minneapolis: University of Minnesota Press, 2006), xxiv.

68. Ibid., xxv–xxvi.

69. Here, McKittrick is specifically working with the critical tools developed in Wynter's essay "Beyond Miranda's Meanings: Un/Silencing the 'Demonic Ground' of Caliban's Women," in *Out of the Kumbla: Caribbean Women and Literature*, ed. Carole Boyce Davies and Elaine Savory Fido (Trenton: Africa World Press, 1990) 355–72.

70. McKittrick, *Demonic Grounds*, xxv.

71. Scott, "The Re-Enchantment of Humanism," 165.

72. For a broad scholarly overview of the debates and critical problematics defining such cultural and institutional reconfigurations in the liberal aftermath of the post–Jim Crow period, see C. W. Watson, *Multiculturalism* (Buckingham, England: Open University Press, 2000); Amy Gutmann and Charles Taylor, *Multiculturalism: Examining the Politics of Recognition* (Princeton, N.J.: Princeton University Press, 1994); Jack Citrin and David O. Sears, *American Identity and the Politics of Multiculturalism* (New York: Cambridge University Press, 2014); Avery Gordon and Christopher Newfield, *Mapping Multiculturalism* (Minneapolis: University of Minnesota Press, 1996); Lawrence Foster and Patricia Susan Herzog, *Defending Diversity: Contemporary Philosophical Perspectives on Pluralism and Multiculturalism* (Amherst: University of Massachusetts Press, 1994); Jacob T. Levy, *The Multiculturalism of Fear* (Oxford: Oxford University Press, 2000); P. J. Kelly, *Multiculturalism Reconsidered: "Culture and Equality" and Its Critics* (Cambridge, UK: Polity Press, 2002).

73. See generally Wendy Brown, *Regulating Aversion: Tolerance in the Age of Identity and Empire* (Princeton, N.J.: Princeton University Press, 2006).

74. "Irruption," *Oxford English Dictionary*, https://www.oed.com/view/Entry /99889?redirectedFrom=irruption#eid November 2019.

75. Lewis Gordon, *Fanon and the Crisis of European Man*, 81; Zakiyyah Iman Jackson, *Becoming Human: Matter and Meaning in an Antiblack World* (New York: NYU Press, 2020); Saidiya Hartman, *Scenes of Subjection: Terror, Slavery, and Self-Making in Nineteenth Century America* (New York: Oxford University Press, 1997).

76. Ruth Wilson Gilmore, *Golden Gulag: Prisons, Surplus, Crisis, and Opposition in Globalizing California* (Berkeley: University of California Press, 2007), 28.

1. "I Used Her Ashes": Multiculturalist White Supremacy/ Counterinsurgency/Domestic War

1. On biopolitical power, see Michel Foucault, *Society Must Be Defended: Lectures at the Collège de France, 1975–76* (New York: Picador, 2003). Regarding the

particular role of "embodiment" in interdisciplinary studies of the body, Casper and Currah write,

> [T]he notion of embodiment in the social sciences and humanities has been foundational for critically grounding body studies. In this scholarship, the Cartesian notion of "the ghost in the machine" has been supplanted by critical approaches that center the phenomenological concept of embodiment. . . .
>
> Much of the scholarship in *Corpus*, however, moves beyond these somewhat obligatory nods to embodiment, complicating the notion, propelling it forward, or even rejecting it as the first point of entry into studies of the body.

See Paisley Currah and Monica J. Casper, "Bringing Forth the Body: An Introduction," in *Corpus: An Interdisciplinary Reader on Bodies and Knowledge* (New York: Palgrave Macmillan), 14.

2. An earlier articulation of the argument developed in the opening part of this chapter appears in "Multiculturalist White Supremacy and the Substructure of the Body," in *Corpus: An Interdisciplinary Reader on Bodies and Knowledge*, ed. Monica J. Casper and Paisley Currah (New York: Palgrave MacMillan, 2011), 39–60.

3. Karen Barad, "Posthumanist Performativity: Toward an Understanding of How Matter Comes to Matter," *Signs: Journal of Women in Culture and Society* 28, no. 3 (2003): 809 (801–31).

4. Ibid., 810.

5. Paisley Currah and Monica J. Casper, "Bringing Forth the Body: An Introduction," in *Corpus: An Interdisciplinary Reader on Bodies and Knowledge* (New York: Palgrave Macmillan), 5 (1–20).

6. Ibid., 14–15.

7. Hortense J. Spillers, "Mama's Baby, Papa's Maybe: An American Grammar Book," *Diacritics* 17, no. 2 (Summer 1987): 67.

8. Stuart Hall, Chas Critcher, Tony Jefferson, John Clarke, and Brian Roberts, *Policing the Crisis: "Mugging," the State and Law and Order* (London: Macmillan, 1978), 394.

9. See Sut Jhally and Stuart Hall, "Race: The Floating Signifier," video recording (Northampton, Mass.: Media Education Foundation, 1996).

10. Cedric Robinson, *Black Marxism: The Making of the Black Radical Tradition* (1983; repr., Chapel Hill: University of North Carolina Press, 2000), 26.

11. See David Theo Goldberg, *Racist Culture: Philosophy and the Politics of Meaning* (Cambridges: Blackwell, 1993).

12. See generally, Reginald Horsman, *Race and Manifest Destiny: The Origins of American Racial Anglo-Saxonism* (Cambridge: Harvard University Press, 1981); Winthrop D. Jordan, *White Over Black: American Attitudes Toward the Negro, 1550–1812*, 2nd ed. (1968; repr., Chapel Hill: University of North Carolina Press, 2012) and *The White Man's Burden: Historical Origins of Racism in the United States* (New York: Oxford University Press, 1974); Denise Ferreira da Silva, *Toward a*

Global Idea of Race (Minneapolis: University of Minnesota Press, 2007); David E. Stannard, *American Holocaust: The Conquest of the New World* (New York: Oxford University Press, 1992); and George M. Frederickson, *The Black Image in the White Mind: The Debate on Afro-American Character and Destiny, 1817–1914* (1971; repr., Middletown, Conn.: Wesleyan University Press, 1987).

13. See Jasbir Puar's examination of "white ascendancy" in *Terrorist Assemblages: Homonationalism in Queer Times* (Durham, N.C.: Duke University Press, 2007).

14. Tiffany Lethabo King, *The Black Shoals: Offshore Formations of Black and Native Studies* (Durham, N.C.: Duke University Press, 2019), xii.

15. Robinson, *Black Marxism*, 28 (emphasis added).

16. Ibid., 10.

17. Ibid., 24.

18. See Michael Omi and Howard Winant, *Racial Formation in the United States*, 3rd. ed. (New York: Routledge, 2015).

19. Ibid., 25.

20. On the dynamic role of race in the production of social, economic, and state hegemonies, see Stuart Hall, "Race, Articulation and Societies Structured in Dominance," *Sociological Theories: Race and Colonialism*, ed. UNESCO (Paris: UNESCO, 1980), 305–45.

21. See Omi and Winant, *Racial Formation*. While there are myriad examples of this scholarly tendency, Omi and Winant's periodization in their paradigm-setting *Racial Formation in the United States* is worth critically revisiting precisely due to the wide influence of racial formation theory in the last fifteen or so years. On the one hand, the authors neatly compartmentalize what they call the period of U.S. "racial dictatorship" between the years 1607–1865, when "most non-whites were firmly eliminated from the sphere of politics" (65–66). On the other, they conceptualize "white supremacy" rather narrowly as the ideological premise of a fringe "Far Right" political reaction to the aftermath of the liberal reforms of the civil rights movement. In their view, beginning in the 1980s this Far Right attempted to "*revive*" white supremacy by "reassert[ing] white identity and reaffirm[ing] the nation as 'the white man's country'" (120). In my analysis, this historical and ideological flattening of white supremacy is both theoretically simplistic and politically dangerous, to the extent that Omi and Winant's presentation does not take seriously the multiple ways that white supremacist social logics (and ideologies) have constituted and/or deformed the institutional conceptions of "democracy," "freedom/liberty," "citizenship," and so on.

22. Silva, *Toward a Global Idea of Race*.

23. See generally Silva, *Toward a Global Idea of Race*; Jordan, *White Over Black*; Goldberg, *Racist Culture*; George M. Frederickson, *The Black Image in the White Mind: The Debate on Afro-American Character and Destiny, 1817–1914* (New York: Harper and Row, 1971); Audrey Smedley, *Race in North America: Origin and Evolution of a Worldview* (Boulder: Westview Press, 2007). David Roediger and Steve Martinot offer two of the most densely engaged scholarly studies of how white

supremacy generates a specific political and cultural formation that is not reducible to the processes of racialization and racial formation. See Roediger, *The Wages of Whiteness: Race and the Making of the American Working Class* (London: Verso, 2007); and Martinot, *The Rule of Racialization: Class, Identity, Governance* (Philadelphia: Temple University Press, 2003).

24. Michael Omi and Howard Winant's historical understanding of racial formation and the "racial state" reproduces precisely the conceptual (and political) errors that I am trying to correct here—namely, that "white supremacy" composes a relatively compartmentalized *moment* in the historical life of racial formation in the United States, and thus "racism" is a kind of "racial project" (or mode of racialization) that is *not* organically linked to the changing historical continuities of white supremacy as a logic of social domination. See especially Omi and Winant, *Racial Formation*, 69–76.

25. See Robinson, *Black Marxism* and Sylvia Wynter, "Unsettling the Coloniality of Being/Power/Truth/Freedom: Towards the Human, After Man, Its Overrepresentation—An Argument," *CR: the New Centennial Review* 3, no. 3 (2003): 257–337. On the anti-Black ontological premise of civil society, see Frank B. Wilderson, III, "The Prison Slave as Hegemony's (Silent) Scandal," *Social Justice: A Journal of Crime, Conflict, and World Order* 30, no. 2 (2003): 18–27.

26. United States Department of the Army, *Counterinsurgency*, Headquarters, Dept. of the Army, 2006 (https://permanent.access.gpo.gov/lps79762/FM_3-24.pdf), p. 1–1.

27. See Public Broadcasting Service (U.S.), and WGBH (Television Station: Boston, Mass.). *LAPD Blues: The Story of Los Angeles' Gangsta Cops & the Corruption Scandal That Has Shaken the Once Great LAPD* (Boston: PBS Online/ WGBH Frontline, 2008), http://www.pbs.org/wgbh/pages/frontline/shows/lapd/bare .html; and Rampart Independent Review Panel, and Los Angeles (CA) Police Commission, *Report of the Rampart Independent Review Panel: A Report to the Los Angeles Board of Police Commissioners Concerning the Operations, Policies, and Procedures of the Los Angeles Police Department in the Wake of the Rampart Scandal* (Los Angeles: Rampart Independent Review Panel, 2000).

28. U.S. v. City of Los Angeles, docket/court 2:00-cv-11769-GAF-RC (C.D. Cal.), 1.

29. Joel Rubin, "Federal Judge Lifts LAPD Consent Decree," *Los Angeles Times*, May 16, 2013, https://www.latimes.com/local/la-xpm-2013-may-16-la-me-lapd-consent -decree-20130517-story.html.

30. See *Gay Games VII: Sports and Cultural Festival Chicago 2006* (DVD) (Wolfe Video, 2007) (135 m.); "10th Annual International Criminal Justice Diversity Symposium," Los Angeles Law Enforcement Gays and Lesbians (LEGAL) website, http://www.losangeleslegal.org/pages/symposium/symposium1-cover.shtml; and William Bratton and George Kelling, "There Are No Cracks in the Broken Windows: Ideological Academics Are Trying to Undermine a Perfectly Good Idea," *National Review Online*, February 28, 2006, https://www.nationalreview.com/2006 /02/there-are-no-cracks-broken-windows-william-bratton-george-kelling/. On the

history and ongoing legacies of "Zero Tolerance" and "Broken Windows" policing, see Rachel Herzing, "No Bratton-style policing in Oakland: Unraveling the fraying edges of zero tolerance," *San Francisco Bay View*, January 22, 2013, https://sfbayview .com/2013/01/no-bratton-style-policing-in-oakland-unraveling-the-fraying-edges-of -zero-tolerance/; Micol Seigel, "William Bratton in the Other L.A.," in *Beyond Walls and Cages: Prisons, Borders, and Global Crisis* (University of Georgia Press, 2012), 115–25; João Costa Vargas, *Catching Hell in the City of Angels: Life and the Meanings of Blackness in South Central Los Angeles* (Minneapolis: University of Minnesota Press, 2006); Bernard E. Harcourt, *Illusion of Order: The False Promise of Broken Windows Policing* (Cambridge: Harvard University Press, 2001); and Christian Parenti, *Lockdown America: Police and Prisons in the Age of Crisis* (New York: Verso, 2000).

31. Rachel Herzing, "No Bratton-style policing in Oakland: Unraveling the fraying edges of zero tolerance," *San Francisco Bay View*, January 22, 2013, https:// sfbayview.com/2013/01/no-bratton-style-policing-in-oakland-unraveling-the-fraying -edges-of-zero-tolerance/.

32. Nelson Lim, Carl Matthies, Greg Ridgeway, and Brian Gifford, *To Protect and Serve: Enhancing the Efficiency of LAPD* (Santa Monica: RAND Corporation, 2009), 4, xix.

33. On policing as domestic war, see Stuart Schrader, *Badges Without Borders. How Global Counterinsurgency Transformed American Policing* (Berkeley: University of California Press, 2019); and Mark Neocleous, *The Fabrication of Social Order: A Critical Theory of Police Power* (Sterling, Va.: Pluto Press, 2000).

34. Mark Neocleous, *Imagining the State* (Maidenhead, Berkshire: Open University Press, 2003), 11.

35. Max Felker-Kantor, "Introduction: The Police Power," *Policing Los Angeles: Race, Resistance, and the Rise of the LAPD* (Chapel Hill: University of North Carolina Press, 2018) (digital edition).

36. On the racial, class, and gender relations of power and state violence that have shaped the historical geographies of Los Angeles, see Mike Davis, *City of Quartz: Excavating the Future in Los Angeles*, 6th ed. (1990; repr., London: Verso, 2006); Scott Kurashige, *The Shifting Grounds of Race: Black and Japanese Americans in the Making of Multiethnic Los Angeles* (Princeton, N.J.: Princeton University Press, 2008); Daniel Widener, *Black Arts West: Culture and Struggle in Postwar Los Angeles* (Durham, N.C.: Duke University Press, 2010); Laura Pulido, Laura R. Barraclough, and Wendy Cheng, eds., *A People's Guide to Los Angeles* (Berkeley: University of California Press, 2012); Laura Pulido and Josh Kun, eds., *Black and Brown in Los Angeles: Beyond Conflict and Coalition* (Berkeley: University of California Press, 2014); and Laura Pulido, *Black, Brown, Yellow, and Left Radical Activism in Southern California* (Berkeley: University of California Press, 2006). While journalistic accounts of LAPD violence are widely available, a recent article in the respected international periodical *The Guardian* provides a symptomatic overview. See Sam Levin, "Hundreds Dead, No One Charged: The

Uphill Battle Against Los Angeles Police Killings," *The Guardian* (U.S. edition), August 24, 2018, https://www.theguardian.com/us-news/2018/aug/24/los-angeles -police-violence-shootings-african-american.

37. See Sandra E. Garcia, "'LAPD Is Hiring!': Recruitment Ad on *Breitbart* Sparks an Inquiry," *The New York Times*, September 29, 2019, https://www.nytimes .com/2019/09/29/us/lapd-recruitment-ads-breitbart.html; Alex Horton, "LAPD Recruitment Ad on *Breitbart* Was So Bewildering That the Chief Wondered Whether It Was a Fake," *The Washington Post*, September 29, 2019, https://www .washingtonpost.com/nation/2019/09/29/lapd-recruitment-ad-breitbart-was-so -bewildering-that-chief-wondered-if-it-was-fake/; and David Zahniser, "The LAPD Opens an Inquiry Into Job Posting on Right-Wing *Breitbart* Website," *Los Angeles Times*, September 28, 2019, https://www.latimes.com/california/story/2019-09-28/lapd -inquiry-job-listing-breitbart-police-chief-michel-moore-recruitment.

38. Tim Arango, "California Today: 'This Is Not Your Grandfather's LAPD,'" *The New York Times*, June 8, 2018, https://www.nytimes.com/2018/06/08/us/california -today-los-angeles-police-chief.html (emphasis added).

39. See Kenneth Bolton Jr. and Joe R. Feagin, *Black in Blue: African-American Police Officers and Racism* (New York: Routledge, 2004); Matthew Horace and Ron Harris, *The Black and the Blue: A Cop Reveals the Crimes, Racism, and Injustice in America's Law Enforcement* (New York: Hachette Books, 2018); and Juan Antonio Juarez, *Brotherhood of Corruption: A Cop Breaks the Silence on Police Abuse, Brutality, and Racial Profiling* (Chicago: Chicago Review Press, 2004).

40. Ian Ayres and Jonathan Borowsky, *A Study of Racially Disparate Outcomes in the Los Angeles Police Department*, ACLU report (October 2008): 27.

41. On the neoconservative movement to end affirmative action and progressive attempts to resist its abolition, see Paul M. Ong, ed., *Impacts of Affirmative Action: Policies and Consequences in California* (Walnut Creek, Calif.: AltaMira Press, 1999); and Lydia Chávez, *The Color Bind: California's Battle to End Affirmative Action* (Berkeley: University of California Press, 1998).

42. Damien M. Sojoyner, *First Strike: Educational Enclosures in Black Los Angeles* (Minneapolis: University of Minnesota Press, 2016), 72.

43. Ibid., 73.

44. The ACLU asserts, "Los Angeles County Jails, with an average daily population nearing 22,000, is the biggest jail system in the world." See ACLU, "LA County Jails," accessed March 2019, https://www.aclu.org/issues/prisoners-rights /cruel-inhuman-and-degrading-conditions/la-county-jails?redirect=la-county-jails. On Los Angeles jails, see Amanda Petteruti and Nastassia Walsh, *Jailing Communities: The Impact of Jail Expansion and Effective Public Safety Strategies*, Justice Policy Institute Report (Washington, DC: Justice Policy Institute, 2008), see especially pages 23 and 26; "Los Angeles County Jail System By the Numbers," *Los Angeles Almanac*, accessed March 2019, http://www.laalmanac.com/crime/cr25b.php; James Austin, Wendy Naro-Ware, Roger Ocker Robert Harris, Robin Allen, *Evaluation of the Current and Future Los Angeles County Jail Population*, JFA Institute report,

April 10, 2012; and Breeanna Hare and Lisa Rose, "Pop. 17,049: Welcome to America's Largest Jail," *CNN*, September 26, 2016, https://www.cnn.com/2016/09/22/us/lisa-ling -this-is-life-la-county-jail-by-the-numbers/index.html.

45. "Frontline: L.A.P.D. Blues," *Frontline*, Public Broadcasting Service, airdate May 15, 2001. For historical context, see Kristian Williams, *Our Enemies in Blue: Police and Power in America* (Cambridge, Mass.: South End Press, 2007).

46. Joel Rubin, "11 LAPD Officers Face Discipline in May Day Melee," *Los Angeles Times*, September 17, 2008, http://articles.latimes.com/2008/sep/17/local/me -mayday17.

47. Melina Abudullah, "Why LA's DA Refuses to Prosecute Killer Cops," Rising Up with Sonali, KPFK 90.7 Los Angeles, Calif., September 29, 2017, https://www .risingupwithsonali.com/why-las-da-refuses-to-prosecute-killer-cops/.

48. Black Lives Matter Los Angeles, "Prosecute Police Who Kill Our People," public petition, accessed March 2019, https://campaigns.organizefor.org/petitions/los -angeles-county-da-prosecute-police-who-kill-our-people. See also, Black Lives Matter Los Angeles, "Sign BLMLA's Petition to Prosecute Police Who Kill Our People," Black Lives Matter website, accessed March 2019, https://blacklivesmatter .com/sign-blmlas-petition-to-prosecute-police-who-kill-our-people/ (emphasis in original).

49. Kate Mather, "L.A. Agrees to Pay Nearly $300,000 to Settle Case of Woman Who Died in LAPD Jail Cell," *Los Angeles Times*, December 13, 2017, https://www .latimes.com/local/lanow/la-me-ln-lapd-settlements-20171213-story.html.

50. Isra Ibrahim, "Woman Throws Ashes of Niece Who Died in Police Custody at LAPD Chief," *The Black Youth Project*, May 11, 2018, http://blackyouthproject .com/woman-throws-ashes-of-niece-who-died-in-police-custody-at-lapd-chief/. See also Kristine Phillips, "'That's Wakiesha!' A Woman Said as She Threw Her Niece's Ashes at the Los Angeles Police Chief," *The Washington Post*, May 9, 2018, https:// www.washingtonpost.com/news/post-nation/wp/2018/05/09/thats-wakiesha-a-woman -said-as-she-threw-her-nieces-ashes-at-the-los-angeles-police-chief/?utm_term= .e7ddaa5c98c6.

51. Robinson, *Black Marxism*, 317.

52. See Sylvia Wynter and Katherine McKittrick, "Unparalleled Catastrophe for Our Species? Or, to Give Humanness a Different Future: Conversations," in Katherine McKittrick, ed., *Sylvia Wynter: On Being Human as Praxis* (Durham, N.C.: Duke University Press, 2015), 9–89.

2. "Let the Past Be Forgotten . . .": Remaking White Being, from Reconstruction to Pacification

1. W. E. B. Du Bois, *Darkwater: Voices From Within the Veil* (New York: Harcourt, Brace and Howe, 1920), 29.

2. C. L. R. James, *The Black Jacobins: Toussaint L'Ouverture and the San Domingo Revolution*, 2nd ed. (1963; repr., New York: Vintage Books, 1989), 33.

3. João Costa Vargas and Moon-Kie Jung, Introduction to *Antiblackness*, ed. João Costa Vargas and Moon-Kie Jung (Durham, N.C.: Duke University Press, forthcoming).

4. On Civilization and savagery, in addition to texts cited elsewhere in this book, see H. L. T. Quan, *Growth Against Democracy: Savage Developmentalism in the Modern World* (Lanham, Md.: Lexington Books, 2012); and Roy Harvey Pearce, *Savagism and Civilization: A Study of the Indian and the American Mind* (1953; repr., Berkeley: University of California Press, 1988). Regarding the genocidal, ecocidal, and land displacing logics of empire and the modern nation-state, see Omer Bartov, *Mirrors of Destruction: War, Genocide, and Modern Identity* (Oxford: Oxford University Press, 2000); Reginald Horsman, *Race and Manifest Destiny: The Origins of American Racial Anglo-Saxonism* (Cambridge: Harvard University Press, 1981); Keith L. Camacho, *Cultures of Commemoration: The Politics of War, Memory, and History in the Mariana Islands* (Honolulu: University of Hawai'i Press, 2011); and Lisa Lowe, *The Intimacies of Four Continents* (Durham, N.C.: Duke University Press, 2015). In addition to the vital work of Sylvia Wynter, i rely on the following authors for their critical approaches to the long humanist project: Winthrop D. Jordan, *The White Man's Burden: Historical Origins of Racism in the United States* (New York: Oxford University Press, 1974); David Theo Goldberg, *Racist Culture: Philosophy and the Politics of Meaning* (Cambridge, Mass.: Blackwell, 1993); Saidiya Hartman, *Scenes of Subjection: Terror, Slavery, and Self-Making in Nineteenth Century America* (New York: Oxford University Press, 1997); and Alexander G. Weheliye, *Habeas Viscus: Racializing Assemblages, Biopolitics, and Black Feminist Theories of the Human* (Durham, N.C.: Duke University Press, 2014).

On white raciality, social/civil death, and personhood, see David R. Roediger *The Wages of Whiteness: Race and the Making of the American Working Class* (London: Verso, 1991); Mae M. Ngai, *Impossible Subjects: Illegal Aliens and the Making of Modern America* (Princeton, N.J.: Princeton University Press, 2004); Patterson, Orlando *Slavery and Social Death: A Comparative Study* (Cambridge: Harvard University Press, 1982); Joshua M. Price, *Prison and Social Death* (New Brunswick, N.J.: Rutgers University Press, 2015); and Geoffrey Adelsberg, Lisa Guenther, and Scott C. Zeman, eds., *Death and Other Penalties: Philosophy in a Time of Mass Incarceration* (New York: Fordham University Press, 2015).

5. Pearce, *Savagism and Civilization*, 91.

6. Stephanie E. Smallwood, *Saltwater Slavery: A Middle Passage from Africa to American Diaspora* (Cambridge: Harvard University Press, 2007), 122.

7. See especially Tiffany Willoughby-Herard, *Waste of a White Skin: The Carnegie Corporation and the Racial Logic of White Vulnerability* (Berkeley: University of California Press, 2015).

8. Willoughby-Herard, *Waste of a White Skin*, 3 (emphasis in the original).

9. See Dylan Rodríguez, "Disrupted Foucault: Los Angeles' Coalition Against Police Abuse (CAPA) and the Obsolescence of White Academic Raciality," in *Active Intolerance: Michel Foucault, the Prisons Information Group, and the Future of Abolition*, ed. Perry Zurn and Andrew Dilts (New York: Palgrave Macmillan, 2016).

10. See Cheryl I. Harris, *Whiteness as Property*, 106 Harv. L. Rev. 1707 (1993).

11. See Giorgio Agamben, *Homo Sacer: Sovereign Power and Bare Life* (Stanford: Stanford University Press, 1998).

12. "13th Amendment to the US Constitution," National Archives, accessed April 2019, https://www.archives.gov/historical-docs/13th-amendment (emphasis added).

13. See generally Richard Delgado and Jena Stefancic, eds., *Critical Race Theory: The Cutting Edge*, 2nd ed. (Philadelphia: Temple University Press, 2000); Kimberle Crenshaw, Neil Gotanda, Garry Peller, and Kendall Thomas, eds., *Critical Race Theory: The Key Writings That Formed the Movement* (New York: New Press, 1996); Mae M. Ngai, *Impossible Subjects*; Mae M. Ngai, "The Architecture of Race in American Immigration Law: A Reexamination of the Immigration Act of 1924," *The Journal of American History* 86, no. 1 (June 1999): 67–92; Leti Volpp, "Citizenship Undone," *Fordham Law Review* 75, no. 5 (April 2007): 2579–86; and Audrey Macklin "Who Is the Citizen's Other? Considering the Heft of Citizenship," *Theoretical Inquiries in Law* 8, no. 2 (July 2007), https://www7.tau.ac.il/ojs/index.php/til/article/view/638/599.

14. Hartman, *Scenes of Subjection*, 21.

15. *Congressional Globe*, February 12, 1847, 29th Congress, 2nd Session, Appendix, 360 (emphasis added).

16. The link between white supremacy and speculative historicity emerges through an against-the-grain reading of the existing scholarship on speculative history and historiography. See, for example, Réal Fillion, "The Continuing Relevance of Speculative Philosophy of History," *Journal of the Philosophy of History* 8, no. 2 (2014): 180–95; and Simon Schama, *Dead Certainties: Unwarranted Speculations* (New York: Vintage Books, 1992). In addition to various other works cited in this book, the notion of speculative historicity as offered here is informed by such texts as: Jace Weaver, *That the People Might Live: Native American Literatures and Native American Community* (New York: Oxford University Press, 1997); Howard Adams, *A Tortured People: The Politics of Colonization* (Penticton, BC: Theytus Books, 1995); Saidiya V. Hartman, *Lose Your Mother: A Journey Along the Atlantic Slave Route* (New York: Farrar, Straus, and Giroux, 2008); José E. Muñoz, *Cruising Utopia: The Then and There of Queer Futurity* (New York: New York University Press, 2009); and Avery Gordon, *Ghostly Matters: Haunting and the Sociological Imagination* (Minneapolis: University of Minnesota Press, 1997).

17. Paula Gunn Allen, Introduction, in *Spider Woman's Granddaughters: Traditional Tales and Contemporary Writing by Native American Women*, ed. Allen (Boston: Beacon Press, 1989), 2 (emphasis added).

18. Sarah Haley, *No Mercy Here: Gender, Punishment, and the Making of Jim Crow Modernity* (Durham, N.C.: University of North Carolina Press, 2016), 62–63 (emphasis added).

19. Glen S. Coulthard, *Red Skin, White Masks: Rejecting the Colonial Politics of Recognition* (Minneapolis: University of Minnesota Press, 2014), 40–41.

20. W. E. B. Du Bois, "The Superior Race," in *The Oxford W. E. B. Du Bois Reader*, ed. Eric Sundquist (1923; repr., Oxford: Oxford University Press, 1996), 62.

21. See David R. Roediger, *The Wages of Whiteness: Race and the Making of the American Working Class* (1991; repr., New York: Verso, 2007); and George Lipsitz, *The Possessive Investment in Whiteness: How White People Profit from Identity Politics* (Philadelphia: Temple University Press, 1998).

22. See Sylvia Wynter, "Unsettling the Coloniality of Being/power/truth/freedom: Towards the Human, After Man, Its Overrepresentation—An Argument," *CR: The New Centennial Review* 3, no. 3 (2003): 257–337.

23. W. E. B. Du Bois, "The Freedmen's Bureau," *Atlantic Monthly* 87 (1901): 357 (emphasis added).

24. *Oxford English Dictionary*, 2nd ed. (1989), s.v. "birthright."

25. See Fanon, *The Wretched of the Earth*, and Sylvia Wynter, "Beyond the World of Man: Glissant and the New Discourse of the Antilles," *World Literature Today* 63, no. 4 (Autumn 1989): 637–47.

26. Wynter, "Beyond the World of Man," 642.

27. Freedman's Aid Societies to Abraham Lincoln, 38th Congress, Session 1, Sen. Ex. Doc. 1 (serial 1176), No. 1, 2.

28. W. E. B. Du Bois, *Black Reconstruction: An Essay Toward a History of the Part Which Black Folk Played in the Attempt to Reconstruct Democracy in America, 1860–1880* (New York: Harcourt, Brace, and Company, 1935).

29. Freedman's Aid Societies to Abraham Lincoln, 5–6 (emphasis added).

30. Colonel O. Brown, Summary Report of Virginia, November 31, 1865, 39th Congress, Session 1, Sen. Ex. Doc. No. 27, 144.

31. Freedman's Bureau Report (38th Congress, Session 1, No. 1, Sen. Ex. Doc. 1 (serial 1176), 2.

32. Paul Skeels Peirce, *The Freedmen's Bureau: A Chapter in the History of Reconstruction* (Iowa City: University of Iowa, 1970), 50.

33. W. E. B. Du Bois, *Black Reconstruction*, 219 (emphasis added).

34. Paul A. Cimbala and Randall M. Miller, Preface, in *The Freedmen's Bureau and Reconstruction: Reconsiderations*, ed. Cimbala and Miller (New York: Fordham University Press, 1999), ix.; and Randall M. Miller, Introduction, in *The Freedmen's Bureau and Reconstruction: Reconsiderations*, ed. Cimbala and Miller (New York: Fordham University Press, 1999), xv.

35. Du Bois, "The Freedmen's Bureau," 359.

36. Miller and Cimbala, *The Freedmen's Bureau and Reconstruction*, xv; Paul Skeels Peirce *The Freedmen's Bureau: A Chapter in the History of Reconstruction* (Iowa City: University of Iowa, 1970), 73

37. See generally, Eric Foner, *Reconstruction: America's Unfinished Revolution, 1863–1877* (New York: Harper & Row, 1988); and Leon Litwack, *Been in the Storm so Long: The Aftermath of Slavery* (New York: Alfred A. Knopf, 1979).

38. Testimony of John H. Wagner before Congressional Joint Select Committee to Inquire into the Condition of Affairs in the Late Insurrectionary States

(Alabama), October 14, 1871, 42nd Congress, Session 2, Sen. Rpt. 41, pt. 9 (Serial Set Volume No. 1492), 927.

39. Report on St. Bernard parish (Louisiana), November 27, 1868, 40th Congress, Session 3, Sen. Ex. Doc. No. 15, 19.

40. In addition to smaller state and local archives distributed across the South, the National Archives has digitized Freedmen's Bureau headquarters records, Assistant Commissioner and education official reports, and field office records, among other archival texts. This chapter relies primarily on Congressional records and testimonials. See "African American Records: Freedmen's Bureau," National Archives, accessed April 1, 2019, https://www.archives.gov/research/african-americans /freedmens-bureau

41. Ibid., 17.

42. Report No. 9, "Reports of Assistant Commissioners of the Freedmen's Bureau," 39th Congress, Session 1, Sen. Ex. Doc. No. 27, 31.

43. Ibid., 32.

44. Frantz Fanon, *Black Skin, White Masks*, trans. Richard Philcox (New York: Grove Press, 2008), xv.

45. See John Hope Franklin and Evelyn Brooks Higginbotham, "Promises and Pitfalls of Reconstruction (1863–1877)," in *From Slavery to Freedom: A History of African Americans* (New York: McGraw-Hill, 2011), 235–59; Paula Giddings, "To Choose Again, Freely," in *When and Where I Enter: The Impact of Black Women on Race and Sex in America* (New York: Bantam Books, 1984), 57–74; and Clyde Woods, "What Happens to a Dream Arrested?" and "The Blues Tradition of Explanation," in *Development Arrested: The Blues and Plantation Power in the Mississippi Delta* (New York: Verso, 1998), 1–39. The in-sentence quotation from Woods appears on page 20 of *Development Arrested.*

46. Woods, *Development Arrested*, 27.

47. See Eric Foner, *Reconstruction: America's Unfinished Revolution, 1863–1877* (New York: Harper & Row, 1988); C. Vann Woodward, *Reunion and Reaction: The Compromise of 1877 and the End of Reconstruction* (Boston: Little, Brown and Company, 1966); and Roy Morris, Jr., *Fraud of the Century: Rutherford B. Hayes, Samuel Tilden and the Stolen Election of 1876* (New York: Simon and Schuster, 2003).

48. Report No. 9, "Reports of Assistant Commissioners of the Freedmen's Bureau," 32.

49. On slavery ledgers and the mundane violence of plantation and slave trade accounting, see Theresa A. Singleton, *The Archaeology of Slavery and Plantation Life* (Orlando: Academic Press, 1985.); Hartman, *Scenes of Subjection: Terror, Slavery, and Self-Making in Nineteenth-Century America*; Smallwood, *Saltwater Slavery: A Middle Passage from Africa to American Diaspora*; Edward E. Baptist, *The Half Has Never Been Told: Slavery and the Making of American Capitalism* (New York: Basic Books, a Member of the Perseus Books Group, 2014); Sven Beckert and Seth Rockman, eds., *Slavery's Capitalism: A New History of American Economic*

Development (Philadelphia: University of Pennsylvania Press, 2016); and Eric Williams, *Capitalism and Slavery* (Chapel Hill: University of North Carolina Press, 1944).

50. Report of Assistant Commissioner's Office (Kentucky), February 15, 1868, 40th Congress, Session 2, H.R. Rep. Doc. No. 329, 4 (emphasis added).

51. Report of Assistant Commissioner's Office (Tennessee), February 11, 1868, 40th Congress, Session 2, H.R. Rep. Doc. No. 329, 35 (emphasis added).

52. Circular No. 10, Freedmen's Bureau Assistant Commissioner's Office (Nashville, Tenn.), December 26, 1865, 39th Congress, Session 1, Sen. Exec. Doc. 27, 4–5.

53. Inspection Report of Brevet Brig. Gen. C. H. Howard, December 30, 1865, 39th Congress, Session 1, 132.

54. Letter to General Fisk from J. Stewart (Bradenburgh, Ky.), January 4, 1866, Sen. Ex. Doc. 27, 39th Congress, Session 1, Sen. Exec. Doc. 27, 8 (emphasis added).

55. Inspection Report of Brevet Brig. Gen. C. H. Howard for South Carolina, Georgia, and Florida, December 30, 1865, 39th Congress, Session 1, Sen. Exec. Doc. 27, 126.

56. Ibid., 128.

57. Report of Assistant Commissioner's Office, Assistant Commissioner Maj. Gen. Clinton B. Fisk (Nashville, Tenn.), February 14, 1866, 39th Congress, Session 1, Sen. Exec. Doc. 27, 10 (emphasis added).

58. Ibid., 12.

59. Report of Assistant Commissioner's Office for the Month of March 1868 (Kentucky), April 10, 1868, 40th Congress, Session 2, H.R. Rep. Ex. Doc. 329, 11.

60. Testimony of Freedmen's Bureau Agent J. C. McMullen, Report of Assistant Commissioner's Office (Tennessee), April 14, 1868, 40th Congress, Session 2, H.R. Rep. Ex. Doc. 329, 38.

61. Ibid., 12.

62. Benjamin R. Beede, "Pacification," in *The War of 1898 and U.S. Interventions, 1898–1934: An Encyclopedia*, ed. Benjamin R. Beede (New York: Garland, 1994), 395 (395–96).

63. U.S. Army, *Counterinsurgency*, 2–12.

64. See Dylan Rodríguez, "'Its Very Familiarity Disguises Its Horror': White Supremacy, Genocide, and the Statecraft of Pacifica Americans," in *Suspended Apocalypse: White Supremacy, Genocide, and the Filipino Condition* (Minneapolis: University of Minnesota Press, 2009); Luzviminda Francisco, "The First Vietnam: The U.S.-Philippine War of 1899," *Bulletin of Concerned Asian Scholars* 5, no. 4 (1973): 2–16; Stuart Creighton Miller, *"Benevolent Assimilation": The American Conquest of the Philippines, 1899–1903* (New Haven: Yale University Press, 1982); William Pomeroy, "'Pacification' in the Philippines, 1898–1913," France-Asie 21 (1967): 427–46; and Christopher J. Einolf, *America in the Philippines, 1899–1902: The First Torture Scandal* (New York: Palgrave Macmillan, 2014).

65. Warwick Anderson, *Colonial Pathologies: American Tropical Medicine, Race, and Hygiene in the Philippines* (Durham, N.C.: Duke University Press, 2006), 3;

Albert J. Beveridge, *Congressional Record*, 1900, 56th Congress, Session 1, Vol. 33, 709 (704–9).

66. The proper designation of people who trace familial genealogy to the Philippines has long been a topic of contention among scholars, activists, community spokespeople, and even elected officials. The implicitly cisgender male normatives "Filipino" and "Pilipino" have long been used as the terms of choice to reference people who identify with a Philippine heritage, while recent terms such as "F/Pilipino/a," "F/Pilipin@," and "F/Pilipinx" have emerged through feminist, queer, and trans* interventions on the rhetorics of collective identity. The terms Pinoy, Pinay, and most recently Pinxy are less commonly seen in academic or formal written discourse, but are widely used in spoken, artistic, and interpersonal vernaculars (including by this author). For the purposes of this chapter, i have chosen to use the term "Filipino" in an attempt to reflect the archive's rhetorical universalization of the Philippine archipelago's many peoples, including numerous Indigenous tribes, linguistic groups, and province-based identities.

67. Renato Constantino, "The Mis-Education of the Filipino," *Journal of Contemporary Asia* 1, no. 1 (Autumn 1970): 20–36.

68. Carter G. Woodson, *The Miseducation of the Negro* (1933; repr., Trenton, N.J.: Africa World Press, 1998).

69. Constantino, "The Mis-Education of the Filipino," 24.

70. See generally Kristin L. Hoganson, *Fighting for American Manhood: How Gender Politics Provoked the Spanish-American and Philippine-American Wars* (New Haven: Yale University Press, 1998); Alfred W. McCoy and Francisco A. Scaran, eds., *The Colonial Crucible: Empire in the Making of the Modern American State* (Madison: University of Wisconsin Press, 2009); and Ken De Bevoise, *Agents of Apocalypse: Epidemic Disease in the Colonial Philippines* (Princeton, N.J.: Princeton University Press, 1995).

Nerissa S. Balce, *Body Parts of Empire: Visual Abjection, Filipino Images, and the American Archive* (Ann Arbor: University of Michigan Press, 2016); Teodoro A. Agoncillo, *History of the Filipino People*, 8th ed. (Quezon City, Philippines: Garotech Publishers, 1990); Renato Constantino, *A History of the Philippines: from the Spanish Colonization to the Second World War* (New York: Monthly Review Press, 1975); Daniel Schirmer, *Republic or Empire* (Cambridge: Schenkman Books, 1972); and Angel Shaw and Luis Francia, eds., *Vestiges of War* (New York: NYU Press, 2002).

71. Balce, *Body Parts of Empire*, 8.

72. Sarita Echavez See, *The Decolonized Eye: Filipino American Art and Performance* (Minneapolis: University of Minnesota Press, 2009), xv.

73. Beveridge, *Congressional Record*, 704–8.

74. In addition to previously cited works, see Reginald Horsman, *Race and Manifest Destiny: The Origins of American Racial Anglo-Saxonism* (Cambridge: Harvard University Press, 1981).

75. See generally Reynaldo C. Ileto, *Knowledge and Pacification: On the U.S. Conquest and the Writing of Philippine History* (Quezon City: Ateneo de Manila University Press, 2017).

76. See generally Martin F. Manalansan and Augusto F. Espiritu, eds., *Filipino Studies: Palimpsests of Nation and Diaspora* (New York: NYU Press, 2016).

77. Rick Baldoz, *The Third Asiatic Invasion: Empire and Migration in Filipino America, 1898–1946* (New York: NYU Press, 2011), 23.

78. Franklin D. Roosevelt, "A Recommendation That Legislation Be Enacted to the Effect That the Philippine Islands Shall Be Granted Their Independence," March 2, 1934, 73rd Congress, Session 2, H.R. Rep. Doc. No. 272, 1–2 (emphasis added).

79. See, *The Decolonized Eye*, xvii.

80. See, for example, "Volume XIV: Acts of the Philippine Commission and Public Resolutions, Etc., from September 24, 1900, to August 31, 1904," Annual Report of the War Department for the Fiscal Year Ended, June 30, 1904, 58th Congress, Session 3, H.R. Rep. Doc. No. 2.

81. "Volume XIV: Acts of the Philippine Commission and Public Resolutions, Etc., from September 24, 1900, to August 31, 1904," Annual Report of the War Department for the Fiscal Year Ended, June 30, 1904, 58th Congress, Session 3, H.R. Rep. Doc. No. 2.

82. "Resolution of the 'Liga Patriotica,' a Civil Organization of the City of Manila, Philippine Islands," May 16, 1935, 74th Congress, Session 1, H.R. Rep. Doc. 253, 1–2.

83. Letter from municipal council of Danao, September 25, 1900, 56th Congress, Session 2, Sen. Doc. No. 234, 1–2.

84. "Report of the Philippine Commission," in *War Department Annual Reports*, vol. 7, 1909 (Washington, D.C.: Government Printing Office, 1910), 49 (emphasis added).

85. Said, *Orientalism*, 40–41.

86. "Report of the Philippine Commission," vol. 7, 1909, 41–42 (emphasis added).

87. Ibid., 44.

88. Ibid.

89. Report on Philippine Independence, submitted by Sen. Millard E. Tydings, March 15, 1934, 73rd Congress, Session 2, Sen. Rep. No. 494, 13.

90. See Cesar Adib Majul, *The Contemporary Muslim Movement in the Philippines* (Berkeley: Mizan Press, 1985).

91. Report on Philippine Independence submitted by Sen. Millard E. Tydings, 6–7 (emphasis added).

92. Ibid., 8.

93. Report on Philippine Independence, submitted by Rep. John McDuffie, March 13, 1934, 73rd Congress, Session 2, H.R. Rep. No. 968.

94. Report on Philippine Independence submitted by Sen. Millard E. Tydings, 4–5.

95. Ibid., 15.

96. Radiogram sent by Manuel L. Quezon to Governor General of Philippine Islands, May 2, 1934, 73rd Congress, Session 2, H.R. Rep. Doc. 355, 2.

97. The author is indebted to the second anonymous reader of this book's draft manuscript for convincingly arguing that such a reading practice must be utilized across archival texts, including and especially Quezon's declaration.

98. David Scott, "The Re-Enchantment of Humanism: An Interview with Sylvia Wynter," 165.

99. See Antonio Gramsci, "The Intellectuals" and "On Education" in Antonio Gramsci, Quintin Hoare, and Geoffrey Nowell-Smith. *Selections from the Prison Notebooks of Antonio Gramsci*. New York: International Publishers, 1971: 3–43.

100. See Stuart Hall, "Race, Articulation, and Societies."

101. See Avery Gordon, *Ghostly Matters*.

102. W. E. B. Du Bois, *Darkwater: Voices from within the Veil* (1920; repr., Hazelton: Pennsylvania State University, 2007), 99.

3. Goldwater's Tribal Tattoo: On Origins and Deletions of Post-Raciality

1. A previous version of this chapter was published as "Goldwater's Left Hand: Post-Raciality and the Roots of the Post-Racial Racist State," *Cultural Dynamics* 26 (March 2014): 29–51.

2. See Dylan Rodríguez, "Goldwater's Left Hand: Post-Raciality and the Roots of the Post-Racial Racist State," *Cultural Dynamics* 26 (March 2014): 29–51.

3. See Denise Ferreira da Silva, *Toward a Global Idea of Race* (Minneapolis: University of Minnesota Press, 2007).

4. See Gilles Deleuze and Félix Guattari, "Savages, Barbarians, Civilized Men," in *Anti-Oedipus: Capitalism and Schizophrenia* (Minneapolis: University of Minnesota Press, 1983), 139–271.

5. Ibid., 220–21.

6. In the forthcoming *White Reconstruction II*, I propose a general definition of racism that focuses on five core logics of dominance: 1) racism as logic of knowledge-dominance; 2) racism as logic of social formation/reproduction; 3) racism as logic of physiological-cultural violence; 4) racism as logic of genocide; 5) racism as logic of proliferation.

7. Sylvia Wynter, "Unsettling the Coloniality of Being/Power/Truth/Freedom: Towards the Human, After Man, Its Overrepresentation—An Argument," *CR: The New Centennial Review* 3, no. 3 (Fall 2003): 322.

8. See for example, Kristian Williams, *Our Enemies in Blue: Police and Power in America* (Cambridge, Mass.: South End Press, 2007); Joy James, ed., *Warfare in the American Homeland: Policing and Prison in a Penal Democracy* (Durham, N.C.: Duke University Press, 2007); Paula Chakravarty and Denise Ferreira da Silva, "Accumulation, Dispossession, and Debt: The Racial Logic of Global Capitalism—An Introduction," in *American Quarterly Special Issue* 64, no. 3

(September 2012): 361–85; Kara Keeling, *The Witch's Flight: The Cinematic, the Black Femme, and the Image of Common Sense* (Durham, N.C.: Duke University Press, 2007); Kelly Lytle Hernandez, *Migra!: A History of the U.S. Border Patrol* (Berkeley: University of California Press, 2010); and Frank B. Wilderson, *Red, White & Black: Cinema and the Structure of U.S. Antagonisms* (Durham, N.C.: Duke University Press, 2010).

9. Michael Omi and Howard Winant, *Racial Formation in the United States: From the 1960s to the 1990s*, 2nd ed. (New York: Routledge, 1994), 67–68 (emphasis added).

10. Clyde Woods, *Development Arrested: From the Plantation Era to the Katrina Crisis in the Mississippi Delta*, 2nd ed. (New York: Verso Press, 2012).

11. See Barbara Ransby, *Ella Baker and the Black Freedom Movement: A Radical Democratic Vision* (Chapel Hill: University of North Carolina Press, 2003); Keeanga-Yamahtta Taylor, *How We Get Free: Black Feminism and the Combahee River Collective* (Chicago: Haymarket Books, 2017); Waldo E. Martin, *No Coward Soldiers: Black Cultural Politics in Postwar America* (Cambridge: Harvard University Press, 2005); Waldo E. Martin, *Civil Rights in the United States*, vol. 1 (New York: Macmillan Reference USA, 2000); Waldo E. Martin, *Civil Rights in the United States*, vol. 2 (New York: Macmillan Reference USA, 2000); Joshua Bloom and Waldo E. Martin, *Black Against Empire: The History and Politics of the Black Panther Party* (Berkeley: University of California Press, 2013); and Robin D. G. Kelley, *Freedom Dreams: The Black Radical Imagination* (Boston: Beacon Press, 2002).

12. Barry M. Goldwater, Personal Journal Entry, January 20, 1961, Personal and Political Papers of Senator Barry M. Goldwater (1909–1998), FM MSS #1, Arizona Historical Foundation, Series I, Alpha files, box 15, folder 5, p. 13 (emphasis added).

13. Malcolm X, with Alex Haley, *The Autobiography of Malcolm X* (1964; repr., New York: Ballantine Books, 1973), 307.

14. Macarena Gómez-Barris and Herman Gray, "Toward a Sociology of the Trace," in *Toward a Sociology of the Trace*, ed. Gómez-Barris and Gray (Minneapolis: University of Minnesota Press, 2010), 4.

15. Lisa Lowe, *The Intimacies of Four Continents* (Durham, N.C.: Duke University Press, 2015), 3.

16. See Walter Benjamin, "Theses on the Philosophy of History," in *Illuminations: Essays and Reflections*, ed. Hannah Arendt, trans. Harry Zohn (New York: Schocken, 1969), 253–64; and Michel Foucault, "Nietzsche, Genealogy, History," in Paul Rabinow, ed., *The Foucault Reader* (New York: Pantheon, 1984), 76–100.

17. Lowe, *The Intimacies of Four Continents*, 2–3.

18. Barry Goldwater for President Committee 1960, Pamphlet, Personal and Political Papers of Senator Barry M. Goldwater (1909–1998), FM MSS #1, Arizona Historical Foundation, Series I, Alpha files, box 95, folder 1.

19. Audra Simpson, "On Ethnographic Refusal: Indigeneity, 'Voice' and Colonial Citizenship," *Junctures* 9 (December 2007): 69.

20. Ibid., 73.

21. See Lisa Lowe, *The Intimacies of Four Continents,* as well as the essay-length articulation of this methodological approach in her chapter "The Intimacies of Four Continents," in *Haunted By Empire: Geographies of Intimacy in North American History,* ed. Ann Laura Stoler (Durham, N.C.: Duke University Press, 2006), 191–212.

22. Avery Gordon, *Ghostly Matters: Haunting and the Sociological Imagination,* 2nd ed. (Minneapolis: University of Minnesota Press, 2008), 8.

23. See Christian Parenti, *Lockdown America: Police and Prisons in the Age of Crisis,* 2nd ed. (London: Verso, 2008).

24. See Robert Alan Goldberg, *Barry Goldwater* (New Haven: Yale University Press, 1995); Barry M. Goldwater, *Conscience of a Conservative* (1960; repr., Princeton: Princeton University Press, 2007); Barry M. Goldwater, *The Conscience of a Majority* (Englewood Cliffs, N.J.: Prentice-Hall, 1970); Dean Smith, *The Goldwaters of Arizona* (Flagstaff: Northland Press, 1986); and Dean Smith and Rob Wood, *Barry Goldwater: The Biography of a Conservative* (New York: Avon Book Division, 1961).

25. See, for example, Avery Gordon, *Ghostly Matters: Haunting and the Sociological Imagination,* 2nd ed. (Minneapolis: University of Minnesota Press, 2008); Herman Gray and Macarena Gómez-Barris, ed., *Toward a Sociology of the Trace* (Minneapolis: University of Minnesota Press, 2010); and Ruby C. Tapia, *American Pietàs: Visions of Race, Death, and the Maternal* (Minneapolis: University of Minnesota Press, 2011).

26. Barry M. Goldwater, Personal Correspondence to Spider Webb, President of Tattoo Club of America, 30 January 1975, Personal and Political Papers of Senator Barry M. Goldwater (1909–1998), FM MSS #1, Arizona Historical Foundation, Series I, Alpha files, Boards and Memberships, Smoki People, 1967–1996, box 46, folder 6.

27. Ibid.

28. Barry M. Goldwater, Personal Correspondence to Dan Stevenson, constituent, March 12, 1980, Personal and Political Papers of Senator Barry M. Goldwater (1909–1998), FM MSS #1, Arizona Historical Foundation, Series I, Alpha files, Boards and Memberships, Smoki People, 1967–1996, box 46, folder 6.

29. Philip J. Deloria, *Playing Indian* (New Haven: Yale University Press, 1998), 136, 129.

30. In addition to Deloria, see Jace Weaver, *Notes from a Miner's Canary: Essays on the State of Native America* (Albuquerque: University of New Mexico Press, 2010); Chad A. Barbour, *From Daniel Boone to Captain America: Playing Indian in American Popular Culture* (Jackson: University Press of Mississippi, 2016); Douglas S. Harvey, *The Theatre of Empire: Frontier Performances in America, 1750–1860* (London: Pickering & Chatto, 2010); and Joshua David Bellin and Laura L. Mielke, *Native Acts Indian Performance, 1603–1832* (Lincoln: University of Nebraska Press, 2011).

31. Deloria, *Playing Indian,* 129–32.

32. See Jennifer DeWitt, "'When They Are Gone . . .': The Smoki People of Prescott and the Preservation of Indian Culture," *The Journal of Arizona History* 37,

no. 4 (Winter 1996): 319–36; Bruce Colbert, "Smoki: The Beginning—Controversial Group 'Basically Saved the Rodeo,'" *The Daily Courier* (Prescott, Ariz.), July 4, 2010, https://www.dcourier.com/news/2010/jul/04/smoki-the-beginning-controversial -group-basically/; and "Smoki People Had Good Intentions" (Editorial), *The Daily Courier* (Prescott, Ariz.), July 6, 2010, https://www.dcourier.com/news/2010/jul/06 /editorial-smoki-people-had-good-intentions/.

33. Barry M. Goldwater, Undated Personal Correspondence to Norman Goldstein, constituent, Personal and Political Papers of Senator Barry M. Goldwater (1909–1998), FM MSS #1, Arizona Historical Foundation, Series I, Alpha files, Boards and Memberships, Smoki People, 1967–1996, box 46, folder 6.

34. Michelle H. Raheja, *Reservation Reelism: Redfacing, Visual Sovereignty, and Representations of Native Americans in Film* (Lincoln: University of Nebraska Press, 2010), 21–22.

35. On Native and Indigenous elimination, see Patrick Wolfe, "Settler Colonialism and the Elimination of the Native," *Journal of Genocide Research* 8, no. 4 (December 2006): 387–409; Wolfe, *Settler Colonialism and the Transformation of Anthropology: The Politics and Poetics of an Ethnographic Event* (London: Cassell, 1999); and J. Kēhaulani Kauanui, "'A Structure, Not an Event:' Settler Colonialism and Enduring Indigeneity," *Lateral* 5, no. 1 (Spring 2016), https://doi.org/10.25158/L5.1 .7. Regarding cultural genocide, Chapter 4 builds a conceptualization of anti-Black and racial-colonial genocide that includes an explication of the term, which challenges the narrow United Nations juridical definition of genocide. See Ward Churchill, *A Little Matter of Genocide: Holocaust and Denial in the Americas, 1492 to the Present* (San Francisco: City Lights Books, 1997).

36. Kauanui, "A Structure, Not an Event."

37. "Smoki to Honor 'Flying Eagle,'" *The Courier* (Ariz.), May 2, 1986, 1b.

38. See Jodi A. Byrd, *The Transit of Empire: Indigenous Critiques of Colonialism* (Minneapolis: University of Minnesota Press 2011); Keith L. Camacho, *Cultures of Commemoration: the Politics of War, Memory, and History in the Mariana Islands* (Honolulu: Center for Pacific Islands Studies, School of Pacific and Asian Studies, University of Hawai'i, Mānoa, 2011); Mishuana Goeman, *Mark My Words: Native Women Mapping Our Nations* (Minneapolis: University of Minnesota Press, 2013); Scott Richard Lyons, *X-Marks: Native Signatures of Assent* (Minneapolis: University of Minnesota Press, 2010); Lyons, *The World, the Text, and the Indian: Global Dimensions of Native American Literature* (Albany: SUNY Press, 2017); and Scott Lauria Morgensen, *Spaces Between Us: Queer Settler Colonialism and Indigenous Decolonization* (Minneapolis: University of Minnesota Press, 2011).

39. Barry M. Goldwater, Letter to Kris Finn of *The Prescott Sun*, May 13, 1986, Personal and Political Papers of Senator Barry M. Goldwater (1909–1998), FM MSS #1, Arizona Historical Foundation, Series I, Alpha files, Boards and Memberships, Smoki People, 1967–1996, box 46, folder 6.

40. On the terror produced by and embedded in the productions of white social life and subjectivities, see Silva, *Toward a Global Idea of Race*; and Sylvia Wynter,

"Unsettling the Coloniality of Being/Power/Truth/Freedom: Towards the Human, After Man, Its Overrepresentation—An Argument" *CR: The New Centennial Review* 3, no. 3 (Fall 2003): 257–337. Regarding the distended temporality of colonial genocide, see Patrick Wolfe, "Structure and Event: Settler Colonialism, Time, and the Question of Genocide," in *Empire, Colony, Genocide: Conquest, Occupation, and Subaltern Resistance in World History*, ed. Dirk A. Moses (New York: Berghahn Books, 2008), 102–32.

41. Sharon Luk, *The Life of Paper: Letters and a Poetics of Living Beyond Captivity* (Oakland: University of California Press, 2018), 3–4.

42. Silva, *Toward a Global Idea of Race.*

43. See João Costa Vargas, *Never Meant to Survive: Genocide and Utopias in Black Diaspora Communities* (New York: Rowman & Littlefield Publishers, 2008); Junaid Akram Rana, *Terrifying Muslims: Race and Labor in the South Asian Diaspora* (Durham: Duke University Press, 2011); and Joy James, ed., *Warfare in the American Homeland: Policing and Prison in a Penal Democracy* (Durham: Duke University Press, 2007).

4. "Civilization in Its Reddened Waters": Anti-Black, Racial-Colonial Genocide and the Logic of Evisceration

1. Some key arguments of this chapter were first articulated in "Inhabiting the Impasse: Racial/Racial-Colonial Power, Genocide Poetics, and the Logic of Evisceration," *Social Text* 33, no. 3 (Fall 2015): 19–44.

2. See Randall Williams, *The Divided World: Human Rights and Its Violence* (Minneapolis: University of Minnesota Press, 2010).

3. Aimé Césaire, *Discourse on Colonialism*, trans. Joan Pinkham (New York: Monthly Review Press, 2000), 37.

4. On the Third Reich's militarization of Aryanism, see Simone Gigliotti and Berel Lang, eds., *The Holocaust: A Reader* (Malden, Mass.: Blackwell, 2005); and Christopher M. Hutton, *Race and the Third Reich: Linguistics, Racial Anthropology and Genetics in the Dialectic of Volk* (Cambridge: Polity Press, 2005). Regarding "industrialized killing," see Omer Bartov, *Murder in Our Midst: The Holocaust, Industrial Killing, and Representation* (New York: Oxford University Press, 1996). While there is wide acknowledgment that the best-known targets of the Nazi movement's genocidal campaigns were generally marked as racial pathologues, non-Aryans, and subhuman, the historical record shows that even these targeted groups—Jews, Romani (Gypsies), Slavs, queer and gender nonconforming, disabled people, and so forth—were nonetheless racially differentiated from peoples of African descent, among others. That is, "non-Aryan" was not necessarily synonymous with "nonwhite," and the fatal gradations of hierarchized difference were largely constructed within a continuum of white raciality: For the Nazis, the mythical Aryan was the supreme white being, against whom inferior and subhuman beings—including other white beings—were defined. By contrast, the historical

evidence indicates that the Nazi regime targeted the racially "black" for sterilization, elimination, and peculiar forms of segregation, while clearly delineating African-derived people as separate from all other non-Aryans.

5. See generally Edward W. Said, *The Question of Palestine* (New York: Vintage Books, 1980); Keith P. Feldman, *A Shadow Over Palestine: The Imperial Life of Race in America* (Minneapolis: University of Minnesota Press, 2015); Sohail Daulatzai and Junaid Rana, eds., *With Stones in Our Hands: Writings on Muslims, Racism, and Empire* (Minneapolis: University of Minnesota Press, 2018); and Norman G. Finkelstein, *Beyond Chutzpah: On the Misuse of Anti-Semitism and the Abuse of History* (Berkeley: University of California Press, 2005).

6. Norman G. Finkelstein, *The Holocaust Industry: Reflections on the Exploitation of Jewish Suffering* (London: Verso, 2003), 47. Finkelstein elaborates,

> The Holocaust is not an arbitrary but rather an internally coherent construct. Its central dogmas sustain significant political and class interests. Indeed, The Holocaust has proven to be an indispensable ideological weapon. Through its deployment, one of the world's most formidable military powers, with a horrendous human rights record, has cast itself as a "victim" state, and the most successful ethnic group in the United States has likewise acquired victim status. Considerable dividends accrue from this specious victimhood— in particular, immunity to criticism, however justified. (3)

> Proponents of Holocaust uniqueness typically disclaim this implication, but such demurrals are disingenuous. The claims of Holocaust uniqueness are intellectually barren and morally discreditable, yet they persist. The question is, Why? In the first place, unique suffering confers unique entitlement. The unique evil of the Holocaust, according to Jacob Neusner, not only sets Jews apart from others, but also gives Jews a "claim upon those others. . . ."
>
> In effect, Holocaust uniqueness—this "claim" upon others, this "moral capital"—serves as Israel's prize alibi. (47–48)

7. See Norman G. Finkelstein, *Beyond Chutzpah: On the Misuse of Anti-Semitism and the Abuse of History* (Berkeley: University of California Press, 2005).

8. Ilan Pappé, *The Ethnic Cleansing of Palestine* (Oxford: Oneworld, 2006), 245.

9. Steven Salaita, "On Colonization and Ethnic Cleansing in North America and Palestine," in J. Kēhaulani Kauanui, ed. *Speaking of Indigenous Politics: Conversations with Activists, Scholars, and Tribal Leaders* (Minneapolis: University of Minnesota Press, 2018), 262–67.

10. Loubna Noor Qutami, "Before the New Sky: Protracted Struggle and Possibilities of the Beyond for Palestine's New Youth Movement" (PhD diss., Department of Ethnic Studies, University of California, Riverside 2018), 69–73.

11. Frantz Fanon, "The Fact of Blackness," in *Black Skin, White Masks*, trans. Charles Lam Markmann (London: Pluto Press, 2008), 87.

12. Omer Bartov, *Murder in Our Midst: The Holocaust, Industrial Killing, and Representation* (New York: Oxford University Press, 1996).

13. Joy James, *Resisting State Violence: Radicalism, Gender, and Race in U.S. Culture* (Minneapolis: University of Minnesota Press, 1996), 46.

14. Sylvia Wynter opens this line of analysis in her extended elaboration of how "Renaissance humanism [instantiated] an extraordinary rupture at the level of the human species as a whole" in a far-reaching 2000 interview with David Scott. See Sylvia Wynter and David Scott, "The Re-enchantment of Humanism: An Interview with Sylvia Wynter," *Small Axe* 8 (September 2000): 177.

15. See Denise Ferreira da Silva, *Toward a Global Idea of Race* (Minneapolis: University of Minnesota Press, 2007).

16. Edward Said, *Orientalism* (New York: Vintage, 1979), 32.

17. See Allen Feldman, *Formations of Violence: The Narrative of the Body and Political Terror in Northern Ireland* (Chicago: University of Chicago Press, 1991).

18. United Nations General Assembly, Convention on the Prevention and Punishment of the Crime of Genocide, 1948, treaties.un.org/doc/Publication/UNTS /Volume%2078/volume-78-I-1021-English.pdf.

19. United Nations General Assembly, *Convention on the Prevention and Punishment of the Crime of Genocide*, United Nations, 1948, https://treaties.un.org /doc/Publication/UNTS/Volume%2078/volume-78-I-1021-English.pdf.

20. Matthew Lippman provides a useful preliminary overview of the UN Genocide Convention in "A Road Map to the 1948 Convention on the Prevention and Punishment of the Crime of Genocide," *Journal of Genocide Research* 4, no. 2 (2002): 177–95.

21. See, for example: Henry R. Huttenbach, "From the Editors: Academia and genocide—degrees of culpability," *Journal of Genocide Research* 10, no. 1 (2008): 1–2; Samuel Totten and Paul R. Bartrop, eds., *The Genocide Studies Reader* (New York: Routledge, 2009). Adam Jones, *New Directions in Genocide Research* (New York: Routledge, 2012); Mark Levene, *Genocide in the Age of the Nation-State: Volume I: The Meaning of Genocide* (New York: I. B. Tauris & Co., 2005); Mark Levene, *Genocide in the Age of the Nation-State: Volume II: The Rise of the West and the Coming of Genocide* (New York: I. B. Tauris & Co., 2005); A. Dirk Moses, ed., *Empire, Colony, Genocide: Conquest, Occupation, and Subaltern Resistance in World History* (New York: Berghahn Books, 2008); Henry R. Huttenbach, "Locating the Holocaust on the Genocide Spectrum: Towards a Methodology of Definition and Categorization," *Holocaust and Genocide Studies* 3, no. 3 (1988): 289–303; Frank Chalk, "Definitions of Genocide and Their Implications for Prediction and Prevention," *Holocaust and Genocide Studies* 4, no. 2 (1989): 149–60.

22. See J. Sebastian, "The Ontological Construction of Universal Rights," in "The Promise of Rights in the Making of Colonial-Modernity" (PhD diss., Department of Ethnic Studies, University of California, Riverside, 2021).

23. Raphaël Lemkin, *Axis Rule in Occupied Europe* (Washington, D.C.: Carnegie Endowment for International Peace, 1944). See especially Chapter IX, "Genocide," 79–95.

24. Samuel Totten, William S. Parsons, and Robert K. Hitchcock, "Confronting Genocide and Ethnocide of Indigenous Peoples," in *Annihilating Difference: The Anthropology of Genocide*, ed. Alexander Laban Hinton (Berkeley: University of California Press, 2002), 70 (emphasis added).

25. See, for example, Yusuf Aksar, "The 'victimized group' concept in the Genocide Convention and the development of international humanitarian law through the practice of ad hoc tribunals," *Journal of Genocide Research* 5, no. 2 (2003): 211–24. Donald W. Beachler, *The Genocide Debate: Politicians, Academics, and Victims* (New York: Palgrave Macmillan, 2011).

26. Bonilla-Silva, *Racism Without Racists: Color-Blind Racism and the Persistence of Racial Inequality in the United States* (Lanham, Md.: Rowman & Littlefield, 2003).

27. A rare and insightful critical response to this scholarly tendency appears in Stener Ekern, "The Modernizing Bias of Human Rights: Stories of Mass Killings and Genocide in Central America," *Journal of Genocide Research* 12, nos. 3–4 (November 2010): 219–41.

28. David H. Jones, "On the Prevention of Genocide: The Gap Between Research and Education," *War Crimes, Genocide & Crimes Against Humanity* 1, no. 1 (January 2005): 39 (emphasis added).

29. Williams, *The Divided World*, 52.

30. João Costa Vargas, *Never Meant to Survive: Genocide and Utopias in Black Diaspora Communities* (New York: Rowman & Littlefield, 2008).

31. See Saidiya Hartman, "The Time of Slavery," *South Atlantic Quarterly* 101, no. 4 (2002): 757–77; Alyosha Goldstein, "Where the Nation Takes Place," *South Atlantic Quarterly* 107, no. 4 (Fall 2008): 833–61; Andrew Woolford, "'Ontological Destruction: Genocide and Canadian Aboriginal Peoples'" *Genocide Studies and Prevention* 4, no. 1 (April 2009): 81–97; Frank B. Wilderson, *Red, White & Black: Cinema and the Structure of U.S. Antagonisms* (Durham, N.C.: Duke University Press, 2010); Zakiyyah Iman Jackson, *Becoming Human: Matter and Meaning in an Antiblack World* (New York: New York University Press, 2020); and Calvin L. Warren, *Ontological Terror: Blackness, Nihilism, and Emancipation* (Durham, N.C.: Duke University Press, 2018).

32. See William L. Patterson, ed., *We Charge Genocide: The Historic Petition to the United Nations for Relief from a Crime of the United States Government against the Negro People* (New York: Civil Rights Congress, 1951); and United Nations Declaration on the Rights of Indigenous Peoples, 2007, www.un.org/esa/socdev /unpfii/documents/DRIPS_en.pdf.

33. Stuart Hall, "Race, Articulation, and Societies Structured in Dominance," in *Black British Cultural Studies: A Reader*, ed. Houston A. Baker Jr., Manthia Diawara, and Ruth H. Lindeborg (Chicago: University of Chicago Press, 1996), 16–60.

34. We Charge Genocide, *Police Violence Against Chicago's Youth of Color*, report submitted to United Nations Committee Against Torture (September 2014): 4. http://report.wechargegenocide.org/.

35. Ibid., 6–11.

36. See Mark Neocleous, *Fascism* (Concepts in Social Thought) (Minneapolis: University of Minnesota Press, 1997).

37. We Charge Genocide, "About," wechargegenocide.org/about/ (accessed February 14, 2015). We Charge Genocide describes itself as

> . . . a grassroots, inter-generational effort to center the voices and experiences of the young people most targeted by police violence in Chicago. Instances of police violence reveal the underlying relationship between marginalized communities and the state. This is a relationship of unequal access to power and resources. This is also a relationship where violence is too often used by the police to silence, isolate, control and repress low-income people and young people of color in particular. . . . We Charge Genocide was started to offer a vehicle for needed organizing and social transformation. The initiative is entirely volunteer-run. We are Chicago residents concerned that the epidemic of police violence continues uninterrupted in our city. We are not a 501c3 and we do this work intentionally outside of the nonprofit industrial complex (which has sometimes silenced community advocates from being able to propose radical ideas and solutions). The name We Charge Genocide comes from a petition filed to the United Nations in 1951, which documented 153 racial killings and other human rights abuses mostly by the police.

38. Michel Foucault, *Discipline and Punish: The Birth of the Prison* (New York: Vintage Books, 1995). Giorgio Agamben, *State of Exception* (Chicago: University of Chicago Press, 2005).

39. See, for example., We Charge Genocide, *supra* note 90, at 6 ("Three police cars arrived on the scene, and police jumped out of their cars with guns drawn, and Roshad ran. Police chase [sic] Roshad through an alley onto the back porch of a house. Several people heard Roshad say, 'Please don't shoot, please don't kill me, I don't have a gun.' People saw him with his hands up when the police shot Roshad 5 times and killed him.").

40. Ibid., 2–9.

41. We Charge Genocide, *Police Violence Against Chicago's Youth of Color*, 7.

42. See Allyson Collins and Human Rights Watch, *Shielded from Justice: Police Brutality and Accountability in the United States* (New York: Human Rights Watch, 1998); Opinion, "To Honor Eric Garner's Life, Reform the Police," *New York Times*, May 15, 2018, https://www.nytimes.com/2018/05/15/opinion/eric-garner-nypd-de-blasio.html.

43. United Nations Convention on the Prevention and Punishment of the Crime of Genocide (1948), https://www.ohchr.org/en/professionalinterest/pages/crimeofgenocide.aspx.

44. See Nada Elia, Jodi Kim, Shana L. Redmond, Dylan Rodríguez, Sarita Echavez See, and Davíd Hernández, *Critical Ethnic Studies: A Reader* (Durham, N.C.: Duke University Press, 2016).

45. See Joy James, ed., *Warfare in the American Homeland: Policing and Prison in a Penal Democracy* (Durham, N.C.: Duke University Press, 2007).

46. Raphaël Lemkin, *Axis Rule in Occupied Europe* (Washington: Carnegie Endowment for International Peace, 1944), 93.

47. Fanon, "Fact of Blackness," 92.

48. See Katherine McKittrick, ed., *Sylvia Wynter: On Being Human as Praxis* (Durham, N.C.: Duke University Press, 2015).

49. Sylvia Wynter, "'No Humans Involved': An Open Letter to My Colleagues," *Forum N.H.I.: Knowledge for the Twenty-First Century* 1, no. 1 (Fall 1994): 2 (emphasis added).

50. "Biggest Prison Strike in US History: Thousands of Georgia Prisoners to Stage Peaceful Protest," press release, December 8, 2010, http://blackagendareport .com/content/ga-prison-inmates-stage-1-day-peaceful-strike-today.

51. The discourse of the Georgia prison strikers echoes the political language of slavery historicized by David M. Oshinsky in his study of the Mississippi State Penitentiary, Parchman Farm. See Oshinsky, *"Worse than Slavery": Parchman Farm and the Ordeal of Jim Crow Justice* (New York: Free Press, 1997).

52. Kung Li, "Georgia Prisoner Strike Comes out of Lockdown," *Facing South*, Institute for Southern Studies, December 16, 2010, www.southernstudies.org /2010/12 /georgia-prisoner-strike-comes-out-of-lockdown.html.

53. Aside from those sources previously cited, the most useful editorial discussions and reportage on the Georgia prisoners' strike include Bruce A. Dixon, "Georgia Inmates Stage 1-Day Peaceful Strike Today," *Black Agenda Report*, December 9, 2010, blackagendareport.com/content/ga-prison-inmates-stage-1-day -peaceful-strike -today; Dixon, "Arrested Georgia Correctional Officer Oversaw Vicious Beating of Prisoner 'in His Capacity' As Supervisor," *Black Agenda Report*, March 15, 2011, blackagendareport.com/content/arrested-georgia-correctional-officer -oversaw-vicious -beating-prisoner-%E2%80%9C-his-capacity%E2%80%9D-super; Dixon and Glen Ford, "GA Prison Inmate Strike Enters New Phase, Prisoners Demand Human Rights, Education, Wages For Work," *Black Agenda Report*, December 15, 2010, blackagendareport.com/content/ga-prison-inmate-strike-enters -new-phase-prisoner-demand-human-rights-education-wages-work; Julianne Hing, "Georgia Prisoners End Protest, But Continue Demands," *Colorlines*, December 15, 2010, colorlines.com/archives/2010/12/georgia_prisoners_strike_for_pay_decent_food .html; Chara Fisher Jackson and Vanita Gupta, "Georgia Prison Strike an Outgrowth of Nation's Addiction to Incarceration," *Daily Kos: News-Community-Action*, January 6, 2011, www.dailykos.com/story/2011/01/06/933848/-Georgia-Prison-Strike-an -Outgrowth-of-Nation-s-Addiction-to-Incarceration; and Michelle Chen, "Georgia Prison Strike: A Hidden Labor Force Resists," *Huffington Post*, December 20, 2010, www.huffingtonpost.com/michelle-chen/georgia-prison-strike-a-h_b_798928.html.

54. The website of the Prisoner Hunger Strike Solidarity coalition (prisoner hungerstrikesolidarity.wordpress.com/) has maintained what is, by far, the most comprehensive, timely, and accurate accounts of the both the Pelican Bay strike

itself and the larger set of institutional (i.e., CDCR) responses and political actions that have followed in the aftermath of the July 2011 mobilization. Its archive of press releases (all available for download) amounts to historical documentation of major and minor developments in the hunger strike and its surrounding contexts. Most germane to the descriptive sketch offered here are the following Prisoner Hunger Strike Solidarity press releases: "Prisoners across at Least 6 California Prisons Join Pelican Bay Hunger Strikers," July 5, 2011; "Pelican Bay Hunger Strike Spreading throughout California System," July 7, 2011; "Medical Conditions Reach Crisis in Pelican Bay Hunger Strike: Advocates Demand Access to Strike Leaders, Negotiations," July 12, 2011; "California Prison Hunger Strike Resumes: Prisoners Cite Continued Torture, CDCR Bad Faith Negotiations," September 3, 2011; and "With 12,000 Participants Last Week, Prisoner Hunger Strike Begins 8th Day: CDCR Bars Family Member Visits," October 3, 2011.

55. While the CDCR officially acknowledged at least 6,500 statewide participants in the strike, support organizations calculated 12,000 participants at the height of the prison strike in fall 2011. See "Pelican Bay Hunger Strike Spreading"; "Prisoners at Corcoran Continue Hunger Strike, Concerns Rise over Health Conditions," Prisoner Hunger Strike Solidarity, February 10, 2012, prisonerhungerstrikesolidarity .wordpress.com/2012/02/10/prisoners-at-cocoran-continue-hunger-strike-concerns -rise-over-health-conditions/#more-1683. Nancy Kinkaid, the federal receiver responsible for overseeing medical care in the California prison system, confirmed the official estimate of 6,500 in an interview with KPCC Radio in Southern California. See "Prison Hunger Strike Over, Official Says," 89.3 KPCC (Los Angeles, Calif.), July 21, 2011, www.scpr.org/news/2011/07/21/27821/medical-official -prisoner-hunger -strike-over/.

56. See "About Prisoner Hunger Strike Solidarity," prisonerhungerstrikesolidarity .wordpress.com/about/ (accessed November 10, 2012).

57. In addition to the resources available through the Prisoner Hunger Strike Solidarity website cited previously, see Victoria Law's excellent summary analysis of the strike, "California Prison Hunger Strike Ends, Conditions of 'Immense Torture' Continue," *Critical Mass Progress*, Criminal Injustice Series, criticalmassprogress .com/2011/10/19/ci-california-prison-hunger-strike-ends-conditions-of-immense -torture-continue/ (accessed November 10, 2012). Other useful reportage on the Pelican Bay strike includes Michael Montgomery, "Pelican Bay Inmates Agree to End 3-Week Hunger Strike," *California Watch*, July 21, 2011, californiawatch.org /dailyreport/pelican-bay-inmates-agree-end-3-week-hunger-strike-11624; SHU captive Mutope Duguma, "Pelican Bay SHU Prisoners Plan to Resume Hunger Strike Sept. 26," *San Francisco Bay View*, September 1, 2011, sfbayview.com/2011/pelican -bay-shu-prisoners-plan-to-resume-hunger-strike-sept-26/; the *San Francisco Bay View* compilation of letters from SHU prisoners Duguma, Paul Sangu Jones, and Randall Sondai Ellis, "Retaliation at Pelican Bay: Letters from the SHU," October 14, 2011, sfbayview.com/2011/retaliation-at-pelican-bay-letters-from-the-shu/; and Ian Lovett, "California Prison Hunger Strike Resumes as Sides Dig In," *New*

York Times, October 7, 2011, www.nytimes.com/2011/10/08/us/hunger-strike-resumes-in-california-prisons.html?_r=1.

58. Angelica Camacho, *Unbroken Spirit: Pelican Bay, California Prisoner Hunger Strikes, Family Uprisings, and Learning to Listen* (PhD diss., Department of Ethnic Studies, University of California, Riverside, 2017), 227–28.

59. Ibid., 232.

60. Ibid., 238–39.

61. Undergraduate research project, Ethnic Studies 177, Critical Studies of the US Prison Industrial Complex, fall quarter 2011, University of California, Riverside. This project entailed the collective work of about a dozen undergraduate students, whose primary tasks were (a) to gather information and biographical testimonials from local (Southern California) extended family members active in the mobilization of free-world solidarity with the Pelican Bay hunger strikers and their demands, and (b) to organize a public forum in which the family members, in collaboration with the students, could discuss the historical context of the strike and articulate the frameworks through which they conceptualized the role of nonimprisoned people (especially college and university student activists) in generating critical narratives regarding the intimate and structural social conditions of racial and class criminalization and incarceration. The summary insights in this article regarding the Pelican Bay hunger strike largely derive from this research project and the public forum produced by it.

62. Avery Gordon, *Ghostly Matters: Haunting and the Sociological Imagination*, 2nd ed. (Minneapolis: University of Minnesota Press, 2008).

63. For a variety of elaborations on radical feminist conceptions of the prison as an apparatus of state violence that both transcends the institutional site of incarceration and focuses gendered technologies of power on imprisoned, formerly imprisoned, and nonimprisoned women, see the late Safiya Bukhari's memoir *The War Before: The True Life Story of Becoming a Black Panther, Keeping the Faith in Prison and Fighting for Those Left Behind* (New York: Feminist Press, 2010); Julia Sudbury, ed., *Global Lockdown: Race, Gender, and the Prison-Industrial Complex* (New York: Routledge, 2005); and Ruth Wilson Gilmore's discussion of the organization Mothers Reclaiming Our Children in *Golden Gulag: Prisons, Surplus, Crisis, and Opposition in Globalizing California* (Berkeley: University of California Press, 2007), 181–240.

64. On homonormativity, see Lisa Duggan, *The Twilight of Equality?: Neoliberalism, Cultural Politics, and the Attack On Democracy* (Boston: Beacon Press, 2003).

65. Bruce A. Dixon, "GA Prison Inmates Stage 1-Day Peaceful Strike Today," *Black Agenda Report*, December 9, 2010, blackagendareport.com/content/ga-prison-inmates-stage-1-day-peaceful-strike-today. See also, Kung Li, "Georgia Prisoner Strike Comes Out of Lockdown," *Facing South* (online), December 16, 2010, https://www.facingsouth.org/2010/12/georgia-prisoner-strike-comes-out-of-lockdown.html.

As i have previously noted, while the Georgia prisoners' strike was unevenly covered by various news and online media venues, the most consistent and insightful reporting was notably undertaken by *Black Agenda Report* (blackagendareport.com/) and Dixon, its managing editor. Dixon's article offered a prompt reproduction of the Georgia strike's initial press release in its entirety, including the full list of demands.

66. "Prisoners' Demands," Prisoner Hunger Strike Solidarity, April 3, 2011, prisonerhungerstrikesolidarity.wordpress.com/the-prisoners-demands-2/. The Prisoner Hunger Strike Solidarity website printed the original "five core demands" upon their issuance and remains the central informational organ for the Pelican Bay hunger strike.

67. In addition to previously cited texts, see "Remember the Hunger Strike," Critical Resistance (online), September 2012, http://criticalresistance.org/resources /current-analysis/remember-the-hunger-strike-2/; "Black August and the Struggle to Abolish Solitary," Critical Resistance (online), August 21, 2015, http://criticalresistance .org/black-august-and-the-struggle-to-abolish-solitary/; Victoria Law, "Two Years After Pelican Bay Hunger Strike, What's Change for People Inside the Prison?" *Truthout* (online), July 8, 2015, https://truthout.org/articles/two-years-after-pelican-bay-hunger -strike-what-s-changed-for-people-inside-the-prison/; and Bruce A. Dixon and Glen Ford, "GA Prison Inmate Strike Enters New Phase, Prisoners Demand Human Rights, Education, Wages for Work," *Black Agenda Report* (online), December 15, 2010, https://blackagendareport.com/content/ga-prison-inmate-strike-enters-new -phase-prisoners-demand-human-rights-education-wages-work.

68. See Orisanmi Burton, "Epistolary Praxis; Prisons, Letter Writing, and Black Radical Kinship," *American Anthropologist*, forthcoming 2020; Burton, *Tip of the Spear: Revolutionary Organizing and Prison Pacification in the Empire State* (book manuscript); Joy James, *Imprisoned Intellectuals: America's Political Prisoners Write on Life, Liberation, and Rebellion* (Lanham, Md.: Rowman & Littlefield, 2003); Dan Berger and Toussaint Losier, *Rethinking the American Prison Movement* (New York: Routledge, 2018); Dan Berger, *Captive Nation: Black Prison Organizing in the Civil Rights Era* (Chapel Hill: University of North Carolina Press, 2014); and Dylan Rodríguez, *Forced Passages: Imprisoned Radical Intellectuals and the US Prison Regime* (Minneapolis: University of Minnesota Press, 2006).

69. Stephen Best and Saidiya Hartman, "Fugitive Justice," *Representations* 92 (2005): 9.

70. João Costa Vargas, "Introduction: The Urgency Imperative of Genocide," in *Never Meant to Survive: Genocide and Utopias in Black Diaspora Communities* (New York: Rowman and Littlefield, 2008), xix–xxxi.

71. See Stefano Harney and Fred Moten, *The Undercommons: Fugitive Planning & Black Study* (Wivenhoe: Minor Compositions, 2013).

72. Fred Moten and Stefano Harney, "Politics Surrounded," *South Atlantic Quarterly* 110, no. 4 (Fall 2011): 985–86 (985–88).

73. See Orlando Patterson, *Slavery and Social Death: A Comparative Study* (Cambridge: Harvard University Press, 1985). A significant and thoughtful reemergence and reinterpretation of Patterson's texts has been well under way over

the last decade, traversing multiple disciplinary and interdisciplinary fields. Here, i am invoking the manner in which Patterson's comparative understanding of the structures of natal alienation, social death, and slave fungibility lends itself to a fluid theoretical appropriation for conceptualizing the material conditions formed by the Thirteenth Amendment to the U.S. Constitution, in which the status of "involuntary servitude" is not abolished but is instead limited to those who have been "duly convicted" of crimes.

74. On bare life, see Giorgio Agamben, *Homo Sacer: Sovereign Power and Bare Life* (Stanford: Stanford University Press, 1998).

75. Omer Bartov, *Murder in Our Midst: The Holocaust, Industrial Killing, and Representation* (New York: Oxford University Press, 1996).

76. Norbert Finzsch, "'It is scarcely possible to conceive that human beings could be so hideous and loathsome': discourses of genocide in eighteenth- and nineteenth-century America and Australia," in *Colonialism and Genocide*, ed. A. Dirk Moses and Dan Stone (New York: Routledge, 2007), 3.

77. See Dan Stone, "Biopower and Modern Genocide," in *Empire, Colony, Genocide: Conquest, Occupation, and Subaltern Resistance in World History*, ed. A. Dirk Moses (New York: Berghahn Books, 2008), 162–82; Michel Foucault, *Security, Territory, Population: Lectures at the Collège de France, 1977–1978* (New York: Picador/Palgrave Macmillan: 2009); Giorgio Agamben, "The Camp as the 'Nomos' of the Modern," *Homo Sacer: Sovereign Power and Bare Life* (Stanford: Stanford University Press, 1998), 95–101; Achille Mbembe, "Necropolitics," *Public Culture* 15, no. 1 (2003): 11–40.

78. Cedric Robinson, *Black Marxism: The Making of the Black Radical Tradition* (Chapel Hill: University of North Carolina Press, 2000).

79. "Ban the Box Movement Sweeps the Country," *All of Us or None* (newsletter), Issue 1 (Fall 2012): 3. Available online at https://www.prisonerswithchildren.org/wp -content/uploads/2013/01/AOUN-Newsletter-9-12-121.pdf.

80. Masthead, *All of Us or None* (newsletter), Issue 2 (Fall 2013). Available at https://www.prisonerswithchildren.org/wp-content/uploads/2013/08/AOUON _newspaper_May_23.pdf.

81. "The Development of All of Us or None," *All of Us or None* (newsletter), Issue 1 (Fall 2012): 1. Available online at https://www.prisonerswithchildren.org/wp-content /uploads/2013/01/AOUN-Newsletter-9-12-121.pdf.

82. See "Hunger Strike! Pelican Bay Human Rights Movement, Stop the Torture!" *All of Us or None* (newsletter), Issue 2 (Fall 2013). Available at https://www .prisonerswithchildren.org/wp-content/uploads/2013/08/AOUON_newspaper_May _23.pdf.

83. Patrick Wolfe, "Settler Colonialism and the Elimination of the Native," *Journal of Genocide Research* 8, no. 4 (2006): 387–409.

84. Ibid., 388.

85. Ibid., 401.

86. Dylan Rodríguez, "Black Studies in Impasse," *Black Scholar* 44, no. 2 (2014): 37–59.

87. Iyko Day, *Alien Capital: Asian Racialization and the Logic of Settler Colonial Capitalism* (Durham, N.C.: Duke University Press, 2016), 31.

88. Ibid., p. 31.

89. Tiffany Lethabo King, *Antipode*, "The Labor of (re)Reading Plantation Landscapes Fungible(ly),"*Antipode 48(4)* (2016): 1034.

90. Ibid., 30.

91. "Eviscerate," *Oxford English Dictionary* (online version), https://www.oed.com/view/Entry/65416?rskey=z39gJZ&result=2#eid.

92. On epigenetics, social determinism, and race, see Louis Maheu and Roderick A. Macdonald, eds., *Challenging Genetic Determinism: New Perspectives on the Gene in Its Multiple Environments* (Montreal: McGill-Queen's University Press, 2011). See especially Section Two, "Social and Ethical Issues Challenging Genes and Environment Interplays," and Section Three, "Interactive Models of Genes and Environment Interplays: Some Examples and Observations."

93. Louis Maheu and Roderick A. Macdonald, Introduction to *Challenging Genetic Determinism*, ed. Maheu and Macdonald, xvi.

94. Dorothy Roberts, *Fatal Invention: How Science, Politics, and Big Business Re-Create Race in the Twenty-First Century* (New York: New Press, 2011), 143.

95. Ibid., 143–44.

96. My use of assemblage in this instance relies on Jasbir Puar's theoretical and methodological interpretation in *Terrorist Assemblages: Homonationalism in Queer Times* (Durham, N.C.: Duke University Press, 2007).

97. Adam Jones, "Gendercide and Genocide," *Journal of Genocide Research* 2, no. 2 (2000): 191.

98. For an excellent example of such a feminist intervention within genocide studies, see Chile Eboe-Osuji, "Rape as Genocide: Some Questions Arising," *Journal of Genocide Research* 9, no. 2 (2007): 251–73.

99. In addition to works cited elsewhere in this book, see Angela Y. Davis (Angela Yvonne), *Women, Race & Class*, 1st Vintage Books ed. (New York: Vintage Books, 1984); Simone Brown, *Dark Matters: On the Surveillance of Blackness* (Durham, N.C.: Duke University Press, 2015); Sherene H. Razack, "Gendered Racial Violence and Spatialized Justice: The Murder of Pamela George," *Canadian Journal of Law & Society* 15, no. 2 (2000): 91–130; Jinthana Haritaworn, Adi Kuntsman, and Silvia Posocco, eds. *Queer Necropolitics* (Abingdon, Oxon: Routledge, 2014); and Setsu Shigematsu and Keith L. Camacho, eds. *Militarized Currents Toward a Decolonized Future in Asia and the Pacific* (Minneapolis: University of Minnesota Press, 2010).

100. See Primo Levi, *Survival in Auschwitz: If This Is a Man*, trans. Stuart Woolf (New York: Orion Press, 1959); and Giorgio Agamben, *Remnants of Auschwitz: The Witness and the Archive* (Brooklyn: Zone Books, 1999).

101. Alex G. Weheliye, *Habeas Viscus: Racializing Assemblages, Biopolitics, and Black Feminist Theories of the Human* (Durham, N.C.: Duke University Press, 2014), 56.

5. "Mass Incarceration" as Misnomer: Domestic War and the Narratives of Carceral Reform

1. Michelle Alexander, *The New Jim Crow: Mass Incarceration in the Age of Colorblindness* (New York: The New Press, 2010)

2. For some of the most rigorously researched and well-argued examples of this reformist narrative, see Peter K. Enns, *Incarceration Nation: How the United States Became the Most Punitive Democracy in the World* (Cambridge: Cambridge University Press, 2016), 157; Glenn C. Loury, *Race, Incarceration, and American Values* (Boston: Massachusetts Institute of Technology Press, 2008), 28; and John D. Pfaff, *Locked in: The True Causes of Mass Incarceration—and How to Achieve Real Reform* (New York: Basic Books, 2017), 162.

3. See Jeremy Travis, President of John Jay College of Criminal Justice, Opening Address at the 2015 National Forum on Criminal Justice: Reducing Mass Incarceration, August 3, 2015.

4. See, for example, Jeremy Diamond and Alex Rogers, "How Jared Kushner, Kim Kardashian West and Congress Drove the Criminal Justice Overhaul," *CNN*, December 21, 2018, https://www-m.cnn.com/2018/12/18/politics/criminal-justice -overhaul/index.html?r=https%3A%2F%2Fwww.google.com%2F.

5. Lloyd Grove, "CNN's Van Jones Secretly Helped Craft the Weak Trump Police Reform He Praised on TV," *The Daily Beast*, June 28, 2020, https://www .thedailybeast.com/cnns-van-jones-secretly-helped-craft-the-weak-trump-police -reform-he-praised-on-tv.

6. Jason Furman and Douglas Holtz-Eakin, "Why Mass Incarceration Doesn't Pay," *New York Times*, Opinion, April 21, 2016, https://www.nytimes.com/2016/04/21 /opinion/why-mass-incarceration-doesnt-pay.html.

7. Adam Gopnik, "The Caging of America," *New Yorker*, January 30, 2012, https://www.newyorker.com/magazine/2012/01/30/the-caging-of-america; Chris Stone, "Ending Mass Incarceration," *Open Society Foundations*, November 7, 2014, https://www.opensocietyfoundations.org/voices/ending-mass-incarceration.

8. The Prison Policy Initiative offers a comprehensive view of U.S. incarceration in its illustrative yearly summary. Peter Wagner and Wendy Sawyer, *Mass Incarceration: The Whole Pie*, Prison Pol'y Initiative (March 14, 2018), https://www .prisonpolicy.org/reports/pie2018.html. PPI clearly distinguishes its quantitative methodology from other criminological sources:

This report offers some much needed clarity by *piecing together this country's disparate systems of confinement.* The American criminal justice system holds almost 2.3 million people in 1,719 state prisons, 102 federal prisons, 1,852 juvenile correctional facilities, 3,163 local jails, and 80 Indian Country jails as well as in military prisons, immigration detention facilities, civil commitment centers, state psychiatric hospitals, and prisons in the U.S. territories.

9. Mark Neocleous, *War Power, Police Power* (Edinburgh: Edinburgh University Press, 2014), 7.

10. Craig Willse, *The Value of Homelessness: Managing Surplus Life in the United States* (Minneapolis: University of Minnesota Press, 2015), 54.

11. On the political geographies of racial capitalism under late neoliberalism, see Ruth Wilson Gilmore, "Fatal Couplings of Power and Difference: Notes on Racism and Geography," *The Professional Geographer* 54, no. 1 (2002): 15–24; Cedric Robinson, *Black Marxism: The Making of the Black Radical Tradition* (1983; repr., Chapel Hill: University of North Carolina Press, 2000). On neoliberalism in its different iterations, see David Harvey, *A Brief History of Neoliberalism* (New York: Oxford University Press, 2005). On the concept of White Being, see "Policing and the Violence of White Being: An Interview with Dylan Rodríguez," *Propter Nos* 1, no. 1 (Fall 2016): 8–18; Alexander Weheliye, *Habeas Viscus: Racializing Assemblages, Biopolitics, and Black Feminist Theories of the Human* (Durham, N.C.: Duke University Press, 2014); Katherine McKittrick, ed., *Sylvia Wynter: On Being Human as Praxis* (Durham, N.C.: Duke University Press, 2015).

12. Stuart Hall, Chas Critcher, Tony Jefferson, John Clarke, and Brian Roberts, *Policing the Crisis: Mugging, the State, and Law and Order* (New York: Palgrave Macmillan, 1978), 19.

13. Dean Spade, *Normal Life: Administrative Violence, Critical Trans Politics, and the Limits of Law* (Brooklyn: South End Press, 2011), 27.

14. See Dylan Rodríguez, "The Political Logic of the Non-Profit Industrial Complex" in *The Revolution Will Not Be Funded: Beyond the Non-Profit Industrial Complex*, eds. INCITE (Cambridge, Mass: South End Press, 2007), 21–40; and Jennifer R. Wolch, *The Shadow State: Government and Voluntary Sector in Transition* (New York: Foundation Center, 1990).

15. See, for example, Angela Davis et al., *If They Come in the Morning: Voices of Resistance* (New York: Third Press, 1971); Manning Marable, "The Meaning of Racist Violence in Late Capitalism," in *How Capitalism Underdeveloped Black America* (Boston: South End Press, 1983); and Prison Research Education Action Project, *Instead of Prisons: A Handbook for Abolitionists* (1976; repr., Oakland: Critical Resistance, 2005).

16. Steven R. Donziger, ed., *The Real War on Crime: the Report of the National Criminal Justice Commission* (New York: HarperCollins, 1996), 31.

17. Select Justice Police Institute publications from this period include: *Cellblocks or Classrooms?: The Funding of Higher Education and Corrections and Its Impact on African American Men* (Justice Policy Institute, 2002), www.justicepolicy.org /downloads/coc.pdf; Tara-Jen Ambrosio and Vincent Schiraldi, *From Classrooms to Cell Blocks: A National Perspective* (Justice Policy Institute, 1997); and Vincent Schiraldi and Justice Policy Institute, *Poor Prescription: The Costs of Imprisoning Drug Offenders in the United States* (Justice Policy Institute, 2000). Prison Activist Resource Center facilitated the publication of two important texts, one of them edited by then-director Elihu Rosenblatt (*Criminal Injustice: Confronting the Prison Crisis* [South End Press, 1996]) and the other an essay pamphlet for activists and teachers authored by former political prisoner Linda Evans and Eve Goldberg, *The*

Prison-Industrial Complex & the Global Economy (1997) (Oakland: PM Press, 2009). Prison Activist Resource Center boasted a highly active website during this time and continues to maintain an online presence at https://www.prisonactivist.org/.

18. See David Garland, ed., *Mass Imprisonment: Social Causes and Consequences* (London: Sage, 2001); Marc Mauer and Meda Chesney-Lind, eds., *Invisible Punishment: The Collateral Consequences of Mass Imprisonment* (New York: New Press, 2002); and Michelle Alexander, *The New Jim Crow: Mass Incarceration in the Age of Colorblindness* (New York: The New Press, 2010).

19. While such rearticulations of "mass incarceration" abound in abolitionist and other radical anti-carceral political communities, some readily accessible examples include the work of Project NIA (niastories.wordpress.com), The Jericho Movement (www.thejerichomovement.com), and Black Agenda Report (www .blackagendareport.com), as well as numerous scholarly publications, including João Costa Vargas, *Never Meant to Survive: Genocide and Utopias in Black Diaspora Communities* (New York: Rowman and Littlefield, 2008); Geoffrey Adelsberg, Lisa Guenther, and Scott Zeman, eds., *Death and Other Penalties: Philosophy in a Time of Mass Incarceration* (New York: Fordham University, 2015); Eric Stanley and Nat Smith, eds., *Captive Genders: Trans Embodiment and the Prison Industrial Complex* (Oakland: AK Press, 2011); Dan Berger, "Social Movements and Mass Incarceration: What Is To Be Done?" *Souls* 15 (2013): 3–18; and Julia Sudbury, "Transatlantic Visions: Resisting the Globalization of Mass Incarceration," *Social Justice* 27, no. 3 (2000): 133–49.

20. See Mechthild Nagel, "Beyond The New Jim Crow," *Peace Studies Journal* 9, no. 1 (2016): 78–97; James Forman, Jr., "Racial Critiques of Mass Incarceration: Beyond the New Jim Crow," *N.Y.U. Law Review* 87, no. 21 (2012): 21–69; Anders Walker, "The New Jim Crow: Recovering the Progressive Origins of Mass Incarceration," *Hastings Constitutional Law Quarterly* 41 (2014): 845–74; and Joseph Osel, "Black Out: Michelle Alexander's Operational Whitewash: 'The New Jim Crow' Reviewed," *International Journal of Radical Critique* 1, no. 1 (2012), https://ssrn .com/abstract=2314109.

21. See David Remnick, "Ten Years After *The New Jim Crow*" (interview with Michelle Alexander), *The New Yorker*, January 17, 2020, https://www.newyorker.com /news/the-new-yorker-interview/ten-years-after-the-new-jim-crow; and Brentin Mock, "Life After *The New Jim Crow*" (interview with Michelle Alexander) *Citylab*, September 30, 2016, https://www.citylab.com/equity/2016/09/life-after-the-new-jim -crow/502472/.

22. Alexander, *The New Jim Crow: Mass Incarceration in the Age of Colorblindness*, 195.

23. Ibid.

24. Ibid., 197.

25. Ibid.

26. See Manning Marable, *Race, Reform, and Rebellion: The Second Reconstruction and Beyond in Black America, 1945–2006* (Jackson: University Press

of Mississippi, 2007), 171; Mark Potok, "The Year in Hate and Extremism," *Intelligence Report*, Southern Poverty Law Center, Spring 2017, https://www .splcenter.org/fighting-hate/intelligence-report/2017/year-hate-and-extremism. According to the SPLC's inventory of racist, nativist, and white supremacist "hate groups" in the United States, there was a numerical historical peak in 2011, and a resurgence during the first years of the Trump presidency. Further, the SPLC notes that its inventory almost certainly underestimates the presence of organized white supremacy and white nationalism by virtue of its mainstreaming in local and national party politics and spreading presence online.

27. See, for example, Patrick Elliot Alexander, *From Slave Ship to Supermax: Mass Incarceration, Prisoner Abuse, and the New Neo-Slave Novel* (Philadelphia: Temple University Press, 2018); Jenna M. Loyd, Matt Michelson, and Andrew Burridge, eds., *Beyond Walls and Cages: Prisons, Borders, and Global Crisis* (Athens: University of Georgia Press, 2012); Martha D. Escobar, *Captivity Beyond Prisons: Criminalization Experiences of Latina (Im)migrants* (Austin: University of Texas Press, 2016); A. Naomi Paik, *Rightlessness: Testimony and Redress in U.S. Prison Camps Since World War II* (Chapel Hill: University of North Carolina Press, 2016).

28. See Jonah Engel Bromwich, "Why Are American Prisons So Afraid of This Book?" *New York Times*, January 18, 2018, https://www.nytimes.com/2018/01/18/us /new-jim-crow-book-ban-prison.html?smid=fb-nytimes&smtyp=cur&fbclid=IwAR1v yAHAGX4DQBvLThag11tS9zkPH7bUv48h5zPN3wZuTPojFRlSQNNzWrI.

29. "Our Mission," Brennan Center for Justice, accessed January 2018, https:// www.brennancenter.org/about. See also Glenn Moramarco, Brennan Center for Justice, "Regulating Electioneering: Distinguishing Between 'Express Advocacy and Issue Advocacy'" (1998), iv, www.brennancenter.org/sites/default/files/legacy/d /cfr5.pdf.

30. Brennan Center, "Shifting Law Enforcement Goals to Reduce Mass Incarceration" (conference agenda), 2–3, https://www.brennancenter.org/sites/default /files/events/092314%20Shifting%20Law%20Enforcement%20Goals%20-%20 FINAL%20AGENDA.pdf.

31. Brennan Center for Justice, conference program for "Shifting Law Enforcement Goals to Reduce Mass Incarceration," September 23, 2014, i (emphasis added), http://www.brennancenter.org/sites/default/files/events/Shifting%20Law%20 Enforcement%20Goals.Program%20Book.pdf.

32. Lauren-Brooke Eisen, Nicole Fortier, and Inimai Chettiar, *Federal Prosecution for the 21st Century*, policy report, Brennan Center for Justice (2014), http://www.brennancenter.org/sites/default/files/analysis/Federal_Prosecution_For _21st_Century.pdf (emphasis mine).

33. Ibid., 13 (emphasis mine).

34. Ibid.

35. Ibid., 14.

36. While the literature on the management of corporate organizational change is vast, the particular inspiration for this reference is a short handbook distributed to

administrators at the University of California, Riverside. Jeffrey M. Hiatt, *Employee's Survival Guide to Change* (2013): 34–43.

37. See Eisen et al., 14.

38. Ibid., 45.

39. Ibid., 4.

40. Ibid., 13.

41. Ibid., 27 (emphasis added).

42. Ibid., 20.

43. See Louis Althusser's discussion of "ideological problematic" in "On the Materialist Dialectics: On the Unevenness of Origins," in Althusser, *For Marx* (1965; repr., New York: Verso, 2005), 161–218.

44. Eric Holder, "Eric Holder's Keynote Address: Shifting Law Enforcement Goals to Reduce Mass Incarceration," Brennan Center for Justice, YouTube channel, accessed August 2015, https://www.youtube.com/watch?v=2xSVJ_VfX-M. See also "Eric Holder's Keynote Address: Shifting Law Enforcement Goals to Reduce Mass Incarceration," Brennan Center website, accessed May 2019, https://www.brennancenter.org/analysis/keynote-address-shifting-law-enforcement-goals-to-reduce-mass-incarceration; and Jacob Sullum "Eric Holder Condemns Mass Incarceration (Again)," *Forbes*, Opinion, November 22, 2013, http://www.forbes.com/sites/jacobsullum/2013/11/22/eric-holder-condemns-mass-incarceration-again/.

45. Oscar Lewis, *La Vida: A Puerto Rican Family in the Culture of Poverty—San Juan and New York* (New York: Random House, 1966); U.S. Department of Labor, "The Negro Family: The Case for National Action," Washington, D.C., U.S. Government Printing Office (1965).

46. "Eric Holder's Keynote Address," Brennan Center (emphasis added).

47. Ibid.

48. See, for example, Heather MacDonald, *The War on Cops: How the New Attack on Law and Order Makes Everyone Less Safe* (New York: Encounter Books, 2016); Alfred S. Regnery, "Police Need Military Equipment to Combat Rising Crime Rates and Police Deaths," *USA Today*, Opinion, August 31, 2017, https://www.usatoday.com/story/opinion/2017/08/31/police-need-military-equipment-combat-rising-crime-rates-and-police-deaths-alfred-regnery-column/613471001/; and Fran Spielman, "FOP [Fraternal Order of Police] Ties Weekend Violence to 'War on Police' That Includes Consent Decree," *Chicago Sun Times*, August 9, 2018, https://chicago.suntimes.com/2018/8/9/18482199/fop-ties-weekend-violence-to-war-on-police-that-includes-consent-decree.

49. Ibid.

50. Ibid.

51. Ibid.

52. Ibid.

53. Ibid.

54. Hillary Clinton, "Hillary Rodham Clinton Speaks Race, Justice," Columbia University School of International and Public Affairs website, April 29, 2015,

https://internal.sipa.columbia.edu/news-center/video/hillary-rodham-clinton-speaks
-on-race-justice. See also Sam Frizell, "Hillary Clinton Calls for an End to 'Mass
Incarceration,'" *Time*, April 29, 2015, http://time.com/3839892/hillary-clinton-calls
-for-an-end-to-mass-incarceration/. Full video of the speech is also available at
Columbia University's YouTube channel, https://www.youtube.com/watch?v
=NnGAy5nIwlo.

55. "Hillary Rodham Clinton," Columbia University.

56. Hillary Clinton (@HillaryClinton), "End mass incarceration. Address
inequality. Restore trust between law enforcement and communities. Read this and
Share," Twitter, April 29, 2015, https://twitter.com/HillaryClinton/status
/593449489207304192.

57. Ruth Wilson Gilmore, "Globalisation and US Prison Growth: From Military
Keynesianism to Post-Keynesian Militarism," *Race & Class* 2, no. 3 (1998–1999): 171–88.

58. Hillary Clinton, "Mrs. Clinton Campaign Speech," CSPAN, January 25,
1996, https://www.c-span.org/video/?69606-1/mrs-clinton-campaign-speech.

59. Barack Obama, "Remarks by the President at the NAACP Conference,"
accessed August 2015, https://www.whitehouse.gov/the-press-office/2015/07/14
/remarks-president-naacp-conference. Full video of the speech is available at
https://youtu.be/UBkFE3sErE8.

60. Ibid.

61. Ibid.

62. "Goldwater's 1964 Acceptance Speech," *Washington Post*, online archive, text
provided by Arizona Historical Foundation, https://www.washingtonpost.com/wp-srv
/politics/daily/may98/goldwaterspeech.htm.

63. In addition to the works of Sylvia Wynter and Frantz Fanon, see David
Marriott, "Inventions of Existence: Sylvia Wynter, Frantz Fanon, Sociogeny, and
'the Damned,'" *The New Centennial Review* 11, no. 3 (Winter 2011): 45–89.

64. See Sylvia Wynter, "Unsettling the Coloniality of Being/Power/Truth/
Freedom: Towards the Human, After Man, Its Overrepresentation—An Argument,"
CR: The New Centennial Review 3, no. 3 (Fall 2003): 257–337.

65. See Chapter 2 in Dylan Rodríguez, *Forced Passages* (Minneapolis: University
of Minnesota Press, 2015).

66. Matt Zapotosky, "3,100 Inmates To Be Released as Trump Administration
Implements Criminal Justice Reform," *The Washington Post*, July 19, 2019, https://
www.washingtonpost.com/national-security/3100-inmates-to-be-released-as-trump
-administration-implements-criminal-justice-reform/2019/07/19/7ed0daf6-a9a4-11e9
-a3a6-ab670962db05_story.html.

67. On contemporary carceral abolitionist praxis, see Dylan Rodríguez,
"Abolition as Praxis of Human Being: A Foreword," *Harvard Law Review* 132, no. 6
(April 2019): 1575–1612; Allegra M. McLeod, "Envisioning Abolition Democracy,"
Harvard Law Review 132, no. 6 (April 2019): 1613–49; Angel E. Sanchez, "In Spite of
Prison," *Harvard Law Review* 132, no. 6 (April 2019): 1650–83; and Patrisse Cullors,
"Abolition and Reparations: Histories of Resistance, Transformative Justice, and

Accountability," *Harvard Law Review* 132, no. 6 (April 2019): 1684–94. See also Abolition Collective, eds., *Abolishing Carceral Society* (Brooklyn: Common Notions, 2018). On the historical context of Black Lives Matter, see Keeanga-Yamahtta Taylor, *From #BlackLivesMatter to Black Liberation* (Chicago: Haymarket Books, 2016). On the Standing Rock struggle, see Nick Estes, *Our History Is the Future: Standing Rock Versus the Dakota Access Pipeline, and the Long Tradition of Indigenous Resistance* (New York: Verso, 2019). Finally, on Idle No More, see Glen Coulthard, *Red Skin, White Masks: Rejecting the Colonial Politics of Recognition* (Minneapolis: University of Minnesota Press, 2014); Kino-nda-niimi Collective, *The Winter We Danced: Voices from the Past, the Future, and the Idle No More Movement* (Winnipeg: ARP Books, 2014); and Kenneth Coates, *#idlenomore: And the Remaking of Canada* (Regina, Saskatchewan: University of Regina Press, 2015).

68. See Angela Y. Davis, "From the Prison of Slavery to the Slavery of Prison: Frederick Douglass and the Convict Lease System," in *The Angela Y. Davis Reader*, ed. Joy James (Maldon, Mass.: Blackwell Publishers, 1998), 74–95; João Costa Vargas, *Never Meant to Survive: Genocide and Utopias in Black Diaspora Communities* (New York: Rowman & Littlefield, 2008); Sarah Haley, *No Mercy Here: Gender, Punishment, and the Making of Jim Crow Modernity* (Chapel Hill: University of North Carolina Press, 2016); Stephanie E Smallwood, *Saltwater Slavery: A Middle Passage from Africa to American Diaspora* (Cambridge: Harvard University Press, 2007); Marcus Rediker, *The Slave Ship: A Human History* (New York: Penguin Group, 2007); Alex Lichtenstein, *Twice the Work of Free Labor: The Political Economy of Convict Labor in the New South* (New York: Verso, 1995); Dennis Childs, *Slaves of the State: Black Incarceration from the Chain Gang to the Penitentiary* (Minneapolis: University of Minnesota Press, 2015); Childs, "'You Ain't Seen Nothin Yet': *Beloved*, the American Chain Gang, and the Middle Passage Re-Mix," *American Quarterly* 61, no. 2 (June 2009), 271–97; David Oshinsky, "*Worse Than Slavery*": *Parchman Farm and the Ordeal of Jim Crow Justice* (New York: Free Press, 1996); Douglas A. Blackmon, *Slavery By Another Name: The Re-Enslavement of Black Americans from the Civil War to World War II* (New York: Doubleday, 2008); Matthew J. Mancini, *One Dies, Get Another: Convict Leasing in the American South, 1866–1928* (Columbia: University of South Carolina Press, 1996); Sally E. Hadden, *Slave Patrols: Law and Violence in Virginia and the Carolinas* (Cambridge: Harvard University Press, 2001); and Loïc Wacquant, *Prisons of Poverty* (1999; repr., Minneapolis: University of Minnesota Press, 2009).

69. U.S. Const. amend. XIII, § 1 (emphasis mine).

70. Frederick Douglass, "In What New Skin Will the Old Snake Come Forth?: An Address Delivered in New York, New York, on 10 May 1865," in *The Frederick Douglass Papers*, ed. John W. Blassingame and John R. McKivigan (New Haven, Conn.: Yale University Press, 1991), 79, 82 (emphasis mine).

71. Ibid., 85.

72. See, for example, Mumia Abu-jamal, *Live From Death Row* (1995, repr., New York: Perennial 2002), 89–91; Safiya Bukhari, *The War Before: The True Life Story of*

Becoming a Black Panther, Keeping the Faith in Prison & Fighting for Those Left Behind (New York: Feminist Press, 2010); Childs, "'You Ain't Seen Nothin Yet,'" 11; Marshall "Eddie" Conway and Dominique Stevenson, *Marshall Law: The Life & Times of a Baltimore Black Panther* (Oakland: AK Press, 2011); Sarah Haley, *No Mercy Here*; Leonard Peltier, *Prison Writings: My Life is My Sun Dance*, ed. Harvey Arden (New York: Crazy Horse Spirit, 1999); Dylan Rodríguez, *Forced Passages* (Minneapolis: University of Minnesota Press, 2015), 146; Dylan Rodríguez, "'Allow One Photo per Year:' Prison Strikes as Racial Archives, from 'Post–Civil Rights' to the Analytics of Genocide," in *The Nation and Its Peoples: Citizens, Denizens, Migrants*, ed. John S. W. Park and Shannon Gleeson (New York: Routledge 2014); Cassandra Shaylor, "'It's Like Living in a Black Hole': Women of Color and Solitary Confinement in the Prison Industrial Complex," *New England Journal on Criminal and Civil Confinement* 24 (1998): 409; *Through the Wire* (P.O.V. Films, 1989).

73. We Charge Genocide, *Police Violence Against Chicago's Youth of Color*, report submitted to United Nations Committee against Torture (September 2014), 4, http://report.wechargegenocide.org/.

74. See Ida B. Wells-Barnett, "Southern Horrors: Lynch Law in All Its Phases" in *Selected Works of Ida B. Wells-Barnett* (1892; repr., New York: Oxford University Press, 1991), 14–45; and William L. Patterson, ed., *We Charge Genocide: The Historic Petition to the United Nations for Relief from a Crime of the United States Government against the Negro People* (New York: Civil Rights Congress, 1951).

75. Regarding the larger context of stop-and-frisk policing, see Michael D. White and Henry F. Fradella, *Stop and Frisk: The Use and Abuse of a Controversial Policing Tactic* (New York: New York University Press, 2016); Kami Chavis Simmons, "The Legacy of Stop and Frisk: Addressing the Vestiges of a Violent Police Culture," *Wake Forest Law Review* 49 (2014): 849–71; Andrew Gelman, Jeffrey Fagan, and Alex Kiss, "An Analysis of the New York City Police Department's 'Stop-and-Frisk' Policy in the Context of Claims of Racial Bias," *Journal of the American Statistical Association* 102 (2007): 813–23.

76. We Charge Genocide, "An Open Letter to the ACLU of Illinois Regarding Stop and Frisk," online letter, August 12, 2015, http://wechargegenocide.org/an-open -letter-to-the-aclu-of-illinois-regarding-stop-frisk/.

77. See Adam Liptak, "1 in 100 US Adults Behind Bars, New Study Says," *New York Times*, February 28, 2008, https://www.nytimes.com/2008/02/28/us/28cnd-prison.html; see also John Gramlich, "America's Incarceration Rate Is at a Two-Decade Low," Pew Research Center, May 2, 2018, http://www.pewresearch.org/fact-tank/2018/05/02 /americas-incarceration-rate-is-at-a-two-decade-low/, showing that while the U.S. incarceration rate in 2016 was at its lowest since 1996, it remained around 860 per 100,000; Peter Wagner, "The Prison Index: Taking the Pulse of the Crime Control Industry," *The Prison Policy Institute* (2003), section 4, https://www.prisonpolicy.org /prisonindex/us_southafrica.html (noting the incarceration rates for all people in apartheid South Africa in 1993 (368 per 100,000), for Black men in South Africa in 1993 (851 per 100,000), and for the African American men in the United States in 2001

(4,848 per 100,000). The scholarship of Professor Nils Christie remains among the most significant sources of radical criminological analysis available, and his versatile book *Crime Control as Industry* is indispensable for its deprovincializing contextualization of late twentieth- and early twenty-first-century incarceration regimes. Nils Christie, *Crime Control as Industry: Towards Gulags, Western Style*, 3d ed. (New York: Routledge, 2000), 13–17. Christie notes that the Soviet Union had an extraordinary incarceration rate of 1,400 per 100,000 in 1950, see *Crime Control as Industry*, 29. Others have remarked upon the Soviet Union's extraordinarily high incarceration rate between 1934 and 1953, see J. Arch Getty et al., "Victims of the Soviet Penal System in the Pre-war Years: A First Approach on the Basis of Archival Evidence," American Historical Review 98, no. 4 (October 1993): 1017, 1020, 1040. Christie's research demonstrates that post–Soviet Union Russia exhibited a rate of incarceration during the latter quarter of the twentieth century that was generally at or below the U.S. rate of the last two decades. Christie, *Crime Control*, 28–31.

78. Marc Mauer, "Americans Behind Bars: The International Use of Incarceration 1992–1993," *The Sentencing Project*, report (1994), http://www .druglibrary.org/schaffer/other/sp/abb.htm.

79. See Franklin E. Zimring, "The Scale of Imprisonment in the United States: Twentieth Century Patterns and Twenty-First Century Prospects," *Journal of Criminal Law and Criminology* 100, no. 3 (2010): 1231; Peter Wagner and Wendy Sawyer, "States of Incarceration: The Global Context 2018," *Prison Policy Initiative* (June 2018), https://www.prisonpolicy.org/global/2018.html.

80. Danielle Kaeble and Mary Cowhig, "Correctional Populations in the United States, 2016," *Office of Justice Programs*, U.S. Department of Justice (April 2018), 2, https://www.bjs.gov/content/pub/pdf/cpus16.pdf.

81. "State-by-State and National Crime Estimates by Year(s)," *Uniform Crime Reporting Statistics*, https://www.ucrdatatool.gov/Search/Crime/State/StatebyState .cfm (select "United States-Total" in column A, all categories in column B, and 1970–2014 in column C).

82. "Criminal Justice Facts," *The Sentencing Project* (2017), http://www .sentencingproject.org/criminal-justice-facts/.

83. Christopher Hartney and Linh Vuong, "Created Equal: Racial and Ethnic Disparities in the U.S. Criminal Justice System," National Council on Crime and Delinquency, Report (2009), 19. It should also be stressed that "Hispanic" is a notoriously vexed U.S. Census demographic classification that erases socially ascribed racial differentiations within the category, and thus underestimates the criminalization of Latinx populations that are racialized and racially profiled/policed as Black, Brown, and/or Indigenous. Carlos Lozada, "Who Is Latino?," *Washington Post*, Opinion, June 21, 2013, https://www.washingtonpost.com/opinions/who-is-latino/2013/06/21 /bcd6f71a-d6a4-11e2-b05f-3ea3f0e7bb5a_story.html?utm_term=.c458043ed185.

84. John Gramlich, "The Gap Between the Number of Blacks and Whites in Prison Is Shrinking," *Pew Research Center* (January 12, 2018), http://www.pewresearch.org/fact -tank/2018/01/12/shrinking-gap-between-number-of-blacks-and-whites-in-prison/.

85. See James Forman Jr., *Locking Up Our Own: Crime and Punishment in Black America* (New York: Farrar, Straus and Giroux, 2017), 10–14, analyzing how the African American community in Washington, D.C., has responded to violence in Black neighborhoods with increased reliance on the criminal justice system; and Ruth Wilson Gilmore, *Golden Gulag: Prisons, Surplus, Crisis, and Opposition in Globalizing California* (Berkeley: University of California Press, 2007), 5–7, analyzing California's prison growth and its disproportionate impact on African Americans and Latinos in the state's urban areas.

86. See Stuart Hall, "Race, Articulation and Societies Structured in Dominance," *Sociological Theories: Race and Colonialism* 37, no. 10 (1980): 339–42, analyzing the United States' particular history of race and slavery as emblematic of the country's hegemonic power struggles.

87. See, for example, Mumia Abu-jamal, *Live From Death Row* (1995, repr., New York: Perennial 2002), 89–91; Bukhari, *The War Before*, 107; Childs, "'You Ain't Seen Nothin Yet,'" 11; Marshall "Eddie" Conway and Dominque Stevenson, *Marshall Law: The Life & Times of a Baltimore Black Panther* (Oakland: AK Press, 2011); Sarah Haley, *No Mercy Here*; Leonard Peltier, *Prison Writings: My Life is My Sun Dance*, ed. Harvey Arden (New York: Crazy Horse Spirit, 1999); Dylan Rodríguez, *Forced Passages* (Minneapolis: University of Minnesota Press, 2015), 146; Dylan Rodríguez, "'Allow One Photo per Year': Prison Strikes (Georgia 2010, California 2011–12) as Racial Archives, from 'Post–Civil Rights' to the Analytics of Genocide," in *The Nation and Its Peoples: Citizens, Denizens, Migrants*, ed. John S. W. Park and Shannon Gleeson (New York: Routledge 2014); Cassandra Shaylor, "'It's Like Living in a Black Hole': Women of Color and Solitary Confinement in the Prison Industrial Complex," *New England Journal on Criminal and Civil Confinement* 24 (1998): 409; *Through the Wire* (P.O.V. Films, 1989).

88. See Rodríguez, *Forced Passages*, 41–47.

89. David Marriott, "Inventions of Existence: Sylvia Wynter, Frantz Fanon, Sociogeny, and 'the Damned,'" *CR: The New Centennial Review* 11, no. 3 (Winter 2011): 79. On sociogeny, see Frantz Fanon, *Black Skin, White Masks*, trans. Charles Lam Markmann (1952; repr., New York: Grove Press 1967), 11; Sylvia Wynter, "Unsettling the Coloniality of Being/Power/Truth/Freedom: Towards the Human, After Man, Its Overrepresentation—An Argument" *CR: The New Centennial Review* 3, no. 3 (Fall 2003): 269.

90. See, for example, Margaret Colgate Love, Wayne A. Logan, Jenny Roberts, *Collateral Consequences of Criminal Conviction: Law, Policy and Practice* (Eagan, Minn.: Thompson Reuters, 2016), 440–48; Jeff Manza and Christopher Uggen, *Locked Out: Felon Disenfranchisement and American Democracy* (New York: Oxford University Press, 2006), 84–90, describing the barriers and challenges that formerly incarcerated people face in restoring their right to vote in various states; Joan Petersilia, *When Prisoners Come Home: Parole and Prisoner Reentry* (New York: Oxford University Press, 2003), 112–26, describing the barriers that formerly incarcerated people face in finding employment and public housing; Donald

Braman, "Families and Incarceration," in *Invisible Punishment: the Collateral Consequences of Mass Imprisonment*, ed. Marc Mauer and Meda Chesney-Lind (New York: The New Press, 2002), 117–18; Loïc Wacquant, "Deadly Symbiosis: When Ghetto and Prison Meet and Mesh," in *Mass Imprisonment: Social Causes and Consequences*, ed. David Garland (Thousand Oaks, Calif.: Sage Publications, 2001), 82, 106.

91. Andrew Burridge, Jenna M. Loyd, Matt Mitchelson, eds., *Beyond Walls and Cages: Prisons, Borders, and Global Crisis* (Athens: University of Georgia Press, 2012).

92. While this chapter is addressing an emergent liberal-progressive institutionalization of mass-incarceration rhetoric, other conceptualizations of the phrase "mass incarceration" continue to circulate through abolitionist and other radical anti-carceral political communities. See, for example, Dan Berger, "Beyond Innocence: US Political Prisoners and the Fight Against Mass Incarceration," *National Jericho Movement* (blog), *Truthout*, July 24, 2015, https://www .thejerichomovement.com/blog/beyond-innocence-us-political-prisoners-and-fight -against-mass-incarceration; and Danny Haiphong, "The U.S. Is a Political Prison, Kamala Harris Is a Prison Guard," *Black Agenda Report*, January 30, 2019, https:// blackagendareport.com/index.php/us-political-prison-kamala-harris-prison-guard. There are also numerous examples of the phrase's use in scholarly publications. See, for example, Julia Sudbury, aka Julia C. Oparah, "Maroon Abolitionists: Black Gender-Oppressed Activists in the Anti-Prison Movement in the U.S. and Canada," in *Captive Genders: Trans Embodiment and the Prison Industrial Complex*, ed. Eric A. Stanley and Nat Smith (Oakland: AK Press, 2011), 293, 296, 301; João H. Costa Vargas, *Never Meant to Survive: Genocide and Utopias in Black Diaspora Communities* (New York: Rowman and Littlefield Publishers, 2008), 11–14, describing an anti-Black genocide continuum that includes the disproportionate incarceration of Black and Brown people; Dan Berger, "Social Movements and Mass Incarceration: What Is To Be Done?," *Souls* 15, no. 1–2 (2013): 5–8, arguing that mass incarceration stems from the government will to suppress political dissidents and rebellion; and Julia Sudbury, "Transatlantic Visions: Resisting the Globalization of Mass Incarceration," *Social Justice* 27, no. 3 (Fall 2000): 134–37, linking mass incarceration in the United Kingdom with trends in the United States.

93. On the linkages between prison/jail reform efforts and the genesis of the US prison industrial complex, see Marie Gottschalk, *The Prison and the Gallows* (New York: Cambridge University Press, 2006), 8–9.

94. Elliott Currie, *Crime and Punishment in America*, 2nd ed. (New York: Picador, 2013), 4–5. For an authoritative study of the emergence of the California prison system in the latter twentieth and early twenty-first centuries, see Gilmore, *Golden Gulag*.

95. Dorothy Roberts, "Foreword: Abolition Constitutionalism," *Harvard Law Review* 133, no. 1 (November 2019): 114.

96. For examples of the extensive scholarship on the expansion of prison under the guise of "reform," see Angela Y. Davis, *Abolition Democracy: Beyond Empire,*

Prisons, and Torture (New York: Seven Stories Press, 2005); Gilmore, *Golden Gulag*, 23, 88–97; Michel Foucault, *Discipline and Punish: The Birth of the Prison*; Terry A. Kupers, *Prison Madness: The Mental Health Crisis Behind Bars and What We Must Do About It* (San Francisco: Jossey-Bass, 1999); John Bartlow Martin, *Break Down the Walls* (New York: Ballantine Books, 1954); Norval Morris, "The Contemporary Prison: 1965–Present," in *The Oxford History of the Prison: the Practice of Punishment in Modern Society*, ed. Norval Morris and David J. Rothman (New York: Oxford University Press, 1995), 227, 249–53; and Alisa Roth, *Insane: America's Criminal Treatment of Mental Illness* (New York: Basic Books, 2018).

97. Angela Y. Davis, *Are Prisons Obsolete?*, 27.

98. Paul Butler, "The System Is Working the Way It Is Supposed To: The Limits of Criminal Justice Reform," *The Georgetown Law Journal* 104 (2016): 1425.

99. Mariame Kaba, "Prison Reform's in Vogue and Other Strange Things . . ." *Truthout*, March 21, 2014, https://truthout.org/articles/prison-reforms-in-vogue-and -other-strange-things/; see also Mariame Kaba, foreword to *Invisible No More: Police Violence Against Black Women and Women of Color*, by Andrea J. Ritchie (Boston: Beacon Press, 2017), xv, advocating against reform as a solution to police violence; Mariame Kaba and Erica R. Meiners, "Arresting the Carceral State," *Jacobin*, February 24, 2014, https://www.jacobinmag.com/2014/02/arresting-the-carceral-state/, addressing a parallel pattern occurring with school "reform" in response to the school-to-prison pipeline; Mariame Kaba and Kelly Hayes, "A Jailbreak of the Imagination: Seeing Prisons for What They Are and Demanding Transformation," *Truthout*, Op-Ed, May 3, 2018, https://truthout.org/articles/a-jailbreak-of-the -imagination-seeing-prisons-for-what-they-are-and-demanding-transformation/, calling for radical change and questioning "reformers'" commitment to ending the carceral violence that has led to mass incarceration.

Epilogue. Abolitionist Imperatives

1. C. L. R. James, *Black Jacobins: Toussaint L'Ouverture and the San Domingo Revolution* (1963; repr. New York: Vintage Books, 1989), 51.

2. Portions of this epilogue have been derived from two previously published articles: Dylan Rodríguez, "Abolition as Praxis of Human Being: A Foreword," *Harvard Law Review* 132, no. 6 (2019): 1575–1612; and Dylan Rodríguez, "The Disorientation of the Teaching Act: Abolition as Pedagogical Position," *Radical Teacher: A Socialist, Feminist and Anti-Racist Journal on the Theory and Practice of Teaching* 1, no. 88 (2010): 7–19.

3. Ruth Wilson Gilmore offers a helpful differentiation between "reformist" logics and abolitionist strategies that make tactical use of reform. Ruth Wilson Gilmore, Foreword to Dan Berger, *The Struggle Within: Prisons, Political Prisoners, and Mass Movements in the United States* (Oakland: PM Press, 2014), vii, vii–viii.

4. To consider abolitionist praxis in the context of particular peoples' systemic, historical endangerment to institutionalized forms of dehumanization, degradation,

and social oppression is to significantly rethink the premises of the United Nations' (UN) canonized conception of "genocide," particularly in regard to the notion that peoplehood *as such* (including self-defined nations, tribes, ethnic groups, and so on) ought to be defined by *cultural* as well as collective physical integrity. For useful points of critical rearticulation and revision of the UN's 1948 Convention on the Prevention and Punishment of the Crime of Genocide, see Ward Churchill, *A Little Matter of Genocide: Holocaust and Denial in the Americas, 1492 to the Present*, 363–92 (1997); and Civil Rights Congress, *We Charge Genocide* (William L. Patterson ed., Int'l Publishers 1970) (1951).

5. David Scott, "The Re-Enchantment of Humanism: An Interview with Sylvia Wynter," *Small Axe* 8 (2000): 165.

6. See *What Is the PIC? What Is Abolition?*, Critical Resistance, http://criticalresistance.org/about/not-so-common-language/; Black Youth Project 100, https://byp100.org/; We Charge Genocide, http://wechargegenocide.org/; Idle No More, http://www.idlenomore.ca/; Nick Estes, "Fighting for Our Lives: #NoDAPL in Historical Context," *Wicazo Sa Review* 32 (2017); Standing Rock Sioux Tribe, https://www.standingrock.org/; Kim TallBear, "Badass (Indigenous) Women Caretake Relations: #NoDAPL, #IdleNoMore, #BlackLivesMatter," *Cultural Anthropology* (December 22, 2016), https://culanth.org/fieldsights/1019-badass-indigenous-women-caretake-relations-nodapl-idlenomore-blacklivesmatter. Dan Berger, Mariame Kaba, and David Stein offer a concise, well-executed rejoinder to simplistic and often ill-informed leftist dismissals of abolitionist praxis. See Dan Berger, Mariame Kaba, and David Stein, "What Abolitionists Do," *Jacobin* (August 24, 2017), https://www.jacobinmag.com/2017/08/prison-abolition-reform-mass-incarceration.

7. Here, collective genius entails the creative labors of community building and cultural-physiological reproduction undertaken under and against conditions of systemic, state-sanctioned violence and what Lewis Gordon has called "institutionalized dehumanization." Lewis R. Gordon, "Fanon's Tragic Revolutionary Violence," in *Fanon: A Critical Reader*, ed. Lewis R. Gordon, et al. (Oxford: Blackwell, 1996). For prior references to this notion of collective genius, see Dylan Rodríguez, "Inhabiting the Impasse: Racial/Racial-Colonial Power, Genocide Poetics, and the Logic of Evisceration," *Social Text*, September 2015, 19, 26; and Dylan Rodríguez, "'Mass Incarceration' Reform as Police Endorsement," Black Agenda Report (February 28, 2018), https://www.blackagendareport.com/mass-incarceration-reform-police-endorsement.

8. Safiya Bukhari, *The War Before: The True Life Story of Becoming a Black Panther, Keeping the Faith in Prison & Fighting for Those Left Behind*, ed. Laura Whitehorn (New York: The Feminist Press at CUNY, 2010), 37. See also Christian Davenport, *How Social Movements Die: Repression and Demobilization of the Republic of New Africa* (New York: Cambridge University Press, 2015), 161–295.

9. Regarding critical theorizations of the politics of demand levied within the purview of liberal state institutions, see generally Wendy Brown, *States of Injury:*

Power and Freedom in Late Modernity (1995); Roderick A. Ferguson, *We Demand: The University and Student Protests* (Oakland: University of California Press, 2017); Stefano Harney and Fred Moten, *The Undercommons: Fugitive Planning & Black Study* (Wivenhoe: Minor Compositions, 2013); and Fred Moten and Stefano Harney, "The University and the Undercommons: Seven Theses," *Social Text* (Summer 2004), 101.

10. On the notion of abolition as a process of building, planning, and making, see Ruth Wilson Gilmore, *Change Everything: Racial Capitalism and the Case for Abolition* (Chicago: Haymarket Books, 2021).

11. See Sylvia Wynter and Katherine McKittrick, "Unparalleled Catastrophe for Our Species? Or, to Give Humanness a Different Future: Conversations," in *Sylvia Wynter: On Being Human as Praxis*, ed. Katherine McKittrick (Durham, N.C.: Duke University Press, 2015), 18, 19–24.

12. See, for example, Clyde Woods, *Development Arrested: The Blues and Plantation Power in the Mississippi Delta* (1998) (examining how postbellum and present-day power and political structures in the Mississippi Delta represent little more than iterations on plantation power structures, clothed with other names).

13. See Douglas A. Blackmon, *Slavery by Another Name: The Re-Enslavement of Black People in America from the Civil War to World War II* (New York: Doubleday, 2008); Erica R. Meiners, *For the Children?: Protecting Innocence in a Carceral State* (Minneapolis: University of Minnesota Press, 2016); Damien M. Sojoyner, *First Strike: Educational Enclosures in Black Los Angeles* (Minneapolis: University of Minnesota Press, 2016). For a more extended theoretical-historical discussion of the U.S. prison/carceral regime as a technology of social power that is (a) not reducible to the sites of criminal justice administration and incarceration, and (b) in long historical continuity with the forms of carceral dominance evident in the hemispheric and transatlantic capture/trafficking of enslaved Africans, see also Dylan Rodríguez, *Forced Passages: Imprisoned Radical Intellectuals and the Prison Regime* (Minneapolis: University of Minnesota Press, 2006), and Dennis Childs, *Slaves of the State: Black Incarceration from the Chain Gang to the Penitentiary* (Minneapolis: University of Minnesota Press, 2015).

14. Achille Mbembe (translated by Steve Corcoran), *Necropolitics* (Durham, N.C.: Duke University Press, 2019); Michel Foucault (edited by Michel Senellart; translated by Graham Burchell), *The Birth of Biopolitics: Lectures at the Collège De France, 1978–79* (Basingstoke England: Palgrave Macmillan, 2008). Regarding the roots of abolition in Black radicalism, see Herbert Aptheker, *Abolitionism: A Revolutionary Movement* (Boston: Twayne, 1989); Lerone Bennett Jr., *Before the Mayflower: A History of Black America* (Chicago: Johnson Publishing, 1969); and Manisha Sinha, *The Slave's Cause: A History of Abolition* (New Haven: Yale University Press, 2016). See generally W. E. B. Du Bois, *Black Reconstruction in America* (1935).

15. In addition to previously cited texts, see Angela Y. Davis, *Are Prisons Obsolete?* (New York: Seven Stories Press, 2003); Angela Y. Davis, "From the Prison of Slavery

to the Slavery of Prison: Frederick Douglass and the Convict Lease System," in *The Angela Y. Davis Reader* 74 (Joy James ed., 1998); Sally E. Hadden, *Slave Patrols: Law and Violence in Virginia and the Carolinas* (Cambridge: Harvard University Press, 2001); Sarah Haley, *No Mercy Here: Gender, Punishment, and the Making of Jim Crow Modernity* (Chapel Hill: University of North Carolina Press, 2016); Alex Lichtenstein, *Twice the Work of Free Labor: The Political Economy of Convict Labor in the New South* (London: Verso, 1996); Matthew J. Mancini, *One Dies, Get Another: Convict Leasing in the American South* (Columbia: University of South Carolina Press, 1996); David M. Oshinsky, *"Worse than Slavery": Parchman Farm and the Ordeal of Jim Crow Justice* (New York: Free Press, 1996).

16. The notion of speculative futurity within abolitionist praxis holds significant, though somewhat underexplored, connections to the artistic and critical work of Afrofuturism. Here, i am especially informed by Octavia Butler's *Kindred* (Garden City, New York: Doubleday & Company, 1979) and Samuel R. Delany's *Dhalgren* (New York: Bantam Books, 1975). See also, Alondra Nelson, ed., *Afrofuturism* (special issue of *Social Text*. 71) (Durham, N.C.: Duke University Press, 2002). Lee Edelman's critical theory of queer politicality beyond and outside liberal and heteronormative futurity is especially helpful within this discussion. See Lee Edelman, *No Future: Queer Theory and the Death Drive* (Durham, N.C.: Duke University Press, 2004), 3 ("[M]y project stakes its claim to the very space that 'politics' makes unthinkable: the space outside the framework within which politics as we know it appears and so outside the conflict of visions that share as their presupposition that the body politic must survive."). Read alongside other works cited here, including writing by Moten and Harney, Cedric Robinson, Bukhari, Kaba, and Woods, Edelman's notion of a politics enacted beyond—or against—the presumption of liberal futurity opens into a robust conversation within the general parameters of what i am referencing here as abolitionist praxis.

17. See Wynter and McKittrick, 15.

18. Bukhari, 61.

19. Martha Escobar, *Captivity Beyond Prisons: Criminalization Experiences of Latina (Im)Migrants* (Austin: University of Texas Press, 2016), 84.

20. Ibid., 13–15.

21. Ibid., 94–95.

22. Among the most durably relevant, historically nuanced explications of this notion remains Cheryl I. Harris, "Whiteness as Property," *Harvard Law Review* 106, no. 1707 (1993).

23. On insurgent futurities, see generally Gaye Theresa Johnson and Alex Lubin, eds., *Futures of Black Radicalism* (London: Verso, 2017); Harney and Moten; José Esteban Muñoz, *Cruising Utopia: The Then and There of Queer Futurity* (New York: New York University Press, 2009); and *Afrofuturism*, special issue of *Social Text* (Summer 2002).

24. Wynter and McKittrick, 21n15.

25. Ibid., 21–22.

26. Ibid., 21.

27. Ibid., 22.

28. Wynter elaborates: "We need to speak instead of our *genres of being human*. Once you redefine being human in hybrid *mythoi* [self-narrated, self-mythologized] and *bios* [bio-physical] terms, and therefore in terms that draw attention to the relativity and original multiplicity of our *genres* of being human, all of a sudden what you begin to recognize is the central role that our discursive *formations*, aesthetic fields, and systems of knowledge must play in the performative enactment of all such genres of being hybridly human." (Ibid., 31.)

29. Ruthie Gilmore has said, "Abolition is a theory of change, it's a theory of social life. It's about making things" (Clément Petitjean, *Prisons and Class Warfare: An Interview with Ruth Wilson Gilmore, Verso* [August 2, 2018], https://www.versobooks.com/blogs/3954-prisons-and-class-warfare-an-interview-with-ruth-wilson-gilmore).

30. On the notion of institutionalized dehumanization as a state of war, see Lewis R. Gordon, *Fanon and the Crisis of European Man: An Essay on Philosophy and the Human Sciences* (New York: Routledge, 1995).

31. On the notion of abolition as pedagogy, see Dylan Rodríguez, "The Disorientation of the Teaching Act: Abolition as Pedagogical Position," *Radical Teacher*, 7–9.

32. See Joy James, "Erasing the Spectacle of Racialized State Violence," *Resisting State Violence: Radicalism, Gender, and Race in U.S. Culture* (Minneapolis: University of Minnesota Press, 1996), 24–43.

33. Angela Y. Davis, *Are Prisons Obsolete?*, 107.

Index

DYLAN RODRÍGUEZ, Professor in the Department of Media and Cultural Studies at the University of California, Riverside, served as Chair of Ethnic Studies from 2009 to 2016, and as President of the American Studies Association in 2020–2021. He is the author of *Forced Passages: Imprisoned Radical Intellectuals and the U.S. Prison Regime* and *Suspended Apocalypse: White Supremacy, Genocide, and the Filipino Condition.* He is a founding member of Critical Resistance and the Critical Ethnic Studies Association.